LIBRARY SERVICES PROJECT -

The Great Fear in Latin America

D1176723

The Great Fear in Latin America

JOHN GERASSI

NEW, REVISED EDITION

ORIGINALLY PUBLISHED AS: *The Great Fear*

COLLIER BOOKS

COLLIER-MACMILLAN LTD · LONDON

© *John Gerassi 1963, 1965. All rights reserved. No part of this book may be reproduced or transmitted in any form or by any means, electronic or mechanical, including photocopying, recording or by any information storage and retrieval system, without permission in writing from the Publisher. Library of Congress Catalog Card Number: 64-23646. First Collier Books Edition 1965.*

Fifth Printing 1969

A hardcover edition of The Great Fear in Latin America *was published originally by The Macmillan Company under the title,* The Great Fear. *The Macmillan Company, Collier-Macmillan Canada Ltd., Toronto, Ontario. Printed in the United States of America.*

This book is dedicated,

pretentiously,

to our Latin American

policymakers.

Assumption

We hold these truths to be self-evident, that all men are created equal, that they are endowed by their Creator with certain unalienable Rights, that among these are Life, Liberty and the pursuit of Happiness. That to secure these rights, Governments are instituted among Men, deriving their just powers from the consent of the governed. That whenever any Form of Government becomes destructive of these ends, it is the Right of the People to alter or to abolish it, and to institute new Government, laying its foundations on such principles and organizing its powers in such form, as to them shall seem most likely to effect their Safety and Happiness.

—Thomas Jefferson, *The Declaration of Independence*

Corollary

That if governments do not derive their just powers from the consent of the governed, it is the right of the people to alter or to abolish them by the means available. That such means include elections, if possible, or force, if not.

Table of Contents

List of Tables

Introduction:

The Need for Reconquest

Latin America's social and economic structure is decadent, corrupt, immoral, and generally unsalvageable.

That a change is coming is obvious. That it will come about through revolution is certain. That revolution entails the possibility of violence is unavoidable. What remains an enigma is: Who will lead the revolution?

The choices are not enigmatic—or, at least, should not be.

No real social change can be effected by what we in the United States are too readily in the habit of calling—erroneously—Latin America's "democratic forces." It is not by accident, as we shall see, that the continent's modern-minded empiricists refer to political crooks, phony reformists, and "enlightened" oligarchs suddenly addicted to the preachings of the Alliance for Progress as just "another bunch of democrats."

Nor can the change in structure be brought about by those who emulate us, no matter how hard we try to convince ourselves that they can. Latin America's history is not our history, its inheritance not our inheritance, its concepts not our concepts, and its passions certainly not our passions.

Who, then, are Latin America's revolutionaries of the future?

The same as those of the present: The Communists, in theory, and the Nationalists, in practice.

Though the two forces may currently form tactical alliances in some countries, they are inexcusably stamped with the same Red label by both our State Department and our

13

press. In fact, they are diametrically opposed. The former are self-assertive internationalists whose adopted values make them view their country within a universal flux. The latter are self-conscious patriots whose repressed instinct is to declare their country the only one valuable. The former are our enemies. The latter are *not* our allies. They are Chileans, Bolivians, or Haitians whose allegiance is to Chile, Bolivia, or Haiti—and to nothing or to no one else.

Once in power, the Nationalists will nationalize American corporations—because it will be in their country's interest to do so. They will trade with the Communist bloc—because it will be in their country's interest to do so. And they will even vote, on occasion, against the United States in the United Nations—because it will be in their country's interest to do so. But they will not be our enemies. Nor will they desert "Western society"—because such desertion will not be in their country's interest.

Which of the two will win out, the Communists or the Nationalists?

That depends on us.

Unless we change our current Latin American policy, unless we reevaluate the Alliance for Progress, unless we realize and accept the choice that faces us, we shall not only see the Communists—despite themselves—win out; we shall also accelerate their victory.

Our current policy in Latin America, as we shall see, supports what I call "medievalists" in their so far successful war against "modernists." True, the former often fool us: They "talk" reforms, even initiate some important ones in their respective domains. But their ultimate criterion is based neither on the dictates of secular law nor on the findings of empirical research.

The medievalist is he whose ultimate allegiance in both official and private life is to an infrastate institution or class, be it religious, economic, or social. The modernist, on the other hand, may oppose the rule of current law, may even espouse "totalitarian" methods, but his criterion is based upon the dictates of impersonal means for impersonal goals for the good of a state that favors neither class nor sect nor group.

When it is *his* law and *his* class that he serves, a medievalist can be a good democrat. When it is "for the good of human beings" that he acts, the modernist can be a ruthless demagogue. The medievalist's main objective is stability, a twentieth century slogan meaning *status quo;* sincerely or not, he claims to believe that liberty is more important than health, and freedom a richer food than bread. The modernist's main objective is nationhood, a traditional slogan meaning dignity; openly or not, he knows that honest exploitation is a greater crime than a bank robbery and that freedom is the result, not the cause, of well-being. The medievalist may shriek foul at the murder of one man. The modernist may approve the execution of a thousand. But the medievalist will keep his people in bondage—with perhaps a "free" press to condemn it—while the modernist will give his people the tools—though perhaps not the press—to build its own true freedom.

Yet it is the medievalists we back. These include not only the self-interested dictators but also the self-interested oligarchies ruling through "democratic" regimes and the self-interested "Democrats" ruling for the rich in the name of the poor. We have worked out a high-sounding, reform-demanding Alliance for Progress whose small black print prohibits true reforms and whose much-ballyhooed loans and grants rarely filter down to the needy. To combat the modernists, we have adopted a policy of branding as "Communists" all reformers who carry out exactly what we claim to want to achieve through the Alliance.

Sooner or later, these modernists will lead Latin Americans to claim that which is denied them—their unalienable rights. To secure these rights they will convert Latin America into an area belonging to Latin Americans, by the gun if necessary. Today, as we shall see, it belongs to foreigners, mostly to citizens or companies of the United States. The great wave that has already begun to form to secure Latin America for its own citizens will be the Reconquest of Latin America. Its overpowering assault is inevitable.

In this light, our current Latin American policy makes sense if, and only if, we are prepared to wage—and win—the Third World War before the full strength of that assault comes down. If so, the immediate advantages gained—and there are many, as we shall see—are well worth the dirty names we are called (and the occasional premature revolts). If not, it is a policy of suicidal shortsightedness, a policy of disaster. Our own rights will never survive a rebellious Latin America united against us.

PART I: An Overview

Chapter 1

Conditions and Realities

Latin America is bigger and potentially richer than we
are. Its borders begin at the Rio Grande and end at the
South Pole, more than ten thousand land miles away.

Latin America is made up of twenty sovereign states
of French, Spanish, or Portuguese origin. It also includes
a series of European and United States colonies (which
are called otherwise) and Jamaica and Trinidad-Tobago,
which gained independence from England on August 1
and 31, 1962, respectively. Though the latter's economies
bear the same characteristics as their Caribbean companions,
they are not ethnically or politically part of Latin America.
Nor is British Honduras, though it should be. Nevertheless,
for purposes of this book, we shall be concerned almost
exclusively with the twenty Latin states, with only fleeting
glances at the others.

These twenty, according to very optimistic estimates,
have an average yearly per capita income of $253, as
listed in descending order on page 20.

Such figures,[1] however, hide the fact that the vast majority
of the population is far, far poorer. In Peru, for example,
more than half the people live outside the money economy
altogether, bartering whatever goods they manage to grow.
Of the other half, 80 percent earn $53 a year, while 100
families own 90 percent of the native (as opposed to

[1] For sources, see page 447.

foreign) wealth, or $1,334,000,000. Of this total, 80 percent is in the hands of just 30 families. Meanwhile, 65 percent of the population is illiterate and 45 percent has never seen a doctor. In Lima, the capital, whose colonial mansions enveloped by ornate wooden balconies help make it one of the most beautiful cities in the world, half of the 1.3 million inhabitants live in rat-infested slums. One, called El Montón, is built around, over, and in the city dump. There, when I visited it, naked children, some too young to know how to walk, competed with pigs for a few bits of food scraps accidentally discarded by the garbage men.

Venezuela	$800
Argentina	530
Cuba	395
Mexico	395
Uruguay	395
Chile	325
Colombia	300
Panama	250
Brazil	240
Costa Rica	240
Dominican Republic	190
El Salvador	140
Guatemala	130
Honduras	120
Nicaragua	115
Peru	115
Ecuador	110
Bolivia	105
Paraguay	95
Haiti	70

United States	$2,060
Norway	1,100
Italy	680

In Chile, unemployment stays doggedly above 18 percent. One-third of the 2,000,000 people that live in Santiago, the capital, are crowded in squatters' huts made of earth or stray planks, with no water, no electricity, no transportation facilities, no municipal garbage disposal system, and no medical attention. One of these slum areas, known as *callampas* (mushrooms) because they have the habit of rising overnight, is in the dead center of town, a dime's throw from the fashionable Crillon Hotel. In that slum, called Colocolo, I saw scores of samples of that traditional sign of extreme substandard conditions: toddlers with bulging stomachs (from starches, their only diet) and hairpin legs (from lack of calcium and other minerals.)

Such scenes are repeated over and over in every Latin American country. Millions of people barely subsist, while occasional oligarchs exhibit a wealth superior to those who in our country can afford yachts, private planes, and houses in Florida, Virginia, and Hyannis Port. Latin American oligarchs manipulate their respective countries' governments to their advantage. To them, the plight of the masses is just "so much sentimental hogwash."

The masses, however, are rapidly becoming a formidable force to contend with. Together, Latin America's twenty nations have already more than 200 million people. In 1900 their population was barely 62 million (4 percent of the world). Fifty years later, it had reached 163 million (6.5 percent). By 1975 it will have jumped to 300 million—more than Soviet Russia's or North America's.

Latin America's yearly rate of population growth was about normal at the beginning of the century (1.8 percent). Today it is 2.8 percent, higher than anywhere else in the world: for instance, it is 1.6 percent in Russia, 0.7 percent in Europe, 1.8 percent in Asia, 1.7 percent in the United States and Canada and, in general, in the world. Table I shows the population in the twenty nations, as it was in 1950, 1960, and as projected for 1970, broken down according to urban and rural areas.

Brazil's present population of about 70 million will pass the 100 million mark at the beginning of the 1970's; biggest among the twenty, Brazil is actually larger than the first forty-eight United States. South America's second country is Argentina, with about 23 million today. And, in our part of the hemisphere, the most populated Latin state is Mexico, with about 37 million people. These three countries account for almost two-thirds of Latin America's population.

The population chart also shows another important Latin American characteristic: urban centers are constantly gaining in proportion to rural areas. The former will actually surpass the latter within this decade. Already five countries—Argentina, Uruguay, Cuba, Chile, and Venezuela—have

Table 1
Latin America's Population
(add: 000)

COUNTRY	URBAN			RURAL			TOTAL		
	1950	1960	1970	1950	1960	1970	1950	1960	1970
Argentina	11,040	14,205	18,000	6,150	6,795	7,600	17,190	21,000	25,600
Bolivia	1,015	1,380	2,000	1,915	2,220	2,600	2,930	3,600	4,600
Brazil	18,815	27,380	40,000	33,160	38,480	45,000	51,860	65,860	85,000
Chile	3,575	5,010	7,000	2,500	2,625	2,800	6,075	7,635	9,800
Colombia	4,170	7,065	11,500	6,975	7,705	8,600	11,145	14,770	20,100
Costa Rica	265	460	700	535	685	900	800	1,145	1,600
Cuba	3,065	4,110	5,500	2,455	2,710	3,000	5,520	6,820	8,500
Dominican Republic	505	865	1,500	1,625	1,980	2,500	2,130	2,845	4,000
Ecuador	910	1,500	2,300	2,285	2,785	3,400	3,195	4,285	5,700
El Salvador	685	1,020	1,700	1,185	1,375	1,600	1,870	2,395	3,300
Guatemala	760	1,205	2,000	2,280	2,775	3,500	3,040	3,980	5,500
Haiti	380	710	1,300	2,730	3,015	3,400	3,110	3,725	4,700
Honduras	430	590	900	955	1,165	1,500	1,385	1,755	2,400
Mexico	11,265	17,510	27,300	15,170	17,605	20,500	26,435	35,115	47,800
Nicaragua	370	625	1,000	690	840	1,100	1,060	1,465	2,100
Panama	285	430	700	470	580	700	755	1,010	1,400
Paraguay	390	565	1,000	1,010	1,060	1,200	1,400	1,625	2,200
Peru	2,975	4,480	7,500	5,195	6,030	7,000	8,170	10,510	14,500
Uruguay	1,895	2,245	2,600	515	515	500	2,410	2,760	3,100
Venezuela	2,675	4,515	7,500	2,300	2,420	2,500	4,975	6,935	10,000
LATIN AMERICA	65,470	95,870	142,000	90,100	103,365	119,900	155,570	199,235	261,900

more people living in cities than on farms, and these five are among the six with the highest per capita incomes. The populations in Mexico, the missing Number 4 in the first six, and Colombia, Number 7, are almost at a 50-50 ratio. Panama, El Salvador, Nicaragua, and Peru will soon follow suit.

The percentage of children in Latin America is higher than in any other area of the world—despite a frightening 20 to 35 percent infant mortality. Slightly more than 32 percent of Latin Americans are one to nine years old (22 percent in the United States), and 23 percent are ten to nineteen years old (17 percent in the United States). The resulting dependency ratio (unemployable mouths to feed) is also higher than in any other area: 50 percent of Latin Americans are either under fifteen or over sixty-five, compared to only 26 percent in the United States. As these proportions increase, dependencies will become more and more of a burden. And as children become adults, a greater and greater demand for jobs will ensue.

One strong reason for the rapid growth is explained by the policy of the Church. If not an actual state religion, the Roman Catholic Church is at least a strong enough unofficial influence to dictate moral standards in almost all Latin American countries. Thus, birth control and divorce are either outlawed (as in Argentina or Colombia, for example) or are extremely difficult to practice or obtain. It is true that many countries in Europe are also Roman Catholic yet have much lower birth rates. But Europe's governments (except Spain's) are fundamentally secular and have limited the Church's influence to a secondary, nonlegal place.

Furthermore, in Latin America the extreme high rate of illiteracy (65 percent) helps maintain the parish priest as primary source of information. Since Latin America's Catholic churchmen are medievalists who consider any increase in population as an increase in the Catholic political force, they actually encourage the poor to view children as new potential working hands rather than as responsibilities. Except in Mexico, where the revolution has cut some of the Church's power, and in Uruguay, where the social reforms of President (1903-1907, 1911-1915) José Batlle y Ordóñez were so popular that his staunch secular principles became laws, Roman Catholicism is not only stronger than any other institution; it is also richer. In some countries, it is the biggest landowner. And though in one (Chile), it has considerably modernized its outlook, the fact remains that the Church is one of the strongest medieval forces retarding Latin America's development.

But the population explosion, which sociologists, economists, and political scientists so fondly blame for most of Latin America's ills, is only one element in the overall explanation. Much more important is the fact that Latin America, unlike other original colonies, such as in North America, was not really settled by its firstcomers, but possessed.

In the United States we are fortunate that our first inhabitants, though owing their allegiance to a foreign power, were nevertheless community-minded. They relied on exports for their currency intake, paid taxes to England, and for a while genuinely considered themselves part of England. Yet they saw the New World as their new home. They established local regulations for their own benefit, as well as for their own safety, and developed their community's economy in such manner as to be self-subsisting and self-rewarding. Having fled England and Holland to seek a new life, they came here to live—and to stay.

The Spanish and Portuguese conquistadores who penetrated into Latin America had no such intentions. They came to suck out its riches for their respective kings, while accompanying Roman Catholic missionaries tried to "Christianize the pagans." To do either, Spain had to send armies. These armies required supply and communications systems and, after a while, some form of home life. Hence Spain encouraged civilians to go to Latin America, where they established settlements. As these grew, the continent was divided into viceroyalties of the Spanish Crown, general captaincies, or other administrative entities.

This type of colonization, however, did not alter the original characteristic of the conquest. As far as Spain was concerned, its armies were in the New World for only one basic reason: to increase Spain's wealth back home. The whole economic and political system of the new possessions remained oriented to benefit Spain only.

Since the Indian cultures of Latin America were extremely complex, unlike those of North America, with extensive mining and farming (rather than hunting) operations, Spain quickly realized that continuing such operations for itself was the best way to reap its wealth. The ores were extracted and shipped home, while cattle was introduced to feed the invaders. Soon Spain began selling not only its Latin American mining products but also its staple and cattle surpluses, encouraging even more extensive farming developments. This in turn stimulated extremes in land tenure: The *minifundio*, tiny plots cultivated by the armies-supporting settlers for their own personal use, offset by the *latifundio*, huge extensions of land cultivated by peons (first Indians, then mestizos) for the Spanish Crown.

Some manufactured goods, mostly artifacts, were locally made, of course; each pueblo had its blacksmith, its forgerer, its carpenter. But the system established powerful aristocrats on one side and on the other, powerless masses who bartered whatever small excesses they might produce, for whatever goods they needed (as the poor whites did in parts of our early South, where Negroes served as the Indians did in Latin America). The aristocracy preferred to import the luxury or even necessary items it needed. In effect, the whole economy was based on exports and imports, not on internal synthesizing or development or self-subsistence.

Spain was far away. As the New World population grew, it became more and more difficult for Spain to control every aspect of its colonies' economies. Thus Spain was forced to let more and more of its riches pass to local hands. Huge land tracts were given or sold to just one family, and it was to that family's economic advantage to keep the peonage system intact.

But the products grown or extracted had to pass through ports, owned by individuals too. Spain, busy with wars and revolutions in Europe, could no longer keep a tight rein on customs. Thus arose a formidable class of middlemen, the merchants, who became a mercantile elite. This elite developed the ports into wealthy centers and became a new oligarchy.

Then, as Buenos Aires, Montevideo, and the port of Lima (Callao) began to compete with one another, the merchants began to offer their goods to all buyers—against Spain's will. Britain always wanted to buy and sell. Spain tried to stop such free-trading. But England, and eventually the United States, which would profit most from free-trading, decided to help the cities, encouraging open rebellion. (British "mercenaries" even joined Bolívar's troops in Venezuela, and he was consistently financed with British funds.) "Independence" was the creation of mercantilism.

Free-trading is only one logical step from freethinking,

and freethinking is only one logical step from all freedoms. Thus the Church and the landed aristocracy fought against the independence that to them represented general economic freedom, that is, the destruction of the peonage system. But the landed gentry was at the mercy of the port merchants. Only through the latter could the former's goods pass. Since the port merchants were as reluctant as the landed gentry to overturn the whole applecart. the situation was finally resolved in favor of both: freedom from Spain and freedom of trade, but no other freedoms. The peonage system remained intact.

The landed gentry became known as the Conservatives. The city merchants became the Liberals. After independence, these two oligarchies began a struggle for power, and except in Colombia, where it is still undecided, the Liberals have won. But this so-called political rivalry was only for economic goals: who would control tariffs, customs, taxes, and so on. Historians like to write fat volumes about the basic differences between the Liberals, who were freethinkers, and the Conservatives, who were Catholic. But in their basic outlook on life, in their total contempt for the masses, in their cult of self-interests, in their allegiance to class and caste rather than to nation, and in their moral precepts on marriage and education, there was no real difference between the Liberals and Conservatives.

This lack of difference among traditional rulers explains in part Latin America's high rate of local revolts. Our press likes to talk of revolutions whenever an ingroup is thrown out by an outgroup. Our press also likes to use the word "caudillo" derogatorily, a sort of loaded synonym for gangster, dictator, party boss, and revolutionary combined. In fact, both concepts are false. A caudillo is not a negative term per se to Latin Americans. There are good caudillos and bad caudillos. José Gervasio Artigas, who fought Britain, Portugal, Spain, and the armies of vested interests in Argentina and Uruguay in the nineteenth century, was a caudillo par excellence, yet he is one of the noblest figures in Latin America's history.

In general, a caudillo is a leader, someone with strength, courage, and perhaps sex appeal. If he is a peasant, his cause is often just. If he is a military man his aim is often greed. But he serves a function—he displaces the ingroup. Except in rare cases—such as Artigas—the caudillo is not a revolutionary. He merely supplants one set of rulers for another, often with the regularity and predictability of our four-year elections. And just as our elections rarely change our structure, the caudillo's revolt does not alter his country's makeup. In Latin America's rigid politico-economic system, the caudillos have served only as means to the changing of government names. Whether Liberal or Conservative, they did not alter Latin America's colonial economic structure.

It is still colonial today. Its basic raw-material production—mineral or food commodities—does not lead to development. Raw materials amount to 90 percent of Latin America's export earnings, but because of rising competition from Asia and especially Africa, and because commodity prices vary and fall, our twenty neighbors do not get enough dollars to pay for their needed manufactured goods (imported mostly from the United States) whose prices are constantly rising. Hence, Latin America's trade is inevitably in deficit, as the list on this page of typical examples from 1960 shows. Venezuela, thanks to her huge oil exports, has usually had a favorable balance of trade; but so few oil dollars benefit the country, as we shall see, that it remains strapped economically.

Since exports amount to a disproportionate share of Latin America's Gross National Product (see Table II), from which budgets get a major part of their funds, Latin

Imports vs. Exports, in Millions of U.S. Dollars, 1960

Argentina	1,249	vs.	1,079
Bolivia	78		51
Brazil	1,462		1,269
Chile	500		490
Colombia	519		464
Costa Rica	110		88
El Salvador	122		117
Guatemala	138		116
Honduras	72		64
Mexico	1,186		760
Nicaragua	72		56
Panama	109		31
Uruguay	244		129

American budgets are also constantly in the red.[2]

In 1958, President Joseph Peter Grace, Jr., of W. R. Grace & Co., which makes huge profits in Latin America dealing mostly with raw materials, said: "We need to bring the revenue Latin Americans receive for their raw materials more in line with the prices they pay for our manufactured goods. Chile, Peru, Mexico and Bolivia have seen the export prices of their metals drop from 40 percent to 50 percent during the last several years. At the same time, since 1951, the average price that Latin America pays for its imports from the United States has risen about 11 percent." (See graph on page 30.)

The argument that we North Americans should pay more for their products and charge less for ours is heard all over Latin America. Even the most pro-Yankee Conservative bigwig complains that Latin America loses more money on the unfair exchange than it gets or can ever hope to get from the Alliance for Progress. In fact, almost everyone in Latin America considers the fall in coffee, banana, cacao, tin, sugar, zinc, copper, meat, or wool prices the worst economic outrage the United States can perpetrate against Latin America.

As our policy now stands, it is. Since our whole expressed objective is to help our neighbors get more dollars to cover the costs of social reforms recommended by the Alliance for Progress, a natural way would be to pay higher prices for their products. This means, in effect, giving their producers subsidies. And it would eliminate the aspect of charity that government-to-government grants imply.

The argument, however, glides over the fact that no government can foot the bill for another's reforms, that the Alliance is based mostly on loans and not grants, and that it is politically unfeasible for us to pay more for their products when we can get the same products for less on the open world market. (It is true, of course, that we control many world market price-setting operations.) Still, why must we take a loss on our manufactured goods

---

[2] There are, of course, other reasons why Latin American budgets go into heavy deficits, for example, arms and "defense" spending, the high rate of evaded taxes, and so on; GNP's include everything produced (calculated at their price value) within a country, and hence include the huge percentage of products (especially minerals) produced by foreign corporations who may pay some taxes but ship most of their profits home.

Table II

Importance of Latin America's Export Earnings to GNP
in 1957 (Typical)
(add $000,000)

	GNP	Exports	Exports as % of GNP
Argentina	8,511	975	11.5
Bolivia	223	74	33.2
Brazil	10,479	1,392	13.3
Chile	1,859	455	24.5
Colombia	2,370	520	21.9
Costa Rica	401	83	20.7
Cuba	2,800	845	30.2
Dominican Republic	656	101	24.5
Ecuador	770	133	17.3
El Salvador	612	138	22.5
Guatemala	645	114	17.7
Haiti	245	34	13.9
Honduras	344	65	18.9
Mexico	8,320	727	8.7
Nicaragua	282	64	22.7
Panama	300	64	21.3
Paraguay	240	33	13.8
Peru	1,815	320	17.6
Uruguay	1,358	128	9.4
Venezuela	6,416	2,366	36.9
TOTAL	48,656	8,631	
Average Latin America			20.0
(United States	440,300	19,506	4.4)

by selling them cheaper in Latin America when one of the reasons they are high is that we have a higher standard of living? Nor is it desirable for our government to use tax money to subsidize our exporters.

These points have rejoinders, but the fact remains that the only lasting solution to this problem is that Latin America must diversify its own production. It must build up its own manufactured goods industry; it must cut down its income dependency on exports; and it must eliminate its commercial dependency on imports. However, it just so hap-

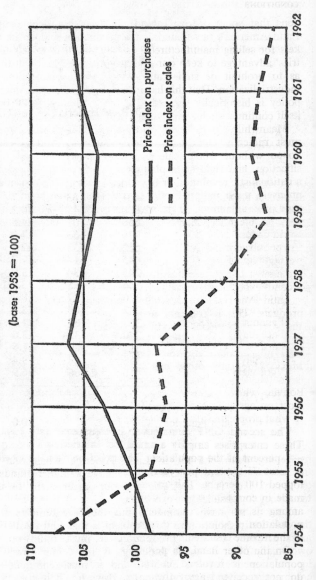

LATIN AMERICA'S TRADE
(base: 1953 = 100)

Price index on purchases
Price index on sales

110
105
100
95
90
85

1954 1955 1956 1957 1958 1959 1960 1961 1962

pens that some of our major industries are dependent on Latin America's raw materials for production and on its markets for selling manufactured goods. Thus, it is to our industries' advantage to keep our policy so oriented and constituted as to prohibit or stall Latin America's diversification and industrialization. That this has in fact been our Latin American policy is historically verified. That the Alliance for Progress itself continues such a policy has yet to be proved.

Meanwhile, to diversify and industrialize, Latin America must radically change its whole structure. And it cannot do so without whole-scale nationalizations, enforced diversification, and rigid state planning, for which it either needs a nationalistic revolution or foreign aid that will be conditioned precisely upon nationalizations, enforced diversification, and rigid state planning. If it gets neither, Latin America will keep its economy colonial and at the mercy of fluctuating world market prices.

The seriousness of this dependency is made clear when we realize that fifteen of the twenty Latin American countries are almost totally dependent on just one (and a much weaker second) export item, as seen in Table III.

Latin America's predominant emphasis is on agricultural products. This is true not only for exports but also within the Gross National Product as well. Argentina, Chile, and Venezuela are the only three countries where agriculture does not account for the largest share of the GNP, and Mexico the only other one where agricultural production is matched by manufacture. All other countries, including Bolivia, which does not export its food commodities, rely most on agriculture for their GNP total. Table IV indicates to what proportions this is true.

The second GNP contributor is commerce and banking. These enterprises employ a small but salaried working force —1 percent of the population. The profit margin, however, is at least 75 percent per year, and in the last few years has topped 100 percent. This means that while huge fortunes are made in commerce and banking, very little of it is distributed among its working force. In other words, 1 percent of the population produces 21 percent of the GNP, but 21 percent of the income is shared by only a handful of individuals.

On the other hand, 55 percent of Latin America's current population is involved in farming. Of these, 80 percent do not receive wages; they are paid in foodstuffs or in

Table III

Latin America's Exports (1959)

Country	Primary Exp.	Producing % of Total Exp. Earnings	Second Exp.	% by Both
(Argentina	meat	26	wheat	39)
Bolivia	tin	62	lead	71
Brazil	coffee	58	cacao	64
Chile	copper	66	nitrates	76
Colombia	coffee	77	oil	92
Costa Rica	coffee	51	bananas	86
Cuba	sugar	77	tobacco	83
Dominican Republic	sugar	48	cacao	65
Ecuador	bananas	57	coffee	75
El Salvador	coffee	72	cotton	88
Guatemala	coffee	72	bananas	85
Haiti	coffee	63	sisal	80
Honduras	bananas	51	coffee	70
(Mexico	cotton	25	coffee	36)
Nicaragua	cotton	39	coffee	73
Panama	bananas	69	cacao	72
(Paraguay	wood pulp	24	meat	46)
(Peru	cotton	23	sugar	38)
Uruguay	wool	54	meat	68
Venezuela	oil	92	iron ore	98

Latin American average export earnings
   from one item: 55.3   from two: 70.3
   (same for 16 out of 20   63.   77.9)

chits redeemable (at 70 percent to 90 percent of their value) at the masters' stores, or in the right to use a tiny section of the masters' lands. (For this right, the user must pay the master a percentage varying from 33 to 80 percent of his yield.) Thus, 11 percent (20 of 55) of Latin America's population participates in the earnings raised by 26 percent of the GNP. This does not mean that this 11 percent shares equally; on the contrary, the majority are employees of big farm corporations and earn low wages.

Table IV

Latin America's GNP Contributions

GOODS	50%
Agriculture	26
Manufacturing	15
Mining	6
Construction	3

SERVICES	50%
Commerce and banking	21
Government	7
Transport and Communications	9
Other Services	15

Since the agricultural peonage system means so little cash outlay (almost no wages) or investments (80-percent-free labor is cheaper than tractors) the *latifundistas* have no intention of changing it. Their control of the land is shown on Table V.

While none of the farm owners in the 0 to 20 hectare bracket owns parcels of land other than his own, the *latifundistas* included in the 1.2 percent do, some owning three, four, or even (in one case I came across in Argentina) fourteen *latifundios* of more than 1,000 hectares each. Thus, the 1.2 percent does not represent 1.2 percent of the population, but much less. I have found that it is not unreasonable to state that less than 1 percent of Latin Americans own 71.6 percent of the farmlands.

One of the results of such unequal distribution of the land is that few peasants or their families can afford to go to school. To make a *minifundio* yield enough to feed a family that has no cash to buy equipment requires that all members of the family work the land. In addition, the children of those held in peonage on the *latifundio* must work the parcels "rented" to the peon because the peon himself has not the time to do so, working from sunup to sundown on the master's property. And most mining

families earn too little from their salary to allow their
children not to work either in the same mines or on other
jobs. The result is that few of the poor ever get to school,
or stay in it, as Table VI indicates.

The average length of schooling for Latin Americans
who attend any school at all is 1.9 years, as compared
to 9 in the United States, 7.2 in Japan, and 4.5 in Puerto
Rico. The Latin American figures would be even lower
had I included Paraguay, where, though official statistics
put illiteracy from a low of 31 percent to a high of 80
percent (depending on which statistical bureau one goes to),
I am convinced, and will indicate why later, that no more
than 2 percent of the population has ever attended school.
On the other hand, the figures would have been much higher
had I included revolutionary Cuba, where illiteracy has
been officially wiped out and where 100 percent of the
children under fifteen are, according to the government,
currently enrolled in schools.

The lack of education, naturally, results in the lack
of teachers, administrators, technicians—and doctors. This
in turn creates a shortage of hospitals, as Table VII shows.
Consequently, every possible disease is not only present
but also widespread in Latin America, and the victims are
increasing: Since 1955, diphtheria has gone up in Brazil,
Colombia, Chile, El Salvador, Panama, the Dominican
Republic, and Venezuela; encephalitis in Argentina, Brazil,
Costa Rica, and Venezuela; typhoid in Brazil, Haiti (by
seven times), Panama, Paraguay, Peru, the Dominican
Republic, and Venezuela; smallpox in Argentina, Bolivia,
Brazil, Ecuador, Colombia, Paraguay and Uruguay; infectious
meningitis in Costa Rica, Haiti, Panama, and Peru; even
leprosy in Brazil, the Dominican Republic, and Paraguay
(where one out of every two thousand inhabitants is infected);
and, finally, the plague that is rising in the blacklands of
Peru. These boosts in the disease rates are only those officially recorded; thousands of cases go unnoticed because
of lack of investigators and communication facilities.

Many Latin Americans die from these diseases simply because they cannot drink uninfected water; 40 million people
living in urban communities and 86 million in rural areas
have inadequate or substandard water supplies. This is already
more than half of Latin America's 200 million population.
And the number is increasing every day. Potable water was

Table V

*Percentage Distribution in 1961 of Agricultural Holdings in 18 Latin American Countries**

Size of Farms by hectares (2.471 acres)	% of All Farms	% of Total Farm Area
0 - 20	74.4	2.9
20 - 100	18.	6.8
100 - 1,000	6.4	19.7
1,000 and over	1.2	71.6
	100.	100.

brought to 21 million people from 1950 to 1960, but the population went up by 30 million during that time.

It is quite understandable that under such conditions so many children die before they are one year old and that the average death rate is so high. Table VIII shows the particulars.

More shocking still, however, is how the surviving live. Three-fourths of Latin Americans are constantly hungry. The average daily calorie intake is 1,200, when normal subsistency is considered 2,400 (and our average in the United States is 3,100). Many Latin Americans actually die from starvation. In Haiti peasants are forced to trap skinny pigeons for food. In Peru and Chile, many eat every other day, and often average as low as 500 calories daily.

In Coquimbo and Atacama provinces, the lower North of Chile, more than 400,000 goats, the chief source of food, died in 1961 from lack of grass or feed. In central Colchagua and O'Higgins provinces, Chile's richest, known

---

* United Nations, the Economic Commission for Latin America, and other agencies' figures are slightly less, but they include Cuba and Bolivia where *latifundios* are illegal and sweeping agrarian reforms almost completed. Since the need for such reforms is our contention, to include Cuba and Bolivia's landholding statistics in this table seems self-defeating. Even if they were, however, the overall injustice is staggering: 1.5 percent of landowners own 64.9 percent of the land.

Table VI

Percentage of Population Attending School in 1961 in 18 Latin American Countries

Country	% Att. School	% Concluded 2 Years	% Completed Prim. School	% Att. Sec. or Tech. School	% Com. Sec. or Tech. School	% Att. Univ.
Argentina	81.4	70.1	19.2	16.0	6.0	3.2
Bolivia	20.9	7.4	1.8	1.0	0.3	0.1
Brazil	44.5	33.8	3.9	3.2	0.8	0.4
Chile	75.4	68.3	15.6	14.1	4.1	2.5
Colombia	57.3	49.6	6.5	5.8	1.4	0.7
Costa Rica	74.4	68.5	16.2	13.8	4.0	1.5
Dominican Republic	38.8	28.4	3.8	3.2	0.4	0.2
Ecuador	51.8	40.1	4.9	4.0	1.5	0.7
El Salvador	36.0	25.3	2.7	2.0	0.4	0.1
Guatemala	24.4	11.2	1.9	1.5	0.2	0.1
Haiti	5.7	2.4	0.9	0.2	negligible—	
Honduras	31.2	22.7	2.8	1.8	0.3	0.1
Mexico	52.5	39.4	7.4	7.1	3.2	1.6
Nicaragua	38.4	24.1	2.1	1.6	0.5	0.2
Panama	64.9	40.0	4.8	4.1	3.3	1.5
Peru	50.8	30.1	3.6	3.0	0.8	0.5
Uruguay	90.2	83.6	24.5	22.6	8.1	4.2
Venezuela	48.3	35.2	3.4	3.0	0.7	0.4
Average for 18:	49.3	38.3	7.0	6.0	2.0	1.0

as *el riñón de la oligarquía* (the oligarchy's kidney), peasants are brutalized by police, penalized for self-defense by judges who are also major landowners, forbidden to attend political rallies, and forced to work six or even seven (illegal) days a week, 17 hours a day, for 70 cents daily paid to them in stale bread (*galletas*) and chits redeemable (at 80 percent of their value) only in the *fundo* (large farm) stores.

In one 800-mile tour of these Chilean provinces, I talked to at least 300 peasants: Not one had ever been

Table VII

Latin America's Hospitals and Doctors (1961)

Country	Hosp. Beds per 1,000 Inhabitants	Inhabitants per Doctor
Argentina	5.3	760
Bolivia	1.8	3,900
Brazil	3.6	2,500
Chile	5.0	1,900
Colombia	3.0	2,900
Costa Rica	5.1	2,700
Dominican Republic	2.7	5,200
Ecuador	3.1	2,900
El Salvador	1.4	5,400
Guatemala	2.1	6,300
Haiti	0.6	9,800
Honduras	2.0	4,800
Mexico	1.0	1,900
Nicaragua	1.8	3,100
Panama	3.6	3,300
Paraguay	0.8	3,700
Uruguay	5.2	830
Venezuela	3.1	2,100
Average	2.8	3,520
(Canada	11.2	900)
(United States	10.6	780)

able to see a doctor during working hours without being docked for it; not one had received the legal minimum in cash; not one had been allowed to use the *fundo* phone even to call a doctor when his wife was about to give birth; not one was permitted to have his family live with him in his *fundo*-provided windowless mud shack unless each member over six years old contributed four hours a day of work free. (And not one, incidentally, had ever seen a United States correspondent before.)

In Paraguay's capital, Asunción, whose population is 202,000, the 60,000 dwellers of the river-swamp Chacarita district live in houses of cardboard where rats are so ac-

Table VIII

Latin America's Life Expectancies

Country	Expect. for All	Expect. for 1-Year-Olds	Number of Deaths per 1,000 (1-Year-Olds)	(2-Year-Olds)	(All)
Argentina	51	56	29	15	95
Bolivia	43	50	70	42	208
Brazil	36	45	51	17	158
Chile	45	52	24	25	140
Colombia	44	51	65	25	170
Costa Rica	50	56	34	14	114
Dominican Republic	45	51	38	16	142
Ecuador	49	56	63	28	176
El Salvador	48	54	59	20	99
Guatemala (Indian)	40 } 42	44 } 46	100 } 90	62 } 57	175 } 157
(White)	50	53	60	31	105
Haiti	29	35	71	46	222
Honduras	47	52	74	30	186
Mexico	34	41	72	34	166
Nicaragua	46	51	78	32	187
Panama	56	59	32	19	98
Paraguay	32	38	69	33	205
Peru	41	46	60	41	139
Uruguay	58	66	25	12	90
Venezuela	49	54	53	21	161
Average	44	50	56	26	153
(Canada	66	68	3.4	1.8	43)
(United States	66	66	2.6	1.2	31)

customed to human beings that neither dodges the other. Some 30,000 people more are crowded in *ana retá í* (the "devil's small village") where malaria, typhoid, syphilis, and hookworm cases outnumber milk-drinking children. In Brazil's Northeast, where men die of old age at twenty-eight, parents feel fortunate when they are able to sell their children into slavery. "My daughter may be used as a prostitute and my son will probably spend the rest of his life working very hard and very long on a São Paulo plantation," one father told me when I asked him why he had sold his two children, "but at least they will eat. My other six children were not so fortunate. They stayed here, and they died."

Why is the United States to blame, if it is, for such conditions? Or more important for our sakes, why must the revolutionaries who try to change such conditions hold us directly responsible? We shall analyze many of the reasons as we go along. But one that is easy for the traveler to notice is envy—not of what the United States may be like, but of the luxury United States companies in Latin America create. As one Villa Miseria (Buenos Aires slum) resident said: "When I go to *el centro,* I see many pretty things, things I want so badly to take home to my wife. But I can never afford them. I will never be able to afford them. They are all United States products."

In Venezuela I got the point with even greater force. With a local friend I had managed to walk about La Charneca, one of those ugly Caracas slums surrounding gigantic ultra-modern glass-and-steel skyscrapers interconnected by huge spiderwebs of multistoried concrete highways. We were able to start a conversation with a small mild-mannered man of forty-odd years who told us that three families—sixteen children—lived in his one-room shack made of discarded or stolen planks. It was a hot and humid day, and almost automatically we began to stare with him at a fifty-foot-wide Coca-Cola advertisement that stood out at the foot of the slum hill. "None of us in this house has ever drunk a Coca-Cola," he said softly. "One day we will kill those who make them."

Chapter 2

News and Facts

To most of us here in the States it seems unfair that we and our government should be hated so much throughout Latin America. All we know, of course, is what we read in our magazines and press, and they tell us that we keep pouring millions of dollars into our neighboring lands. We send them technicians, build them factories, houses, roads, and bridges, even pay them higher than world market prices for such commodities as sugar. "The more we give them, the more they hate us," we often feel. "It's the old story of biting the hand that feeds them."

What we never hear about, however, is just *how* we feed them and under what conditions. We know that our businessmen, like any other businessmen, are not all very scrupulous about making a dollar. That's why we have laws regulating all forms of business practices.

It can happen even in the United States, of course, if the deal is big enough, that bribes get passed around like pinup calendars: to judges, district attorneys, government officials, even—and we have such cases in our recent history —to presidential aides. Big advertisers have a way of silencing many of our newspaper editors. But, sooner or later, someone will talk; some new investigator will begin to dig; and some politician will squawk, even if only for his own gain. There's always someone whose interest has been hurt, and there's always someone who can make it his interest to tell the story.

40

In Latin America, the story is rarely told. Generally, the rules are made by the unethical businessmen, either local or foreign—and usually in partnership. These businessmen are Latin America's modern oligarchies, and although they may govern under many names, their interests remain the same. Even our Senate is aware of this; in 1960 a study prepared by Harvard's Center for International Affairs for the Senate Committee on Foreign Relations reported:

> Traditionally, ideology played a very minor part in Latin American political life. "Conservatives" distinguished themselves from "Liberals" in respect of such matters as the proper role of the Church and the extent of the formal powers of government. But the division was essentially spurious, since politics was regarded as exclusively the concern of a small ruling oligarchy, to which both "Conservatives" and "Liberals" belonged, and neither party was interested in initiating social or economic change. . . . It is not at all farfetched in view of Latin American history that the state had been traditionally little more than an instrument of class oppression.[1]

Today the oligarchies control most of the armies, police forces, banks, congresses and, in general, the state machinery. And those who denounce this control—smeared as Fascists not long ago—are branded Communists by Latin America's press as well as our own. Corruption is common in every Latin American country. Courts never condemn the rich. Union leaders who complain of wage and living conditions are "traitors," while those who make deals with management and government are the so-called democrats or Free Unionists.

Latin America's press, from which most United States correspondents copy the information they send us to read

---

[1] The report goes on to say that conditions are slowly changing, mainly because "with the incorporation of the urban and increasingly the rural masses, and particularly with the rise in political importance of the middle groups, the ideological issues have become increasingly significant." The reason given is certainly correct, but not the implication that the oligarchy has stopped using government as "an instrument of class oppression," nor that it has any intention of doing so.

at home, is usually a party press—an organ of political parties that, in turn, represent the oligarchies. Some countries allow true opposition papers to operate, and these often print the story as it is, say, for example, that a United States loan of $7.5 million at 3 percent to Peru for low-cost housing projects is used by the country's Premier (who owns the Housing Institute) to reloan to high-cost constructors at 12 percent.

Generally the facts are not printed, just the news. It is news, for example, that a United States oil company, given the right to exploit 1,000,000 Argentine acres, is investing $200 million. It is fact that the money is deposited in New York and is taken out as a loan in local currency in Argentina, resulting in no benefit to the local economy.

There are other kinds of hidden facts, too. Most United States corporations claim to make only a decent profit on a huge investment. One company in Peru, for example, claims its investment to be more than $283 million; but in fact (as we shall see) it invested only $32.6 million, the remainder being paper loans and write-offs.

To find the facts in Latin America is officially hard but actually easy. In Bolivia, for example, I first went to our embassy, hoping one official might arrange an interview for me with Vice-President Juan Lechín. "Impossible," I was told. "He won't see an American correspondent now except under special circumstances." A few minutes later, from my hotel, I dialed his office and without even identifying myself got him on the other end. I told him I wanted to hear his side of Bolivia's story, and he scheduled an interview for the very next day. (Down with grippe by then, he received me and I had the interview as promised—at his bedside.)

Our embassy also told me that I would never get to see President Paz Estenssoro—"too busy." I called the palace, told a press secretary what I wanted, and I had an interview at the palace that very evening.

In Paraguay, a vicious dictatorship, our embassy told me not even to try to talk to the pro-Castro Febreristas—"We have never been able to see them ourselves." I looked up the names of two known Febrerista lawyers in the phone book, went to their offices, explained to their secretaries that I wanted to talk to them "to get the whole picture," and was told that the men in question "no longer participate in politics." Two hours later I was being followed, obviously by Febreristas. Seeing that I was poking about, with obvious journalistic curiosity—walking through slums, talking with workers, scrutinizing reports at the Finance Ministry, even interviewing their archenemy, Dictator Alfredo Stroessner— they finally stopped me on a street corner, rushed me into a building through one entrance, pushed me out through another, hustled me into one car, another, then a third, blindfolded me and led me from one alleyway to another until we got to their secret headquarters. The Febreristas then showed me that part of the city that I would never have seen had I relied only on our embassy. The Febreristas also put me in contact with the Communist underground leaders and militiamen.

Nowhere did I find a door closed. Everywhere, even where persecution is at its worst, it was possible to interview the extremes, Right or Left. Occasionally I had to travel by mule and sometimes by foot, but never were the hardships so bad that my wife could not accompany me and, once there, methodically take down every word said as my secretary. What was shocking to us both is that in every country we visited—and we visited every country of Latin America except Cuba—we came across not only peasants and workers but also their leaders and politicians who said, "You are the first North American correspondents ever to try to see us."

In Latin America, the French, German, and British correspondents, even the loner from Yugoslavia's *Politika*, try, as a matter of course. Perhaps they are more accustomed to lying, corrupt governments and press, and thus, unlike United States correspondents, know that facts are rarely officially announced and more rarely still unofficially published. Therefore, they are more apt to "dig" out a story from its sources. Unfortunately our correspondents do not. Inevitably, they get their story by reading local newspapers, making a phone call to an official source to "verify" what they have read, then filing it home.

I have found Associated Press and United Press International completely unreliable in Latin America. To the people of Latin America AP and UPI are United States Government agencies. And it is not hard to see why: Their dispatches turn every politician that criticizes the United States into a "Leftist," most peasant leaders that demand a better living standard into "demagogues," and all Castro supporters into "Communists." (This would mean that a majority of the people *are* Communist, since a majority of Latin Americans *are* pro-Castro—at least whenever they identify Castro with rebellion against United States domination. Why many Latin Americans are both pro-Castro and anti-Communist, and why this is not a contradiction, will be made clear later.)

UPI and AP are factories. But what about newspaper correspondents? Unfortunately, the same is generally true. One Latin American *New York Times* man, for example, told me that Uruguay's only hope was Senator Pedro Berro who is a member of the Conservative Blanco Party and a wealthy aristocrat with a vision narrowed by decades of do-nothing petty politics. Why pick Berro, then? Berro is honest, he said. Undoubtedly, Berro is pro-United States, he added. Unquestionably. That was all.

In Argentina another *Times* man told me back in December, 1961, that then-President Arturo Frondizi would never be toppled. Having written an article for the *Baltimore Sun*[2] in which I said that Frondizi would and should fall, I naturally was ready to argue. "Listen," the *Times* man said, "Frondizi is pro-United States. That's what counts. He's a crook and a fraud, granted, but he's pro-United States. D'you realize what would happen if he fell? We might get another Perón!" I agreed, but is that a reason to predict that Frondizi would not fall?

At the second Punta del Este Conference, Cuba's President Osvaldo Dorticós made one of the most brilliantly demagogic speeches any of us had ever heard. He was often interrupted by applause. Not only spectators but most of the Latin American press corps were deeply impressed. Later, many wrote that Dorticós' speech was boring and that no one clapped. "I have to write such lies," the correspondent for Buenos Aires' *Noticias Gráficas* told me. The question, however, is: Do we, the North American reporters, have to lie too? No United States newspaper that I saw reported Dorticós' impact, not even the text of his speech. "You know what they want to hear in Florida," a correspondent from that state told me. "That's what I give them." Another

---

[2] Whose permission to incorporate my articles in this book is gratefully acknowledged.

explained it this way: "Today I can pick up the phone and get right through to Frondizi, Prado, Betancourt, or almost any other Latin American President. If I write the truth, I'll never even get to their barbers. Back home that means I'm not doing so good! Besides, my paper wouldn't print it anyway."

Unfortunately, that is sometimes true. After the first Punta del Este Conference, Cuban delegate Ernesto "Che" Guevara made a speech at the University of Montevideo. In it he said—and I quote from my dispatch to the *New York Times*—"Killing is evil. . . . All countries are different and progress should be achieved by peaceful means wherever possible. The members of this government [Uruguay] do not agree with our ideas yet they allow us to express such ideas. That is something you should cherish." This quote was cut out in the *Times'* printed version; undoubtedly the *Times*, pressed for space, felt it was not newsworthy enough. After Guevara's talk, there was a demonstration that was broken up by the police, and one man was killed. As a consequence, Uruguay's executive body took up the motion that Guevara be declared *persona non grata*. This is what the *Times* printed, as I had filed it: "At a special meeting of the Government Council, one member [whom I had identified as Councillor Benito Nardone] moved that Major Guevara be declared unwelcome in Uruguay." However, the *Times* did *not* print the following paragraph:

Furious that his motion was not passed by the nine-man Government Council, Sr. Nardone then said, "If the government does not govern there are some here who are willing to do it." Taken as a veiled threat of a *coup d'état*, Sr. Nardone's statement was immediately denounced by members of both houses of Uruguay's Congress.

Again, there is no doubt that the *Times* judged the latter paragraph to be lacking in news value. It is only circumstantially odd that Nardone was the most loudly anti-Communist member of the council, was the only one to be officially invited to the United States, where he was given an honorary degree at Fordham University, and in general is considered by some (but not all) of our embassy people as Uruguay's "greatest democrat," when in fact he is no democrat at all.

When Brazil President João Goulart appointed Francisco Brochado da Rocha as Premier, the *New York Times* reported on July 11, 1962, that "Dr. Brochado da Rocha is a member of the conservative Social Democratic Party, the largest in Congress." The late Premier was indeed a conservative, but he was also a Nationalist. That means he was interested in his nation's welfare. And, since it is Brazil's interest to push its foreign policy as close to a neutralist position as possible, the Premier, conservative as he was, insisted that under his direction Brazil would maintain a hands-off-Cuba policy: That, presumably, made him anti-United States. On July 14th, after Brazil's Congress approved President Goulart's appointment, the *New York Times* said: "Premier Brochado da Rocha is a member of the middle-of-the-road Social Democratic party." Then, on the very next day, July 15th, a *Times* editorial referred to the Premier as "a Leftist." Perhaps we should not question the discernment of the *New York Times*. Perhaps Premier Brochado da Rocha, who was fifty-two in July, 1962, experienced a quick evolution: After decades of conservative party politics, he suddenly saw the light, moved from Right to Center in three days and from Center to Left overnight.

It is true that correspondents in a hurry to get foreign news are often at the mercy of our State Department (through our embassies), USIA or other official channels. There the truth, if it is being concealed, is harder to find. Examples are numerous. Here's one of little significance in itself. When the first Punta del Este Conference ended, Richard Goodwin, one of our delegates, and "Che" Guevara met at a Brazilian diplomat's party and spent an hour chatting together informally. No secrets were revealed, no deals were made, no special amiabilities exchanged. Nevertheless, fearing the political consequences back home, our delegation and our Uruguayan Embassy "categorically" denied the meeting. Had not the Brazilian diplomat confirmed it (as did Goodwin thereafter), we would have branded the Cuban delegate a liar. Goodwin, upon his return home, was asked to appear before a congressional committee to explain the meeting. This, presumably, is what our State Department wanted to avoid by denying it in the first place. A foreigner's declaration was required for us to get the truth.

Incidents like this happen every day. The State Department

may have a million reasons for lying—all of them "for the good of the United States"—but the point remains: Unless we are willing to accept blindly the State Department's criteria about what is our good, we must hunt for the truth much harder outside the United States than we are accustomed to doing at home. Then, when we do, we are apt to find that our good is not always being served.

This can even be the case at home—in matters pertaining to Latin American policies, at least. Here's another example. On April 15, 1961, not too many hours before Cuban exiles invaded Cuba's Bay of Pigs, the island was bombarded by B-26's. Cuban Foreign Minister Raul Roa immediately denounced the attack in the United Nations as United States aggression, claiming both the planes and the pilots were ours. Ambassador to the United Nations Adlai Stevenson called the State Department to check. He was told that the planes were Cuban, flown by Cuban deserters. Believing his sources, Stevenson repeated as much in the United Nations, and stuck to that defense even after Roa asked Stevenson to furnish just one Cuban pilot. Later, of course, it turned out that the planes had been ours—painted over by our Central Intelligence Agency.[3] Would we have known the truth had the invasion succeeded?

If our press misrepresents the facts on Latin America, if our economic policies disregard Latin America's needs, if our political policies support Latin America's medievalists bent on profiting from such disregard, then perhaps we can understand why Latin Americans hate us. They would no longer be biting the hand that feeds them, but, rather, biting the hand that hurts them.

[3] According to Stewart Alsop, Stevenson protested to Kennedy, but did not resign when he discovered the truth.

PART II: The Pacesetters

PART II. The Framework

Argentina, Brazil, and Mexico are Latin America's biggest countries. Significantly, they lead the rest in opposition to United States influence, which nevertheless remains very strong. Not counting Cuba, they are the only Latin American countries that have nationalized United States corporations and, in the case of the last two, that are still occasionally doing so.

Argentina, which has yet to find its political course for the 1960s, has a long history of "independence" from the United States, and its only popular government since 1923 remained at least cool toward us until its fall. This is perhaps the real reason why our homegrown critics called it—and its leader, Juan Domingo Perón—"Fascist."

Brazil barely escaped a civil war in 1961 on the basic issue of whether it should be an unquestioning ally of the United States or follow its own independent course. The actual government, a highly repressive right-wing military dictatorship, must use cops and soldiers to keep the country from going neutralist.

Mexico has had its nationalistic revolution. It may yet have to undergo a second, as we shall see. But even today's conservative and pro-United States government feels obliged to maintain an "independent" foreign policy. Anti-Yankeeism is too firmly rooted in the hills and dust of Mexico for any government to ignore.

There is much more unrest in all three countries than

51

is reported in our press. We often hear of the infighting carried on by Brazilian and Argentine politicians and military. We rarely hear, however, of the vast number of peasants and workers and intellectuals who are slowly being prepared for their country's forthcoming declaration of economic independence.

Not all of Argentina's militarists are conniving, power-lusting pawns of vested interests; some are "Nasserites" convinced that a strong neutralist regime is the country's only salvation. As Argentina's last election proved, the majority of the people agree. In Brazil the tensions raised by the struggle between Nationalist and "anti-Communist" forces overshadows a much more fundamental struggle being waged between landless peasants and land-hoarding barons. In Mexico the dictatorial powers of the ruling party usually squashes news of small peasant rebellions solidly rooted in the old revolutionary tradition.

It was no accident that Brazil's conservative President Jânio Quadros welcomed Communist guests at his palace, that Argentina's President Arturo Frondizi, totally dependent on the United States, ordered his delegate at the Second Punta del Este Conference to vote against us, and that Mexico's middle-class President Adolfo López Mateos was compelled to cast Latin America's only No vote against an Organization of American States motion to deal with the "threat" created by Cuba's conversion to Communism. These three presidents reflect their people's pulse. And that pulse has only recently begun accelerating.

Because the peoples of Argentina, Brazil, and Mexico add up to almost two-thirds of Latin America, this pulse is of primary importance. If any of their veins burst, blood can flow on the whole continent. They are Latin America's leaders. Argentina, Brazil, and Mexico set the pace. Sooner or later the others must follow.

Chapter 3

Argentina

Of the three, Argentina is the most unstable. A powerful country with vast resources and a huge extension of lush flat land called *pampa*, where, as the saying goes, "one spits and out comes grass," Argentina is underpopulated and overendowed. It has enough oil to be an exporter, enough natural gas to provide heat for all its inhabitants, and enough rivers to light twenty times more houses and factories than it now does. It was, once, Latin America's economic leader. Today it is its most insolvent, its most irresponsible—and its most unpredictable.

Argentina's past events, however, were very predictable. The first Latin American country to break with Spain, even in 1810 it was divided into the typical two camps: the landed gentry, or Federalists, versus the city merchants, or Unitarians (*unitarios*). Both, in their own way, were out to milk the poor, the peons and the Indians who were not yet viciously persecuted. Both were unpatriotic in the genuine sense of the word: they felt no true love or respect for their country, aping England and France in Buenos Aires, Spain in the interior. Of the two, however, the landed gentry had the more native roots and, as Federalists, the greater vision of their country.

Because the merchants were allied to British traders, British imperialism had no difficulty spreading its claws throughout the country. The landed aristocrat fought back with his gauchos (cowboys) as best he could, but rarely succeeded. There were exceptions, of course, and Juan Manuel de Rosas was perhaps the greatest of these.

53

A blue-eyed, Buenos Aires-born aristocrat who was raised
on the pampa and who used his loyal gauchos to bully
himself to power in 1829 (at the time, the governorship
of Buenos Aires Province), Rosas crushed the Unitarians
for many years. But while he championed federation, his
real interest was Rosas; he betrayed, executed, and destroyed
whoever he pleased for whatever reason pleased him.
Nevertheless, he fought England and France and launched
Argentina toward the powerful status it went on to achieve
in the last century. That no monument to Rosas exists
in all Argentina and that no plaza or street bears his name
is not proof of his barbarism or cruelty, his self-interest
or self-indulgence. It is proof, rather, that Argentina was
finally won and controlled by the city merchants, the residents
of the port of Buenos Aires, known as *porteños*.

The best known *porteños* are Bartolomé Mitre and
Domingo Faustino Sarmiento, whose rise to presidential
power and whose worst claim to fame are based on their
hatred of what was genuine in Argentina—the gauchos.
To Sarmiento, Mitre, and their followers, the gauchos,
the *campo* (the fields), and the majestic beauty of Argentina's
harsh countryside was *"La Barbarie."*

True, these *porteños* chalked up sound accomplishments.
Mitre formulated Argentina's first all-encompassing judicial
code and established a court system, extended the postal
service and telegraph lines, federalized customs, created
a national credit bank, encouraged immigration and, more
basically, achieved national unity for which he had systematically to wipe out Argentina's numerous *caudillos*. Sarmiento
extended the railroads, built bridges, began the modernization
of the port of Buenos Aires, organized the Banco Nacional
and, always obsessed by the honest earthiness of his people,
whom he called "loafers, drunkards, useless fellows," launched
Argentina's primary school system and reorganized its educational methods.

Both Mitre and Sarmiento, however, lacked moral principles. Mitre tried a political comeback through force.
Sarmiento used fraud to win elections. As President, Sarmiento
fled to Europe when Argentina was struck by a yellow-fever
epidemic (while even many of his fellow oligarchs stayed
behind to help.) As governor of La Rioja Province, Sarmiento
relentlessly pursued Angel Vicente Peñaloza, known as

"El Chacho," the last of the major caudillos, finally cornered him and caught him by surprise, had him tied, pierced with a lance, shot, and decapitated. With the approval of Mitre, who was then President, Sarmiento had El Chacho's head jammed atop a pike, and commented happily, "If the head of that inveterate rogue had not been cut off and displayed, the rabble wouldn't have quieted down in six months."

Such cruelty or amorality was not abnormal. Both Mitre and Sarmiento belonged to a class that found such activities natural. This "enlightened" minority was extremely Europhile, convinced of its mission in the progress of Argentina, a firm believer in free trade because it profited from it, and, of course, conservative politically. It favored immigration in order to acquire cheap labor, but it felt only contempt for the *gringo* (Italian) and the *gallego* (Spaniard) newcomers. In order to attract foreign capital, it did not refrain from making undue concessions. These investments brought roads, electricity, railroads, and so on, benefiting mainly their foreign owners and the Argentine minority known as "the oligarchy."

With a tight hold on political power, with *La Prensa*, *La Nación* (founded by Mitre), and the rest of the press to support its actions, and with the big export-import firms to control trade, the oligarchy ruled Argentine life from top to bottom. It maintained "democracy" through such undemocratic means as suppression of constitutional guarantees, election frauds, and frequent federal interventions in the provinces. Until it cut its own throat when President Sáenz Peña let ballots be secret, the oligarchy was the law.

But the unavoidable had to happen. The hordes of Spanish and Italian immigrants who settled mostly in Buenos Aires brought with them new ideas on trade and work and laws. As they grew in number and means (after years of penny-pinching saving), they began to form a new class, the bourgeoisie, and demanded a new party to be their voice. Launched just before this century by a romantic idealist named Leandro N. Alem,[1] then enlarged and system-

[1] Who committed suicide with a farewell evaluation of his own career that has come to characterize the life of Argentina's radicalism: "It is better to die than to live sterile, useless, and humiliated."

atized by his conniving nephew, Hipólito Yrigoyen, the
new party was the Unión Cívica Radical.

Yrigoyen finally won the presidency in 1916 and again
in 1928. But, suspicious of his aides while overly confident
of himself, he tried to do everything himself and consequently
did almost nothing well. He enacted some social legislation
—nothing compared to what was being done next door
in Uruguay—but failed even to tackle Argentina's main
problem, the enormous disparity between land and city,
peon and oligarch. While he floundered, his aides, more
crooked than not, milked the treasury to such an extent
that Argentine Historian Félix Weil lamented that "an
honest President may be much more expensive for the
country in the course of time than a 'run-of-the-mill'
politician."

General José Félix Uriburu overthrew Yrigoyen in 1930,
clamped Argentina within a ruthless but efficient dictatorship,
tried to set up a vague kind of corporative state based
on some badly digested concepts imported from Mussolini's
Italy, and failed.

Backing him was a group of pseudointellectuals who
called themselves Nationalists but were in fact reactionary
oligarchs. They opposed universal suffrage and democracy,
which they called demagogery, favored some sort of fascistic
corporative representation directed by a strong man, and
rabidly defended the Catholic Church, which they considered
the main pillar of society. They were also usually pro-British
and always anti-United States, especially after the coming
of the New Deal. These "oligarcho-nationalists" played
an increasing role in Argentine politics, gaining followers
as they went along, and becoming, after Hitler enacted
the Nürnberg Laws, violently anti-Semitic. They published
a whole series of newspapers and magazines, one of them
subsidized by Germany's Nazi Embassy—*El Pampero.* The
group's revered publication was *Sol y Luna,* whose hero
was Spain's dictator Francisco Franco and whose major
contributors will reappear in our history.

In the November, 1931, elections, meanwhile, the Radicals
proved how unradical they were. Prohibited from presenting
candidates, they either boycotted the election or backed
Conservative General Agustín P. Justo, instead of Lisandro
de la Torre, the Socialist and Progressive Democrat parties'
candidate.

Justo's way of helping Argentina recover was by encouraging European, especially British, and United States corporations to move into the country by the boatload. By 1942 Britain owned three-fifths of the $2,500,000,000 foreign investment in Argentina, and the United States, 20 percent. Justo seemed to agree with Mitre who had called England "the principal factor in the country's political, social, and economic progress." Justo even outlawed Buenos Aires *colectivos,* the small locally owned buses that took most of the slow British-owned trolley's traffic, and gave Britain a new citywide monopoly charter with a guaranteed return of 7 percent. The genuine Nationalist outcry did not stop the giveaways.

These giveaways, leading back further than Mitre, must be understood well before one quickly brands what followed Justo as "Fascism." Germany, be it of Kaiser Wilhelm II or Adolf Hitler, was not imperialistic in Argentina (though German officers trained the Argentine Army). But economically, England was. So, to a lesser extent, was the United States. Besides, Argentina's traditional aspirations for the leadership of Latin America conflicted with our own designs. During World War I, President Yrigoyen had kept Argentina firmly neutral, selling to both sides even after German subs had sunk Argentine ships. It was good business to be neutral, and Argentina felt unmoved by any other issue in that "War of the Imperialists."

But by World War II there existed issues: Democracy versus Fascism, World Morality versus World Domination. But not to the Argentines. Democracy had not worked in Argentina. Fascism had not been tried. Many Argentines had sympathized with the Spanish Republic during the Spanish Civil War of 1936-1939. But many, especially those under the influence of the Church, which was (and is) one of the most reactionary forces in Argentina, had been partisans of Franco. World morality was (and is) no issue to Argentines: they have never seen a moral government. And, as to world domination, who dominated what in Argentina? The British had 60 percent, we had 20 percent, the French and Belgians the rest—Allies all! The Argentine hated his British-owned railroad: it ran late, used old equipment, broke down often, charged high prices. The *porteño* hated his British-owned trolley: it ran slow, was old and worn, and had no competition.

Until 1943 President Ramón S. Castillo, an oligarch's pawn strongly backed by the "neutralist" oligarcho-nationalist group, ran Argentina down, but kept neutralism up, and had no trouble. But when he hand-picked Robustiano Patrón Costas to succeed him, he sealed his fall. Patrón Costas was (and his family is) the owner of hundreds of thousands of sugar hectares where peons and Indians imported from Bolivia are brutally treated. But what angered the "neutralists" was that his financial monopolies dealt with the British. Thus, on June 4, 1943, before the elections ever came off, a military junta once again took the government.

From June 7th until February, 1944, Argentina was ruled by General Pedro P. Ramírez with iron and blood. University critics were fired. Pro-Allied organizations were closed. Demonstrations were suppressed. Even Jews were persecuted for a while. Our Secretary of State, Cordell Hull, who had rushed the United States into recognizing the coup—not because it was "democratic," for it certainly was not, nor was it meant to be, but because it might be anti-Nazi—pressured and threatened until, finally, Ramírez broke relations with the Axis. But it was not a popular act. The majority of the Argentines were neutral—and not just the oligarchs, but the people. Those who took trains (the oligarchs take planes) and those who rode trolleys (the oligarchs ride taxis) were more anti-British than anti-Nazi. Ramírez fell.

The man who masterminded the new coup, the man who understood and used public opinion best, was Colonel Juan Domingo Perón.

Ever since the early days of the 1943 coup, Perón had played a strange and important role from behind the scenes. As leader of a group of Nationalist officers known as GOU (Grupo de Oficiales Unidos), Perón had a strong following among the military. Now he set out to woo and win the masses, whose strength he never underestimated (until he finally overestimated it). He took over a job no one wanted—the Labor Department. From there he worked quietly and carefully to build up a loyal labor movement.

Tall, with a winning smile and fiery tongue, Perón decreed labor and social laws, built up strong unions in the meat-packing houses (*frigoríficos*) and even in the sugar plantations

where union supporters only months before had been
ruthlessly murdered. He forced employers to yield to
union demands. Wages went up. Social-security funds were
launched. The Statute of the Peon gave the eight-hour day
and the minimum wage to the field hand. More important
still, Perón gave the workingman a consciousness—of his
class, his strength, and his importance.

Jealous of Perón's power, and allied to the oligarchy
that feared him, a group of officers staged an anti-Perón
golpe, or coup, on October 9, 1945. They imprisoned Perón
but vacillated long enough at the Casa Rosada (the Pink
House, Argentina's White House) for Perón's labor friends
and his wife-to-be, Eva, to rally the workers. They showed
up more than 100,000 strong and literally took over Buenos
Aires. Perón was released. "I am back!" he shouted to
the crowds. "We have won!"

He *was* back: Within five months Perón was elected President in a fair election by a sweeping majority, and his
followers captured almost two-thirds of the House and
all but two of the Senate seats. And the masses had also
won: Unions were organized in every industry; social security
was spread to cover all activities; education was made
free to all who qualified; vast low-income housing projects
were launched and completed, and were actually turned
over to low-income earners—unheard of in Latin America.

Paid vacations became standard. A working student was
granted one paid week off before every major examination,
and a mother-to-be received three paid months off before
and after giving birth. All workers, even white-collar (banks,
insurance, and so on), were guaranteed free medical care
and half of their vacation-trip expenses. Workers' colonies
were built all over Argentina. One especially impressed
me. Built on the side of three man-made lakes in the lower
Sierras on the road from Córdoba to Río Cuarto, this
colony is a complex of eight hotels, scores of family cabins,
movies, swimming pools for adults and children, coffee
shops, medical centers, churches, well-planned gardens, amuse-
ment halls, riding stables with horses for adults and ponies
for children, and so on. Elegant, aesthetically modern, in
white brick and natural mahogany, clean and spacious,
this resort was available to workers for fifteen days once

a year at fifteen cents a day per person, all services included.[2]

One of GOU's (and Perón's) promises was the "economic emancipation" of Argentina from foreign vices. To accomplish this, Perón created the Argentine Institute for Promotion of Exchange, a monopoly handling all basic commodity exports, which bought Argentine products low and sold them overseas high. With its earnings, and with Argentina's sterling blocked in England during World War II, Perón bought out Argentina's IT&T company from the United States and the railroads and trolleys from England. He paid off Argentina's debts (though he was forced to borrow again in 1950) and launched his Five-Year Plan (1946) that covered everything from women's vote to shipbuilding but focused most on industrialization.

By 1954 Perón had completed or solidly under way 45 major hydroelectric projects designed to produce 2 billion kilowatt-hours of energy, twenty times what was available in 1936. By 1947 he could boast, exaggerating only slightly, that Argentina had its own "iron and steel industry, coal mines, and various other raw materials; makes all powder and explosives needed in the country and makes all its arms, munitions, and vehicles." It did in fact make farm and industrial machinery, planes, a few cars, and produced enough steel to take pride in its heavy new industry. During his ten-year rule, Perón also increased Argentina's Merchant Marine by 500 percent to more than 1,500,000 tons.

But Perón failed. His economic measures were not too sweeping; they were not sweeping enough. He raised rural wages and forced landowners to sell cheap, but when they balked (all *latifundistas* were opposed to Perón) he did not take the next logical step: nationalize the land. Thus the amount of land under cultivation dropped from 21,814,000 hectares in 1934-1938 to 17,254,000 in 1955. So ruthless and efficient in silencing political and intellectual opponents, Perón not once dared to use his arbitrary power to silence Argentina's landed oligarchy. Perón failed because he was not a revolutionary.

Self-centered and self-interested, Perón wanted only to

[2] Many of these colonies have been sold to private clubs since the fall of Perón; this one, however, was still for workers when I visited it in 1962, but charges were then $1 a day, which at our price scales was the equivalent of $8.

stay in power, be revered as a world statesman, and assure himself a place in history. He founded and propagated a quasi-philosophy, called *Justicialismo,* that claimed to keep the four dialectical pulls of history (idealism and materialism, individualism and collectivism) at equal distance from each other—a third position, as he said, between Communism and capitalism. Actually, he had neither ideological groundings nor empirical convictions—except to "play it by ear." He knew how to control the army and how to dominate the General Confederation of Labor (CGT). But he never learned to differentiate between a Nationalist who sought a truly emancipated Argentina and a nationalist to whom "emancipation" simply meant wiping out foreign competition. Perón had opposition labor leaders shot. Why did he not have Patrón Costas shot? Those industrialists, financiers, speculators, and land barons who were not in his private circle were 100 percent against him. Yet Perón crushed not one. Perón was not a Fascist, as numerous critics call him; he was not in the last analysis anything else than a Peronist. But he gave the masses their first political conscience, and for this he indeed won himself a place in history.

Morally (not to mention financially) corrupt himself, Perón was naturally surrounded by many other crooks. Like rats on a sinking boat, these crooks—so vociferously pro-Perón only months before—turned against him when the going got tough. The revolt that overthrew Perón in 1955 was not a popular revolt. It was carried out by a bunch of despicable "apes"—forgive me the word, but that is, in fact, what they are called: *Los Gorilas.*

The gorillas were top army, air force, and navy officers whose rise they owed to Perón himself; one Admiral Isaac Rojas, who led the navy against Perón and who then became Vice-President in the transitional government of General Pedro Eugenio Aramburu, used to brag, when he was Perón's naval attaché in Rio de Janeiro, that no man could be more Peronist than he. Aramburu himself owed his status to Perón.

The gorillas had not the remotest respect for democratic law and order; during their two-year rule, more "enemies of the state" were executed by firing squad without trial than had been silenced by Perón himself during his whole reign. In fact, so quick was gorilla justice that some non-

Peronists were shot by mistake during one infamous night's work known as *Operación Masacre*.

The motive for the 1955 coup was lust for power, and its success was possible only because the structure of Perón's regime had begun to disintegrate from within. It was then that Perón overestimated the strength of the masses. They would have fought and died to defend his right to "brutalize" them, as our press used to say, had they been armed. But, unable to fight back, they went home after suffering a few deaths from bombs dropped indiscriminately on the main square, the Plaza de Mayo, by brave gorilla pilots.[3]

The gorillas have either ruled directly or used their power as veto ever since. The first provisional government lasted but a few months, ousted as it was by General Aramburu and Admiral Rojas. These ex-Peronists banned all Peronist activities and repressed the Left as well, but because General Aramburu wanted to be a "constitutional" President, allowed free elections to take place in 1958.

The first to announce his candidacy was a former small-time corporation lawyer named Arturo Frondizi—one of Latin America's shrewdest politicians. With mild manners to conceal razor-edged irony and thick horn-rimmed glasses to camouflage sharp eyes, Frondizi was capable of fooling many people for a very long time. A Radical who had risen fast but not, in his own estimation, high enough in his party, Frondizi suddenly broke away from Yrigoyen's old apparatus and set up his own, Unión Cívica Radical Intransigente (UCRI), and wooed away much of the younger blood. The old Radicals thereupon called themselves Unión Cívica Radical del Pueblo (UCRP), elected their own slates —and the campaign was on.

To Argentines, Frondizi was not an unknown. He had been a vice-presidential candidate a few years before, and had gained fame with a rabidly nationalistic book on Argentina's oil problems, *Política Petróleo*. Nevertheless, he seemed too much of an upstart to be a presidential candidate. But he had one huge asset—an ex-Communist

[3] Some youthful members of Perón's Alianza Libertadora Nacionalista fought tanks and cannons with pistols and rifles until their Buenos Aires headquarters was pulverized to rubble.

turned multimillionaire entrepreneur named Rogelio Frigerio. A cold, ruthless calculator who, according to one of his top aides, defines democracy as "that system where money talks louder than principles." Frigerio poured his energy, considerable talent, and especially money into the job of creating a Frondizi image. He launched a magazine called *Qué*, and hired for it some of Argentina's best political essayists, such as Dardo Cúneo and Noé Jitrik, and journalists, including Marcos Merchensky, Rogelio García Lupo and Osiris Troiani, the latter two staunch, quasi-Falangist Nationalists who believed Frondizi to be, as he claimed, one of them.

These writers not only edited *Qué* and other pamphlets and newssheets but, with the writer Ismael Viñas (another Nationalist, out of the left wing of the Radicals), also wrote Frondizi's speeches, blasted his critics, waged a brilliant campaign over radio and TV. Convinced that Frondizi would finish what Perón had begun—to make Argentina "politically sovereign, socially just, and economically free" —they helped to make him into an aggressive, popular hero, and to win the allegiance of Left and Right extremists, including such an oligarcho-nationalist as Marcelo Sánchez Sorondo.[4]

Frigerio, meanwhile, had little trouble swinging over the military. Obeying Mexico's revolutionary President Alvaro Obregón, who once said, "I do not know a single general able to resist to a cannonade of one million pesos," Frigerio fired peso cannonballs right and left, and got no less than two hundred generals on the boards of corporations he either influenced, controlled, or owned.

Once elected, Frondizi gave a few top Peronists their amnesties and returned their confiscated properties; he allowed them to hold on to their union posts once they regained them. Simultaneously he gave the oligarchy "development" tax concessions and lucrative contracts. He talked interested foreign firms into partnership with the oligarchy in new industries that, under cover of "Argentine companies," opened Argentina to foreign investments. (To prove the sincerity of his "free enterprising" economy, he

[4] Who, after years of plotting in the air and on the Right, seems to have finally set his feet on solid ground, and currently edits *Segunda República,* whose editorial policy is "Either a nationalist dictatorship or a free, uncancellable election."

agreed to pay American & Foreign Power Company about $60 million for twenty-two plants expropriated by Perón.) To satisfy the army, Frondizi kept in operation Perón's Plan Conintes (*Conmoción Interior del Estado*) whereby the country was legally under military rule, the brass being allowed to arrest and judge its civilian enemies secretly and with military appointed defense lawyers. Frondizi also assured Aramburu of his support in the 1964 presidential elections. Aramburu and his friends rallied behind Frondizi.

But other militarists—not all fifteen thousand high-echelon officers on active duty could be bought—remained restless. When their restlessness became plots and an army command or two prepared to rebel, Frondizi aides easily convinced Peronist labor leaders that their necks were at stake; the labor men staged one- or two-day general strikes, and the militarists, fearful of a Peronist revolution, quickly switched their support back to Frondizi. Then, when Peronists became too loud, Frondizi let his federal police clamp a few score or even hundreds into jails for two weeks of cooling off. And when they persisted, Frondizi's contacts within the army "arranged" a new military coup.

Meanwhile, his so-called "economic program" continued. Mainly limited to giving away oil exploration concessions and boosting production of manufactured goods, this program was quite successful. The once barren deserts of Patagonia, in the South, were transformed into bustling mining centers, with old and new wells gushing out 70 percent of the country's daily needs of 250,000 barrels. (United States oil companies increased their contracts to a value of $1 billion; Standard Oil of New Jersey alone exploited 1,184,000 acres in Patagonia.) Manufactured goods also went up significantly, especially in cars and vehicles.

But other heavy-industry projects were flops. Frondizi's much-repeated goal of making Argentina self-sufficient in steel was a total fiasco. By 1962 it was producing 600,000 tons when it needed 3,000,000. Furthermore, the emphasis on heavy industry hurt agricultural production. Meat dropped from 145,000 metric tons a year during the Perón regime to 87,000 at the end of 1961; cereals and vegetables dropped to 5 percent below World War II's level; wheat dipped steadily since 1955, 30 percent in 1961 alone. Even electricity, a basic item for industrialization, went down sharply at first (Perón's incompleted projects were discontinued), and then slowly, from 646 million kilowatt-hours in 1959 to 630 million by 1962.

One result, of course, was trade imbalance. In 1960 the deficit was $237 million; in 1961, $450 million; in 1962, around $640 million. These imbalances, in turn, caused money to become tighter than it already was, and inflation outran wage increases. Since the fall of Perón, salaries went up 400 percent, food 750 percent, other items 800 percent. Thus, the per capita yearly consumption of meat (Argentina's staple food) dropped from 92.3 kilos in 1955 to 64.8 by 1962, milk from 96 liters to 81, eggs from 56 to 20, potatoes from 63 kilos to 39.5. Frondizi, short of money, had to raise taxes, In 1955 indirect taxes, which hurt the poor most, amounted to 51.8 percent of the government revenue; by 1962 they were 74.3 percent.

With the masses losing their buying power, their restlessness became more acute. To cope with it, Frondizi cut away one civil liberty after another. He kept Argentina under a state of siege (besides Plan Conintes), and the police took advantage of their right to arbitrary arrest, seizure, search, confiscation, and indefinite detention. One midnight in September, 1961, for example, the police raided the homes of Spanish Republican exile leaders, hauled off to Las Heras Penitentiary all those present, including friends, visitors, and families, and kept them incommunicado for weeks. The official explanation was "Communist activities," but leaders of Buenos Aires' Basque, Galician, and Catalán clubs were known as fervent anti-Communists. In Buenos Aires, people became more afraid of police than of thieves. Not having one's documents or being in a café after midnight with a member of the opposite sex who was not a spouse was grounds for arrest. Victims were generally held forty-eight hours; families were not notified; young girls were sometimes raped.

Torture became more common than under Perón; the usual method was the *picana,* a 12,000-volt electrical device that, attached to sexual organs, nipples, or soles of feet, caused unbearable pain (and eventual sterility) without leaving traces. On July 1, 1961, a congressional investigating committee, which had turned up evidence of widespread police torture practices resulting in 38 innocent deaths, was dissolved after a group of policemen fired 200 shots against the Congress building, wounding two bystanders.

Policemen were not fired or prosecuted; instead their salaries were raised 35 percent, and on July 25th Frondizi declared a National Police Week.

Censorship became unbearably rigid. Movies were heavily cut. Newspapers and magazines were constantly confiscated; more than thirty were permanently banned. And while police proudly upheld Argentina's moral values, such Fascist groups as Tacuara, which denounced the United States as a "Judeo-capitalist" state led by "Communist" Kennedy, went unmolested. Tacuara hoodlums tossed stink bombs into theaters showing anti-Nazi films (*Mein Kampf,* for example, which my wife and I had to see through tears), and broke into Jewish cultural centers or into university seminars armed with submachine guns. They wore identifiable armbands or lapel buttons, made the Fascist salute, published anti-Semitic tracts, and owned offices in the center of town, yet not one of them was hauled off to jail while I was there. (Since then, in June, 1962, one Tacuara pug was arrested for murdering a Jewish boy, but was released four days later for "insufficient evidence" despite a neighborhood full of witnesses.)

Reasons for Tacuara's police protection exist. When Nazi hangman Eichmann, who was kidnapped from Argentina by Israeli agents, was being tried in Jerusalem, early in 1962, members of the Argentine Army's equivalent of the CIA (each armed service has its own espionage system) told leaders of the Buenos Aires Jewish Community: "There will be a great deal of anti-Semitic activity now. We can assure you that no one from your community will suffer, physically or materially, if you cooperate with us. We want the names of every Communist Jew."

Others never arrested for their activities were the Rightist gorillas who increased their plots (thirty-five by March, 1962) as the situation worsened. The rebellious military, Frondizi told the people, "acted, perhaps misguidedly, from an intense anti-Communist patriotism." And to prove he meant it, he sent to Congress late in 1961 a new Law for the Defense of Democracy that prescribed jail terms for "all members or nonmembers of movements or parties that are Communist or might be favorable toward Communism in the future." The law was to be retroactive for three to five years.

Naturally, this form of democracy was nothing Frondizi's

aides bargained for; García Lupo, Troiani, Viñas, and the others quickly went into vigorous and at times persecuted[5] opposition. So did Frondizi's hand-picked Vice-President Alejandro Gómez, who resigned.

But one group did not; on the contrary. Typical of this group, the oligarcho-nationalists, was Juan Carlos Goyeneche, known about town as "The Viceroy," one of the directors of *Sol y Luna,* who had deserted Perón when he had begun raising the wages of peons. Goyeneche made his comeback with the gorillas, whom he served as a press secretary. In an interview early in 1962, after his return from a trip to the United States, he told me he had "found, especially in the West Coast where the Crusades and the John Birch Society are so strong, a very healthy rejuvenation, proving there was still hope in the United States." Another *Sol y Luna* contributor was one Máximo Etchecopar who used to refer to democracies as "backward" and who then became one of "Democrat Frondizi's" ambassadors. Worst of all was Mario Amadeo, another *Sol y Luna* director, who in 1946 said that neither the United States nor Russia could save the world, since "in both reigns the predominance of the masses with all its nefarious consequences, hate of personality, vulgar tastes, contempt for traditions, crude utilitarianism, absence of refinement," while only "two nations today appear with the great historic possibilities for the exercise of that mission [saving the world]: [Franco] Spain and [Perón] Argentina." Amadeo became so pro-gorilla that he served as the transitional government's Minister of Foreign Affairs, and so pro-Frondizi as to merit the post of Ambassador to the United Nations, where he was often cited as an example of Latin America's defenders of democratic principles.

There was one other Frondizi aide who was perfectly happy: Rogelio Frigerio. Having quietly acquired control of half of all TV and radio channels in Argentina, he was convinced that the elimination of the Left and of the non-Peronist Nationalists was in his interest. Hence he decided

---

[5] Viñas' apartment was bombed, fortunately when he was absent; but his books, paintings, files, manuscripts (some without copies), and so on, were burned. García Lupo was sought by DIPA (the "antisubversion" secret police) which ransacked his belongings. Troiani went into exile.

to tighten his grip on the country even more. Thus, late in 1961, Frondizi and Frigerio (FF) went all out against their major enemy: not the Peronists, not the Communists, not even the military, but their old party buddies—the democratic, harmless, senile People's Radicals.

Most of Argentina's provinces let only the winning and first minority party split up, proportionally to their vote, all elective offices. The Frigerio-Frondizi plan was to permit Peronists (by then handily divided by FF manipulation) to present candidates, hoping that their strength would politically eliminate the People's Radicals. In a series of by-elections a few weeks later, the formula worked: FF's men came in first, one faction of the Peronists second, and the People's Radicals became unemployed. Fortified by this success, FF decided to let the Peronists participate in the general provincial and parliamentary elections of March, 1962. "We shall wipe the People's Radicals from Argentina's political map," rejoiced one FF lieutenant.

There was another, more subtle reasoning behind FF's apparent madness. They knew that the Peronists would make a strong showing, perhaps actually win in a few provinces. Peronists are potential troublemakers. After his fall, Perón had ordered his forces to plot for his return: some two hundred or three hundred terrorists had tossed a few bombs, and some Peronist officers had tried a few minor coups, but no Peronist leader had ever become strong enough or the party disciplined enough to launch a revolution —against a well-armed army. But by its very size, his following remained a danger.

Frondizi and Frigerio also knew that no matter how much they gave in to the military's demands, increasing its budget, its pay, and its power, they would never be totally free from their military shadow, which would always be able to throw them out. However, should the country function well *with* Peronists in key jobs but *without* real power, the military might be curtailed. The whole country, then, would be against the military. And so was born a weird philosophy: integrationism.

With Perón in no position to quibble, Frondizi and Frigerio offered him a pact: Peronists would be integrated if they promised to behave. To Perón the deal had certain advantages. If his men could take over some "democratic" posts, and pose as good, corruptible Democrats, the oligarchy-military alliance against him might let them slowly acquire real power. It was worth a try.

To FF the deal had very distinct advantages. If the Peronists fared badly, they would never be a menace again. And if they came through strongly, two possibilities would arise: (1) the military would allow the Peronists to take their posts, in which case the former would lose some of its own power, or (2) the military would toss the Peronists out, in which case the latter (unable to launch or win a revolution) would no longer represent a threat. Either way, FF were convinced they would gain.

But in this ingenious plan, FF did not once consider the possibility that the military would throw them out along with the Peronists. Integrationism was a lovely tactic, it seemed, for FF to have their cake and eat it. If it worked, they would be the masters of Argentina. If it failed, two of their enemies (Peronists and People's Radicals) would be eliminated and, allied with the gorillas, FF could develop more fully Argentina's form of Francoism.

Then, suddenly, all seemed to go wrong: From his plush exile in Spain, Perón, unsure of his personal future in this "integrationist" maneuver, ordered his followers to vote blank. Fortunately for FF, Peronist leaders in Argentina realized that another round of protest votes (twice Peronists had voted blank) would spell their political eclipse. "We can't control the masses," complained syndicalist Augusto Vandor to his boss after a hurried trip to Spain. "They're angry, outraged against the government. They want to vote—or fight." Reluctant to start a fight that he knew would fail, Perón opted for the vote. The Peronists united and presented strong candidates.

Then the army warned FF that they would be held personally responsible if UCRI lost the election. So an unwritten agreement between FF's Interior Minister Alfredo Vítolo and Crisólogo Larralde, chief of the Buenos Aires Province People's Radicals, was worked out promising Larralde the presidency in 1964 if he would help the Intransigentes in 1962. But a month before the elections, Larralde died of a heart attack, and his successors were not so naïve as to believe an FF promise.

Next, a deal with the old man himself was attempted. One Jacobo Timerman, a small-time TV producer turned never-writing Roving Reporter for Frigerio's *El Mundo* (and then Director of the prestigious newsmagazine *Primera Plana*) called on Perón for an "interview." He came back empty-handed. Finally, the Peronists received millions of pesos to torpedo their own chances; they gleefully accepted and, having learned from FF that double cross equals shrewdness, used the money to step up their campaigns.

They did not need to. With democracy discredited, real democrats voted for the Peronists either in protest or because the Peronists represented Argentina's only mass-based party. As expected, the Socialists and Communists followed suit. When the returns were in, Peronists, with 2,528,000 to FF's 2,038,000, took 44 of the 86 congressional seats at stake, nine of the 14 governorships (including crucial Buenos Aires), and wiped out FF majorities in almost all elected assemblies or councils.

Before Frondizi could figure out the next deal—or double cross—the army occupied La Plata, capital of Buenos Aires Province, and presented him with an order "intervening" (that is, firing all elected officials) in the five most important provinces where Peronists had won. Frondizi signed "in the name of democracy" the rape order of democratic process. But it did not save him. He was arrested. Frigerio fled to Uruguay. Frondizi tried to stand his ground, refusing to sign his resignation "for the defense of democracy."

It was an empty gesture. The only debating still heard was which branch of the Armed Forces would give Frondizi his *coup de grâce*. United States Ambassador Robert McClintock, rushing frantically (but never so fast as to forget his constant companion—his dog), huddled with military leaders. It does not matter if he told them "leave Frondizi alone or get no more aid" as they claim and he denies; the fact that he personally intervened (could he not have used intermediaries?) convinced the masses that we had abandoned Frondizi. The masses hated Frondizi and would not have done anything to save him, but our "intervention," as McClintock's moves were immediately characterized, did add fuel to the already strongly burning fires of anti-Yankeeism.

The military gorillas put Senator José María Guido, the next highest elected official, into the Pink House (after he had sworn never to enter it under force), told him to do as they ordered, and thus naïvely hoped to have saved "democratic legality"—a gimmick needed by ambitious Gen-

eral Aramburu to allow him to run for the presidency as
soon as the situation simmered down enough for his gorillas
to schedule an election. The farce was over.

Frigerio and Frondizi failed because they had over-
confidently dismissed Argentina's militarists as stupid. That
such a characteristic is not to be overlooked is clear enough.
It was they, for example, who fabricated the "Cuban documents" meant to force Frondizi to break relations with
Fidel Castro, a job so badly done (names were wrong, Argentine slang was used, events were described in "letters"
dated before they occurred) that Frondizi found himself
in the ridiculous position of having publicly to brand the
documents false. But the gorillas were not so stupid as
not to see the threat that FF's integrationism posed. If
it succeeded, they realized, General Aramburu, who dreamt
of the presidency with nymphomaniacal lust, would have
less chance to win it in the next election. But with Frondizi
jailed, Frigerio in exile, UCRP defeated, the Peronists
outlawed, and UCRI split (President Guido is a UCRI),
Aramburu would have the best of chances.

There was, moreover, one other reason for the gorillas'
coup. Frondizi had refused to break relations with Cuba,
Russia, or her satellites. Frigerio, the businessman, had
refused to cut off Argentina's trade with these countries
as well. At the second Punta del Este Conference, Argentina
had been one of the six countries to refuse to vote with
the United States against Cuba. Since it has been our consistent policy in Latin America to "convince" governments
to break such relations and cut off such trade (even if
we ourselves maintain them), the gorillas were under strong
pressure from our military missions to force Frondizi's
hand. Despite Frondizi's occasional maverick vote in the
Organization of American States, our State Department
claimed not to want him out; he was, in fact, a strong "free
enterpriser," and our own companies profited most from
this. But our tough-lining Pentagon apparently was not
impressed; its mission chiefs in Argentina said so to
the gorillas, and thus Frondizi fell. And, proving that
even our State Department was not so unhappy, we quickly
recognized his illegal successor.

As far as our companies are concerned, what followed
Frondizi was even better. The military victors kept on
feuding among themselves, even to the point of beginning—but

not finishing—a minor civil war in September, 1962. But their Economics Minister, Alvaro Alsogaray,[6] increased the rate of giveaways and, until general discontent forced him out in December, attracted dollar loans.

Eventually, of course, the gorillas thought they were ready to win an election. So they scheduled one for July 7, 1963, and their candidate, naturally, was Gen. Aramburu. By then, Frondizi had been released from Martin García, the Plate River island prison where he had been kept by the gorillas. But he was under a form of exile and surveillance in Bariloche, and was not allowed to participate in the elections. Nevertheless, backed by Frigerio and allied to most Peronist leaders, he pushed his Frente Nacional y Popular into the elections and, when the gorillas ordered the Frente to withdraw, told his followers to vote blank.

That, too, was a mistake: it risked letting Aramburu win by default, a prospect extremely distasteful to Argentina's masses and middle class. So they voted for an aging gentle country doctor named Arturo Illia, the candidate of the sterile UCRP.

Illia won, and a month after taking office, he kept his campaign promise to annul Argentina's contracts with foreign (mostly U.S.) oil companies. For a few days, Washington was worried. Could Illia be a Nationalist at heart? Actually such an annulment would have hurt Argentina's economy, but it was all a grandstand play anyway. Illia turned the issue over to the courts and promised the U.S. that its oil companies would get a fair shake. Then, while unemployment, prices and the ratio of small business bankruptcies (already highest in Argentine history) kept

---

[6] Known to Argentines as "Esso-garay," this Machiavellian Big-Business puppet told Buenos Aires' *La Nación* in 1962, after the Frondizi-Frigerio fall, that since 1956 "Mr. Frigerio . . . has done more for Communism in Argentina from above than what the Red organizations and leaders could do from below." But, he added, Frigerio's actions "would not have been possible if he had not had the tolerance of President Frondizi." Alsogaray, of course, learned the art of making such hypocritical statements as Frondizi's longtime Economics Minister, and, as such, was more responsible for Argentina's internal policies than any other official.

rising, Illia simply printed more money to pay immediate bills, and gleefully sat back to let the Alliance for Progress handle long range problems. Though the old likable radical meant well, his program-less government quickly convinced reform-minded Argentines that the Frondizi-Perón-Frigerio Frente was not so bad after all. At least, the Frente was willing to make as well as receive a few dollars.

But Argentina needs more than dollars to rise anew. Perhaps it needs, as most Argentines are hoping and as is more likely everyday, a Nasser-type strongman to put an end to the gorilla's rule and our Pentagon's advice. It certainly needs cohesiveness, honesty, morality, pride, strength, courage, and faith in itself—all nonexistent since the Gorilla Revolution. It is a nation divided into Buenos Aires, a city of crammed subways, and *campo,* fields of hushed exploitation.

Badly copied from dozens of European postcards, the capital is a huge (4,000,000 people; 8,000,000 in greater Buenos Aires), personality-less conglomeration of rude, unhappy people who hide their shame behind masks of chauvinistic superiority. There are agreeable spots: the quaint Italian La Boca waterfront district, the Fifth Avenue shops along swank Avenida Santa Fe and bustling Calle Florida where overfashionable *pituca* (snob-class) girls resemble Champs-Elysées streetwalkers, or the Paris-style portable bookstalls in front of the Palace of Justice. But most sidewalks are full of holes, plush apartments full of cockroaches, and public bathrooms full of lice. Telephones never work when it rains; telegrams always arrive after the sender; and newspapers rarely print news. Thirty years ago *La Prensa* had more correspondents, more foreign and local news than either the London or the New York *Times;* today, it is like its competitors—full of cheap propaganda, more or less badly written, and ever open to the "advice" of local or foreign big money interests. Rents are so high ($100 monthly and up) that newlyweds (who earn at most $200 together) must remain with their parents. Customs men, police, phone inspectors (who must approve waiting orders on lists ten years long), and government officials are all bribable. Tipping is 24 percent by law (on the bill), 10 percent more by expectation (on the table). Civil servants are rarely paid on time; some go months without their checks, and one plan hatched between Guido and the military was to pay them with bonds. Milk runs short two or three days a week. Trolleys stop dead because of lack of power. And, finally, the people—with some marvelous exceptions, friends I shall always cherish—are insufferable; but perhaps justifiably so; for, as one Argentine told me: The *porteño* gets up at six, shaves with cold water because the furnace is dead, rushes to his train, which is late, crowds into a *colectivo* where his wallet is pickpocketed, gets to his office late and is bawled out, returns the way he came, doesn't watch TV because the electricity is cut, and has to go to bed early because there is no heat."

Outside Greater Buenos Aires the living conditions are worse but the people are nicer. The gaucho, tough and ever ready to use the long knife he keeps in his belt, is friendly and extremely hospitable. The poor live in shacks of corrugated tin, warm in summer, ice-cold in winter. The only good roads are the tourist roads (to the summer resort of Mar del Plata, for example, or along the Sierra Lake region). Even the main artery between the cities of Córdoba and Santa Fe is in terrible condition, though it was once paved—back in the twenties. One interstate dirt road had a sign reading "Men at work, road under repair"; seeing neither workers nor machinery, I asked the police chief of a charming town called Arrufo what had happened. "I've been here since 1936," he answered, "and so have the signs."

In the *estancias* where Argentina's main products, meat, wheat and corn, are raised, there are no electricity lines and no phones. Where conditions are best, peons live three to six in 8-by-4-foot heatless shacks and are happy when they earn the equivalent (at our cost of living scales) of $36 a month. Their families, who are not allowed on the *estancias,* must survive in the nearest town on whatever part of the $36 the man chips in. They live in makeshift shacks, see no doctor, and their children rarely go to school. "Ask any peon if he is not happier seeing his family only on Sunday!" *estancieros* remarked. Considering under what conditions the families are forced to live, I was surprised the peons visited them at all.

In United States-owned Aguilar coal mines in backward Jujuy Province, seven hundred families toil for pittance at 12,000 feet above sea level, and when they go to one of the two latrines a vigilante clocks their time. In Yaví,

Jujuy, on the Bolivian border, where Indians live outside the money economy altogether, 75 percent carry tuberculosis. In Salta Province sugar plantations, where no Indians or peons can read or write, one *ingenio* (sugar plantation) owner gave me this explanation: "These peons can cut cane just as well without being able to read."

They can also rebel without being able to read. "Someday Perón will lead us again, or else we too will get our Castro," is a remark I often heard from Argentina's peons.

Perón will not lead again.

Chapter 4

Brazil

Like Argentina, Brazil owes its awakening to a dictator. Like Argentina too, Brazil has long been run or directed by the army. But unlike the Argentine military, Brazil's has often been patriotic, nationalistic, and relatively free of self-interest.

As the biggest nation on the continent, Brazil needed only to declare itself free to obtain independence. Portuguese King João VI's twenty-three-year-old son Pedro—"a grand fellow," as Brazilian novelist Erico Verissimo has written, "sentimental, impulsive, romantic, sensual, and spoiled"—was admiring the muddy waters of São Paulo's foul-smelling Ipiranga River on September 7, 1822, when he suddenly ripped the Portuguese colors from his vest, and shouted: "Independence or Death!" Then, obeying his wise father's advice ("If Brazil demands independence, grant it, but put the crown upon your own head"), and appealing to the British Navy for support, he proclaimed Brazil an empire.

Pedro I irritated Brazilians; he abdicated in 1831. Pedro II was born in Brazil, educated in Brazil, and loved by Brazilians—until he began to rule with a firm hand. Then he became "a sort of Queen Victoria in Breeches," as sociohistorian Gilberto Freyre has written, "who watched his statesmen like a moral detective." He freed his slaves upon assuming the throne, personally congratulated the Benedictine Order in Rio de Janeiro when it freed its own in 1866, and wept from joy ("What great people!") when Parliament voted total emancipation in 1888. But abolition was not enough; in 1889 the army forced Pedro II to abdicate. He refused a pension and sailed for Europe, where he died, lonely and forgotten, in 1891.

The military dictators or presidents that ruled the First Republic (1889-1930) were not especially bad. The very first, General Deodoro da Fonseca, turned Brazil into a federation of twenty states called the United States of Brazil, and severed all ties between Church and State. Others built up Brazil's exports, her foreign trade, her place in the society of nations. But all were traditional, unconcerned with Brazil's social needs, and unpreoccupied by the influx of foreign companies that were rapidly turning Brazil's political sovereignty into the economic dependency of powerful international trusts. By 1930 the general restlessness demanded a change. It was time for Getulio Vargas.

Getulio, as everyone called him, was not an impressive-looking man. He was five feet four inches tall, wore glasses, and had a sardonic sense of humor. He lived quietly, played golf on Sundays, and spoke badly. Born in Rio Grande do Sul, Brazil's southernmost province, Vargas began his career in the army, went on to study law, shot up the ranks of state politics, and became governor in the late 1920's. To the gubernatorial Pirantiní Palace he attracted a group of young, passionate, brilliant men who soon united in a Liberal Alliance to break Brazil's traditional order. While they talked, Vargas listened. He was, in the words of Gilberto Freyre, "silent, introspective, subtle, realistic, distant, cold," but also "instinctive, fatalistic, proud, dramatic."

In 1930 Vargas ran for the presidency—and lost. But his new ideas had appealed to a group of young, nationalistic army officers who had been itching to take matters into their own hands for almost a decade. These officers, known as the Tenentes (lieutenants), had staged three unsuccessful revolts in 1922, 1924, and 1926. After the last try, a young captain named Luiz Carlos Prestes (who had been stationed mostly in Rio Grande do Sul), eluded his pursuers for almost two years, leading his men more than a thousand miles across Brazil's jungles and into Bolivia. "Prestes' Long March" is as famous in Latin America as the Chinese

Communists' Long March is famous in Asia, and many of the former's participants went on to play important roles in Vargas' later governments. In 1930 the Tenentes joined the Liberal Alliance, and overthrew the old order.

Vargas became provisional President, set up a dictatorship, and immediately tried to save Brazil's economy, which was near bankruptcy from internal mismanagement, and totally helpless against the Great Depression. To encourage national industry, he enacted tariffs, launched a foreign-exchange monopoly that favored the importation of heavy equipment and materials but penalized the importation of competitive goods, and constructed roads and railways. He also drained swamplands, opening them to farming.

Vargas then tried to enlarge Brazil's steel output. He created the National Steel Company (1941) and erected the Volta Redonda Plant, ninety miles from Rio. In 1938 he had organized the National Petroleum Council to find oil and keep it in Brazilian hands.

Vargas also gave the workers their first social legislation, as well as higher wages, medical care, housing, and so on. He created a new Ministry of Industry, Commerce, and Labor and granted unions legality and recognition (though he forced them also to register, ·which destroyed their undercover militancy). He established social-security funds to cover most workers, and raised the number of students in secondary schools from 60,000 in 1930 to 450,000 by 1945 (still pitifully low). Finally, Vargas destroyed some of the power held by provincial oligarchies on their provinces by tearing down states' rights barriers, abolishing the independent state judiciaries, sharply cutting (then eliminating) interstate tariffs, wiping out *caudilhismo,* and ruling through federally appointed "interventors."

That Vargas was an absolute dictator is undeniable; his reach spread everywhere. But Vargas did not kill his opponents, or cause them to "disappear." He did not allow elections, but his democratic predecessors had allowed only fraudulent ones. He sometimes closed down an opposition paper for a day or two, but his democratic predecessors had controlled them all every day.

On the other hand, Vargas was immensely popular. He often strolled in the streets without bodyguards, never outlawed free speech (and some of the jokes making fun of him, as vicious as they were, amused him more than

anyone else). And though corruption was widespread in
his government (as in all those that had preceded his),
Vargas himself was scrupulously honest—and Brazilians
knew it.

During his first reign there were four revolts against
him—and these indicate, by a reverse elimination process,
just where Vargas' regime stood. The first, in 1932, was
led by São Paulo's oligarchy. Ever since the creation of
the republic, two states (that is, two local oligarchies) had
dominated Brazilian politics: Minas Gerais and São Paulo.
Every President had come from one or the other. Then,
by Vargas' coup, the Paulistas were cheated of power;
hence they rebelled. They were quickly defeated and quickly
pardoned. But Vargas thereafter increased his vigilance
over Paulista financial interests.

The next uprising, in 1935, was led by the National
Liberation Alliance, a popular front of Socialists, some
of the old Tenentes disappointed with Vargas' moderate
program, and the Communist Party. For President, the
alliance chose Luiz Carlos Prestes, the famous leader of
the Long March who had spent a few exiled years in
Russia and had come back to Brazil a confirmed Communist.
That revolt also failed. Prestes, caught in 1936, was jailed
until 1945.

In 1934 Vargas had enacted a new constitution, promising
free elections within three years. But in 1937 he staged
a lightning-fast coup, dumped the constitution in favor
of another that he and his Minister of Justice Francisco
Campo had secretly written, and declared Brazil an "*Estado
Novo.*" This New State called for the complete reorganization
of Brazil, its economy, its government, and its habits.
It put all workers and all employers into government-
supervised *sindicatos* with the power to regulate production
and quotas, salaries and profits. In theory, Getulio's New
State was a Brazilian version of Mussolini's Corporative
State. In practice, however, it served only to give Vargas
more control (generally to the workers' advantage). But
it also created the impression that Brazil was moving to
the extreme Right, without due consideration for Brazil's
real Fascists, who were now banned. Led by a brilliant
crackpot named Plinio Salgado, who mixed anti-Semitism
with sun worship, and the green shirt uniform with Greek
identification symbols, Brazil's Fascist Party, called Inte-

gralismo, had few members, much money (from the German Embassy), and top Brazilian oligarchs for fronts. Thus, in May, 1938, Integralista militants bribed their way into Rio's presidential Guanabara Palace, occupied its gardens and, armed with submachine guns, ordered Vargas to surrender. With his daughter and four guards, Vargas opened fire from the palace windows, and held the invaders off until an aide sneaked out through the roof and called for reinforcements. (The Fascists had cut phone lines.) Salgado went into hiding, then into exile in Portugal.

The fourth and last coup against Vargas (in his first reign) came in October, 1945. The dictator had promised free general elections for December, giving his word not to be a candidate. In May he had released all political prisoners. (In his first public appearance, Communist Chief Prestes told 100,000 people crammed into Rio's Vasco da Gama Stadium that he would back Vargas' candidate as the least of all evils despite the fact that he had been in jail nine years and that Vargas had deported his German-born wife to Germany, where she was executed.) But the oligarchy, our corporations in Brazil, our government, and some military leaders were afraid Vargas would pull off another coup. Our ambassador, Adolf Berle, openly intervened by commenting on the situation and on the hope we held for Brazil's new democracy. Finally, during the night of October 24-25, 1945, army tanks surrounded the palace, and Vargas was forced to resign.

The oligarchy returned to power. But by 1950 Vargas was back in politics as candidate of the Brazilian Labor Party (PTB). The army, by then purged of its nationalistic elements, was solidly opposed to him. But since the generals were on the inside (the government), they did not realize that to the outside (the people), five years of democracy had brought only lower wages, more foreign corporations, and less national dignity. Thus fooled, the generals allowed the election to take place. Vargas was overwhelmingly elected.

But his position was weak. Like a cougar, the army was constantly perched above him, ready to pounce. Early in 1953, Vargas appointed as new Minister of Labor a young politician from his home state—João Goulart. Working fast, Goulart reorganized trade unions into a powerful force, helped them gain many favorable contracts, ended the government's interference in unions (by "receivers" appointed by Vargas' Democratic predecessor), and raised minimum wages—before the army finally ordered Vargas to fire him a year later.

Still, Vargas was strong enough to start a national development program to be financed by $500,000,000 worth of credits from the United States, and a state oil corporation, Petrobras, to exploit Brazil's oil resources for Brazilians. Vargas' nationalism obviously did not please the Eisenhower administration. It canceled, unilaterally, the United States-Brazil Development Agreement after delivering only $180,000,000 of its commitment. Simultaneously the Brazilian oligarchical press began a vicious attack against Vargas and his nationalism, while most of the independent press, subjugated to threats of advertising boycotts, remained silent.

The biggest pressure came from United States oil companies to which Vargas and Petrobras represented competition. And the loudest criticism was printed in *Tribuna da Impresa,* owned by an oligarch named Carlos Lacerda. Vargas, who had been freely elected this time and whose projects were always submitted to (and often rejected by) Congress, was now described as "dictator" and "Fascist."

Nevertheless, he tried to push through his program. As late as mid-August, 1954, according to Gilberto Freyre, who is known for his anti-Vargas stand, Vargas called him to the palace and offered him the directorship of an institute about to be created to map out a land reform that would include the expropriation of *fazendas (Latifundios).* That was too much for the oligarchy. They decided to act, and the army gave Vargas an ultimatum.

On August 24, 1954, Vargas wrote a flamboyant, emotional letter to his people in which he accused "international economic and financial groups," without specifically naming our corporations, of national "domination and looting" insofar as "profits of foreign enterprises reached 500 percent yearly." He accused the "international groups" of having joined forces with the "national groups." Then, dramatically (see Appendix A for the whole text), he wrote: "I gave you my life. Now I offer you my death." And he shot himself dead.

Though vain, self-centered, obsessed with his place in history, and more personally ambitious than convinced of

Brazil's needs for reform, Vargas accomplished more for his country than had any other of its presidents. He tried to cut down the giveaways and to put a stop to excess profits. (Such a law failed to pass his Congress.) He stimulated national industries and exploited Brazil's national resources. And he forced Brazilians to become aware of their problems. Having awakened his country, Vargas could not be quietly buried. *Getulismo* has retained its strength in Brazilian politics ever since his death.

It was that strength that got Juscelino Kubitschek and João Goulart elected President and Vice-President in 1955. Immediately rumors grew of another army coup, but nationalistic War Minister Henrique Teixeira Lott staged a "preventive" coup first, and guaranteed the winners their posts.

On January 28, 1956, Kubitschek and Goulart took over the government, and shortly afterward many of Vargas' aides were back in the palace. Nationalism again became a hot issue. Kubitschek even expropriated some United States property while remaining our strong ally. But obsessed with "opening up the interior," he carried out no reforms, and instead spent most of his energy and funds building Brazil's new capital, Brasília, six hundred miles inland from Rio.[1]

Most of Brasília's tab was handed to the man who took over from Kubitschek early in 1961. Jânio da Silva Quadros, a weird, eccentric politician from São Paulo, was a conservative anyway; he was already a firm believer in tight money policies. He thus clamped down hard on unions, sent federal troops to the Northeast hunger dens to squash protest rallies, jailed disobedient students, tightened credit, stopped most federal subsidies, fired government featherbedders, and devaluated the cruzeiro almost to its free market level. But Quadros was also honest. He refused to favor friends, cleaned out one federal agency after another, ordered his government prosecutors to dig up and expose as much dirt as they could find. And, finally, he was pro-Brazil. That meant that as long as he was President, Brazil would

---

[1] An incredible achievement, Brasília was built from wilderness up in less than four years (1956-1960), already functions more or less smoothly as a capital, and will surely prove to be a great boon to the development of the country.

maintain a *Brazilian* foreign policy.

Quadros had made his views perfectly clear during his campaign. He had even warned Brazilians not to expect betrayals. "I will not be another Frondizi," he had said. Once elected, he kept his word. "Why should the United States trade with Russia and her satellites but insist that Brazil trade only with the United States?" he asked. So, Quadros began negotiations with Russia and other Communist countries to establish diplomatic and commercial relations. He was, in a word, independent.

The export-importers weren't very happy. Neither was Washington nor our corporations. But what could we say?

Quadros was, after all, a Conservative. Thus, when First Astronaut Yuri Gagarin and Secretary of the Soviet Presidium Michael Georgadze visited Brazil and Quadros gave them Brazil's *Cruzeiro do Sul* medal, no one much protested. Every visiting foreign dignitary has received that medal—as part of protocol.

But in August, 1961, Quadros sent his Congress a profits bill. It called for a new tax on all earnings, domestic or foreign, of 30 percent—with one important proviso: profits reinvested in industries that benefited public service or set up new industries, especially in the Northeast, would be taxed only 10 percent. Since there already existed a 20 percent tax on all exported profits, our companies shipping their earnings home or local companies investing their profits abroad would thereafter be taxed 50 percent—still lower than corporate taxes in the U.S. itself.

That did it: just as in 1954. Local oligarchies launched an intensive anti-Quadros campaign. He was smeared as an eccentric, an oddball, or a madman. Then, when he received Cuban Minister Guevara on the latter's way home from the first Punta del Este Conference and gave him the *Cruzeiro do Sul* medal, he was branded a Communist. On August 24, 1961, exactly seven years to the day of Vargas' suicide, old oligarch Lacerda, now governor of Guanabara (Rio de Janeiro), went on a radio-TV nationwide hookup to denounce Quadros, who had been elected by the greatest majority ever given a presidential candidate. Quadros is a dictator plotting to close down Congress and establish a Cuban-type regime in Brazil, said Lacerda.

On the very next day, General Corderio Farías, commander in chief of the army, told Quadros to change his "pro-Communist" foreign policy or else.

According to one version, namely Quadros' secretary, the President then shouted: "You are under arrest!"

"And you are deposed," Corderio Farías supposedly retorted.

This version has it that Quadros was, thereupon, whipped off, incommunicado, to an air force base, then on to a slow boat to England, Quadros was permitted only to write a "resignation" letter. Another version insists that Quadros, frustrated and angry, simply walked out of the government.

Whatever the version, he did write a resignation letter which, reminiscent of Vargas', attributed his failure to "reactionaries" and to "the ambitions of groups of individuals, some of whom are foreigners . . . the terrible forces that arose against me." When he returned home, in March, 1962, Quadros named some of those "foreigners"—former United States Ambassador John Moors Cabot, former Latin America Task Force Chief Adolf Berle, Secretary of the Treasury Douglas Dillon, West Germany Ambassador Herbert Dittman, and so on.[2] Quadros also accused Lacerda and other oligarchs.

As formidable as these men and their interests are, Quadros had run from a fight. He had abandoned Brazil. Would the army have shot him, had he refused to resign? Would their coup have not aroused an outcry, perhaps a revolution, had he told the truth from the ship's radio? (It was not a Brazilian ship, and Quadros was free to do as he pleased.) But Quadros was a democrat. He had fled to avoid the crisis.[3]

The crisis was far from over. By law, Vice-President João "Jango" Goulart (who had been reelected, as permitted for Vice-Presidents by the Brazilian Constitution) was to take over. But Goulart was a *real* Communist, the army,

---

[2] Quadros had sent a trade mission to East Germany that had greatly worried Washington and the Adenauer government, even though, when asked if "this implied a revision of our position on the Berlin question, I answered in the negative, although we would trade with ten Germanys if they existed."

[3] Quadros tried for the comeback in 1962, running for the governorship of the State of São Paulo. He was defeated.

Washington, and the oligarchy agreed. He was, in fact, at that very moment visiting Communist China, and on the night Quadros was overthrown, Goulart had dashed off these words to his host, Mao Tse-tung: "I congratulate Your Excellency on the triumphs achieved by the people and government of the Chinese Republic in its heroic fight for progress and the raising of the standard of living of the people."[4]

Goulart is a millionaire *fazendeiro* on whose property the best livestock in Brazil is raised. Goulart is a Catholic who wears a medal of the Virgin around his neck. As Brazil's Vice-President he had also visited anti-Communist countries and had issued "congratulatory" thank-you notes to each, as protocol required. Nevertheless, he was branded a Red by Brazil's military and the oligarchy, and a Leftist by Washington and our press.

The military took over. They closed down newspapers, occupied radio stations, intervened among unions, stopped all commercial traffic, and jailed their critics, including some congressmen. On the 26th Marshal Odilio Denys, head of the army and War Minister (since Marshal Lott resigned to run against Quadros), told a United States correspondent that Goulart would be arrested if he returned. When asked why, Denys retorted: "Would you like it if your sons became Communists? Well, the moment has come when Brazil must choose between Communism and democracy." He was then asked why Marshal Lott, who opposed the coup, was under arrest. "Subversive!" Denys shouted straightfacedly. The reporter laughed. "Careful," Denys said, "I feel like arresting people these days."

On the 27th Goulart reached Paris.

On the 28th his military-appointed successor told the Senate that the military had agreed on "the absolute inconvenience, for reasons of national security, of Goulart's return." Students reacted by staging a huge pro-Goulart rally. It was broken up by army bayonets. (A UPI reporter

[4] That message was sent and made public to the press on August 25th, the day of Quadros' "resignation." It was not distributed by AP or UPI in South America (or especially in Brazil) until the 27th—after the militarists publically denounced Goulart as a Communist and were looking for evidence to "prove" their charge. Surely another coincidence. There are so many of them.

must have seen it because its dispatch said that Denys was in "complete control," having the support of the artillery, the tank corps, and those soldiers who carry "loaded weapons.")

Meanwhile, in Rio Grande do Sul, where Vargas and Goulart were raised, a stiff, conservative general commanded the Third Army. His name was General Machado Lopes, and he was one of those rare Latin American militarists who had ever fired a weapon at an *armed* enemy (he fought in Italy with the Allies during World War II). His ideas about taking orders were very conventional: "The Constitution states that Sr. Goulart is President. Did he appoint Marshal Denys as my superior? Until I know just who is my legal superior my orders will come from the Constitution itself."

"Traitor!" reacted Denys, Lacerda, & Co. Soldiers with "loaded weapons" were sent down to jail the "rebel." But Rio Grande do Sul was being governed by one Leonel Brizola, Goulart's brother-in-law, a follower of Vargas and, though a Rightist by inclination, a Brazilian Nationalist by sentiment. Brizola gave the order: defend the constitution. Rio Grande do Sul got set for an invasion.

Students were armed. The army deployed, taking the students under its wing, and *President* Goulart, who by then had reached New York, was invited to come to take command. In Rio de Janeiro the press reported Rio Grande in "open rebellion."[5] The aircraft carrier *Minas Gerais* was rushed into action, to squash the rebellion. The Fourth Army, in the North, was ordered to stay put; the North had long been on the point of revolution. The First Army was told to keep Marshal Lott arrested, suppress students, and break strikes. The Second Army was told to attack the South.

But Denys did not have the support of Brazilians. The

---

[5] One whose newspaper again shouted loudest was Governor Carlos Lacerda, who clamped a rigid censorship on all Rio newspapers (except his own, of course), and later explained, "I chose censorship to help the military to avoid civil war." This incredible cynicism was uttered at the Inter-American Press Association convention held in Manhattan in October, 1961, and was approved by such outstanding free-press advocates as *Time, Life, Chicago Tribune*, UPI, AP, and so on.

governor of Goiás, northwest of Rio, declared his allegiance to "Jango" Goulart. A colonel, ordered to fire upon Third Army troops, refused. Machado Lopes sent his men to Rio Grande do Sul's borders, but instead they charged all the way to Florianópolis, a port 150 miles up the coast of the next state, Santa Catarina, and were cheered the whole way. The navy (with its *Minas Gerais* in the lead) declared such an advance "intolerable"—then withdrew.

Goulart had reached Montevideo. Rio Grande's gauchos sent him a message, begging him to take personal command and to let them finish this civil war started by "imperialists and Brazilian enemies of Brazil." Northeast leaders let it be known that they would fight if victory meant the social restructuring of the country. Union chiefs got set to tie up Rio and São Paulo. Students were already in the streets of most cities. Victory was certain.

But Goulart *is* a millionaire *fazendeiro*. His interests were not reforms but power. And, afraid that a civil war would bring another Castro-like revolution, Washington quickly changed its tactics. Denys and his aides were pressured to find a compromise. A constitutional amendment was presented by Plinio Salgado, by now deputy, the only freely elected Fascist in the world. On September 2nd the constitution was thus amended. "Under military pressure," as Kubitschek, now a senator, said, Brazil would become a parliamentary democracy. Goulart would be President, but his power would be cut. Goulart accepted.

I was in Pôrto Alegre, capital of Rio Grande do Sul, during the *Legalidade* (the fight for constitutional legality). It was something to see. Soldiers and students, for decades bitter enemies, now slept side by side, or joked together guarding bridges, manning anti-aircraft machine guns, or protecting the gubernatorial Piratiní Palace. Old men volunteered for fire detail, as arm carriers, and munition bearers. Young women, their hair still fashionably up in bouffant pyramids, set up first-aid stations, while their mothers made up improvised bandages, flags, and stretchers.

At one point I came across a wealthy factory owner standing near the palace. He had argued for twelve hours with a leader of UNE (União Nacional dos Estudantes) about the nationalization of major industries and utilities. Shaking his head, he told me: "I must be crazy. I have gone without my sleep to listen to this Bolshevik tell me that I should have all my wealth taken away to be distributed to the poor." Then, smiling, he smacked the student on his back, and said, "He even told me I should be shot." The two were members of the same Committees for Defense of the Constitution and for Democratic Resistance.

Pôrto Alegre's 1961 leaders risked civil war to defend "democracy." But if they were wise enough to understand that true democracy in Brazil is impossible without social reforms first, they were naïve to hope that backing one man was enough to achieve it. They were not ideologically mature enough to go beyond the immediate causes of the potential struggle. When their hero let them down, their hopes were crushed. It was to be expected; Goulart was not guided by the conviction that Brazil's most important need was social reform. To have thought differently was to court defeat—a defeat that the people of Pôrto Alegre expressed on their walls, where one could read, three months later: "Jango, traitor, coward."

The "treason," of course, was the deal by which Goulart retained his presidency in a parliamentary system. Nevertheless, he managed to keep a tight hold on this system, seeing to it that Quadros' popular "independent" foreign policy remained intact, a course our press found most "confusing." In November, 1961, for example, *Time* magazine wrote: Goulart "accepted an anxiously awaited invitation to Washington from U.S. Ambassador Lincoln Gordon—and then immediately confused everybody again by awarding Communist Poland's Foreign Minister Adam Rapacki the Order of the Southern Cross," that is, the *Cruzeiro do Sul*. Apparently *Time* thinks that any President who wants to visit us must necessarily hate our enemies as a consequence, and is "confused" whenever this does not occur. But, of course, *Time* magazine is so unused to the word "independent" that an independent foreign policy must be very confusing indeed. In South America, where everyone would like to follow an independent foreign policy but where only Brazil has, at times, the courage, no one was confused.

After the crisis, "Jango" ably pitted one power group against another. He did not let his prime ministers deviate from his own policies. Always, his ultimate goal was to resume full executive power either through a plebiscite, (which he won by an overwhelming five to one majority on January 6, 1963) popular pressure, or military action.

He deftly placed generals faithful to him in key positions, and patiently waited for the right moment to force the issue—which caused Lacerda, naturally, to foam that "those in power are trying to assassinate Brazilian democracy from the back."

And while Goulart played out his game, he enacted no reforms, letting the economy deteriorate at the fastest clip in Brazilian history (prices were inflated by 95.89 percent in 1963). Meanwhile, our press concentrated its attacks on Brizola, the only Brazilian to have carried out reforms since Getulio Vargas. I had seen Brizola, who is Goulart's brother-in-law, in action during the *Legalidade* period, and he had impressed me as neither a Leftist nor a revolutionary, but as a Nationalist, very Catholic and very anti-Communist, who tried to raise living conditions through peaceful means. Like Goulart, he was a constitutionalist, who would fight *against* the generals' coup but not stage a coup himself. He was convinced—or he hoped so strongly that he thought he was convinced—that under the constitution Goulart would carry out the reforms on a nationwide scale that he, Brizola, was carrying out in Rio Grande do Sul. He was not anti-United States, but he could not understand why Brazil (or any other Latin American country) must see itself (to borrow the analogy from Juan José Arévalo) as a meek sardine trying to please a powerful shark (us) with its every action, when some of these actions do not benefit the sardine. Brizola would hate to see his country a satellite of Russia, but he would also hate to see it a satellite of the United States—or so, at least, it seemed to me then.

But the *Legalidade* crisis was perhaps not a good moment to judge such things. Rio Grande do Sul was in total upheaval; the whole state was united for one purpose—saving the federal government. Hence, I decided to return there later. I did, in March-April, 1962. I traveled throughout the state, visiting farms, *fazendas,* and government-owned cooperatives, talking to peasants and land-owners, to agronomists, engineers, economists, and opposition leaders, and, of course, to Brizola and his aides. I wrote a long article of which the following is part:

"There are only two alternatives: reforms by evolution or reforms by revolution. And when I say 'reforms,' I

don't mean a Free Trade agreement that takes twelve years
to show meagre results, a 'colonization' program that
gives ten or twenty or even fifty thousand peasants plots
of arid land without the machinery, credit and know-how
to render them fertile. I don't even mean reforms financed by a ten-year Alliance through local oligarchs, no
matter how well intentioned. Latin America needs thousands of new schools *this* year, a vast agrarian reform that
will start giving land to millions of landless peasants *today*,
an industrialization program that will develop dormant resources and create new jobs *now*. In sum, we need to change
the whole structure, economically and socially, of our continent. And it *will* change—whether by violence or not.
Here in Rio Grande do Sul, we are staking our very lives
on the belief it can be done in peace."

The speaker was Leonel Brizola, the dashingly handsome,
controversial governor of Rio Grande do Sul, Brazil's
southernmost state—and one of its poorest. Accused of
being a Fascist, a Communist, and a demagogue by the
world's conservative press, Brizola has become, in the short
three years of his mandate, Latin America's most popular
hero, topping even Northeast Brazil's fiery, Socialist Peasant League Leader Francisco Julião. The reason is simple:
While Julião harangues, Brizola works.

Born January 22, 1922, in a small Rio Grande agricultural center called Caràzinho, Brizola was more fortunate
than his fellow gauchos. Though his Italian-born father was
poor, his mother was literate and she taught young Leonel
to read and write. At fourteen, he journeyed (mostly on
foot) the three hundred miles to the state capital, Pôrto
Alegre, where he went to work as an elevator operator
while continuing to study. Entering the city's Faculty of
Engineering, he soon developed a second calling—politics.
With a group of fellow students in 1946, he founded Rio
Grande's branch of Vargas' Brazilian Workers Party (PTB)
and the following year won himself a deputy's seat in
the state Parliament. . . . In 1957, Brizola was elected
governor by a sweeping majority and even before he moved
into the state's gubernatorial Piratiní Palace, he had his
program—and his top-level advisers—on the ready.

"Most crucial was education," he says. "It's a prereq-
uisite for the development because only education can

prepare the poor to enjoy the fruits of progress. Without it, development serves only the rich." Though Rio Grande do Sul is a fertile state of 100,000 square miles (about the size of Nevada) with more than 400 miles of Atlantic coastline, 9,400,000 head of cattle, 12,600,000 sheep and produces 75 percent of Brazil's wines, its 6,000,000 people are among the country's poorest—their toil being at the service of powerful São Paulo trusts, absentee land barons, and foreign corporations. Thus Brizola launched first his educational program.

In 1958 Rio Grande had 1,795 schools and 300,000 students. Today, there are 4,500 schools with an enrollment of 605,000 students plus 30,000 more in 69 technical centers. There are also 12,370 new teachers, and the illiteracy rate in the state (34 percent) is far lower than anywhere else in Brazil (average: 70 percent). To foot the bill for his three-year achievement, Brizola earmarked 15 percent of the state's approximate $100,000,000 annual budget, added occasional millions more through special bond-sale campaigns. To build the schools themselves, he launched a state construction firm, then also started up adult education schools, teacher-training courses and a student-scholarship system whereby recipients served six to twelve months as rural teachers. "We can't expect top quality in so short a time," Brizola admits, "but the first job is to get all our people to be able to read and write. We've done as much as we could in three years in that respect." . . .

Though education came first, Brizola did not wait to push the rest of his program. He upped electricity output from 300,000 kilowatt-hours in 1958 to 635,000 today, hopes to cross the 1,000,000 mark before his term ends in December. Roadbuilders are trying to link the coastal ports with the interior's backwoods. And finally, Brizola is driving through two other crucial aspects of his program, which in recent months have focused public attention on his administration: agrarian reform and the nationalization of ill-functioning public utilities. . . .

Like the rest of Brazil and Latin America, Rio Grande do Sul is farmed by millions but owned by few. . . . In Rio Grande the figures are not extreme, but bad enough: there are 8,964 *latifundistas* with 52.2 percent of the land, 57,293 medium farmers with 28.1 percent, 277,806 small farmers with 20 percent and 450,000 with no land at all. The first task performed by Brizola's agrarian reform advisers (including agronomists, economists, and land engineers, et cetera) was to verify the oft-repeated statement that small farms are uneconomical. They compared Livramento, a rich area of 736,000 hectares with 58,850 people, near the Uruguayan border, which is owned by a handful of absentee landlords, to Santa Rosa, a central, less fertile area of only 57,700 hectares owned mostly by its 22,570 inhabitants. Both raised cattle and sheep. The results showed that while Livramento produces 18,816 agricultural tons a year, Santa Rosa turns out 147,027. Relative to cost, a peon's output in Livramento is 1.2; his counterpart in Santa Rosa has a 2.7 ratio. Heavily populated Livramento's contribution to state tax revenue is 1.4 percent; less than half in size, Santa Rosa pays 4.5 percent. In the former, infant mortality is 14 percent, in the latter 7 percent. Anxious to show the moral differences as well, the *Movimento dos Agricultures Sem Terra* (MASTER), Rio Grande's equivalent of the Peasant Leagues, also came up with another set of figures: in Livramento 20 percent of the children are illegitimate, in Santa Rosa only 2 percent.

Armed with such data, Brizola's agricultural experts insisted upon a strong redistribution program. Nevertheless, Brizola preferred to proceed slowly, so far has distributed (armed by Articles 145, 173, and 174 of the state constitution) 150,000 hectares to 5,000 families (all the land was state-owned except one *latifundio* of 60,000 hectares for which the state is offering cash at current market value). Each time land was given to peasants, the state furnished farmers with tools, machinery, and long-range, no-interest credit facilities, built them simple but pleasant one-story housing units, and provided them with on-the-spot expert advice. Machinery, costly and scarce, is owned on a cooperative basis, and farming is coordinated to avoid waste or uneconomical haphazardness; otherwise each new peasant-owner is master of his land. Because the program has proved such a success—the first 2,000 families have had time to show production results—it is now being accelerated so as to give land to another 6,000 families before Brizola's term ends. But most observers agree that the next administration, no matter what its politics, is bound to continue the program. As one MASTER leader puts it:

"Those who have always been thirsty only beg, but those who have their water taken away, demand."

The uproar on Brizola's nationalizations centers around his taking over IT&T's Rio Grande Subsidiary, Companhia Telefonica Nacional (CTN). Of the state's 6,000,000 people only 28,648 have phones; Pôrto Alegre's 670,000 inhabitants own but 14,300 (compared, say, to Minneapolis, which has 650,000 inhabitants and more than 200,000 phones). In the capital there are 30,000 priority (businesses, doctors, newspapermen) requests on waiting lists. When it rains, all phone communication breaks down. Equipment is old, often broken. . . . CTN explained that because its costs were in dollars and its receipts in inflation-prone cruzeiros, it could not afford to modernize. Brizola, thereupon, appointed his own commission, which, after a year of study, recommended that the state start its own telephone company, drawing funds from public sale of shares and from an investment of CTN of 25 percent of its worth. The company agreed, appointing one of two experts who would investigate CTN's assets. The experts agreed on the figure 1,350,000,000 cruzeiros (about $3,250,000); the state Parliament made the new company a fact (Law 4,073, December 30, 1960); and shares went on the open market.

A month later, CTN rejected the experts' finding. Brizola set up a new panel of experts to check it again. They upheld the figures. CTN again refused. Finally, two months ago, Brizola decreed CTN's nationalization, using laws existing in Rio Grande's 1947 constitution to do so. Though the state will abide by the payment price set by the courts, its offer was a low 149,758,000 cruzeiros (less than $500,-000), a figure arrived at by taking CTN's previous evaluation and deducting various liabilities, a list of which have been presented to the court. One is especially interesting: IT&T, according to state publications, owns 370,308 of CTN's 374,970 shares (about 90 percent), yet is also its biggest debtor with arrears to the subsidiary of 1,270,443,-930.60 cruzeiros (about $3,000,000)—a proof, say state auditors, that though CTN claims to be constantly losing money, all actual capital has long been sucked out of Rio Grande and shipped home.

Brizola's various reforms sound extreme. He is deemed a revolutionary. Actually, he is not even a Socialist. "I

will try to help achieve economic development and bring
social justice to Brazil by law and always within the
democratic process," he says.

I have dedicated so much space to Brizola because I
am convinced of his importance—one of the few Latin
American statesmen to have tried reforms peacefully yet
the one most criticized by our press (besides Cubans).

Since I wrote the above article, Brizola has changed.
According to some of his former friends and advisers,
he has abandoned the cause in favor of self-interest, and
they point to his wealth as evidence. Perhaps. But he has
so identified himself with a particular line that he could
not switch from it without ruining his political fortune.
That line is still nationalist, still religious, and still anti-
Communist. But it now incorporates two crucial and fundamental points. First, the "democratic," that is, the laissez-faire
development of Brazil, may bring about industrialization
but does not help the people. Brizola now realizes that
big industry tends to be monopolistic and that even where
competitive, it becomes highly centralized. Aside from
creating a rapidly rising inflationary spiral for the whole
country, economic intensification brings about a geographic
disequilibrium. During Kubitschek's regime, for example,
industrialization surged ahead. But where? In São Paulo,
in Belo Horizonte and, less so, in Rio de Janeiro. Such
industrialization there, with new jobs, a bigger flow of
currency, more buildings, and so on, stimulated inflation,
which affected all Brazilians, including those who, like
some of the gauchos of Rio Grande do Sul, have not seen
a new factory spring up in decades. Frozen by the lack
of employment choices, these gauchos did not receive wage
increases yet have had to pay more and more for their
necessities. Brizola concludes that in such underdeveloped
countries as Brazil, industrial centralization must be avoided;
hence, economic development must be undertaken by the
state.

Second, Brizola has become aware that undirected industrialization tends to eliminate small businesses, and this
restricts social mobility. This develops the antidemocratic
structure of society. As Brizola's brilliant economic aide
Franklin de Oliveira has pointed out, the elimination of
small businesses in developed countries is less drastic, since

services that thrive from and around huge assembly-line plants can accommodate much of the dislocated manpower. But even then, as in the United States, where a special congressional committee is dedicated to small businesses, such elimination can be critical. In underdeveloped countries in the process of industrialization, it is disastrous—another reason why the state must lead and control economic development. And this, as Franklin de Oliveira says in his book *Rio Grande do Sul: um Novo Nordeste,* is Socialistic development. "Let's say it that way, without fear, because there is no other way for us." For Rio Grande, the Northeast, or any other area or country that needs to jump from the Middle Ages to the twentieth century, only some form of Socialism can be applied. This is what India, Egypt, Cuba, China, Ceylon,[6] Ghana, Indonesia, and so on, have realized. Perhaps the free enterprise of capitalism is the last stage of development. In underdeveloped countries, however, it cannot be a transitional phase.[7]

[6] Where Mrs. Sirima R. D. Bandaranaike, the Prime Minister, has nationalized Roman Catholic Church schools, the Bank of Ceylon, transport services, life insurance, the Port of Colombo, almost two hundred Esso, Caltex, and Burmah-Shell gas stations and oil depots. When our ambassador reminded Mrs. Bandaranaike in July, 1962, that President Kennedy can suspend aid to any country that expropriates our property without proper compensation within six months, the lady ruler replied: "The best form of foreign aid the U.S. can give to small countries is to abstain from interfering in their affairs."

[7] The argument would have this interesting political parallel: Russia was underdeveloped under the czardom; the revolution that overthrew the old regime had to make a jump of centuries in a few decades, hence was ruthless and totally totalitarian; today, Russia has almost caught up to the United States, hence cannot retain such a degree of ruthlessness, and therefore is beginning to liberalize. Once a country becomes "bourgeoised" economically, it must become "bourgeoised" politically. Starving, hungry, or exploited peasants and workers can be regimented, dominated, and exploited "for the sake of the future." One who knows suffering in himself can be taught to sacrifice himself for others. But not a well-fed bureaucrat. He talks of the "finer things in life," says that bread is not enough, or, to quote a famous title, says that he lives "not by bread alone." The argument is strengthened by what is happening in China

Today, Brizola is a Socialistic Nationalist who feels that public services and utilities (transportation, electricity, gas, telephone, water, and so on) are a right, not a luxury. Says he: "Just as every family is entitled to a house or apartment, and sufficient food and clothing, and as children are entitled to schooling, the whole family to medical and dental care, and the family provider to a job that *can* provide, so the family is entitled—in the twentieth century of jets and interplanetary satellites—to a telephone, to electricity, and to some form of transportation. Because private enterprise must make profits, it cannot, and does not want to, run such services at a loss. The state, therefore, must take them over and operate them, not at a profit, but as truly public services."

Brizola also insists that Brazilian peasants, like peasants or farmers anywhere in the world, are entitled to at least the *opportunity* of buying their own land. Under Brazil's current landownership system this is impossible. The only land available is the 50 percent that is inaccessible. The other half is owned by less than 2 percent of the population. There is no alternative to agrarian reform.

To carry out such a reform democratically, (that is, by paying reasonable compensation) is too costly. Nevertheless, Brizola was willing to try. He and his aides calculated that it could be done if local centers of wealth donated $140,000,000 a year for ten years and some exterior power $300,000,000 for the start. On March 1, 1962, Brizola said that the owners of heavy industry, banks, trusts, and so on, had a "social obligation" to participate. He showed how, if all participated (foreign companies included), the $140,000,000 could be easily and painlessly raised. Then he asked that the United States, through the Alliance for Progress, put up the other $300,000,000.

where a medieval, not to say prehistoric, economic structure has only recently been overturned. Until China is economically developed, its political system will be absolutely rigid. Following this line of economic determinism, then, it is no accident that Russia and China (supported by Albania, the poorest of the satellites) are in conflict. They are in different stages of economic development, hence in different political stages as well. This whole argument would put democracy to the Left of Communism.

Instead, our Congress passed the 1963 foreign-aid bill with a proviso specifically aimed against Brizola: that no country receive aid if it expropriates United States property and does not make "appropriate" recompense within six months.

If Brizola has now lost the patience he had in 1961, so should Brazil. The world's biggest coffee exporter, potentially one of the greatest powers on earth, with more arable land than all Europe, 15 percent of the world's forests and 35 percent of its iron deposits, it remains a country where half of its 70 million people are underfed, barefoot, and sickly. In six states, one out of six children dies before he or she is one year old, and one out of six suffers from goiter. Technology is incredibly bad. A hectare in Brazil renders 1,000 kilos of corn and 1,500 kilos of rice; in Italy, an identical (in quality) hectare gives 1,600 kilos of corn and 4,600 kilos of rice. With a potential hydroelectric power of 80 million killowatts, the world's best, Brazil produces only 5,000,000, less than the city of New York.

In the immense northeastern bulge inhabited by 25 million people, food riots degenerate into peasant massacres. Trying to piece out a living on the *sertão*, the soft brown hills of hard arid land where drought reigns eight to ten months a year, the peasant of the bulge works as a share-cropper on *latifundios* owned by a handful of feudal landlords. He has to pay two-thirds of his crop as "rent," is forced to sell the rest to the owner at one-third its value, but has to buy his tools and supplies at 40 percent above standard prices from the owner's store. His way of life is rigidly controlled by the owner, who in one case posted these regulations:

All residents of this property are prohibited from:

1. Carrying arms of any type.
2. Drinking *aguardente* or any other alcoholic beverage.
3. Playing cards or any other game.
4. Spending their free time anywhere except on the property.
5. Hunting or allowing strangers to hunt.
6. Fighting with his neighbor or anybody else.
7. Attending sick friends.
8. Holding a dance without permission of the owner.

9. Spreading gossip.
10. Feigning illness to avoid work.
    Any who do not comply have twenty-four hours
    to get off.

In Rio Grande do Norte, 463 of every 1,000 children die before one year. Diets are manioc flour and molasses, never milk and often no water. Landlords consider all complaints the work of "packs of thieves and Communists."

"We are generous men," explained one Paraíba landlord, Joacil Pereira by name. "If a peasant dies, or his wife dies, or his child dies, who pays for the funeral? The landlord." But when Rio Grande do Norte Sharecropper Antonio Avelino Acca planted a banana tree without Landlord Antonio Moreira's permission, the latter reacted by burning Avelino's house and crops to the ground. In such conditions, even Catholic priests become revolutionaries, as, for example Father Emerson Negreiros, who told his parishioners in Santa Cruz (Rio Grande do Norte): "You should raise a goat to give milk to your children. If the landlord comes to kill your goat, he is threatening the lives of your children. Do not let him kill your goat! Kill him first."

The priest, however, had no suggestion on how to obtain a goat, in the first place. Most peasants could not even afford the rope to stop it from escaping. There are about 2,000,000 who are literally starving (less than 100 calories a day) at any one period of the year. Many of them sell themselves or members of their families into slavery to escape. One Belo Horizonte newspaper discovered as many as 50,000 victims (sold for $1,500,000), and one reporter, to prove it, bought a man and his wife for $30. "I have seen many a good man starve," explained the slave; "that is why I did not mind being sold." When one slave dealer was arrested in São Paulo in 1959, he admitted having contacts with São Paulo ranchers, coffee plantations, and construction projects for his commodity—except teenage girls, who were sold to brothels.

But it is not only in the bulge where Brazilians die of hunger or disease. In Rio's *favelas,* the hillside slums where population runs to 1,000,000 (out of Rio's total of 3,000,-000) and where the only running water is the rain that causes occasional landslides and the makeshift houses to come tumbling down, a pregnant woman told me: "My first two babies died within a few months of their birth. Now I hope only that this one will be a boy and that he will grow up to be strong so he can avenge his dead brother and sister." I asked her who she thought was responsible. Her answer was blunt:

"You!—and all the others like you who can afford those shoes and that suit. I think just the money you paid for that pen could have saved one of my children."

Neither she nor her children have yet been saved but, according to our State Department, Brazil has! In the spring of 1964, the U.S., the right-wing faction of the Brazilian army, and our old friend, power-lusting Carlos Lacerda, ganged up on Goulart to "prevent Brazil's Communization." The army *golpistas* then installed one of their fellows, Marshal of the Army Humberto Castelo Branco, as President, arrested some 40,000 moderates and Nationalists (but not one member of the Communist Party central committee), and deprived of their political rights every politician, statesman or leader who opposed them—including Quadros, Goulart, and Kubitschek. The U.S. applauded; President Johnson sent his "warm wishes" to the new regime before Goulart had yet left Brazil for exile in Spain. Brizola, who also lost his rights, first went underground and tried to lead the resistance. But when he realized that moderates and reformers do not fight, he too went into exile—but in nearby Uruguay from which he could work for the revolution. Having eliminated the center, Brazil's reactionaries seemed in a rush to make Gilberto Freyre's prophecy come true—that Brazil would soon be "a tropical China."

Chapter 5

Mexico

In this hemisphere of endless suffering Mexicans have perhaps suffered the most—from wars, occupation, exploitation, and the visible extremes of wealth and poverty. The land itself is certainly one of the hardest to dominate: Only 10 percent can be tilled, and most of this is neither fertile nor level nor well watered. On this 10 percent live and labor more than 50 percent of the Mexicans.

They are nothing like the myth that we have created about them. Mostly of Indian blood, Mexicans work hard and long. They are not grumblers and they are not meek. If given half the chance to enjoy the fruit of their labor, they will dance and sing and laugh, even with the United States *gringo* they consider the thief of so much of their ancestors' land. If pushed too hard, too long, Mexicans know how to rebel—and fight.

They have fought many times, but their most glorious fight was against themselves. The famous revolution that began in 1910 was not meant to be a "social" revolution—at least, not to the politicians who led it at first. To them, it was to be just a change of guard, a way of getting rid of the long (but not too cruel) dictatorship of Porfirio Díaz. But leaders sometimes become led, and the forces they unleash can often swell beyond their expectations.

Francisco I. Madero, who led the first revolutionary wave, was certainly honest and well principled. But he was also a wealthy landowner who perhaps understood but certainly could never feel the burning thirst for change that Mexican Indians and peasants suffered. This thirst demanded a new type of leader, men like Pancho Villa and Emiliano Zapata—and a flood that has not yet completely stopped even if recent Mexican "revolutionary" regimes have managed to control it temporarily.

Madero was assassinated. His successor was driven out. Venustiano Carranza, who followed, was already part of the flood. Though personally incapable of fathoming its significance, he was guided by the brilliant tactician Alvaro Obregón, who let the flood soak the whole land. By 1917 Mexico had one of the most advanced constitutions in the world.

Despite President Woodrow Wilson's oft-repeated warnings that Mexicans should respect United States property, followed by our armed intervention (General John J. Pershing's Expeditionary Force), Mexico's new constitution included (Article 27) a revolutionary doctrine of property: "The ownership of land and waters . . . is vested originally in the nation . . . [and] the nation shall have at all times the right to impose upon private property such restrictions as the public interest may require . . . in order to conserve and equitably distribute the public wealth. . . . In the nation is vested direct ownership of all mineral fuels, petroleum, and all hydrocarbons—solid, liquid, or gaseous." Article 130 smashed the power of the Church. Article 123 gave the workers their rights. In theory, Mexico had reconquered itself.

But practice is often less dramatic than theory. After Carranza tried to pick his own successor, side-stepping Obregón who thereupon rebelled, the revolution settled down. Obregón, elected in 1920, Plutarco Elías Calles (in 1924), and the three Calles protégés who followed, solidified the revolution. They or their aides may have been corrupt, as our historians like to point out at length. They or their aides may have committed dozens of errors, carried out numerous excesses, rigged elections, and destroyed democratic process. But they began the distribution of land; they launched education reforms and developed national culture (especially Obregón's able Minister of Education José Vasconcelos); they gave workers higher wages; they curbed the power of Mexico's viciously reactionary Church and they established order[1]—within the revolutionary context.

But by 1934 Calles and his crew had grown too rich to care anymore. They wanted to rest. They decided it was time to halt the revolution and its reforms. Thus, in 1934, Calles had one of his aides elected: an Indian from Michoacán with only three years of schooling, a man who had supported his family since he was twelve, who had fought well (at sixteen) under General Calles during the revolution and had served him even better in the Cabinet and as a governor of Michoacán—in sum, a loyal aide that kept his mouth shut and did as he was told.

That man was General Lázaro Cárdenas, Mexico's greatest President—and its revolutionary conscience today.

Cárdenas must have shocked Calles as soon as the 1934 campaign began. Though assured of election, Cárdenas took it seriously, traveled extensively, supposedly to campaign, actually to renew his contact with the people. Once elected, he broke Calles' hold on Mexican politics by slowly getting rid of the ex-President's pals from the army, and by arming unions and peasant groups to offset army power. A few generals balked, some *Callistas* even bolted (San Luis Potosí's General Saturnino Cedillo was maneuvered into yielding all power or rebelling; he chose the latter, and was killed). Finally, Calles had to surrender—and leave Mexico.

But as shrewd as Cárdenas was, his victory was ultimately made possible only by the people. Cárdenas was undoubtedly Mexico's most popular hero, and still is today. He lived simply, opened his house and office to all, and did his self-imposed job as best as he could. That job, he decided, was to return the temporarily stilled revolution to its birthplace, the peasant community.

With superhuman energy that exhausted his aides, Cárdenas visited thousands of villages, spent endless hours listening to their problems, and handed down remedies that were fair and honest and meaningful. He personally supervised the transfer of hundreds of haciendas into community *ejidos*, distributing more than 45,000,000 acres in his six-year reign. When it ended, almost one-third of Mexicans had received their own parcel.

---

[1] Though Obregón was assassinated in 1938 by a Catholic fanatic, and a military revolt almost erupted.

Cárdenas also strengthened the labor movement. The Confederation of Mexican Workers (CTM) under Vicente Lombardo Toledano became a powerful Cárdenas ally, and the Lombardo-Cárdenas-inspired Confederation of Latin American Workers, organized in 1938, won the adherence of all Latin America unions, even the support of unions in the United States (John L. Lewis' UMWA) and France (Léon Jouhaux's CGT).

The major crisis during Cárdenas' presidency began in May, 1937—over oil. Some 17,000 oil workers had struck the oil corporation owned by the British (60 percent) and by the United States (40 percent) for better wages. The companies had refused to yield. The conflict then was taken to Mexico's Labor Board, which, cleaned out by Cárdenas, was not for sale. The board pointed out that while real wages of our oil workers here at home had risen 8.75 percent since 1934, real Mexican oil wages had actually dropped 23 percent and that while United States oil net earnings at home were 1.44 percent, in Mexico they were 17.82 percent. The board, therefore, ordered the United States-British oil corporations to grant the increases. The companies reacted by buying full-page ads in Mexico's press denouncing the board. They declared that they would not comply with its decision. Cárdenas' conciliation attempts were rejected. Finally, on March 18, 1938, Cárdenas quietly signed a decree, based on the Spanish law of 1783 (Charles III: "The mines are the property of the Royal Crown") and Article 27 of the Constitution, ordering the expropriation of the companies. Cárdenas agreed to pay $23,995,991 to cover "actual sums invested, less depreciation incident to their various operations." (The companies demanded some $450,000,000, finally got what Cárdenas offered.) Under Cárdenas, Mexicans had finally begun their reconquest in practice as well as in theory.

The practice was quickly stopped or curtailed by Cárdenas' successors—Avila Camacho (1940-1946), Miguel Alemán (1946-1952), Adolfo Ruíz Cortines (1952-1958), and the current President Adolfo López Mateos (1958-1964). The next one, Gustavo Díaz Ordaz, nominated and therefore sure of election at the time of this writing, is not expected to change the pattern. These presidents have pushed Mexico to the Right, creating a climate for high-level corruption, and have twisted the Institutional Revolutionary Party

(PRI) into a Tammany-like machine.

Controlling the registration lists as well as the polls (where no voting booths exist) and the counting, PRI runs everything in Mexico. The party had had such power since 1928, but after Cárdenas, it was a party of the middle class at the service of the middle and upper classes.

Since Cárdenas, PRI's police and federal forces have sometimes concentrated their power against PAN (National Action Party), which is the far-Right opposition, but most often against the Left. PAN has never had a chance of winning elections, even if they had been free. Nevertheless, PRI police broke up PAN rallies with tear gas in 1958, kidnapped and beat up PAN leader Carlos Piñeda in Campeche in 1959, and killed five PAN demonstrators and arrested four hundred more for protesting a fraudulent election in Yucatán, also in 1959. In Sonora in 1961, leftist Ricardo Topete, an old 1910 peasant-general, tried to enter the PRI convention as a candidate for governor, but police road blocks stopped his supporters; and when they protested, PRI police dispersed them with tear gas and machine-gun fire, then roughed up Topete himself. Near Acapulco that year, PRI police told 11,000 squatters to get off property coveted by speculators, and made their point with machine-gun fire, wounding nine, six of them women and children.

In September, 1961, peasant rebellions erupted in various parts of Mexico; some 200 hungry peasants, for example, rushed the army post at Jáltipan, Veracruz, with a few rifles and machetes on September 15th. In all, 100 peasants were killed and hundreds more were injured. President López Mateos reacted, not by alleviating their conditions, but by jailing 1,000 suspects in 50 towns from Yucatán to Baja California. In general, since 1940, on the false thesis that Mexico has a huge middle class,[2] PRI has ruled against the peasants, despite the much-publicized distribution of lands that are occasionally announced.

Since 1940, distributed parcels have inevitably been from Mexico's poorest, unirrigated land. Today, about 50 percent of Mexico's cultivated land is in the hands of peasants (the other half is made up of *latifundios* worked by 2,000,000

[2] The middle class is bigger in Mexico than in most other Latin American countries, but not so big as sociohistorians would have us believe.

peasants). But only 10 percent of the landed peasants can obtain federal credits; the rest have become tied to their land, as if to absentee landlords of the old days, through the local money centers, controlled by Mexico's new "revolutionary" oligarchy. López Mateos has not distributed irrigated land nor has he aided the *ejidos* with credits, machinery, or technical help. Thus the *ejidos*, once Mexico's pride, have become marginal farms.

Mexican law limits land property to 100 hectares. However, because only 4,000,000 of Mexico's 40,000,000 hectares of arable land are irrigated (and only 7,000,000 could be irrigated), 100 hectares of irrigated land represent an extremely valuable property. In addition, the *latifundistas* get around the law by having 100 hectares "owned" by each member of their families. Hundreds of presidential friends have been given land and, accumulated at 100 hectares per family member, they have become today's big *latifundistas*. López Mateos had promised that irrigated land would be distributed to the *ejidatarios*. He has not kept his promise.

A product of Mexico's new middle-class bureaucracy, López Mateos[3] is personally honest, but his own limited political framework restricted him from giving his regime audacity. It made a stab here, another there, but did not plan or execute coordinated attacks against Mexico's remaining misery, backwardness, and its imbalanced industrial development. López Mateos' executive body executed the policies of powerful interests (1 percent of the population collects 51 percent of the income) that became at times viciously counterrevolutionary.

One recent example of such counterrevolutionary activity involves a man named Rubén M. Jaramillo and his family.

Jaramillo was born with this century in the hills of the state of Morelos. Still young, he joined Zapata for the *Tierra y Libertad* (Land and Liberty) crusade against oppression. When armed fighting stopped, Jaramillo returned to Morelos, where he became a peasant leader, constantly threatening rebellion if agrarian reforms were not carried out. Often he led his men onto undistributed land, and stayed there until it was parceled out or until federal troops

---

[3] Mexicans like to call him "the belly button—neither at the right nor at the left and good for nothing."

forced him off. He was tough, at times cruel, perhaps occasionally too hotheaded to avoid mistakes. But he was a genuine peasant leader in the tradition of Emiliano Zapata.

During Cárdenas' presidency, Jaramillo had no reason to fight. But after Cárdenas, he became vocal. As long as some agrarian reforms were enacted, he kept his activities peaceful. When Ruíz Cortines halted reforms completely, Jaramillo took his men to the hills. He was pursued by tanks, cavalry, artillery, and the air force, but, aided by Morelos' peasants and familiar with Morelos' terrain, he was never caught.

When López Mateos became President, and offered him an amnesty, Jaramillo went home. He met López Mateos, told him what he had fought for, and that he would continue to fight if land reforms were not renewed. López Mateos promised to bring the revolution back to Morelos, and the two men hugged each other in a Latin-style *abrazo*. The scene, photographed by witnesses, became known throughout Mexico. Jaramillo proudly decorated his walls with it.

But López Mateos forgot about Morelos. Jaramillo waited and waited. Then, in 1961, he decided to wait no longer. With five thousand landless peasants, he occupied a series of *latifundios* and unused plots in Michapa and El Guarín, especially the vast untilled tracts owned by a wealthy landowner named Ramón Espín, the protégé and friend of Morelos PRI Governor Norberto López Avelar. The case went to the Department of Agrarian Matters and Colonization (DAAC), which found that the land was indeed unused and should be distributed. Jaramillo, his aims accomplished, left his men on their new land. Then, a few weeks later, DAAC reversed itself, and declared Jaramillo an outlaw for trespassing on private property.

Early in 1962, the Secretariat of Hydroelectric Resources announced that the Alto Amacuzac and San Jerónimo rivers were to be tapped for a dam, electric power and irrigation project which would transform Michapa and El Guarín's 40,000 hectares into the breadbasket of Morelos. DAAC had not known about the project when it announced its first decision. Said Professor Roberto Barrios, DAAC's boss: "I did not know. We were going to give a gold mine to those people! And great political power." Thus on February 13, 1962, General Pascual Cornejo Brum, chief of Morelos' military zone, was ordered to clear the occupied lands. Jaramillo again sought a peaceful solution. On March 18th he tried to see López Mateos, but was refused an audience, and returned to his home in Tlaquiltenango, Morelos, a modest single-floor, poured-concrete house where he lived with his pregnant wife, Epifania Zúñiga, and his three adolescent sons.

They were all there on May 23, 1962, at 2:30 P.M. when sixty soldiers and civilians suddenly arrived in two army trucks and two jeeps, surrounded the house, leveled submachine guns at its two entrances, and ordered Jaramillo to come out. When he did, besiegers rushed into the house, brought out Epifania and the three sons, pushed all five into the vehicles, and drove away. Up to this point, there are scores of witnesses—the neighbors and passersby.

Two hours later, near the Xochicalco archaeological ruins, peasants found the whole Jaramillo family dead. Each of the five heads had a *coup de grâce* .45 bullet in it; in each of the five bodies was a handful of Thompson submachine-gun slugs.[4]

Witnesses, slugs, history, and facts notwithstanding, Mexico's press—and, naturally, *Time* magazine—tried to make the murders sound like "a private affair" of "revenge." But there can be no doubt that the Jaramillos were killed, on orders from the PRI top, because they represented the Mexican peasants' unfulfilled demands from the revolution.

---

[4] The cartridges, found all around the bodies, were stamped Fábrica Nacional de Municiones (1953 and 1954), a supplier that distributes only to the army. Morelos Police Chief Captain Gustavo Ortega Rojas told reporters a few hours after the assassination that the Federal Judicial Police had called him the night before to ask for arms and a jeep, but that when the *Federales* never showed up and he called them, he was told: "It is no longer necessary; everything has been taken care of." The time: 1 hour 30 minutes after Jaramillo's death. (Ortega later denied this conversation when questioned by official "investigators.")

PART III: The Followers

A social revolution in Costa Rica may create interest, arouse solidarity, or ignite revulsion; it may even affect diplomatic history as far as Argentina. But Argentina's economic and political structure will certainly never collapse or be radically changed directly because of such a revolution. A social revolution in Argentina however, will have some very direct repercussions even as far as Costa Rica. These repercussions may not necessarily lead the latter to imitate the former. But a nonrevolutionary Costa Rica would never feel safe with a revolutionary Argentina staring back even from halfway down the globe. Such are the unbalanced facts of political life when countries, small and poor, must share a continent with countries large and rich.

It is even more obvious that a revolt in Argentina would shake Chile, Paraguay, and Bolivia from the very first gunplay; that Brazil, a giant whose frontiers reach out like claws into every country in South America except Chile and Ecuador, need only to rock for the whole continent to roll; that Mexico, which cushions the rest of the hemisphere from "the blond monster up north," can easily let its waters flood all Central America. For better or for worse, Argentina, Brazil, and Mexico have the strength to guide the continent along their own paths. United, the three have the power to fashion it in their image. As social revolutionaries proud of their "independence," the three would inevitably compel the continent's other Latin American states to follow suit.

111

Chapter 6

Chile

Long in the mood to jump the gun, Chileans may yet reconquer Chile before its neighboring giant snaps out of its military stupor—and they may even do so through the ballot.

Perhaps one reason for such prospects is Chile's great political sophistication. And perhaps one explanation for this political maturity comes from Chile's racial mixture, the same that has produced the hemisphere's prettiest women—a combination of Spanish, German, Italian and, to a lesser extent, English, Irish, French, and Yugoslav immigrants with Arauco Indian natives.

Such immigration never attained astronomical figures, but, except for a German colony near Valdivia, the immigrants rapidly became Chileanized. They intermarried, discarded their native languages, and almost automatically injected into Chilean customs a sense of compromise, which is the basis for efficient democracy. Indeed, Chile has suffered less from *Caudillismo* or military dictators than any other Latin American country. Its original inhabitants, the Arauco Indians, elected their *caciques,* refused to accept foreign domination, and constantly revolted against invaders—first the Incas, then the Spanish conquistadores. When General Bernardo O'Higgins, though the nation's first hero and one of its liberators from Spain, who was chosen Chile's first President, tried to set up a dictatorship, he was overthrown.

But such a democratic tradition and political sophistication have not spared Chile from a whole series of disastrous democratic regimes. Until 1879 it was run mostly by Conservatives, usually big landowners who had little vision of their country's future. Nevertheless, the Liberals, though just as conservative in matters of economy, were always raising their heads; in 1865 they won a major victory when non-Catholics were granted freedom to worship (without public display) and have their own schools. In 1875 Congress abolished Church courts and gave their civilian counterpart jurisdiction over priests, a measure that was not revoked despite the archbishop's excommunication of all congressmen who had voted for it.

There were other Liberal victories, but none, of course, that affected the welfare of the masses. In 1879, however, the War of the Pacific erupted, and its consequences did change the structure somewhat. The war was fought over nitrates, the huge deposits centered in what is now the North of Chile, the desert region from Copiapó to Arica. Part of the desert was owned by Peru, part—including the port of Antofagasta—by Bolivia, and only the southern fringe by Chile. But Chile was exploiting the mines in all three parts, and its new-rising industrialists were in no mood to pay royalties to their neighbors. The matter was complicated by the fact that a great deal of foreign capital was involved, particularly British, German, and United States capital. Finally, Chile went to war against both Peru and Bolivia, and Nationalists of the three countries refer to it as the Imperialist War.

Chile won, annexed the whole region up to and including Peru's port of Arica, and thus cut Bolivia off from the sea. The defeat was disastrous for Bolivia (and was one of the minor reasons why it waged the Chaco War against Paraguay, hoping to gain an outlet on rivers leading to the Atlantic). But to Chile, victory brought immediate benefits. Tax receipts doubled almost at once, sufficiently to cover half of the national budget. Public projects were encouraged. Chile's economic pace quickened. Its foreign trade increased. Industrial expansion soared. And a working class was born.

But the long-range effects were unfortunate. In the first place, a disparity between city and country set in, never to be eliminated. Second, because the new industries were owned by a relatively small group of autocrats who were either also involved in the mining or were within the ruling circles, industrial development was neither balanced nor beneficial to the country as a whole. Third, Chile rapidly overextended its reliance on mining earnings; by the war's end in 1881, 78.5 percent of its exports were mining ores; a few years later Chile was totally dependent on foreign markets for her economic salvation. And, finally, the rapid off-balance industrialization (plus unredemption of wartime bonds) created an inflation (and the devaluation of the peso) that has never been seriously stopped. Chile's economy has been under constant need of an emergency boost ever since, and has been characterized by patchwork.

Meanwhile returning Pacific War veterans, restless and often unemployed, turned toward new ideas imported from Europe—Anarchism, Socialism, Syndicalism and, later, Fascism. The constantly increasing bureaucratic class, known today as white-collar workers, demanded representation, and swelled the ranks of a new Radical Party. In 1909 a typesetter named Luis Emilio Recabarren organized the Workers' Federation of Chile and in 1919 led it into affiliation with the labor movement headquartered in Moscow. Finally, in 1920, all these new forces united in one Liberal Alliance to elect an offbeat northern (Tarapacá Province) deputy belonging to one faction of the Liberal Party: Arturo Alessandri, known as "the Lion of Taracapá."

Alessandri was a vain, conniving, shrewd, disproportionately ambitious egotist, convinced of his own destiny and his place in history, oligarchical by taste but humble and "proletarian" by political insight. Nevertheless, his election was extremely significant. It was not a simple electoral change. "The passive obedience of the masses of the country to the old oligarchic circles," as one Chilean historian, Alberto Edwards, has put it, "had ceased to exist."

Alessandri, as he said himself in his first address to Congress in June, 1920 wanted to decentralize the government, abolish the parliamentary regime, separate Church from State, establish monetary stability, social security, and government control of banks and insurance companies, and institute universal suffrage. He achieved almost none of these goals. Until September, 1924, his congresses torpedoed them. Then the deadlock was broken by the military.

In the first blatant intervention in almost a century, the army, which had not been paid while the deputies had voted themselves boosts in salary, forced Congress to approve the labor code.

This code recognized labor unions and collective bargaining, established child-labor laws, a health-insurance plan, a social-security system, accident compensation—and a raise in army and navy pay. Once the code was enacted, the army took over completely and sent Alessandri off to Europe. But in March, 1925, another coup put Colonel Carlos Ibáñez del Campo as head of a new junta that called Alessandri back. He managed to get one more reform through —the separation of Church and State. But the old Lion was tame. And when Ibáñez refused to resign as Minister of War, Alessandri quit instead. Ibáñez then ruled Chile until 1931.

At first, Ibáñez sounded and acted nationalistic enough to get Leftist support. He launched costly public projects of railroads, irrigation, and docks, set up the Chilean Nitrate Company partly with government and partly with private capital, and raised Chilean wages. But it soon became apparent, as the famous Chilean historian Ricardo Donoso has said, that Ibáñez' "fundamental idea was the restoration of the authority of power, the maintenance at all costs of public order, and the resolute combating of the extremism of the Left." Hence the Left went into opposition. Disturbances against Ibáñez mounted.

Chilean politics are so complicated that no opposition movement of principle ever belongs to Right or Left exclusively. The furor against Ibáñez was no exception. The students, mostly Leftists, who rioted against him were also aided by the oligarchy, not because Ibáñez had hurt it (he *did* enforce Alessandri's labor code, but this affected more the small industries of the middle class than the monopolists or land barons), but because Ibáñez had opposed the oligarchy's parliamentary system. Thus, when the students barricaded themselves in the university, they received food from the swank Club de la Unión—prepaid. The oligarchy-outfitted and -financed Republican Militias, reactionary youths wearing blue shirts, joined the extreme Left against Ibáñez. Finally, as crisis followed crisis, Ibáñez fled to Argentina.

On June 4, 1932, a new coup brought about a Socialist state. Led by antimilitary, antioligarchical youths grouped

in NAP (New Public Action) and directed by Eugenio
Mate Hurtado, this strange coup was backed by Marmaduke
Grove who, aside from having such a weird name, was
also chief of Chile's air force. Thereupon, the various factions
involved integrated into one party, the Socialist, and hence
was born Chile's first Socialist Republic.

It did not last long, being downed by another coup a
few weeks later. But ever since, the Socialist Party has
played an extremely important role in Chilean politics,
and it has kept its *golpista* (coup-prone) reputation. Meanwhile, new elections were called, and by the end of 1932
Alessandri was back—this time the candidate of the Right.
He had become a purely social lion.

Alessandri executed some noteworthy projects, but he
also had sixty-three young Nazis massacred after they
had surrendered. He increased press censorship and repressed
strikes with force. The result was that Democrats, Radicals,
Radical-Socialists, some Socialists, and Communists united
in a Popular Front and succeeded in getting their candidate,
Radical Pedro Aguirre Cerda, elected at the next contest.

Aguirre Cerda was a wealthy landowner, winegrower,
and oligarch. Nevertheless, his regime was fair. It was characterized especially by the creation of various mixed (private-
state) corporations to stimulate national industrialization.
Most famous among these was what is now called the Corporación de Fomento de la Producción (CORFO). If it
has achieved nothing except some excellent studies, surveys,
and reports, that is because subsequent presidents never
modernized or updated CORFO's original purpose, expressed
thus by one of its first directors:

> I can tell you that never has the Corporation interfered
> with private . . . initiative. It is in particular the indus-
> trialists themselves who very often, not always, seek the
> form in which the Corporation may help them. The cases
> in which they themselves have sought association with the
> Corporation are innumerable; but never has the corpora-
> tion come to control the businesses which it aids or in
> which it participates. The Corporation intervenes as a
> capitalistic partner. . . .

Unfortunately, this is still true today. Consequently, Chile's
industrialization remains totally imbalanced.

Radicals or moderates ruled Chile until 1952. In 1946 the Popular Front candidate, Gabriel González Videla, a Radical, was elected with Communist support in a deal promising the Reds three ministries. But when the Communists won one-sixth of the vote (80,000) in municipal elections five months later, González Videla double-crossed them, banned the Communist Party, broke relations with Russia, Czechoslovakia, and Yugoslavia, tossed Communists into concentration camps, and even unseated Senator Pablo Neruda, one of the Spanish language's two greatest living poets.[1] This last act prompted a sharp denunciation from ex-president Alessandri, by then the octogenarian president of the Senate—his last notable deed before his death in 1950.

Chile's moderate presidents were businessmen. Their lack of moral stature, fiscal responsibility, or concern for social development and national pride caused old Colonel—now General—Ibáñez to win the 1952 election. That Chileans saw in this lifelong plotter, *golpista*, and former dictator, an example of probity, honor, uprightness, loyalty, and strength is perhaps the best reflection on the worth of his predecessors.

Ibáñez blundered from one crisis to another. He could do nothing against inflation that, using the index 1940 = 100, had reached 511.1 in 1950 and 624.8 in 1951, then skyrocketed to 763.4 in 1952, 956.8 in 1953, 1,648.0 in 1954, 2,887.1 in 1955, and 4,942.1 in 1958. Within the structure of Chile's economy, Ibáñez had only three choices: (1) clamping the country into "austerity" (no government subsidies, a wage freeze, devaluation, and so on), which causes recession and puts construction workers out of jobs in the first of a bottomless pit of social problems and which only erases some of the symptoms without attacking the illness; or (2) attacking the illness itself by rebalancing the distorted industrialization through state planning, alleviating the city-country disparity through land reform, curbing currency manipulations and speculation by nationalizing banks and controlling exchanges; or (3) doing nothing.

Ibáñez called in a mission of economic advisers from the Washington, D.C., firm of Klein-Saks. The advisers

---

[1] The other, Rafael Alberti, also a Communist, is a Spanish Republican exile who shuttles between Argentina and Rome.

recommended the first alternative. Immediately, almost all academically trained Chilean economists protested that in underdeveloped countries such short-visioned recommendations (which follow International Monetary Fund policies) never help anyone except those companies or individuals that have extensive fluid assets. Ibáñez therefore abandoned the notion. But he also rejected the second alternative, which would have required federal control of the economy. So he did nothing—except legalize the Communist Party and retire when he was supposed to.

Joining the Socialists in a new Popular Front, this time called FRAP (Popular Action Front), the Communists came out of hiding. They were strong and ready. And the Socialists, active, aggressive, and well led since the 1930's, were even stronger. Together the two (and smaller regional parties) pushed FRAP candidate Salvador Allende, a witty, sophisticated, extremely sharp and observant Socialist senator and doctor, to within 29,000 votes (out of almost 1,000,000) of winning the 1958 elections. Had 70 percent of Chile's peasants not been disqualified as illiterates, Allende would have won overwhelmingly.

In 1961's midterm election FRAP fared even better, obtaining more votes than any other party or political block, but gained only a few congressional seats because Chile's system of proportional representation by province is such that even if one party gets an absolute majority of the votes it cannot obtain even half of the electoral posts. See page 119 for the 1962 congressional breakdown.

Because the Radicals tended to abstain when not under official pressure, the government had to stake its name on all bills it wanted passed; otherwise the FRAP-Christian-Democrat voting alliance carried. But because the government was aware that the majority of Chileans were opposed to its policies, it was reluctant to identify itself with any issue. Thus, very little was accomplished in Chile since 1958.

From that time on, all Chileans seemed preoccupied with only one thing—the 1964 elections. As the date neared, it became clearer and clearer that only FRAP's Allende or the Christian Democrats' Frei could win. Either way, the Right would be defeated.

The Right did win the 1958 election, however, and its candidate, Arturo Alessandri, son of the "Lion of Taracapá," became Chile's President. His regime, which ran until late

Parties		House		Senate	
	Pro-government	84		26	
Conservatives			⎧ 17		⎧ 4
Liberals	The Right	84	⎨ 28	26	⎨ 9
Radicals			⎩ 39		⎩ 13
	The Opposition	63		19	
Independents			⎧ —		⎧ 2
	Center	23	⎨	6	⎨
Christian Democrats			⎩ 23		⎩ 4
Independent			⎧ —		⎧ 1
Padena (Partido			⎪ 12		⎪ —
Demócrata Nacional)			⎪		⎪
Vanguardia Nacional	The Left	40	⎨ —	13	⎨ 1
del Pueblo	(FRAP)		⎪		⎪
Socialists			⎪ 12		⎪ 7
Communists			⎩ 16		⎩ 4
TOTAL		147		45	

1964, was inept and morally corrupt. The economy went progressively down. As a banker and industrialist, Alessandri, Jr., sacrificed all social-progress reforms to push, obsessively, only one measure: stabilization. Backed by the International Monetary Fund and aided by United States handouts, including Alliance funds (which were not used for reforms but for bolstering the budget), Alessandri sought only to stop spiraling inflation. By pumping Chile's reserves into the economy, he succeeded in cutting it down from 38 percent in 1958 to 10 percent in 1963.

But at what cost? Reserves fell to $5,000,000 by 1962. Government deficits (at 1960's value when the escudo, invented to make inflation seem less severe, was worth 1,000 pesos, or about one dollar) rose; namely, 121,000,000 escudos in 1958, 184,000,000 in 1959, 190,000,000 in 1960, 195,000,000 in 1961, and approximately 292,000,000 in 1962. Alessandri devised a ten-year plan called National Program for Economic Development, aimed at increasing the GNP to 5 percent a year. But despite huge foreign loans (mostly United States) that covered 70 percent of the plan's cost, the GNP increase stayed at a low 1.4 percent (and population growth at 2.5 percent). Meanwhile, Chile indebted itself for decades to come (though it refused to up property or income tax above 16 percent). Alessandri himself said in 1961, "The tax resources do not suffice to cover the normal expenses and the amortization of debts."

Unemployment went up to 18 percent. One third of Santiago's 2,000,000 people continued to live in unsanitary squatters' huts, despite Chile's advanced social laws. With "austerity" in application since 1958, salaries have only doubled, but the resulting housing slump caused rents to jump 500 percent. Government cancellation of subsidies forced food production to drop, causing prices to go up 400 percent (self-sufficient in agriculture twenty years ago, Chile now earmarks 20 percent of its import budget to food). And, as a result, workdays lost to strikes soared from 196,000 in 1958 to 6,000,000 in 1961. That year alone, private housing starts dropped 25 percent and public housing fell 69.8 percent.

Nevertheless, most of Santiago remained a cheerful capital, framed on both sides by a split in the majestic Andes peaks. Its boulevards were elegant, its swank stores full. It was in the rest of Chile that misery became overpowering. Rarely more than 110 miles wide but 2,800 miles long, Chile is like a ribbon that runs from the very tip of the continent up the Pacific Coast to the arid, mineral-filled desert range of central South America. In the South, farmers, many of them descendants of Arauco Indians, try to earn a living on plots surrounded by huge forests, and live isolated in their sad gloom. In the North, half a million people subsist on sand and rocks in wooden shacks while huge corporations take $350,000,000 annual net worth of copper, nitrates, gold, and silver out of the Andes heights. And in the central *Riñón de la oligarquía,* as we saw in Chapter 1, most peasants are held in a peonage that differs from slavery only to legal minds. The peasant or agrarian worker (known as *obligado,* the obliged one, or as *inquilino,* the lessee) who manages to get a contract, as is required by law, does not fare much better. The following contract, copied and translated verbatim, is typical (explanations follow):

WORK CONTRACT FOR HIRED HANDS

Fundo: San Miguel de Challeuque
Owners: Bisquerit and Munito
Signed on May 1st, 1961, by the Society Bisquerit & Munito
and by Antonio Farias Rodríguez, single, 20 years old.
   The latter will work as an agricultural worker, in the
fields, and will live in a house furnished by the *fundo*.

Pay: 197 pesos 50 centavos a day [13.2 U.S. cents]
Regalía: half a *cuadra* of land
Ration: two biscuits a day
   The right to have four animals graze on the *fundo* fields
and to cultivate the land immediately around his designated
house

Contract for one year

Note:
   1. The above not withstanding, the owner may terminate
the contract without notice or severance pay for the following
reasons:
   a) For negligent work or lack of conscientiousness
      in fulfilling obligations.
   b) For dishonesty, flagrancy, grave insults, immoral
      conduct.
   c) For material damages caused intentionally to tools,
      animals, etc.
   d) For not showing up to work for two consecutive
      days without justification or without providing a re-
      placement.
   e) For keeping pigs loose.
   f) For lodging anyone in *inquilino* houses without per-
      mission or for holding drinking sessions.
   2. It is compulsory for all persons living in *obligado*
houses to work the *fundo* fields whenever required by
the *fundo*.
   3. All *obligados* must send other *obligados* to replace
them whenever the former are working their *regalía* land.
                                                   [signatures]

Fundo is the Chilean word for *estancia* or hacienda or
ranch. The pay, 13.2 cents, is in flagrant violation of
minimum-wage laws, which set agriculture wages at 900
pesos (60 U.S. cents). The word *regalía* is used somewhat

as we use royalty. It is not a gift, however, since it is subtracted from the pay, as is the ration, in this case two hard flat breads called biscuits, which are about six inches in diameter. A *cuadra*, meaning a block, is about one acre, so that Antonio, here, was allowed half an acre plus six feet around his house. The house itself was eight feet long and four feet wide with a five-foot rectangular hole for a door and a one-foot-square hole for a window. It was made out of earth and hay, had no floor and, of course, no kitchen, bath, electricity, or running water. To keep warm in winter, Antonio used old discarded boards to plug both holes and build a fire in the house. There was no furniture. Antonio slept on hay.

Compared to others I saw, these conditions were quite good. Antonio figured that after raising corn and vegetables on his half-acre for two years, he could afford a sheep, and after eight sheep he could start selling an animal or two each year. Antonio was full of hope: After ten years, he said, he would get a scooter, and after twenty he would take a vacation to see the sea (140 miles away) he had heard so much about.

Despite the restrictions imposed by *fundo* owners and police, the *rotos* (broken ones, that is, the poor) were becoming more and more conscious of their lot. Whether at night or on their way to Sunday church, they managed to congregate to listen to political agitators. Since only FRAP representatives constantly denounced *fundo* conditions in Congress—naming names and bringing in the uneatable bread for dramatic proof—FRAP attracted most of the ears. Running second in popularity but first in votes (since, as pointed out, most of the population cannot vote) were the Christian Democrats, whose leaders, Senators Eduardo Frei and Radomiro Tomic, sounded so Leftist for a while that they frightened the United States.

Eventually, Washington realized that Frei was the lesser of the two "evils"—he, at least, would not nationalize the copper mines without paying for them. The United States, therefore, decided to back him, pouring in millions of dollars through fake foundations. The Communists, meanwhile, did their best to torpedo Allende's chances (for reasons we shall analyze later), and in September, 1964, Frei was elected President.

Chapter 7

Paraguay

Stuck in the lower center of South America, Paraguay is beyond belief. It might be almost enough to say that one-third of its current population is in exile, mostly in Argentina; that is, 1,800,000 are in, 600,000 are out. There is every justification for it.

I realized this within one hour of my arrival in Asunción, but the point was driven home later when I was taken to a middle-class sector. Along the eight-foot-tall wall, in huge black letters, was painted: RAMON ESCOBAR—AS-SASSIN—TORTURER. Facing the letters were fifteen university students, stripped to the waist. Watching from across the red-clay street were some thirty black-faced men, women, and children. And watching the watchers were fifty head-shaved soldiers, each clutching a submachine gun. "Start scratching off the letters!" ordered an officer. Immediately six other soldiers slashed the students' backs with long-handled horsewhips, and the students began ripping away the cement with their bare nails. Fifteen minutes later, one student fainted. A whistle was blown and two white wagons drove up. Students, soldiers, and spectators disappeared.

"That is modern Paraguay," explained my guide, a member of the opposition. "Those boys had nothing to do with that sign. That's the way the regime breaks down the opposition. Whenever anybody speaks out, the police swoop down on the university or into the workers' district, pick out the first batch they see, and put them through torture like this."

We walked on, climbed a gray hill just a few blocks away, still within the city limits. There, grown men were also being whipped, only much less frequently. In their case, however, the outdoor session went on from sunup to sundown, for they were the political prisoners of Cantera de Tacumbú, where rocks are split by hand for the city's hand-paved streets. "Believe me," said my guide, whose scars were proof of his knowledge, "these prisoners are lucky; they could be in Peña Hermosa, the Chaco island concentration camp where death is as common as leprosy."

Despite these scenes—or rather because of them—in 1962 Paraguay was relatively calm. Known opposition leaders were allowed to work, write, and distribute their antigovernment manifestos, even to stage clandestine interparty elections where 25,000 voters chose new chiefs under the eyes of ruthlessly efficient secret policemen. Arbitrary arrests, "disappearances," and rapid executions without trials were still very much part of Paraguay; they occurred less frequently, however, than they did up to 1960. Some prisoners managed to get to the courts: Julio Rojas, Alfredo Alcorta, Ananías and Antonio Maidana, for example, were ordered freed by judges in 1959, 1958, and 1957 respectively; they are still in jail. José Prieto waited three years for his trial, then was condemned to ten years of Chaco banishment; instead, he was shot. Some one hundred prisoners are now in jail for opposition to the regime. In 1959 the figures ran into the thousands.

One reason for the government's relative benevolence is its desire to appear bloodless enough to receive Alliance for Progress dollars. Another is its knowledge that as long as innocents suffer for acts of protest, most oppositionists' consciences will keep plots confined to parlors. Sooner or later, however, the lid will be torn off, and Paraguay will rock with violence.

It will not be the first time. A landlocked subtropical country of 1,800,000 people and 157,047 square miles of pastures and forests, with poor access by river to the Atlantic 900 miles away, Paraguay has seen more wars and revolutions than most Latin American nations. Except those working in Jesuit missions, the basically Indian population (native Guaraní is still spoken more than Spanish) was enslaved by Spanish adventurers until Paraguay's independence in 1811, and by dictators until 1864. That year, Dictator Francisco Solano López declared war against Brazil on the pretext that the latter had interfered in Uruguayan affairs, but actually to stretch Paraguay's northeastern border. But he soon found himself at war with Brazil, Argentina, and Uruguay in what is called the War of the Triple Alliance. Paraguay's soldiers fought with incredible bravery until 1870, losing two-thirds of the country's 600,000 population. At the war's end only 29,000 males were alive.

Revolutions, especially from 1922 to 1923, continued to plague the country. Nevertheless, by 1928 Paraguay had slowly begun its recovery, when interest focused on the Chaco, wild western Paraguay and southeastern Bolivia, where oil was said to abound. Britain's Royal Shell was exploring in Paraguay; our Standard Oil was in Bolivia. The rivalry that led to hostilities is known as the Chaco War or as the Petroleum War, and once again Paraguayans died uselessly: for though Paraguay won the war and received a good chunk of Bolivian Chaco, oil was found only on the part remaining in Bolivia.

In February, 1936, another popular uprising brought to power Colonel Rafael Franco, the Chaco War's greatest hero. His government, though short-lived (eighteen months), gave Paraguayans their first social laws, even an Agrarian Reform (Decree 1060). As a result, his party, quickly known as Partido Revolutionario Febrerista, became the one great hope of Paraguay's common man, who until then had been forced to obey one of two traditional and oligarchical parties, the Liberals and the Colorados.

It was the latter two, however, that went on to rule—by force and often by repression. A short but violent civil war in 1947 failed to upset the habit. And by far the worst of the rulers is the latest, Colorado Dictator Alfredo Stroessner, a cold, cruel, crew-cutted general of German extraction who has toyed with power since 1940 and held it tight since 1954. Favoring only his beloved military chums —with whom he can drink and dance until sunup seven days a week—and army-connected oligarchs, Stroessner has let Paraguay degenerate into one of the poorest, sickest, and least socially just countries in the world.

Only 25 landowners hold 130,000 square kilometers, the equivalent of Denmark, Belgium, and Holland combined;

1,552 people own 317,500 square kilometers, three-fourths of Paraguay. There's an Agrarian Reform Institute; its budget is $275,000 a year, of which $261,000 goes for administrative salaries. Per capita income is $95 a year, and is that high only because computers include the millions "earned" by Stroessner's army pals. Only 158 miles of road are paved. In Asunción, a dull, drab city of 270,000 people, only a few downtown streets are asphalted, and even they have no gutters, resulting in the city's total paralysis whenever one of the numerous flash rainstorms occurs. Between 42 and 50 percent of the national budget is taken up by the military and police, which outnumber workers 40,000 to 20,000; less than 20 percent by education, culture, and health combined. Illiteracy is officially estimated at 80 percent, but actually must run close to 98 percent. In 1940, with the population at 1,200,000, there were 2,077 schools; today, the population having increased 50 percent, there are only 1,813 schools. One out of every 2,000 people people has leprosy.

In 1940 Paraguay had 2,732 industrial firms; today there are 700. The agricultural index has dropped from 113.8 in 1955 to 77.6 today, meat production (Paraguay's main export) from 121 in 1950 to 105 in 1955 to 100 today, construction from 114.7 to 90.2. Since 1956 the cost of living has jumped 48 times, wages only 40 times. Only 1 percent of the total area is under cultivation; 75 percent is forest land, yet wood exports have dropped from 229,000 tons in 1956 to 142,000 tons in 1961, though demand continues to increase.

United States aid, meanwhile, goes to waste. ICA, for example, furnished funds and engineering skill for roads. But roads are built by the army, which pockets at least two dollars for every one it spends on public works. The army, the first priority on Paraguay's meat supply, actually takes it all and sells its surplus abroad for its own profit. The army is in charge of all contraband operations, run mostly from Puerto Stroessner to Uruguay's free port, Nueva Palmira. A just opened thirteen-story luxury hotel called the Guaraní, in the center of town, was built for a Brazilian contractor in part by the trucks and men of Asunción's Escolta Battalion, the Presidential Guard corps. While the men were just working off their recruitment time, their commander, Colonel Fretes Dávalos, charged the contractors standard rates and pocketed the payroll. Colonel Ramón Escobar, aside from being the city's top torturer, is also said to operate its freight transportation system—using the vehicles of his command.

That none of these facts appears in the local press is understandable: all newspapers are officially official (*La Tarade, Patria*), unofficially official (*El Pais*), officially "opposed" (*Tribuna Liberal*), or so officially independent (*Tribuna*) that it is the only daily in Latin America without an editorial page. The facts, however, are known; living conditions teach only too well.

Nowhere is progress needed so badly as in Paraguay. Nowhere must so much be done so fast with so little. To do it, a popular government is bound to be extremely radical. Already in 1962's Febrerista clandestine but fair elections, the winners were the nationalistic Leftists, who are pro-Castro but non-Communist. So far, Communists have not been able significantly to increase their followers. But they will continue to gain with the simple tactic of pointing out the wavy-roofed, air-conditioned United States Embassy, Paraguay's swankiest building complex, as Stroessner's Number One supporter.

And in fact it is. Even such staunchly pro-United States oppositionists as Liberal Party President Carlos Pastore, a member of the oligarchy self-exiled in Uruguay, has become bitter. When most polite, he says, "If all United States aid to Stroessner stopped today, democracy might still be salvageable tomorrow."

When I repeated this to United States Embassy officials in Asunción, they answered, "But Stroessner is anti-Communist." The argument that anti-Communist butchers accelerate Communist takeovers seemed to carry no weight. "In the last analysis," I was told, "our policy is one of survival. Thus a sure anti-Communist, no matter how despicable, is better than a reformer, no matter how honest, who might turn against us."

Hasn't that been said before?

Chapter 8

Peru

Peru's Pacific coastline, a narrow strip 1,410 miles long, is a sandy desert spotted with 40 oases watered by 52 little rivers that wind their way down from the snow-topped Andes never more than a few dozen miles away. Although the coastline occupies less than one-tenth of Peru, more than a fourth of the country's inhabitants live there. The Andes ranges, including ten peaks more than 20,000 feet tall, take up about 40 percent of the land and as much as 73 percent of the people. The eastern slope of the Andes, known as the *montaña* as opposed to the range itself which is called the *sierra*, makes up the rest of Peru, which is never more than 800 miles wide. In the *montaña* a quarter of a million inhabitants live in thick wet jungles and forests surrounded by powerful rivers.

In the coastal zone are Peru's first and third cities: Lima, the beautiful, charming, Spanish-colonial capital, has almost 1,500,000 dwellers (counting Callao, twenty minutes away); and Trujillo, a quaint city of old churches, numerous small plazas, with the remains of a wall King Charles V ordered built around it in 1686, and a filthy market in the center of town, has less than 75,000. Peru's second city, Arequipa, of some 140,000 people, is in the *sierra*, 7,500 feet up and at the foot of the 19,200-foot volcano El Misti. The *sierra* also houses the famous cities of Cuzco, Puno, and Ayacucho. The only city of note in the *montaña* is Peru's port on the Amazon, Iquitos, which once prospered from the rubber trade but has slowly lost all economic significance since 1915.

Almost all of Peru's 1,100,000 whites (10 percent of the population) live along the coast where, despite the deserts, are grown most of the country's cash crops—cotton, sugar cane, and rice in the North, grapes, fruits and olives in the South. Oil, too, comes from the coast. This small strip consumes most of the country's imports and supplies most of its exports.

The oligarchy, thirty families at the top and no more than a few hundred in all, is proud of its Spanish conquistador background. It owns all the coastal plantations and most of the *sierra*'s larger ones. The Indians, Quechua-speaking Inca descendants, are restricted to pastoral farming and a bit of agriculture in the deeper *sierra* valleys. Theirs is a bleak, hard life in barely fertile land cluttered with rocks. There are about 5,000 Indian communities, where land is tilled and llamas or goats are raised on the communal holding system of the Incas. But the Indians rarely own land where the soil is fair, having lost it to the oligarchy, which used the armies as personal conquerors. Even now, some Indian complaint that the land is being taken by the federal police and given to a stranger is often reported.

More than 70 percent of the Indians and mestizos (mixed bloods, known in Peru as Cholos), that is, about 5,500,000 Peruvians, live outside the money economy, eating what they can manage to produce and weaving cheap textiles for themselves or for barter. They chew cocaine-producing coca leaves to still hunger pains, and average 500 calories a day. Where there is grass, the Peruvian Andes Indian eats it—and also the sheep he kills when it gets so hungry that it begins tearing another sheep's wool off for its food. The peons who work the land of the whites average one sol (4 cents) a day, and not only labor from sunup to sundown but must also furnish servants for the master's hacienda or Lima house.

There are about 100,000 Indians employed in the big *sierra* mines, where pay is better (up to $1 a day) but where conditions (minerals lie at up to 17,000 feet above sea level) and poisonous fumes make a man of thirty-five look sixty—if he has survived that long in the first place. Many companies, including some of our own mining corporations, distribute coca to the Indians before they enter the pits so as to render them semiunconscious of dangers, hardships, and the internal pains the fumes create.

Sooner or later, someone will lead Peruvians to change these conditions. The United States is currently hoping that the leader will be a man called Victor Raúl Haya de la Torre. Until the appearance of this man, Peru's overall history is boringly repetitious (an oligarch ousted by an army coup replaced by another oligarch), though Peru has had its share of glorious epochs—the Inca civilization was one of the most developed, stratified, and organized societies known to man, and the Spanish conquest launched by Francisco Pizarro, Diego de Almagro, and the priest Fernando de Luque was one of the cruelest and bloodiest but also most spectacular in the history of man.

Born in Trujillo in 1895, Haya de la Torre belongs to the oligarchy, with blood ties going back to Juan de la Torre, one of Pizarro's lieutenants. Haya's father was a congressman, and his uncle was Augusto Leguía's vice-presidential running mate in the 1920 elections (canceled when Leguía seized power by force). Thus, when he came to Lima to attend the University of San Marcos, Haya had no trouble finding an "in"—a prominent lawyer and top Leguía backer who put him to work as a clerk and gave him the chance to get a good look at practical politics. At the university, however, Haya became a constant agitator. He joined, then presided over, the Student Federation, campaigned for "university reform" (autonomous status), for a labor code, and for setting up popular adult-education universities in the interior. Then, after the Student Federation joined the Labor Federation to protest Leguía's decision to "dedicate Peru to the sacred heart of Jesus," and the demonstration was broken up by police and bullets, Haya was jailed, then deported to Panama.

For the next eight years Haya wandered in Central America, Mexico, the United States, Europe, and Russia. He was named honorary president of Havana University's Student Federation, worked as Mexican Education Minister José Vasconcelos' private secretary, and launched a new movement to carry out his ideas—APRA (American Popular Revolutionary Alliance). He also wrote numerous articles, talked politics with Leon Trotsky, and attended the Fifth Congress of the Communist International and the 1927

Communist-organized World Anti-Imperialist Congress (where
his coolness toward Communists led to final rupture). He
studied at the London School of Economics, was jailed
in Switzerland and then escaped, and finally headed home.
But, landing in Panama, he was seized *outside* the Canal
Zone, and inside the "independent" sovereign nation of
Panama, by Canal Zone United States officials, was tossed
into prison, and forced to fork out $90 for his ship passage
—to Germany.

Nevertheless he reached home in 1931, after Leguía had
been ousted and new elections called. Haya decided to
throw his newly formed APRA party into the election.
Its changes were good. APRA was a fiery, idealistic revolutionary party with aims at liberating not just Peru but
all of "Indo-America." It sought to oppose imperialism with
a grand "Alliance" of workers, peasants, intellectuals, and
the bourgeoisie. It demanded the political unity of Latin
America, the nationalization of land and industry, and the
internationalization of the Panama Canal. Wrote Haya
in *El antimperialismo y el Apra:*

> Our historic experience in Latin America, and especially
> the very important and contemporaneous experience of
> Mexico, show us that the immense power of Yankee impe-
> rialism cannot be confronted without the unity of the Latin
> American peoples. But since this unity is conspired against
> jointly by our governing classes and imperialism, and since
> the former aid the latter, the State, instrument of oppression
> by one class of another, becomes an arm of our national
> ruling classes and [of] imperialism to exploit our producing
> classes and to keep our peoples divided. Consequently,
> the fight against our governing classes is indispensable; po-
> litical power must be captured by the producers; production
> must be socialized, and Latin America must constitute
> a Federation of States. This is the only road to victory
> over imperialism, and the political objectives of APRA as
> the International Revolutionary Anti-Imperialist Party. . . .

In those days, Haya insisted that the only effective way
to combat imperialism was through state capitalism, "which
must *direct* the national economy [and which] will have
to deny individual or collective rights in the economic field
when the use of these rights implies an imperialist danger."

In *Impresiones de la Inglaterra Imperialista y de la Rusia Soviética,* Haya added:

> What Aprismo considers ruinous for Peru is that in the name of our need for foreign capital, the country is converted into a slave of this capital, and instead of foreign capital serving the progress of the country, the country becomes its servant.

But Haya was no Communist:

> The Communist Party in Indoamerica lacks the force and the authority to lead the anti-imperialist struggle. . . . The anti-imperialist current among our peoples is older than the Third International and more vast than the exclusiveness of their class party. In order that one class in Indoamerica could be able by itself to victoriously lead the anti-imperialist struggle, it would have to achieve the conditions which Marx set forth for the effective class leadership of a revolution: "For the emancipation of a people to coincide with the emancipation of a given class within bourgeois society, it is necessary that the class as such represent all society." And this exactly is not the case with our nascent proletarian class, and even less with the weak Communist Party in Indoamerica, which does not even represent the proletariat.

Under APRA, Haya saw a bright future for Indoamerica:

> With production intensified, organized on the basis of the restoration of the agrarian community, evolved, modernized, and provided with all of the elements of modern technology and organized cooperatively, Indoamerica will be the granary and stable of the world. The revindication of the Indian as a man and of his system as a method of production are imperative for economic reasons. The index of production will rise extraordinarily. Adapting the system to the man and the man to the system and extending it to all of the Andean zone under the form of state cooperatives, the economic transformation of South America will accelerate prodigiously. If we try to extend the system to industry as it develops—especially to mining, adopting all

of the most modern production elements and methods—we will add another factor to the vast panorama of total economic transformation, axis of anti-imperialist resistance. The base, as the reader will have noted, is in the million of indigenous workers of the countryside and of the mines, who will keep as a sacred aspiration for the future the restoration of a social system of the past. Restored in its essence and modernized by contemporary technology, we will have used the past as has no other people to establish favorable conditions for growth in the future.

Thus, Haya in the early thirties was a Nationalist, proud of his heritage, anxious to elevate his people, repulsed by the idea of subjugating their will and tradition to anyone but themselves. He was also a Socialist convinced that Peru's or Indoamerica's only open road to the twentieth century was one of strict government-directed economy. The combination—National Socialism—perhaps resembled its European counterpart in theory, but neither Haya nor APRA were Nazis or Fascists in the form applied in Germany or Italy. Haya was then a modernist who hoped that peaceful revolution was possible. He entered Peru's 1931 elections as a democratic participant.

Through fraud, by control of the electoral machinery, with the army used to supervise voting, and by means of stiff examinations to eliminate "illiterates," Peru's General Sánchez Cerro was proclaimed the "winner" 150,000 to 110,000. APRA knew that it had won the election. Nevertheless, Haya accepted the fraud in order to keep its political activity legal. But "democracy" would have no such thing; President Sánchez Cerro consolidated his armed forces, then declared APRA illegal, jailed Haya and scores of other leaders, and, after rank-and-file Apristas rebelled in Trujillo, killing 200-odd soldiers, launched a vicious program of persecution; in 1932 alone, more than 5,000 Apristas were killed, many of them in jail.

Until 1945 a limited but often extremely bloody war ensued between APRA on the one hand and the oligarchy and its military pawns on the other. The latter often wiped out whole villages; the former fought back through its well-disciplined shock troops, called búfalos, with assassinations (including that of Sánchez Cerro in 1933), ambushes, and even occasional uprisings. APRA was by now a highly organized grassroots party run on a cell system; it was prepared for underground existence. How many people were killed in this undeclared civil war is impossible to estimate, but every oligarch family claims at least one martyr.

By 1945, however, it became clear that something was wrong with Haya, APRA, or both. If the party was as popular and as mass-based as it claimed, why did it never dare come out and fight—with general uprisings, sabotage, guerrillas, or terrorism? Surely Haya must have realized by then that Peru's "democracy" would never allow his brand of democracy to take over. Nor could Haya insist that his moral principles rejected violence. In the first place APRA did not keep its hands clean; the *búfalos* fought hard, and fought to kill. Second, Haya never ordered his Apristas to wage a Ghandian-like war of nonviolence. Third, if conditions were as bad as he said—and they were—then Indians were dying anyway, from hunger, disease, and exposure, in which case, a revolt to end such deaths was morally justifiable. However, if Haya's aim was personal political power, then compromises, practical politics, and deals with the oligarchy were certainly more advantageous, even more so if economic advantages were also involved.

In the 1945 election Haya made a deal with the oligarchy. He ordered APRA to support the conservative candidate, José Bustamante y Rivero, who won overwhelmingly. For a while, after the election, it looked as if there were two presidents in Peru, Bustamente in the Casa de Gobierno (Government House) and Haya in the Casa del Pueblo (People's House). Apristas even became Cabinet ministers—in a reactionary government. Still, few people doubted the motives of Haya. APRA set up a Peasant and Indian Bureau, took over the Confederation of Peruvian Workers from the Communists but kept up its militancy, and sent mobile health units into the *sierra*.

Nevertheless, some Apristas were unhappy. No basic changes were being carried out. The government *was* conservative. United States capital was entering, not leaving, Peru. On October 3, 1948, the dissatisfied Apristas rebelled. Haya immediately repudiated the revolt, and it was crushed. But neither did the Bustamante government survive. It was overthrown later that month by General Manuel A. Odría, who went on to rule until 1956.

Odría banned APRA, offset mild persecutions (Haya

spent five years in the Colombian Embassy) with a series of public projects that gave most of the poor good jobs even if it gave all of the rich more wealth. The rich, however, did not like Odría's hand-picked candidate in the 1956 election, and chose instead an aging playboy oligarch and ex-President, Manuel Prado y Ugarteche, whose family is supposedly the richest among Peru's "thirty families."

APRA, prohibited from running, obviously could not choose to back Odría's candidate. Nor could it support Architect Fernando Belaunde Terry, who was running on a newly formed Popular Action Party. Belaunde was an oligarch, but he had long supported APRA, and his Acción Popular Party platform was full of such slogans as Agrarian Reform and Independent Foreign Policy. Unknown a few months before the election, Belaunde was rapidly gaining wide popular support. Therefore, Haya gave the order that APRA back Prado, who in turn put Apristas on his congressional lists. Haya finally made his true intentions clear—to those who wanted to see.

The people did not—not yet. Prado won. Belaunde was a fair second, 106,000 out of 1,250,000 votes behind. On his first day in office, Prado kept his side of the APRA-oligarchy pact: he legalized the (by now in quotes) "Revolutionary" Party.

It was a different party. No longer did the *búfalos* fight—out of self-defense—against the oligarchy's goons or dragoons. Now they attacked Belaunde's men and, when true Apristas abandoned Haya to form APRA Rebelde, their ex-comrades as well. Yelling "Communist!" at all opponents, Haya's shock troops broke up rallies, beat up critics, even killed old allies. In Parliament, Haya's representatives supported Prado's Prime Minister Pedro Beltrán, an overwealthy land baron, press lord, and financier whose much-heralded "agrarian reform" was no more than a colonization project aimed at keeping Peru's restless Indians away from Lima while his own and friends' vast *latifundios* went untouched. As payment for their support, Apristas received some choice appointments (for example, control of Peru's United Nations delegation) and some lucrative jobs (bank directorships). The old rebels, settling down comfortably in swank San Isidro (Lima's silk-stocking district) mansions, passed their brass knuckles to younger men, who were told to fight all grumblers because they

were Communists. APRA became the great friend of the
United States, and our State Department began to propagate
Haya's merits.

For six long years Prado and Beltrán ruled the country
as they wanted because Apristas in Congress backed them.
No reforms were carried out. No industry was nationalized.
No armed forces were curtailed. Peru was ruled for the
rich by the rich, and APRA said not a word. It was interested
in only one thing: winning power in 1962. Behind the scenes,
it plotted, connived, and manipulated to make sure this
would come about—one way or another.

As the 1962 elections neared, hundreds of known, *proved*
cases of Aprista fraud (giving false documentation, registering
minors, and so on) were reported in the Peruvian press,
including, for example, those uncovered by Judge Antonio
M. Villar of the First Judicial District of Lima, whose court
challenged no less than nine hundred registrants—all Apristas.
These fraud cases were denounced *before* the election to
Prado's National Election Board. But Prado was in favor
of APRA.

Haya de la Torre was the industrial and banking oligarchy's
candidate in 1962. His most dangerous opponent was Belaunde, also representing the oligarchy, but its mining faction.
This time, he had no platform and no ideas, but plenty
of slogans ("Peru is my Doctrine") and a plan of building
a huge Pan American highway on top of the Andes (average
height 18,000 feet) which, he told me seriously, would benefit
the poor of five countries and eliminate the need of an
agrarian reform. The real beneficiaries, of course, would
be his construction and mining industrialist friends.

One more candidate was considered important: durable
General Manuel Odría, who was the front for the old-style
oligarchs who were still fanatically anti-Apristas despite
APRA's turnabout. It was an oligarchy's election, and unless
Haya won and the old-style Aprista-hating militarists stopped
him from taking power, it would be an oligarchy's victory.

The campaign was tough. The very day I returned to
Peru, just before the election, I noticed *búfalos* breaking
up a Belaunde and a minor Leftist rally, fighting *with*
the police against the people. I soon noticed, too, that
APRA was not the great mass-based party I thought and
all the correspondents swore it was. In 11,440-foot high
Cuzco, once the spectacular capital of the Incas, in other

southern cities, in the northern oil regions of Talara and
Negritos, even in Haya's hometown of Trujillo, APRA no
longer seemed to be the party of the humble. At first I
was impressed by the size of APRA rallies. But the APRA
machine, with its network of trucks and busses that hauled
thousands from town to town to swell rallies, with its rhythmic
chanters, banner and handkerchief wavers, and with police
(but not military) protection, was somewhat frightening.
It reminded me of the same organized frenzy in Germany
in the late thirties.

Then I had a long interview with Haya. A big, bulky,
yet somewhat effeminate bundle of old nerves and worn
energies, he appeared to be simply an "anti." For three
solid hours he spoke only of Communism, which he saw
everywhere—in Belaunde's Popular Action, in the press
(including the oligarchical *El Comercio* and *La Prensa,*
the latter owned by Beltrán, his ex-ally, who was then
considering being a candidate himself[1]), even, incredibly,
in Odría's *Unión Nacional Odriista.* (Later, APRA's daily,
La Tribuna, followed Haya's lead and published an accusa-
tion that 30 percent of both parties were Communist.)
Land-occupying peasants, no matter how miserable their
lot, are pushed by Communists, he said. Nationalists who
want to nationalize mines or industries are Communist
tools. "Imperialism is a form of development in underdeveloped countries," said the anti-imperialist. "Imperialism
is *necessary* for Latin America's development."

At least on the question of agrarian reform, I thought,
the great "friend of the Indian" would stick by his old
principles. "It is not a question of taking wealth from the
one who has it but of developing what exists," he said.
Surely, I insisted, one cannot deny that all arable lands
are in *latifundios* owned by the few and that what remains
underdeveloped is poor lands. "There are many wrong ideas
about the *latifundio,*" he retorted. "When people say that
there is a hacienda as large as Switzerland [there is], it
might be that that particular land is not very productive
[it is] and that the owners [one of the thirty] need a large
amount ot it." I started digging out my file; I was ready

[1] Beltrán did try. He rented a whole building as campaign headquarters, scheduled a mass meeting, and gave up his ambitions
when only 200 people showed up.

to argue with examples. Haya stopped me. "Times have changed!" he shouted. Then, smacking his fist, he shrieked "Our *only* fight is against Communism!"

A few days later, I talked to a group of Inca-descended Indians whose traditional common lands had long been taken over by Lima-based land barons. They had never heard of Fidel Castro, or of Stalin or Khrushchev. But they had also not let an APRA delegation enter their last remaining possession, a plot 30 by 20 feet on the road to Ayacucho, where they grew a calorie-low mountain corn on which they lived. These Indians distrusted all parties and never allowed a politician to enter their "home." When I met them (through an Indian guide) they were mourning the death of one of their members—killed by *búfalos* who had accused them of being Communist for not letting them pass.

On June 10, 1962, Peruvians went to the polls. They gave Haya, Belaunde, and Odría about the same vote. Officially Haya won by 14,000 votes. Belaunde yelled Fraud! The army, too, said that there had been fraud. And every Peruvian knew that there had been fraud. Everybody, that is, except the *New York Times* correspondent who reported that there had been no fraud because the National Election Board said so. The *Times* thereupon carried numerous editorials criticizing everybody except Haya, the board, and President Prado. It did not once mention that the board chairman was José Luis Bustamante y Corzo, an oligarch and Prado's excellent personal friend for many years.

Meanwhile, Haya rushed around making deals. First, the anti-Communist leader wanted a pact with Belaunde, who was 30 percent Communist. Belaunde turned Haya down. The former went home to Arequipa, his stronghold, threw up barricades, called for a revolution to give him his rights, and went to sleep. So did his supporters. Had the military not come to his support, Belaunde would have brilliantly maneuvered himself into oblivion.

Haya then went to see 30 percent Communist Odría, who did not turn him down. Shrewd and slippery, Odría had impressed me as the only candidate with some political sense. Now he used that sense. If a man of such great "principles" as Haya, whom he had jailed, persecuted, haunted, and deported, can come sniveling up to him for a deal,

Odría must have gloated, obviously he's a phony. Odría knows how to handle phonies. The two enemies made a deal. The man Haya hated most for so long was to be President, while APRA was to have few choice plums.

But on June 18th the Armed Forces, disgusted by the whole show, put an end to all deals. Staging a finely executed coup, they took over the country and canceled the elections. It was now Kennedy's turn to cry foul. We broke relations with Peru and said we'd cut off all our aid. The *New York Times* applauded Kennedy (except for the columnist James Reston, who kept his sense of critical objectivity and calmly reminded his readers that Kennedy's "pique" is not to be confused with diplomacy).

Haya fled for cover. The great fighter told his APRA to keep fighting—and they called a general strike—while he would hide out. The strike failed. Thus ended, in effect, the great forty-year-long Aprista crusade.

As for President Kennedy, he had no choice but to accept his failure. Within days of the coup, the State Department started grinding out stories about the junta's assurance of free elections, of civil liberties, and soon—all of which the junta had clearly guaranteed the day it took power. But Kennedy needed to rejuvenate such assurances to save face. When he thought he had, he recognized the junta.

And as for the *New York Times*, it too had to save face. Its Peru correspondent found that "there is no militant anger" against the coup, while editorials suddenly reminded its readers that Haya, the great popular leader, had not even got one-third of the votes. And, of course, it praised Kennedy, who had "struck a blow for democracy."

Actually, neither Prado, Odría, Belaunde, Haya, Kennedy (or Johnson) nor the *New York Times* could do a thing for Peru's democracy. That would have to wait for the coming of a new, popular leader.

In the meantime, Peru is ruled by President Belaunde, who won the 1963 elections staged, as promised, by the junta. It is ruled badly, mainly because the Apristas and Odriistas, who together control Congress, have ganged up to torpedo Belaunde's program—smearing him as a Communist.

Overly ambitious, Belaunde has fought back the best he could. He encouraged landless Indians to seize untilled *latifundios* so as to force through Congress his land reform bill. He helped Communists seize union directorates so as to break APRA's strangle-hold on Labor. And he is pushing for various nationalizations, so as to win the support of the masses. An impatient demagogue, he has wooed and won the support of most of the Left—and the Nationalist army officers—and, in crucial municipal elections in December, 1963, captured 51 percent of the vote. Now, he is known to toy with the idea of setting up a "popular dictatorship" in order to eliminate Haya-Odría's legal sabotage. Considering his program—and his enemies—such a move would obviously not be detrimental to Peru.

---

[2] Watered down by compromises, the Bill finally passed in May 1964, whereupon Belaunde immediately set to work putting it into practice; by June, he had expropriated 937,500 acres.

Chapter 9

Ecuador

So poor that luxury houses seem drab, Ecuador is in a state of decay. The stone-walled government palace, on one side of Quito's Independence Square, and the Majestic Hotel, supposedly the best in the capital's downtown, on the other, go without paint—too expensive. Tourists rarely stay more than one day. Beggars outnumber workers. Though the country is essentially agricultural and 71 percent of the people work the land, only 5 percent is under cultivation. All of that, plus 25 percent of the rest, is owned by 1 percent of the population—4,200 individuals.

Almost all of the country's 2,400,000 Indians are illiterate. Living in the generally infertile *sierra*, they subsist, outside the economy, on 600 calories a day. Still under the *huasipungo* system, the Indians get paid in the right to use parcels of the master's land (no cash), but must also send their womenfolk (especially the young) to his house to serve his *every* desire.

As in most other Latin American countries, Ecuador has Liberals and Conservatives—both at the service of the oligarchy. In impoverished Ecuador the same oligarchy owns both the land (bananas, coffee, cacao) and the commerce (export-import), in conjunction with United States interests. As a result, politics have generally been an intramural game of the rich and for the rich.

The one politician who has been an exception is José María Velasco Ibarra, a powerful *caudillo* who never lost

141

an election and who late in 1961 had shouted that "only law or Providence will oust me from the Presidency before the end of my term." Four times Ecuador's President and three times ousted before the end of his term—by neither law nor Providence—Velasco is now a bitter old warrior in exile in Argentina, where I went to see him.

Tall and thin, his deep black eyes ever concealed behind dark prescription glasses, his bald dome offset by a thick snow-white moustache, Velasco Ibarra is modern Ecuador's best known politician—and its unluckiest. Though his family tree grew in the country's bluest fields (his mother's branch leads back to the founder of the city of Ibarra and to revolutionary hero Simón Bolívar), Velasco owns neither land nor legacy; his father, a noted Quito mathematician, was one of those rare Latin American wonders, an honest politician.

So was Velasco. "I do not even own a house," he said proudly. "In all my years as a popular leader, I accepted only one of the thousands of gifts offered me, a small ranch near Guayaquil, which I sold to buy this Buenos Aires apartment during my last exile. I own nothing else, except my books."

Velasco was born in Quito on March 19, 1893. He studied law hard and entered politics early. A Conservative like his father, he rapidly became Ecuador's fieriest orator; his feverish singsong hypnotized masses; his glowing charm disarmed critics; his erudite penetration converted skeptics. Thus, in the presidential elections of 1933, he was swept to victory as the Conservative Party candidate backed by the Liberal Party.

But his former supporters, firmly entrenched in Congress, had no intention of letting him keep his campaign promises, or so he said: "They were interested only in their own benefits. And that's the way it's always been. To them, politics was a fight among individuals for the sheer vanity and utility of having power. Never did they consider the interest of the people, never did they have national programs. What they wanted was to reap the fruits of power, nothing else." When Congress went on strike in 1935, refusing to consider government bills, Velasco dissolved it and called for a new constitutional assembly. But it never convened. Less than one year after his term began, Velasco was overthrown by a military coup.

The wartime dictatorship of Liberal President Carlos Arroyo del Río brought Velasco back. Aided by the Democratic Alliance, a coalition that included Socialists and Communists, he staged his only successful coup and made himself President in 1944. But the following year, the Alliance enacted a new constitution that was, he said, "barbaric, absurd, utopian, and impossible, a typical example of the idiotic *criollo* Communism that congratulates itself for filling theaters and lecture halls with illiterate Indians." So, in 1946, "I smashed the radical constitution and set up a new one."

Fashioned after ours in that it divides the government into three branches, Velasco's constitution is still Ecuador's law of the land. It made voting at eighteen compulsory for literate men and optional for literate women; to keep the military from wielding disproportionate influence in politics, it denied the vote to the Armed Forces and police. As a result, Velasco was ousted by the army in 1947.

Elected President once again in 1952, Velasco finally had the chance to work. He launched road and rail projects to link the *sierra* with the fertile coast. He almost balanced the budgets by stimulating exports; Ecuador became the world's No. 1 banana exporter, shipping out 600,000 metric tons a year, and a petroleum exporter by half of its yearly 400,000 tons' yield. To Leftist complaints that most of the better banana plantations were owned by the United Fruit Company and that 90 percent of the oil wells belonged to British firms, Velasco retorted: "Ecuador has no native capital. Only foreign investments will bring in such capital, needed to develop the country." Velasco also made sure that his perennial enemy, the Armed Forces, felt appeased. He bought them ships and planes, built them schools and forts, raised their salaries, and increased their benefits. "They owe me everything they have," he shouted at me. Velasco finished his term.

His efforts had not basically changed Ecuador. It was still poor, and even its biggest industry, textiles, could account for only 50 percent of national demand. Once world commodity prices began sinking, Ecuador's per capita export value became the lowest in the Southern Hemisphere.

But Velasco was still strong, and in 1960 he won an overwhelming election victory. This time, however, he found his people different, influenced not by events at home but by those hundreds of miles away—in Fidel Castro's

Cuba. "Everybody was mad," he said. "Peasants wanted land. Workers wanted higher wages. Peoples called for nationalization. Politicians talked of a new future. It seemed to me as if the Right had become Left and the Left, Right. Even the Army agitated for unrealistic reforms."

Velasco tried to reunite his people—with old history. Hapless Ecuador, once a fair-sized nation of 400,000 square miles, had been whittled down to 275,000 by 1900— still bigger than Mexico, though. Then, in 1904, it lost 27,000 square miles of Amazonian territory to Brazil. In 1916 it lost 65,000 more to Colombia. Finally, in 1941, Peru invaded Ecuador, defeated its ill-prepared, outnumbered army and stole another 70,000 square miles (legalized by the Rio Treaty), making Ecuador smaller than the state of Colorado. By renewing his country's feud with Peru, Velasco hoped to rally his people together.

To cope with Castroites, by far the majority of political Ecuadoreans, Velasco launched what he called his "Independent" foreign policy. "I have always been a vigorous advocate of the autodetermination of peoples, of the principle of nonintervention, and of the equality of countries regardless of size. Cuba presented me a test case; I stood firm." When United States Ambassador to the United Nations Adlai E. Stevenson visited Ecuador before the first Punta del Este conference, "I told him: 'The United States must sit down with Cuba and the rest of the continent at a round table. Let each side say what it has to, and let us all discuss the differences.' Mr. Stevenson told me that this was impossible because the United States does not accept Cuba as an equal. I said this was wrong, and furthermore I made it clear that Ecuador would oppose any form of punitive action against Cuba. As a result, naturally, Ecuador's oligarchy, United States corporations (despite all the help I gave them), and extreme Right became my enemies."

But Velasco's "Independent" policies were not one-sided. When Vice-President Carlos Julio Arosemena decided to tour iron-curtain countries during Stevenson's visit, "I was absolutely opposed. I told Arosemena that not only was his trip timed to insult Ambassador Stevenson but was also aimed at ruining Ecuador—which, after all, had asked the United States for financial aid." Velasco publicly disowned Arosemena's trip. As a result, the Left, too, became Velasco's enemy. "That the Right teamed up with Communists is beyond my comprehension," he said, though such coalitions are nothing new to Latin America, as we shall see.

Controlling Congress, the Right-Left coalition passed laws raising public salaries without appropriating the necessary funds. "I needed new money right away," Velasco explained, "so I had to levy indirect taxes. It was only a temporary move, while we worked out a general income-tax plan. But they did not give me time. They screamed that I was milking the poor in favor of the rich. Even Arosemena, who, as a member of the cabinet, had voted in favor of the taxes, denounced them later as favoring the oligarchy. And when I presented a fiscal reform, a reform that would have canceled most of the indirect taxes, Congress ignored it completely. They also ignored my agrarian reform plan, which I also presented at that time [1961] and which called for the expropriation and distribution of unused land. Even the press, the oligarchy's press, was silent. I had to go to the people to tell them myself. But it was too late."

To gain back at least support from the Right, Velasco raised salaries of the Armed Forces and the police. Then he freed the sucre (which, long frozen at 15 to the dollar, immediately tumbled down to 30). "Freeing the sucre had to be done," he insisted. "The International Monetary Fund had warned us that exports would continue to fall unless we did. It was the only way to save our economy. But the Communists yelled I was raising the cost of living. They organized strikes everywhere. Labor unions' protests were read in Congress but I was not allowed to defend myself. Then students rioted. Finally, on October 4th, a general strike turned into a revolution." It was the end.

"I did not quit!" Velasco told me over and over, waving his arms in hate. "I never resigned! I was stoned out of the government palace. Then the air force turned against me. I had done everything possible for the Armed Forces, everything!" Then, sinking back in his worn armchair, in his poorly furnished three-room apartment, he seemed to fall into a dream. "I await the people's reaction," he finally said softly, more out of bitterness than out of hope. "I await their vengeance."

Vengeance never came. Arosemena became President, defended Velasco's "Independent" foreign policy, refused to vote with the United States at Punta del Este, and lost his power—to the military. At first, the generals ruled behind Arosemena's back, letting him keep the title of "President." Then, when he showed up drunk once too often for a public function, they overthrew him altogether, and ruled outright from a four-man military Junta. It is completely at the service of the U.S. (indeed, some evidence indicates that the coup was instigated by the CIA), and Nationalism is now dead in Ecuador.

Velasco Ibarra, however, was not the Nationalist he thinks or claims to have been. But he rode the nationalistic ticket. More out of political instinct than conviction, he understood that no matter what he did, he had to sound Ecuadorian. A brilliant demagogue, who had a charismatic hold on Indians, he always won his elections through his mass appeal: "Give me a balcony and I will govern," he used to say. But even in poor backward Ecuador now, there is more to governing than talking from a balcony. Thus, it was not enough for his foreign policies to be independent. Velasco should have been independent internally as well. He should have crushed the oligarchy of which he complained so much, and then, had he called upon his people to defend him, he could have also crushed the military.

Velasco thought his people had to be placated, not led. Hence, he planned a mild agrarian reform and a milder still tax revision while he tried also to increase exports and attract more foreign capital by granting better concessions to the rich. But, by attempting to soothe everyone, he was finally opposed by all—including, because of his foreign policy, the United States. Our press spoke badly of him. We supported the coup against him. We did not break relations, or even think of it, when "democratic process" was being torn to shreds, as we did in Peru. In Peru we liked who was being ousted. In Ecuador we did not.

When Velasco's successor, ex-Vice-President and then President Carlos Julio Arosemena, finally took over, we suddenly got scared. Arosemena had clamored for true tax, agrarian, and educational reforms, and was therefore deemed a dangerous Leftist (despite the fact that we insist on precisely such reforms). To make matters worse, Arosemena had visited Russia, and for some reason *Time*, Washington, and even the *New York Times* seem to consider all Kremlin visitors (except, presumably, such United States citizens as Richard Nixon) either avowed or undercover Reds. Thus, we found in Ecuador, as one newspaper put it, "the danger of an educated Leftist."

Educated Arosemena certainly was. A wealthy banker-aristocrat whose father was President from 1947 to 1948, Ecuador's last President was shrewd, sharp, and refined, a very articulate and extremely *simpático* bon vivant to boot. Tall, sporting a bushy moustache, his hair parted in the middle somewhat in the style of an old barbershop-quartet singer, he also had an artist's flair for saying neutral platitudes about friend or foe while his intense eyes communicated the most incisive, unattributable, but vicious criticism of the same subject.

As for being a Leftist, he may well have been—in his heart. But, like Brazil's President Goulart or Argentina's ex-President Frondizi—both of whom once also scared Washington for their "Leftist" inclinations—Arosemena's personal opinions had nothing to do with hard politics, and he, like the others, was a hard politician—or so he thought. This brand of politics is above all pragmatic. All three men obviously feel that all compromises are valid as long as they stay in power, presumably to achieve, ultimately, their true goals. Goulart seems, however, to be showing that his true goal is just that—to keep and increase his power. Frondizi proved that after three years of debasing compromises, no goals ever remain true. And Arosemena never got the chance to show any goal at all.

One reason is that his position was weak. Having assumed the presidency after a coup from the far Right and Left, he found himself totally alone. Once Velasco was out and Arosemena was in, the oligarchy-Communist alliance was over, and both sides returned to their game of pressing for their own advantages.

President Arosemena, like Frondizi before him in Argentina, evaluated the sides and chose what he thought was the stronger. The Right demanded that Ecuador break relations with Cuba; Arosemena complied. But his heart was obviously not in it. When 50 URJE (Revolutionary Union of Ecuadorian Youth) youngsters took to the hills in Castro-like rebellion and were quickly apprehended, Arosemena gave the order to treat them well, as if prisoners-of-war. There was no persecution of the Left, not even of known Communists. Nor was Castro's news agency Prensa Latina shut down despite the break in relations.

Yet Arosemena knew Ecuador cannot stay as it is. What, then, was his game?

Convinced that he could not change the structure alone, he had decided to wait "for the right moment," as one of his trusted aides told me. "It will come. It is only a question of still being here, when it does." And while they waited, the medievalists consolidated their power to keep the old structure unchanged.

In Ecuador that consolidation took place very rapidly, and Arosemena was tossed out. The two traditional parties—Conservative and Liberal—approved whole-heartedly. Basically unchanged since Ecuador's Independence in 1830, they both currently support the army. As for the Catholic Church, it is one of Ecuador's most medieval forces—and the nation's biggest landowner to boot. (In Quito's Iglesia de la Compañía, where men and women must still enter through separate doors, not only the altar but every bit of decoration, even posts and beams, are made of gold—enough gold to give that 60 percent of Ecuador's people who lack shoes and houses both.)

"Those fifty guerrillas were young, hotheaded, untrained, innocent," one nonpolitical intellectual told me, "but their rebellion was the first. They failed. So will the next, and the next. But unless our structure changes, there will be another 'next'—and it will not fail."

But while Ecuador awaits its new hotheads, the ruling junta sinks the country lower and lower into feudalism. Students are jailed, University departments are "reorganized," professors are fired, strikes are repressed by guns, and Washington lamentably talks of the junta generals as "modern" and "enlightened." Once again, the sole criteria is: Does Ecuador vote with us?

Chapter 10

Colombia

The Colombian presidential elections, held on May 6, 1962, were hailed in the United States press as a decisive test for democracy. After the election returns were in and what had to happen naturally happened—the majority faction of the Liberals and the majority faction of the Conservatives saw their mutual candidate, Guillermo León Valencia, win—our press praised the outcome as a great victory for democracy. Our press even went further. The *New York Times,* for example, printed an AP dispatch under the headline COLOMBIA VOTERS IN LARGE TURNOUT.

Nothing could be further from fact. The elections did not decide anything. There is no democracy in Colombia. Two of the other three candidates were declared illegal and their vote annulled even before the elections. And the "large turnout" report was absolutely false. What makes it worse is that every newspaper in Colombia, including all the dailies that supported the farcical elections that had taken place, admitted the turnout was poor. In a front-page headline the Conservative *El Siglo* reported that the election aroused "little interest." The Liberal *El Espectador* headlined "absolute calm in the country. There was strong abstention," across its front page. And this should have been obvious, even to AP's correspondent. In any case, this is what I saw, as I cruised through the streets of Bogotá, the capital of Colombia, and then reported to the *Baltimore Sun*:

> Along the drab, dirty streets of Bogotá, thousands of white-helmeted, rifle-clutching security policemen shifted uneasily from foot to foot as they stood guarding small, makeshift sidewalk cabins. Inside, a handful of somber officials waited drowsily. Occasionally a citizen entered one of the gray cabins, identified himself, dropped an envelope into a squat wooden box, then dipped his right index finger into a bowl of indelible red ink—proof that he had voted in a presidential election billed as one of Colombia's most crucial.
>
> In fact, however, the election proved that the country's political system is absurd—and that most of the population knows it. Of 16,000,000 inhabitants, 9,000,000 could have registered, but only 6,000,000 did, and less than half of these voted (counting a probable 500,000 fraudulent votes).

The official figures, when they came in, certified the above, thus:

CANDIDATES			
	A	1,324,502	
	B	223,929	
	C	448,321	(annulled)
	D	47,186	(annulled)
Total		2,043,938	

Registered voters according to official data: 5,877,000
Abstention: 3,833,062

The winner: The abstainers by 65 percent (even with fraud).[1] Sixty-five percent of the vote represents the people. But in Colombia's democracy the people do not count, hence the winner was candidate *A*.

---

[1] Aside from just adding numbers to the vote (as was done in Colombia's last election)—of which no one complains since the numbers are added to all parties—fraud in Colombia is done by local *caciques,* or town rulers, who control local militias and police. Anyone who is a Liberal can vote as he wishes *once*

An unpredictable, tense, eccentric professional politician, Valencia has no nonpolitical profession but does hold an honorary doctor's degree from the university of his hometown, Popayán, a small colonial city where its dwellers claim Don Quixote's bones are buried. The son of Colombia's greatest poet of the same name (who twice ran unsuccessfully for the presidency), Don Guillermo is a Conservative whose victory was possible only because of the Liberals—and whose presidential career may be cut short by the Liberals. This is the natural outcome of Colombia's sordid history.

Soon after Colombia became independent in 1819, two rival factions began to jockey for power: the first claimed liberator Simón Bolívar as their mentor, and espoused his form of Centralism which later evolved into Conservatism, while the second preferred liberator Francisco de Paula Santander's form of Federalism which later evolved into Liberalism. Though ideological differences were also proclaimed (the Liberals were anticlerical, the Conservatives

he's inside the polling station in a Conservative town, but usually, if he is known to be a Liberal, something happens to him *before* he ever reaches the station. And vice versa, of course, in Liberal towns. Notice, for example, the following statistics:

In Iquira, Candidate A (Valencia), 8; B (Jorge Leyva, Conservative opposition). 1,238; C (López Michelsen, Liberal opposition), 0; and D (Rojas Pinilla, Independent on Conservative list), 0.

In Saladoblanco, A—261; B—681; C—0; D—0.

In Puerto López, A—198; B—1; C—1,501; D—2.

In Cucutilla, A—2,656; B—637; C—0; D—0.

In Musticua, A—1,062; B—0; C—0; D—0.

In Floridablanca, A—1,225; B—0; C—0; D—0.

In Galán, A—1,525; B—0; C—0; D—0.

It is impossible to believe that in Puerto López there is only one voter in favor of Leyva who *can* be elected, but 1,501 voters for López Michelsen who cannot, while in Cucutilla, just a few miles away, 637 voters favor Leyva, 2,656 favor Valencia, and not one voter favors López; or that in Iquira only 8 people voted for Valencia (the winner), while 1,238 voted for the loser. In the big cities, however, where political murders or accidents are not so common, the proportions become reasonable:

In Barranquilla, A—33,547; B—2,710; C—12, 555; D—370.

In Bogotá, A—144,456; B—21,851; C—33,296; D—7,089.

strongly Catholic), the two parties' basic rivalry was economic: the Liberals were mostly city merchants, hence free-traders; the Conservatives mostly ranchers, hence protectionists.

The Conservatives ruled until 1930, when they were ousted by the Liberals who stayed in power until 1946. That year, the Liberal Party, by then a strong majority, was split by a demagogic but sincerely social-minded dark-skinned lawyer named Jorge Eliécer Gaitán, who awakened in his party's humble and poor something unknown until then: class consciousness. The split, however, allowed Conservative candidate Mariano Ospina Pérez to win, and his regime soon launched a program that has since been labeled the "homogenization of Colombia"—the wiping out of the Liberal majority through systematic murder.

Then one day in 1948, while the Bogotá Conference of Hemisphere Foreign Ministers was in session, Gaitán himself was murdered. The culprit, Roa Sierra, was conveniently shot and killed on the spot, and no proof has ever fallen upon his employers. Both the Conservative and the traditional Liberal parties have been accused of the crime, and both certainly stood to gain from the death of a leader whose rising popular support threatened both party oligarchies.

After his death, Gaitán's followers took to the streets, and the resulting riot has passed into history under the name of the Bogotazo. Police squashed the capital's rebellion. But Colombia fell into civil war. By 1953 more than 300,-000 Colombians were killed—Liberals shot from above (army, police), Conservatives from below (guerrillas, rebels).

In 1953 a military coup brought to power General Gustavo Rojas Pinilla, who, described as Colombia's most vicious dictator, was in fact its best pacifier. He limited violence to occasional banditry, crowded the country with public projects, enriched himself and his cronies, and tried to stay in power on the grounds that civil war between the Liberals and the Conservatives would return if he left. To prove him wrong, a fashionable Liberal Journalist named Alberto Lleras Camargo, then Secretary General of the Organization of American States (OAS), rushed home from Washington and hunted for a friendly Conservative. His find was Guillermo León Valencia, the current President.

Liberal Lleras Camargo's tactic pleased Conservative Chief Laureano Gómez, an ex-President of Fascist leanings who was itching to return from his exile in Dictator Francisco

Franco's Spain. Thus, Lleras and Gómez got together on Catalonia's splendid coast and worked out one of the continent's weirdest pacts, which gave birth to Colombia's current *Frente Nacional*.

Deciding, most naturally, to exclude all other parties from Colombian political life, Lleras and Gómez agreed to split their country between themselves thus: all public jobs from ministers and congressmen to porters and chambermaids would be filled half by Liberals, half by Conservatives; all laws (except for national emergency) would require a vote of two-thirds; and the presidency would rotate from one party to the other every four years.

The *Frente Nacional* worked: Rojas fell. Laureano Gómez thereupon vetoed the candidacy of party-mate Valencia, and Lleras became President in 1958. In the 1960 midterm parliamentary elections, however, Gómez lost control of his half of Congress to old strong-man Ospina Pérez; and President Lleras, while holding on to most of his Liberal half, lost enough ground so that his Liberal opponents, plus the Ospina Conservatives, controlled more than one-third of Congress. President Lleras needed another pact, and this time turned to his own party rivals, led by cousin Carlos Lleras Restrepo.

The deal came at a high price. Meeting at the house of old reactionary Liberal patriarch Eduardo Santos, owner of Bogotá's truths-discriminating daily *El Tiempo*, Carlos Lleras and Alberto Lleras came to an understanding: Carlos got both the Liberal Party leadership and the vice-presidency, while the President got his two-thirds vote. But the new Vice-President had party power—and he used it. He made a pact with Ospina's Conservatives, rejected all of Lleras Camargo's suggestions for the 1962 presidential candidacy, and supported Valencia.

Valencia won and became President on August 7, 1962. Immediately rumors began to fly that retiring President Lleras Camargo (now chairman of the editorial board of U.S.-directed, arch-conservative *Visión*) would direct a campaign to unseat Valencia either by discrediting him enough to force a coup or by pressuring him to resign or at worst by having him locked up in an insane asylum. But Alberto Lleras underestimated cousin Carlos, who had no intention of losing his grip on the Liberal Party or allowing the *Frente* to disintegrate. Convinced that if Valencia finishes his term, he himself would be the next president, Carlos foiled Alberto's plans.

Nor was Valencia willing to be pushed around. "I will never resign!" he assured me after the election. He was quite familiar with the rumors. "I am neither a Quadros [who quit Brazil's presidency under pressure] nor a Velasco Ibarra [who let himself be ousted from Ecuador's presidency]. Let me assure you: no one pushes Valencia around," he affirmed emphatically.

He has, nevertheless, had a tough time—even without brilliant political manipulators against him. Though Colombia is one of South America's richest countries—and one where the Alliance for Progress is showing most results—the yearly population increase (2.9 percent) is higher than the rise in Gross National Product (2.5 percent). Contrasts between rich and poor are enormous: 3.5 percent of landowners control 65 percent of the land; 320 individuals own 56 percent of all capital; 50 percent of the population lives outside the money economy altogether, earning low wages (for long hours) in low-calorie foodstuffs. Violence is still rampant: guerrillas, some with ideological bases, operate freely—and kill more than thirty Colombians every week (despite intensive and often unfairly cruel government measures). A big business-managed and financed Mano Negra (Black Hand) interferes with freedom of the press through advertising blackmail. Corruption, on a national scale, is up to Rojas standards, and because of the fifty-fifty split in public jobs (and because no old employee was fired) the public payroll has doubled. The only bright spot is the low level of anti-Yankeeism, but even that is being ruined slowly by some United States businessmen's participation in the Black Hand.

To bring social justice to all his countrymen, as he promised to do, President Valencia should have fought both Liberal and Conservative oligarchies whose political rivalry is always subservient to their financial interests—as proved by their *Frente Nacional* pact. "I will recognize no demands," Valencia told me, "save those from the people." But observers noted that he owed his election to the *Frente*, not the people, and the *Frente*, that is, the oligarchy, is against the people. Thus, though Valencia did enact some austerity measures which, with a 1963-64 rise in coffee prices, brought Colombia a slightly higher standard of living, no meaningful reforms were put into practice. Agrarian reform remains a piece of paper, and Colombians are no better off than ever before.

Chapter 11

Venezuela

Nowhere in Latin America has the United States so much at stake as in Venezuela. Yet nowhere in Latin America is the future so hard to predict. Even the military are unpredictable: Venezuela has become the first and only hemisphere nation where Armed Forces officers, traditionally the dependable, obedient tools of the extreme Right, have occasionally joined the extreme Left as active partners. These officers have proved their new allegiance by launching revolts. The first, in May, 1962, was weak: a dozen men were killed, and it failed. The second, in June, 1962, was stronger: 400 people died and 2,000 people were wounded, but it too failed. Eventually, especially now that President Betancourt has finished his term, one may not fail.

The reason, unfortunately, is clear: nowhere in Latin America has a regime received more official United States support as a "truly great, reform-minded democracy" than in Venezuela. Yet nowhere has a regime done more to discredit democracy and make a farce of reforms than that of the ruling Acción Democrática. Caracas, the capital, knows this. So do many officers. But so far neither the interior nor Liberal apologists in the U.S. recognize this, mainly out of loyalty to AD's great leader, Rómulo Betancourt.

Small, squat, and shrewd, Betancourt was once a Communist plotter against Dictator Juan Vicente Gómez, the "Tyrant of the Andes," who came to power with the aid of the big foreign oil corporations (three of whose executives

155

stayed on as his advisers), ruled ruthlessly (as "President" or from behind the scenes) from 1908 to 1936, and died peacefully in his bed at the age of seventy-eight. It was during Gómez' reign, incidentally, that foreign oil concessions were distributed by the gallons; and it was then, too, that our corporations displaced Britain's as prime beneficiaries.

By 1945, however, President Isaías Medina Angarita had launched Venezuela's first democratic reforms, allowing political parties (but not Communists) to organize, and had enacted the country's first Petroleum Laws. But that year, returned-exile Betancourt, now leader of the non-Communist Leftist Acción Democrática Party, teamed up with young Rightist military men, including Captain Marcos Pérez Jiménez, and overthrew Venezuela's only democratic regime of the century.

Betancourt's critics point to this as proof that he was never a democrat and that he had already become the willing pawn of oil corporations. (They also have a very telling piece of evidence, namely, that *Fortune* magazine, which is as pro-United States business interest as is possible, referred to Betancourt's AD and Standard Oil's Venezuelan subsidiary, the Creole Oil Corporation, as "allies," in an evaluation of Betancourt's 1945-1948 regime.) His backers, on the other hand, insist the coup was necessary because President Medina's measures were too moderate. Whatever the truth, Betancourt became a member of the ruling Junta, passed no new oil laws, and spent most of his energy setting up a cell-system party machinery throughout the interior. He lasted only three years, however. In 1948 his old army allies rose up anew—and tossed him back into exile.

The new rulers (Pérez Jiménez from behind the scenes until 1952, as "President" thereafter) were at first both feared and hated by our oilmen. But soon it became clear that "P.J." was interested only in the good life—his—and a working harmony was quickly established. He became the continent's most vicious dictator since the Spanish conquista- dores and one of its worst thieves to boot (after five years of exile in Miami, he was finally extradited home to stand trial for embezzling $250,000,000 in public funds); yet he was awarded the United States Order of Merit for services rendered "before and after becoming President," and his Gestapo Chief Pedro Estrada became a friend of our ambassador.

But one day in 1958, a general strike degenerated into a revolution. The army and Estrada's hoods could have handled it (the latter killed 300 students), but the navy, led by Admiral Wolfgang Larrazábal, made it stick. Larrazábal then set up a provisional government that promised free elections within that year.

The AD men returned immediately. Betancourt wasted no time launching his presidential candidacy. Twenty days before election day, the Left united behind Larrazábal who carried the capital 5 to 1. But Larrazábal had no time to campaign outside Caracas, where AD's cell-system organization, still intact, was too thorough. Betancourt was the narrow overall winner, though with only 49 percent of the vote.

At first he seemed to remember his promises of reforms. He approved Larrazábal's 60 to 40 oil-split law, pressed Agronomist Salvador de la Plaza and AD Peasant League Leader Ramón Quijada to work out an agrarian reform law, and assured industrial reformist Domingo Alberto Rangel, an AD deputy and loyal Betancourt backer, that the regime would enact all types of reforms. Betancourt even formed a coalition Cabinet, giving top posts to Larrazábal's Unión Republicana Democrática (URD) Party.

The oligarchy and the oilmen got frightened. Therefore, the military acted. Coup after coup was attempted and failed —though some came very close to succeeding. To stay in power, Betancourt realized he had to reassure the Right. Hence, he fired his URD allies, hired in their place leaders from COPEI, the Catholic Party he had denounced as "the reactionary tool of the oligarchy" only a few months before. Big business was encouraged, and tax "concessions" were liberally dispensed. Military salaries and fringe benefits rose even higher than during the P.J. regime. Finally, constitutional guarantees were abolished under the State of Siege, and old Pedro Estrada men returned to their familiar jobs.

Understandably, Betancourt's reform-minded allies deserted him. First, of course, went the URD; then good friend Rangel bolted, splitting AD wide open by launching a new Movement of the Revolutionary left (MIR). Finally, such old aides as Salvador de la Plaza and Ramón Quijada abandoned Betancourt, Quijada taking a group of AD congressmen with him into an opposition block then called

AD-ARS. He explained it to me thus: "It took me a long time to leave the old man. After all, he had passed my Agrarian Reform Law. But finally I realized nothing was really being done. You hear a lot of talk about Agrarian Reform, especially in your [U.S.] newspapers. True, Betancourt has given away thousands of land titles to landless peasants. But no loans, no roads, no equipment, generally not even the land—just the titles. My law, our law, has become a farce."

Indeed, almost ninety thousand land titles have been distributed, with much fanfare, by Betancourt. But only two thousand new owners are actually working their lands satisfactorily. "I got my title two years ago," one peasant told me, "but I can't even get the government to show me where my land *is*." Most of the given land is from old, inaccessible government holdings. Some have been "expropriated" from rich *latifundistas*. One of them candidly told me about it: "I sold the government two thousand hectares for the Reform. It was my worst land. I couldn't work it, even with machinery—too hilly. But I got a better price for that land than my best land could bring me on the open market. There's a dozen families working it now. They'll go bankrupt in less than two years and I'll buy the land back at 10 percent—with the road they themselves have had to build." Quijada later reacted: "I am against violence. I am anti-Communist and anti-Castro. When my men occupy land by force, I tell them to give it back, to wait. But how long will they wait, how long *can* they wait?"

Many of the peasants are not waiting. Some, though very few, have joined students as guerrillas. But most are flocking to the big cities in search of nonexisting jobs. In 1936 the rural population was 67 percent; in 1950, 46 percent; today it is 30 percent. Meanwhile, Caracas has soared from 150,000 inhabitants to more than 2,000,000.

Venezuela, South America's northernmost country, the size of Germany and France combined, could be one of the richest in the world; from its soil flows about 140 million tons of oil and almost 30 million tons of iron every year. At current prices that should bring the country an income of approximately $4 billion, enough to give each of its 6,000,000 people almost a Park Avenue standard of living.

But reality is otherwise. The oil is in the hands of foreign corporations; so are the iron, and the means of transporting both to our or the world's markets; Bethlehem Steel's El Pao mine pays Venezuela one bolivar (about 20 cents) per hectare exploited on a fifty-year concession; U.S. Steel pays one bolivar per ton extracted (which sells at about $7 at embarkation point). Thus, the country earns only $1 billion from its natural resources.

The land itself is highly fertile, enough so to feed all its inhabitants and also furnish a slight surplus for export. Yet because only 3 percent of the population owns 90 percent of the land (counting the new titleowners in the 3 percent), and the landed oligarchy grows only cattle for export, Venezuela must spend $150 million or more a year on food. Hence, instead of being one of the richest countries, Venezuela is the most expensive, twice as dear as New York, with eggs imported from Florida and corn from Iowa. One-third of Caracas' inhabitants live in hillside slums (*ranchos*) in plain view of the luxurious skyscrapers built mostly for the oil companies or by the oil revenue.

As Betancourt's "reform program" increased poverty on one side and the already formidable fortunes on the other (Venezuelan oligarchs export about $200 million a year to Swiss or United States banks), more and more people began losing patience with democracy. Even Caracas' conservative but fair Catholic daily *La Religión* became critical. Betancourt lost his once-solid parliamentary majority and soon could rule only with the gun.

Armed AD shock troops combed the country for "opponents." They broke up opposition rallies, wrecked its meeting halls, smashed its printing presses (*Clarín, La Tarde,* and *La Hora*), and burned or bombed offices or businesses that advertised in the world-famous Leftist but anti-Communist daily *El Nacional.* Political assassinations became common, and opposition congressmen, who were forced to walk with bodyguards, even feared to check their pistols at Parliament's door. Students were shot down indiscriminately. During my stay in Caracas, Eduardo Antonio Espinoza, twenty, was machine-gunned as he left Block 21, one of the capital's low-cost housing projects where police are afraid to enter. Student Enrique Leonardo Pérez Rodríguez was killed when his bus was machine-gunned near a cemetery at noon; Enrique was then only a few feet away from his home, and his father, a pro-AD supporter of the Catholic

COPEI, was a witness to the shooting, attributed by Betancourt to the Left. "It was the police," said the father. "I saw the police fire."

Not only university students were the victims. High-school student Mario Guillermo Woermer was fourteen when AD hoods fired into a protest march. So was Alvaro Ruíz González, killed as he stepped out of his high school, clutching books in both hands. Why so much killing? One nonpolitical Colonial History professor explained it thus: "The government wants the students to react, to fight back. Then it can have a pretext to invade the university grounds [autonomous by law] to shoot or arrest all suspected Leftists. Since 1960 more than three hundred students have been killed. It has become impossible for an honest man to support this government, even if he is a Conservative."

Such is also the explanation given by so many young officers who have become plotters—allied to the Left. Captain Jesús Teodoro Molina, Commander of Marine Battalion 3 stationed in Carúpano, less than one hundred miles down the east Caribbean coast from Caracas, was no Left-trained plotter when he rebelled in May, 1962. "If Betancourt is democracy, I want no part of it," he told friends when he formed the Movement for Democratic Recuperation for "A return to morality! A stop to the giveaway of our national resources! An end to persecution!" and invited all Betancourt opponents to join. The Communists did (one Red deputy, Eloy Torres, was caught with him later). If these nationalistic officers are becoming the unconscious tools of the Communists, however, the fault is with Betancourt. Until social and economic justice returns to Venezuela, there will be more rebellions, "guided" by more Communists.

Yet many United States Liberals point to Betancourt as the supreme example of a "Leftist," "Nationalist" Latin American leader who brought about economic reforms without destroying democratic process. No Latin American President was more praised, respected, and aided than Betancourt. Numerous supposedly serious books on Latin America, when they get to Venezuela, fall all over themselves to "prove" how great social justice was under Betancourt. Why?

Most important is the fact that Betancourt, like his friends Haya de la Torre and Costa Rica's José Figueres, is well known throughout Latin America, that he has a long reputation of having fought against dictatorships, that he used to be violently anti-imperialist, that is, anti-United States, and yet—and this is the crucial point—then became solidly pro-United States. And Betancourt never expropriated or nationalized United States property.

That to our State Department this is ample reason for supporting Betancourt is excusable. But why must such so-called Liberals as William Benton, Harry Kantor, Frank Tannenbaum, Robert Alexander, and so on,[1] give Betancourt such a clean bill of health? Because they cannot understand that *not* to be pro-United States is not necessarily to be anti-United States.

In Montevideo, an intelligent, up-to-date United States press attaché, who spoke fluent Spanish and in every way represented the best of our Foreign Service, told me once, when we were analyzing the famous Uruguayan Nationalist Carlos Quijano (editor and publisher of the continent's best neutralist weekly, *Marcha*), "In the final analysis, he is a Communist." Quijano, who is also his country's top economist, had only recently attacked the Russian multi-megaton bomb tests, had been the main speaker at the commemoration of the Hungarian Revolution (against Russia), and had written two long, passion-packed editorials against Castro for declaring himself and his Cuban regime "Marxist-Leninist." However, Quijano was also anti-United States corporations in Latin American and said he would continue to defend Castro's regime for its policy of expropriating our private property interests which—and we can never allow ourselves to forget this—under Batista had owned more than 60 percent of Cuba but had not contributed even shoes to the undernourished, illiterate, or homeless peasants. "I know all that," retorted my press attaché friend, "but when the chips are down, whom will Quijano fight for? For us?" No, but he would not fight for Russia either, I replied. He would fight only for Uruguay or Latin America. "Never mind that," my friend insisted; "the point is he won't fight for the U.S., and that means that in the last analysis he's a tool of the Communists, which is the same, for practical purposes, as *being* a Communist."

If neutralists are to be considered our enemies, then, of course, the most "Leftist" friend we have in Latin America *is* Betancourt. Thus, our American "Liberals" are pro-Betan-

[1] See Bibliography.

court. They justify their support by "listing" his "reforms," which they could not do for other pro-United States Latin Americans, such as Stroessner or Alessandri or Valencia.

Betancourt made a choice, and made it early: I cannot nationalize the oil industry; therefore, I cannot be "independent." Hence since the oil belongs mostly to the United States and I cannot be against, I must be pro. That Betancourt could not—during his 1959-1964 regime—nationalize the oil is correct. Here are the reasons in his own words (1956):

> We had always rejected the possibility of applying, in the beginning of an administration with a revolutionary orientation, a similar measure to that which is the greatest claim to fame of the Mexican regime of Lázaro Cárdenas, because there are substantial differences between the situation of Mexico when it nationalized petroleum, and that of ourselves. Petroleum was and is in the Mexican economy a factor of importance, but complementing others of considerable size. As a result, the country did not experience a serious drawback to its normal evolution when the international oil cartel and the governments in agreement with it decreed the boycott of nationalized oil. In contrast, when we took over the government [1945], practically all of the Venezuelan economy and an appreciable part of the fiscal activity of the government were dependent on petroleum.

The implication is clear: Venezuela must develop other industries and other sources of income, must nationalize other industries (iron, for example), and when it is in a position to weather an oil boycott (it could always sell to Scandinavia, India, Egypt, and other neutralist countries, even other countries of Latin America, like Chile), then, and only then, must it nationalize the oil. To this argument, all Nationalists and Leftists agree. Even a Communist deputy told me, "We can't eat oil, can we?"

But all true reformists also agree that the government dependency on the oil revenue should be cut. Betancourt actually increased that dependency. In 1945 oil contributed 92 percent of Venezuela's Foreign Exchange, 31 percent of its budget, and required only 8 percent of the working force. In 1962, however, oil accounted for 92 percent of Foreign Exchange (the same figure), 63 percent of the budget (more than double), and only 1.4 percent of the labor force. To bring the point home harder still, unemployment in 1945 was 6 percent, while by 1962 it had jumped to 17 percent. That Betancourt, under such conditions, felt obliged to give in to the dictates of oil companies is understandable. I am not the first to say this: in his excellent book *Arms and Politics in Latin America*, written for and under the auspices of the Council on Foreign Relations, Professor Edwin Lieuwen calls our Venezuelan oil corporations "an economic dictator."

But that Betancourt is a Venezuelan Nationalist and, as Liberal Professor Robert Alexander states, "a Latin American Nationalist," is sheer distortion. Alexander, for example, defends the fact that Betancourt and AD joined forces with Right-wing militarists to overthrow the Democratic regime of Medina Angarita thus:

> Many have argued that Acción Democrática betrayed its own democratic profession when it seized power in collaboration with a faction of the army. The author believes that the AD's actions were justified. The Acción Democrática leaders themselves maintain that the young army officers would have overthrown Medina Angarita in any case. . . .

In other words, what this Rutgers Professor of Economics and admirer of nonrevolutionary "democrats" maintains, in effect, is that the John Birch Society is perfectly justified to join forces with the United States Communist Party to overthrow the Democratic regime of President Johnson, because the Birchers are convinced (as they are) that the Communists will overthrow it anyway. The analogy is not so farfetched: the officers who participated in the 1945 coup were Gómez-trained; that is, they belonged to the regime that had been Betancourt's most bitter enemy.

Alexander is so intent on painting a glowing picture of Betancourt that he insists all Betancourt's aides were just as pure as the old man. Thus Alexander explains that Major Mario Vargas and Colonel Carlos Delgado Chalbaud, who were pro-AD, tried to stop Pérez Jiménez' 1948 coup against AD but when they saw it was hopeless they "joined the movement with the hope of diverting it into less harmful channels." Delgado Chalbaud became president

of the junta that took over from AD; he immediately banned
AD and had its leaders arrested and deported. But presumably
the colonel, though president of the junta, was opposed
to it just the same. As proof, Alexander writes that in
November, 1950, *two years later*, Chalbaud was kidnapped
and killed, and the man who shot him was shot by the police
"so that he did not implicate those who were in the conspiracy
with him." One is supposed to deduce, I gather, that Delgado
Chalbaud, as head of the junta, was still pro-AD simply
because the loyal friends of loyal Betancourt never betray,
and because two years later, after all the AD persecutions,
the other members of the junta realized that their boss
was a traitor and had him done in (of which there is no
proof either). If this is a valid argument, then how can
Alexander explain the scores of Betancourt friends, Quijada,
Rangel, de la Plaza, and so on, who then denounced Betancourt as a traitor to the interests and the people of Venezuela?

Alexander and the other Liberal defenders of Latin American democrats are, unfortunately, very important. They
have created a myth about Haya de la Torre, Figueres,
and Betancourt that has permeated not only our universities
but also our State Department, where honest men, even
if they began to doubt, would surely feel reluctant to oppose
or contradict the "findings" of such "learned" men.

That Betancourt did a great deal for Venezuela during
his first term is undeniable. He built 5,000 houses, got real
wages to rise substantially (64.7 percent in money over
only 29.4 percent in costs), got school attendance to jump
from 142,500 to 522,000, adding 5,000 new classrooms.
That Betancourt only masqueraded as a reformer since
his 1957 return is equally undeniable—despite the findings
of our Liberals.

Many such Liberals have strongly condemned this book
because of what I have just said about Betancourt. Friends
of mine on the Washington *Post*, *The New York Times*,
and in various universities have told me that my book
would be the best of its kind "except for your blast on
Betancourt." When they heard that I was updating it for
a new edition, they tried to convince me to change it,
or at least to modify my description of life in Venezuela
under AD rule.

Their arguments are mainly two: 1) Betancourt has at
least tried to enact reforms, more so than any other non-

revolutionary leader in Latin America; and 2) because of
the strength of the Castro-Communists, he had no choice
but to be tough. But what in fact has Betancourt done?
He did launch a literacy campaign, on a wider scale than
any other "democratic" reformer. That's true. But this
is no comparison. If the argument is meant as proof that
democratic reformers are better than non-democratic reformers
—that is, Castros—then one must compare Betancourt's
"reforms" to Castro's.

In such light, Betancourt's program becomes ludicrous.
He could have closed all schools for one year, for example,
drafted all students and teachers, sent them out to teach
illiterates how to read and write. He did not. He could have
hit the oil companies much harder, forced them to finance
his agrarian reform, an act which because he was our friend,
the United States would have accepted. He did not. He
could have taxed luxury imports heavily enough to pay
for slum clearance. He did not. He could have ordered
the army to clear jungles, build roads, put up water lines,
sewage systems, etc. (like Bolivia's army). He did not. He
could have tried to cut down the military's vast privileges,
the oligarchy's strangle-hold on the economy. He could
have forced profit sharing, even a very mild one, onto
the big money makers. He could have levied a special tax
on profits leaving the country and ordered a special dispen-
sation on profits reinvested in job-creating industries. He
did none of these things. For all his prestige as a reformer,
he did not even curb unemployment.

"He couldn't do a thing," a Liberal answers me, "because
the Pérez Jiménez wing of the military would have overthrown
him." So what? Frondizi used the same excuse, though he
at least industrialized Argentina far, far more than Betancourt
did Venezuela. How long must do-nothingism be defended
on the fear of a Rightist take-over? If Betancourt had been
a true reformer, he would have dared, risked—and fought
the Right, not just the Left.

"He did not have a Congressional majority," is another
argument used. "He wanted to become the first democratically elected president in Venezuelan history to finish his
term, so as to set up a precedent," is still another argument
in his defense. Both are fallacious. In the first place, he
had a majority until he abandoned his reforms. His friends
and allies went into opposition *after* he gave in to demands

of the Right. Secondly, what good is a "democratic precedent" if no democracy filters to the people, if the only ones to profit from democracy are the rich and the military?

Had Betancourt fought for his country's much-needed reforms, I would have been the last to condemn his toughness. So backward is Latin America that repressions cannot be damned just because violence *per se* is wrong. Each child that dies of hunger dies a violent death. If the only way to give him enough food is to use violence, fine. But *only if* the goal is to end hunger. Winning "democratic elections" is no justification for violence, because such elections are not an end in themselves. They are justified only if it can be shown that as a result of such elections, the poor will stop getting poorer and the rich richer. And contrarily, had Pérez Jiménez, for all his vicious repressions, enacted and enforced those needed reforms mentioned above, his regime would have been more praiseworthy than Betancourt's.

In any case, Betancourt succeeded: he did become Venezuela's first democratically elected president to finish his term. In the 1963 elections, Leftists were not allowed to run. MIR and the Communists were outlawed, their leaders jailed. AD's candidate, Raul Leoni, a colorless Tammany-style pro, won 32 percent of the vote. Next came COPEI's chief, Rafael Caldera, with 22 percent. United, the two parties have a working majority. It represents a rousing defeat for the Left, which had asked the people to abstain —and tried to convince them with terrorism and threats of increased violence.

Che Guevara once wrote (in his book on *Guerrilla Warfare*):

> Where a government has come to power through some form of popular vote, fraudulent or not, and maintains at least an appearance of constitutional legality, the guerrilla outbreak cannot be promoted, since the possibilities of peaceful struggle have not yet been exhausted.

Venezuela's Leftists, who so admire the Cuban Revolution and whom the Cuban revolutionaries so gladly help, had obviously not done their homework. Their failure—and the Right's success—will be hard to overcome in the near future. In the meantime, Leoni is President—and the poor continue to get poorer, and the rich richer.

Chapter 12
Central America

The six countries that make up Central America—Panama, Costa Rica, Nicaragua, Honduras, El Salvador, and Guatemala —are among the most backward in the whole hemisphere. One is almost totally Indian (Guatemala); another is almost totally white (Costa Rica); the rest are basically mestizo or mixed-blood (Spanish, Indian, and Negro). All six have been ruled by dictators, and most have served as a playground for our Marines; as such, much of their suffering falls within the scope of Chapter 17.

Costa Rica has had a lukewarm Nationalist revolution that, though frustrated, corrupted, and abandoned, nevertheless deserves a separate Chapter 14.

The others have never had even the chance to judge the merits or demerits of true democracy. To their people, mostly illiterate and apolitical, "democracy" means the corruption of the many, whereas "dictatorship" means the corruption of a few.

Before taking a closer look, we must spend a few pages on a fruit. No understanding of Central America is possible without an analysis of—bananas!

This little crescent-shaped, easily perishable food is the world's most important fruit, as shown by the table on page 168. Since some 40 percent of the world's fresh fruit trade (and consumption) is in bananas, it is clear that their production is of great importance—all the more so when we learn that bananas, residents of the tropics, do not grow in the United States. We must, therefore, import all

167

Percentage of Fruit Trade in the World

	% Fresh	% Total
Fresh Bananas	40.7	36.4
Oranges and Tangerines	32.8	29.4
Lemons and Limes	4.2	3.7
Grapefruit	2.0	1.8
Apple, table	11.4	10.2
Pears, table	3.0	2.7
Grapes, table	3.5	3.1
Pineapple	2.4	2.2
Dried Dates		4.9
Raisins		4.0
Prunes		0.7
Figs		0.7
Other		0.2

our needs, and apparently we need bananas more than does any other region:

	% of world imported
U.S. and Canada	57%
Europe	36%
South America	4%
Africa, Asia, Oceania	3%
TOTAL	100%

The next background fact that we should know is that Latin America is the world's Number One producer:

Central America	23.2%	
South America	45.6%	68.8% of world total
Asia	23.2%	
Africa	6.4%	
Oceania	1.6%	
TOTAL	100.0%	

Almost 70 percent of the world's bananas are grown in Latin America. The world's total production of bananas (what is exported *plus* what is locally consumed) is about 26 billion pounds. Therefore, at the average retail banana price of $0.17 a pound, Latin America should earn 70 percent of 26,000,000,000 times 17, or more than $3 billion a year. Latin America consumes exactly half of its own production, meaning that if Latin America owned its banana crop, and the bananas were distributed and sold by Latin Americans, about $1.05 billion ($1.5 billion less 30 percent export markup) would be circulating in Latin America.

If the production was owned by the governments, Latin America's profits would be $357 million in local currency (34 percent of $1.05 billion). Furthermore, its gross revenue from exports would be $450 million (70 percent of $1.5 billion going for shipment, jobber and retailer costs), of which $351 million (production costs and shipping to local embarkation points being 22 percent) would be net profits. Crystallizing these figures, we find that if Latin America's governments owned their banana production (but not local distributors or retailers):

$1.5 billion in currency would circulate in Latin America,
of which $450 million would be in dollars;
$708 million in hard currency profits would be added to national budgets,
of which $351 million would be in dollars.

Yet Latin America receives an average (1951-1960) of only $192,100,000 yearly. Most of the difference belongs to an octopus corporation, chartered out of Boston, called the United Fruit Company.

Owning almost 2,000,000 acres in six Latin American countries (Guatemala, Honduras, Costa Rica, Panama, Ecuador, and Colombia)—plus thousands of acres in sugarcane, cacao, and oil palm, about 1,500 miles of railroads, some 60 ships, sugar refineries, whole ports (from land and houses to streetcars and lampposts), communication networks (including the Tropical Radio Telegraph Co., which operates throughout Central America)—United Fruit holds between 30 and 40 percent of the world's banana market, more than 60 percent of United States sales, and 60 percent of the six countries' banana exports; or if Ecuador (where banana competition is stiff) is excluded, 80 percent of the five. Of United's acreage, only about 5.2 percent is farmed; the rest is held in reserve.

United Fruit can be said to dominate Panama completely since the country's bananas account for 70 percent of all exports and since the company's share is 93 percent, that is 93 times 70, or 63 percent of Panama's foreign-exchange earnings. Also, United almost dominates (and is the strongest economic power in) Costa Rica and Honduras, controlling 41 percent and 42 percent of their respective foreign-exchange earnings.

But United Fruit brings into the six countries only about $145 million yearly, on which it pays about $18 million in yearly taxes. Whether the company makes or surpasses the net profit it claims—$26 million—is hard to judge, for various reasons: (1) it buys much of its services and material from its own subsidiaries, where prices, costs, and so on, can be juggled to fit the need; (2) it charges itself for local transportation, since it also owns its rail and trolley network (at least one country has accused United Fruit railroads of being the most expensive and the worst rail systems in the world); and (3) it charges itself whatever overseas transportation prices it wants, since it owns its own shipping fleet. (Fleet earnings are taxable where ships are registered, not where the freight is picked up.) But even if one accepts United Fruit's profit reports as accurate, it becomes clear that the company has earned back its investment over and over again, since the company itself claims its foreign investment to be only $159 million.

Whether it is true or not that United Fruit uses its position, economic power, and near monopoly holdings to influence, alter, dictate, or frustrate native government economies or policies is not for us to decide. There has been proof of such intervention in the past,[1] and Nationalists insist it is still going on today, even to the extent that United Fruit finances revolutions (including the one in Guatemala in 1954) and *coup d'états* to ensure "friendly" regimes. True or not, it is shocking enough that United Fruit has the power to so intervene if it wishes—on its own.

And that United Fruit has at least near-monopoly power is proved by the fact that the United States Department of Justice was moved to sue it for antitrust-law violations

[1] See Chapter 17.

(Civil Action 4560, filed July 2, 1954, as amended January 12, 1956). Said the government: "With the exception of land in Ecuador, United owns, leases or otherwise controls 85 percent of the land in the American tropics suitable for banana cultivation."

Early in 1958, the antitrust suit was settled through a "consent decree" (approved by the company on April 16, 1958) that, while not proving United Fruit guilty as charged, did order it to comply with the following (among others):

1. Divest itself of its stock ownership of the International Railways of Central America by June 30, 1966;

2. Get rid of part of its producing lands, purchasing arrangements, shipping facilities, and distribution networks by 1970;

3. Get rid of its Banana Selling Corporation, a Mobile, Alabama, subsidiary;

4. Desist from engaging in jobbing operations, exclusive sales contracts, entering into collusive agreements with or coercive tactics against competitors, forcing its customers to use specified transportation media, boycotts, transportation monopolies, and so on.

Since then, United Fruit has got rid of more than 40,000 acres of banana land. But under these conditions: land has been rented or sold to local "associate producers" who are helped with United Fruit loans and technicians and to whom United Fruit supplies such services as weekly spraying (at a charge, naturally) on varying types of arrangements, including a fifty-fifty split in profits and an exclusivity-clause contract. In September, 1962, United Fruit announced its intentions of investing about $1,000,000 to raise bananas on 25,000 acres of virgin land in Colombia. The venture was to be in partnership with the Corporación Financiera Colombiana de Desarrollo Industrial, a private company which had negotiated a $6,000,000 loan from the First National Bank of Boston.[2] United-CFCDI's plan is to clear the land, then let Colombians use it to raise bananas that must be sold to United Fruit. To United's President Thomas Sunderland, the deal was "the first sizable effort by private enterprise to put into actual practice the objectives of the Alliance for Progress to aid the advance and prosperity of Latin America." In fact, it served to increase United

2 A bank with many close associations with United Fruit.

Fruit's influence in Colombia, previously small.

United Fruit's new "arrangements" may not be considered monopolistic according to United States legal concepts, but its hold on the economy of Latin American banana-producing countries has remained unchanged, especially in Central America.

Panama has the least amount of people of any Latin American country—barely over one million. It has, however, one of its greatest assets—the Panama Canal.

Unfortunately for the people of Panama, the Canal's existence helps them very little. Work was originally begun on it by a French company, in an agreement with Colombia, in which Panama was then a state. Later, after quite a bit of our shenanigans, Panama rebelled, got United States aid, was recognized as an "independent" country—and we took over the Canal's construction.

Colombia was paid $25 million as compensation, the French company $40 million for its rights, Panama a booby-prize gift of $10 million. Panama thereupon agreed to grant the Zone, a ribbon that slices the country in two, to the United States for $250,000 a year *for ever,* which, if not illegal, is immoral. That fee has been upped to $1,930,000 a year today. We take in about $54,000,000 in tolls every year.

Aside from the numerous moral outrages perpetrated by our Canal Zone authorities, such as classifying our workers as "gold" and anyone else as "silver," and paying the golds twice, thrice, or even five times as much as the silvers for the same work (setting up this discrimination even in Canal post offices where windows were marked "gold" and "silver"), the Canal has brought only hardships to Panamanians.

Until fairly recently fences and guard posts got our extra-territorial status across rather harshly. Most fences are gone today, but the country is still divided by ten miles of "foreign" territory. (Unequal pay scales, incidentally, continue, despite a 1955 Remón-Eisenhower treaty promising the contrary.) Next, the United States constantly interfered in Panama's internal affairs, insisting its government be "well disposed" toward us.

Until 1936 Panama was an official protectorate of the United States. We policed Colón (on the Caribbean sea) and Panama City (the capital, on the Pacific); we had the "right" to appropriate lands and waters at will, and to sell "commissary" goods to anyone.

After 1936 we kept our interference indirect, through diplomatic pressure. We also insisted that a National Police Force be created, and it has controlled politics ever since. Corrupt and arbitrary, it has made "elections" meaningless. The country has had twenty-nine presidents, five of them seated, then unseated, by one police chief, José Antonio Remón, who finally decided to become President himself in 1952.

Remón turned out to be a maverick, betraying his self-interested friends. He improved government services, forced public employees to work for their pay, cut down graft, began paying off Panama's debts, and was slowly developing into a lukewarm Nationalist. He was, therefore, assassinated in 1955, and the oligarchy, represented by such names as Arias or Chiari, returned.

The oligarchy, at the time of this writing, is in power through millionaire President Roberto Francisco Chiari; it will still be in power by the time this book is in bookstores, since the "election" of Marco A. Robles, Chiari's handpicked successor, will only have changed the names. This oligarchy has lived off the Canal and supporting businesses (services, retail stores, tourist trade, and so on) without doing one thing for the country. Even in the center of Panama City slums abound. One, called "Hollywood," has neither water nor plumbing nor electricity, not even streets. Both Colón and the capital are poor, dirty, full of bugs, prostitutes, pickpockets, and drug addicts. Naturally, the big banana plantations are owned by United Fruit. Those I saw in Chiriquí Province had slave-age conditions.

In the interior, peasant union organizers are persecuted. Early in August, 1962, a group of peasants seized a strip of land in Pacora Valley, and demanded that a primary school be erected thereon. A few weeks later, landless peasants occupied the valley's larger estates. About that time, too, university students went on strike in support of demands for better living conditions. On August 21st Major Manuel José Hurtado led eighteen *carabineros* into the jungles near Balboa, the beginning of a guerrilla operation. (Hurtado was trained in guerrilla warfare at our Zone's Fort Sherman.) In general, violence occurs much more frequently than is reported in Panama's newspapers (owned by the oligarchy) or in ours.

Until Panamanians get rid of their oligarchical rulers, they will remain poor, illiterate, and unsovereign. Unless we change our Canal policy, however, that will not occur—peacefully. In fact, most of current violence is actually stimulated by the oligarchy which wants more money from the U.S. for the Canal—money of course, which never filters down to the people. Thus it is that each of the major riots that have caused clashes between the U.S. and Panama —the most important of which occurred early in 1964—was sparked by Panama's rulers. Naturally, each time blood is spilled, these oligarchs blame the U.S. to their people, and local Nationalists to the U.S. So far we have reacted by giving in to this blackmail, and the Canal has remained a political football, helping to keep the Panamanians down.

No conscientious Latin American, however, considers our position on the Canal morally just. Even Panama's Christian Democrats, who are pro-United States, unhesitatingly insist that the Canal must be nationalized. We have got our investment back ten times over; we could at least offer to sell it back to Panama. Or we could take Panama in as an equal partner—disbanding the Panama Canal Company and withdrawing our Armed Forces. We could always insist, in legal writing, that shipping must never be interfered with (and that the Canal must be operated, defended, and totally controlled by us in case of war). But until the Panama Canal has a different status, one that recognizes Panama's sovereignty, our reputation in Latin America will never be favorable. Perhaps we don't care. If we do, no Alliance for Progress can ever hope to offset actions, and to Latin Americans, our actions in Panama are inexcusable.

Nicaragua, the biggest of the Central American republics, is by far the worst. It is so poor and rundown that one corner of Managua's main square, where Congress, the cathedral, the tourist headquarters, and the oligarchy's club are located, is an empty lot. Along main Roosevelt Avenue are a few stores and a hotel or two, the swankiest of which (the Gran Hotel) is an ugly, hot, wooden monstrosity that, except for its swimming pool, would compare adversely with a dozen Times Square roach dens.

The only impressive buildings are located on top of a hill at the other end of Roosevelt Avenue from main square. There stand two huge palaces: the President's and the National Guard commander's. Around them on one side are officers' quarters, barricades, fortifications, checkpoints, and fences. In back, after a hundred-foot precipice, is a small lake where Managua's womenfolk gather, coming from the far side, to wash their clothes. And between the military installations and the lake, on the only exposed flank, is, appropriately, the United States Embassy complex.

Aside from these buildings, Managua and the rest of Nicaragua is a filthy, year-long-hot, depressing hovel where only high military officers and a few well-connected oligarchs can escape the misery around them by flocking to the plush air-conditioned country club which, though not a military but a private club, is guarded by soldiers. But then, the whole country is run by soldiers—for the Somozas.

Papa Somoza, named Anastasio and known as Tacho, was assassinated in 1956 after ruling Nicaragua as his personal slave camp for twenty years. Before he died he accumulated a $200 million grafted fortune that included a sugar mill, cement plant, and cotton gin, sugar, cotton, and coffee plantations, thousands of top farmlands and thousands of cattle, newspapers, the country's only TV station, and radio station, and an airline and steamship company.

After he died, his two sons—"President" Luis and National Guard Commander General Anastasio ("Tachito") Somoza—took over the country—and the looting. The only difference between their behavior and Papa's is that the sons are more cowardly; they exchange rooms and beds in their huge palaces every night.

"President" Luis finally "decided" to allow "free" elections in February 1963—so as to get his share of Alliance goodies. The winner, naturally, was the official candidate, René Schick. A long-time Somoza pal and often a Somoza cabinet minister, Schick will nevertheless not reign with full Somoza trust: Tachito retains control of the National Guard, that is, remains the true ruler of Nicaragua.

Officially, however, the regime is now being referred to as a Democracy, and we can be expected to keep our dollars going in, as the Somozas predict. It does not seem to matter to us that the election was meaningless, that only candidates approved by the Somozas were allowed to run, and that their leading opponent, Conservative Fernando Agüero, had withdrawn before election day because of the obvious fix. Agüero had another reason to withdraw— fear. Back in July 1962, for example, when he returned from the United States and was met at the airport by some fifteen thousand Conservatives, who then marched peacefully back to town, Somozas' soldiers reacted by spraying them with bullets. In Nicaragua, even Conservatives had to learn the hard way that democratic process means Somozan success.[3]

Honduras is quaint—that's all. Tegucigalpa, the capital, with 120,000 people, even has a pink château for a presidential palace. The city is built on Mount El Picacho and some picturesque streets, lined with stuccoed houses painted in gay colors, are stepped—somewhat a handicap to the scooterbug. The city, like the countryside, is clean. Communications are almost nonexistent. Huge empty spaces separate small Indian farming centers, some of which we discovered had not heard of World War II, much less of the first—or the possibility of a third.

United Fruit has done its best work in Honduras, building schools, experimental farms, and clinics. It also has taken over the choicest lands and coasts the country has to offer. It owns Puerto Cortés through which more than half of Honduras' trade passes (I wonder how Massachusetts residents would feel if Texas' King Ranch owned Boston?) and the port of Tela. Competitor Standard Fruit Company owns another port, La Ceiba.

Most people in Honduras are peaceful. The main exceptions are the land barons who often shoot down disobedient or complaining peons in cold blood ("They're armed, aren't

[3] It was to this bastion of democracy that José Miró Cardona, the leader of the anti-Castro Cuban Revolutionary Council came seeking arms. After four hours with Somoza, Miró Cardona told newsmen that he was touring Latin America's "democratic countries to seek arms with which to fight the totalitarian regime of Fidel Castro. We free Cubans will provide the fighters, because direct action to overthrow that regime will come. But we need the material help from the democracies." He had come to the right place.

they?" one told me; "they could use their machetes."), and the army officers who see their function in life as the seizing of the government for themselves or for their oligarchical patrons.

Honduras has seen ten constitutions drafted and ignored, and a whole flock of dictators, succeeding themselves in rapid order through military coups. Until late 1963, it was ruled by a "democrat," President Ramón Villeda Morales, who talked well and recognized that Honduras is "the country of the four 70's—70 percent illiteracy, 70 percent illegitimacy, 70 percent rural populations, 70 percent avoidable deaths." Villeda Morales did wonders for democracy: his was one of the most corrupt regimes in Honduras' history. But a few days before elections to choose his successor came off, the Conservatives pushed the military to throw out Villeda, and the country is now ruled by a bunch of corrupt non-democrats instead of corrupt democrats.

El Salvador is the tiniest country in Latin America: its 2,700,000 people are squeezed 320 to the square mile. Its gold holdings are fair—$30 million. Its balance of trade is favorable—$133 million exports in 1959 versus $100 million imports. Its economy is stable—the colón has remained frozen at 2.5 to the dollar for years. But there the positive statistics end.

The country has been run by a handful of coffee and banking families (called the Big 14) ever since the Spaniards left 140 years ago. Wages are incredibly low (top agricultural salary is $0.60 a day), unemployment high (30,000 in the capital, San Salvador, alone). More than half the population is illiterate. El Salvador and Uruguay have about the same number of people, and though the former's living conditions produce more illness than the latter's, El Salvador has one-third the hospitals, one-fourth the hospital beds, and one-seventh the doctors.

Since 1954 Salvador's poor have been getting poorer since real wages (cost rises over salary boosts) have dropped 30 percent; hence, they have withdrawn whatever bank deposits they might have had. The rich, on the other hand, have been getting richer, as proved by the fact that bank deposits have gone up from $35 million in 1954 to $42.6 million in 1961. In addition, the amounts invested abroad jumped from $10 million a year in 1954-1959 to more than $25 million since. In the last six years, the Big 14 have about doubled their real worth (without even counting their local reinvestments, which have tripled).

The Big 14 have ruled El Salvador through military dictators ever since anyone can remember. For four years, until October, 1960, President Colonel José María Lemus kept opponents in jail, using United States-equipped police to terrorize grumblers. Dictator Lemus came to the United States in March, 1959, was warmly received by President Eisenhower, and was awarded a Manhattan ticker-tape parade. Upon his return, Lemus apparently decided he had been too lenient, and began liquidating critics.

Then, in September, 1960, he outlawed all political rallies. Some five thousand San Salvador students staged a protest. Lemus' police broke it up, jailing scores of students. When students protested again, the police went after them with more brutality, followed some into the university, systematically smashed every office, classroom, and laboratory (one of which had been built with Rockefeller funds). "Every single blackboard was broken," a student told me. Goons also beat Dr. Napoleón Rodríguez Ruíz, the university president, bayoneted students, killed a librarian, and raped dozens of coeds. Finally, when seven thousand more students amassed anew, Lemus ordered his troops to open fire— point-blank.

Horrified, El Salvador's moderates acted to save their country from further bloodshed, and especially from open rebellion, possibly of a Castroite texture. They deposed Lemus, set up a six-man junta, and promised free elections by 1962. But our State Department refused to recognize the new government. Ambassador Thorsten Kalijarvi, who had never met the three civil members of the junta, returned to Washington a week after the coup and branded the junta, which Castro had not recognized, as pro-Castro. His main argument, apparently, was that the junta had released political prisoners (mostly students) and promised every *legal* party free participation in the 1962 elections (not, however, the Communist Party, which remained illegal). The evidence was obviously deemed overwhelming; we delayed recognizing the junta until December. By then it was doomed.

The oligarchy, which had regrouped Lemus' militarists, staged a new coup and set up a government of rightist colonels that, when confronted with a new student demonstration, resorted to former practices—police again dispersed "rioters" with point-blank gunfire. This time there was no hesitation in Washington, no talk of "undemocratic" juntas. The Kennedy administration recognized the new government. In October, 1961, after launching such weak reforms as a seventy-cent-a-day wage minimum and a 33 percent cut in slum rents, the new strong man, Colonel Julio Adalberto Rivera, resigned to organize a "new" political party "to defend the reform program." He called it the National Conciliation Party, and presented candidates to fill every Constituent Assembly seat. There were 800,000 registered voters and seven opposition parties. But the army was in charge of the polls. Result: Rivera's men won all fifty-four seats.

A presidential election was called for April, 1962. This time the seven opposition parties refused to present candidates, charging that fraud was to be perpetrated again. Just a few days before the election, the entire crew of computing-machine operators, who insisted on releasing voting tabulations themselves without presenting them to army supervisors for "correction," were fired. Rivera wanted a good showing—500,000 votes—despite the fact that he was unopposed.

Even with army help, however, he managed only 370,000. Heavily criticized for fraud in the Assembly election, he had finally admitted observers to the polls for the presidential one—after it was too late to inscribe other candidates. Most observers reported that blank ballots far outnumbered the progovernment ballots. I spoke to six poll watchers, all members of the conservative but fair Christian Democrat movement. "No one was allowed to count the blank ballots," one said, while the others nodded agreement, "but the mutilated ones, which we could spot by their shapes, outnumbered the announced government ballots three to one. I don't believe the 370,000 count."

Rivera is President. The Big 14 are happy; they can go on with their practices. We recognized Rivera, and no report of election fraud was published here.[4] AP did report, however, that he "is a strong supporter of Washington's

---

[4] Though the *New York Times* did report, on September 30, 1962, that a viciously undemocratic "anti-Communist" law had become effective at midnight on the 28th and that "mass arrests" were reported.

Alliance for Progress." Not for attribution, of course, one high official of our Foreign Service in San Salvador told me: "It's just as if Lemus was back; a smarter Lemus perhaps, but the same clique. Unfortunately, nothing is going to change around here."

Guatemala has had few dictators—but their reigns have been long. From 1838, when the short-lived United Provinces of Central America disintegrated, to 1865, the boss was an Indian illiterate *caudillo* named Rafael Carrera, who was very Catholic (and Conservative), signed Latin America's first concordat with the Vatican, intervened in neighboring lands to establish Conservative regimes there, and kept Indians in peonage to the big Creole landowners because "to be against private property is to be against God."

His successor, Liberal Justo Rufino Barrios, an anticlerical, proscribed religious processions, forbade the wearing of clerical habits, confiscated Church property, made civil marriage obligatory, and kept the Indians in peonage to big landowners (now including some German immigrants) because the latter were whiter and "Indians think like priests—kneeling."

From 1898 to 1920, Manuel Estrada Cabrera, who was reelected "unanimously" just about every other month, developed a secret police to track down critics, and kept Indians in peonage by allowing the United Fruit Company, to which he granted huge concessions, to use private armies as "pacifiers." Then, from 1931 to 1944, the next dictator, Jorge Ubico, altered the pattern.

Just as ruthless, bloody, and corrupt as his predecessors, Ubico was also intelligent. Thus, he managed to refill the treasury coffers, balance budgets, restore Guatemala's international credit, and build more roads and hospitals than all his predecessors combined. By decree, he theoretically ended peonage; he posed as the Indians' friend. But in practice he let the landowners and United Fruit continue as they always had. Ubico also pilfered more funds than his predecessors, and discovered more plots against him, hence executed more. He mastered the art of handling men, as the following tale by Guatemalan writer Jorge García Granados illustrates:

In 1934, he [Ubico] uncovered a conspiracy against

him. . . . Seventeen men were seized, given a farcical trial in which they were not even permitted defense attorneys, and sentenced them to be shot. Although I had no part in the conspiracy, I wrote Ubico a strong letter charging that the trial was a mockery of the law, and urging him to pardon the condemned.

Ubico replied by sending a squad of police to arrest me in my home, take me to the place of execution, and force me to be an eyewitness to the shooting of the seventeen. Then I was thrown into prison and held in solitary confinement for months, not even permitted to receive news from my family.

Ubico was considered one of our good friends in Central America, and we openly supported him. Nevertheless, he was overthrown by a revolution in 1944. Free elections were called, and in 1945 Juan José Arévalo came to power.

Arévalo and his legally elected successor, Jacobo Arbenz Guzmán (1950-1954), began what is now commonly called the Social Revolution. To Latin Americans everywhere, they were Social Reformers and Nationalists. To our State Department and press, they were Communists and Russian agents "who led the people like sheep." That at least this last point was false has been proved by a United States social scientist[5] who based his report on a thorough research project that included a vast number of interviews. His conclusions:

It has been commented that "these people were being led like sheep"; in the writer's opinion, this is not supported. It is clear that the population interviewed was in general interested in some phase of the past [Arbenz] government's activities. . . . It may be said that these people were being led in that they did what the Communist wanted; on the other hand, they were doing things which they too wished to do. The Communists were successful in identifying their goals with those of certain portions of the rural population; this can be laid to the cleverness of the Communists, but not necessarily to the "sheep-like" qualities of the population.

[5] Stokes Newbold, with the collaboration of June and Manning Nash: *A Study of Receptivity to Communism in Rural Guatemala.*

No serious historian or sociologist questions the fact that Guatemala needed social change: before Arévalo the right of labor, whether in factories or in fields, including United Fruit plantations, had never been recognized; unions, civil liberties, freedom of speech and press were outlawed; foreign interests had been sacred, their privileges were monopolistic and their tax concessions beyond all considerations of fairness; counting each foreign corporation as a person, 98 percent of Guatemala's cultivated land was owned by exactly 142 people; only one-third of schoolchildren could attend classes—there weren't any more schools—and only 10 percent did.

Arévalo and Arbenz changed these conditions. As long as they pressed forward for education reforms, no one grumbled too much. Free speech and press were established. Then unions were recognized and legalized, and many passed into Leftist control. Perhaps some were Communist; after all, according to our Senate Investigating Subcommittee, there were 1,000 Communists in Guatemala, and these 1,000 must have been doing something.

On June 17, 1952, Arbenz proclaimed a wide-sweeping program (Decree 900) of land reform. It called for the expropriation and redistribution of uncultivated or fallow lands above a basic acreage, specifically exempted all intensively cultivated lands (only 5 percent of over-1,000 hectare farms were then under cultivation), ordered all absentee-owned property to be redistributed, offered compensation in twenty-year bonds at 3 percent interest assessed according to the declared tax value. Even our own agronomists approved. On page 179 of *Latin American Issues,* published by the Twentieth Century Fund, one can read: "For all the furor it produced, Decree 900, which had its roots in the constitution of 1945, is a remarkably mild and a fairly sound piece of legislation."

But, since much of Guatemala's plantation land (including 400,000 acres not under cultivation) belonged to the United Fruit Company, we naturally became concerned. And when Arbenz gave out the company's land to 180,000 peasants, we began seeing Red.

"The Communists have been able to move in easily," agreed at the time the late, staunchly anti-Communist Columbia University teacher Jésus de Galíndez. But, he added, "social-economic reform is absolutely necessary in Guatemala.

To condemn it is to help Communism."

We condemned it just the same. Having refused to sell arms to Guatemala since 1948, we intercepted and confiscated a shipment from Switzerland—a fact reported in Latin America by no United States agency, only by the British service Reuters.[6] Then, in 1954, we got the OAS to convene its foreign ministers in Caracas (home of Dictator Pérez Jiménez). Secretary of State John Foster Dulles showed up just long enough to bulldoze a declaration censuring Guatemala, and sped home.

Fortified with this declaration, we went to work getting rid of Arbenz. We found another Guatemalan colonel, Carlos Castillo Armas (a graduate of the United States Command and General Staff School at Fort Leavenworth, Kansas), fed him arms (including six F-47's piloted by US "volunteers") and dollars to set up a rebel force in Honduras and Nicaragua (home of Dictator Anastasio Somoza), and helped him overthrow Arbenz. Armas thereupon became a ruthless dictator, closed down opposition newspapers (which Arbenz had never done), smashed student rallies, tortured and murdered his critics, gave back Arbenz-expropriated lands, allowed plantation owners to cut down wages 30 percent, and awarded friends $1,000,000 a year through legal *confidenciales,* and millions more through other channels.[7]

Armas was assassinated in 1957, and elections were scheduled. The moderates won, so the military immediately annulled the election and scheduled a new one. This time the army made sure of the outcome: conservative General Miguel Ydígoras Fuentes became President early in 1958. Husky, informal, and good-natured in appearance, Ydígoras was thereupon billed as a great democrat—in the United States (thanks mainly to such agile PR men as former Secretary of Interior Oscar Littleton Chapman).

But in Guatemala, as everywhere else in Latin America, he was known for what he was: a dictator who is perhaps not

[6] Guatemala finally got some arms from Czechoslovakia.

[7] One friend and beneficiary was Thomas J. Dodd, ex-Representative, now Senator from Connecticut, who was hired to represent (i.e., lobby for) Guatemala in the United States for $50,000 a year—the same Senator Dodd who in 1962 almost (he refused because he was "too busy") led the Senate investigation on sugar lobbies.

so bloody as the average Latin American strong man but who nevertheless ruled with hoods, goons, and his United States-equipped army. There was little freedom of the press in Guatemala, and persistent critics were inevitably silenced or taught a painful lesson.[8] No land reform has been attempted since Arbenz' fall, nor was any tried under Ydígoras, since the land is mostly owned by our companies or Ydígoras' pals. When he took over Guatemala, the government still owned 88 coffee *fincas;* only a handful remains today. Ydígoras, whose official, *legal* pay was $1,094,000 a year, had been giving the *fincas* away or selling them cheaply to friends and political partners. For example, one plantation, which made more than $200,000 a year, went to moviemaker Ramiro Samayoa, a personal friend of Ydígoras. Meanwhile, of course, no serious attempt was undertaken to reduce illiteracy, disease, or poverty.

Unfortunately, the United States is held partly responsible for these conditions. The reason is that Ydígoras and our State Department were so tightly linked that most Latin Americans were convinced that the Guatemalan government did not make a single move without first being so ordered by the United States. Unfortunately, there were some facts to back up this contention.

When Guatemala was rocked by revolt in November, 1960 —a revolt of Guatemalan conservative army officers against Ydígoras—it wired Washington (via United Fruit-owned

---

[8] One incident is worth detailing. Early in 1960, a frail, pretty, twenty-two-year-old newspaperwoman named Irma Flaquer, who supports her two children, started a column of criticism, *Lo que otros callan* (What Others Hide), in the capital's afternoon daily *La Hora* (15,000 circulation). She denounced Ydígoras' corruption and ridiculed his policies; she campaigned against poverty, slums, and alcoholism. At first, the government was reluctant to use strong-arm measures against a girl; so, instead, Information Chief Augusto Mulet Descamps branded her "treasonable" and a "whore." When she persisted, however, she was jumped by one Gloria Castillo, a tough 150-pound political troubleshooter and boss of the pro-Ydígoras market women's union. Saying "the old man is fed up with you," Gloria kicked and punched Irma unconscious, then ripped out chunks of Irma's hair. The Information Ministry passed off the beating as "a street incident."

Tropical Radio) a series of badly coded messages, which were monitored by a whole flock of Latin American radio operators (including hams as far down as Colombia). The messages were easily decoded and then made public. Message 1,788, sent on November 14th, at 12:50 P.M., ordered the Guatemalan United States ambassador to get OAS help, but ended with this now famous sentence: "Get in touch immediately with [then Assistant Secretary of State for Inter-American Affairs] Thomas Mann to coordinate your action." Eight hours later, Cable 1,793 told the ambassador to apply for our naval and air support, concluding, "Convenient coordinate immediately with State Department."

Is Guatemala so "sold out" to the United States, asked Latin Americans, that even in a moment of crisis—a revolution—it must first get clearance for its acts from the United States? For their answer, Latin Americans unfortunately looked at the results: without waiting for OAS action, the United States dispatched warships to the Guatemalan coast. The revolution was doomed. Latin Americans asked: Was the payoff the Retalhuleu Base? (On January 10, 1961, the *New York Times* described this base as a training center for Cuban exiles and as a launching pad for their unsuccessful Bay of Pigs invasion of Cuba; the Kennedy Administration then admitted it, but Ydígoras denied it to the day he was overthrown.)

Early in 1962, it seemed as if Ydígoras was through. Students, teachers, even Ydígoras-controlled unions were demanding his resignation. There were riots every single day for a month, and Guatemala refused to issue any entrance visas. Then, suddenly, came absolute silence. Not one protest, not one rally, not one public complaint were reported. When I arrived a few days later, the country was completely calm. I asked my contacts to explain. "We have never seen such efficient lightning-fast repressions," they told me, "and we know for certain that the whole government apparatus was taken over by the CIA." I would have doubted such an explanation much more had my contacts in Guatemala, as in all Central America, not been the Christian Democrats. Pro-United States and anti-Castro (though pro-reforms), they stood only to lose from such a tale. True or not, the country had undoubtedly been cowed into total passivity by the time I arrived. When Ydígoras was finally tossed out of office, the tossers, of course, were army officers from the extreme Right. After that the atmosphere had the same quiet thickness common to Nicargua or Paraguay.

Nevertheless, Guatemala impressed me as one of the most charming countries on this continent. Its people are hospitable, its sights overpoweringly attractive, its plazas or main squares picturesque, its buildings old and poor but enchanting. True, half of Guatemala City's 400,000 inhabitants live in swampside slums, and true, many peasants live in mud huts without sanitation while the huge master's home that overlooks them could easily house all the peon families in luxury and still leave a dozen-room wing for the owner. Yet, wherever one travels in Guatemala one finds smiles, even on poverty—perhaps not smiles of happiness but certainly smiles of hospitality.

In the hazardous mountainous passes on the western side of Lake Atitlán, which is one of the continent's real marvels, Indians would rush up to us every time we stopped our jeep—not to beg for money, as we were warned, but to help push, thinking we were stuck (the zigzag climb on mud, dirt, or rocks is at sixty degrees, with precipices for shoulders). Around the lake itself, where each town's women wear identically colored bright garments and wave to all newcomers, in the mountain paths from Totonicapán to Huehuetenango or in the jungle trails (called roads) behind Copán; in fact anywhere we journeyed in our vista-packed 2,000-mile trip through Guatemala the only discourteous, inhospitable individual we met was a United States engineer named La Rue who ordered his armed private cops to stop anyone from using a road he had built (from Tres Encuentros to San Cristóbal) because the United States company he worked for had not been paid by the government.

So beautiful, so friendly, so enchanting is Guatemala that it seems doubly a crime that it is run so unjustly for the benefit of so few.

Chapter 13

The Caribbean

Perhaps some man of leisure, fortune, and persistency has visited all the islands crammed in the 2,000-mile Florida-to-Venezuela Caribbean Sea. Certainly no reporter has; there are thousands of them (the British Bahama group alone includes 3,000-odd islands). There are all types—fat ones, tall ones (volcanic), tiny ones, and so on. Most are colonies; some are "Overseas Departments"; a few are independent. Venezuela owns a couple, France and the Netherlands a handful, Britain a stackful. We own two sets: Puerto Rico and Vieques, taken from Spain, and three Virgin Islands bought from Denmark in 1917. Cuba[1] and the Dominican Republic became independent from Spain. Haiti, which shares the island of Hispaniola with the Dominican Republic, broke from France. Jamaica, and Trinidad and Tobago got their independence from England in August, 1962.

All the Caribbean Islands, large or small, are graced by warm sunshine and cool evening breezes. All produce sugar, some form of rum, and tourist attractions in their clean white beaches and clear green seas. Most islands are coral reefs surrounded by more coral reefs—a guarantee against sharks and unsurmountable waves. Some have Indian descendants (the Caribs and Arawaks); all have Negroes.

[1] Put off limits by our State Department, Cuba is the only country in Latin America I did not visit, hence no description of Cuban life can appear in this book.

Most are run by whites, and all have "color" problems.

In the Spanish (independent) islands, color lines are drawn only by social snobs. In the British and United States islands, discrimination is illegal but exists in businesses as well as in social clubs. In the French-owned islands, which are Departments of France (sending deputies to Paris and governed by a Paris-appointed prefect), the "Continentals" or "Europeans" view the native Negroes with such derision and treat them with such contempt that one easily understands the hate that Algerians have for the French *colon*. In both Martinique and Guadeloupe, which are filthy though picturesque volcanic islands,[2] the Negroes, who form 95 percent of the population, live in rat-infested slums, while the *colons*, who own all of the island's wealth, enjoy fashionable seaside villas, yachts, and air-conditioned cars.

In Trinidad, one of the biggest of the Windward series, rivalry between the big East Indies immigrant population and the Negroes leads to occasional violence. Trinidad, and its smaller neighboring island Tobago, are run by Prime Minister Eric Williams, a short, Negro, former Howard University professor, who sticks to English traditions while he recites nationalistic slogans and practices Tammany Hall tactics. The islands were members of the British West Indies Federation until it collapsed when Jamaica, the richest, broke away two years ago to prepare for its independence. In Trinidad-Tobago, Williams had always been cool toward the Federation anyway. He too wanted independence. The people, however, were generally opposed. "Just having embassies in the major countries," one luncheonette clerk told me, "will cost us more than our whole budget does now. And who will pay so that the big shots can live in Paris or Rome? We, the people."

Statistically, Trinidad is not so poor. It is a big producer and exporter of asphalt (more than 50,000 tons a year) and sugar (about 200,000 tons) and breaks about even in its trade. Its 800,000 inhabitants are increasing at a rate of more than 3 percent yearly, and its capital, Port of Spain, is mostly an unimpressive wood-and-nail city.

[2] In 1902, some 2,000 people were killed by an eruption in Guadeloupe, and 40,000 people, as well as the old capital of Saint-Pierre, were wiped out in Martinique.

Still, wages have been rising at a slightly higher rate than prices for the last few years.

The other eight island members of the defunct Federation now want to go it alone. All are impoverished, though none has the slums of Martinique or even Jamaica. Barbados, one of the nicest of the Windward islands, is to be the capital of the new Federation, and its Premier Errol Barrow is in favor of it. England, which would have to help out with financial aid, is still hesitant. Under its rule, Barbados or Antigua, the loveliest isle of the Leeward series, or any of the other six, have had few problems. Dependent upon sugar exports and tourist imports, the islands cannot hope for a much brighter future, but, as Barrow puts it, "Are you better off by yourself or together?"

Our islands are studies in contrasts. Both the Virgin Islands, with their tax-free enticement to Miami and Westchester County playboys, and Puerto Rico, with its lax gambling laws, exhibit some of the most ostentatious luxury sights this side of Monte Carlo. But in both, local inhabitants profit little from the imported wealth. In the Virgin Islands, where the Negro majority keeps strong tabs on illegal discrimination practices, whites are settling in so fast that the former may soon lose their rein on the local government. Poor and excluded from high society, the Negroes would then be deprived of legal power as well.

In Puerto Rico, which seems to have become the brothel of the Caribbean since Castro's puritanical squads drafted the prostitutes into the militias, one luxury hotel crowds another along San Juan beaches. Each hotel has its own casino, and in each thousands of dollars are tossed at a wheel every night. A few miles away, thousands of Puertorriqueños are jammed into waterless slums. Governor Muñoz Marín's much heralded "Operation Bootstrap," which has brought the island dozens of factories, thanks to attractive tax concessions, has created some jobs. But Bootstrap is obviously not the least bit what it claims to be.

Instead of making Puerto Rico a showplace for Latin Americans to see what democratic capitalism can do, we have not even wiped out dire poverty. The (visiting) Latin who sees the same illiteracy he has at home, the same extremes in wealth, and the same social injustices is also shocked by Puerto Rico's disappearing personality. Not Spanish, not American, P.R. is a sort of illegitimate child, a place where signs read "Salida de trucks," instead of "Truck exit" or Salida de camiones.

Jamaica is very much like its music—enchanting and steel-drum strong at first glance, hollow and repetitious as one gets to know it. A fair-sized (4,500 square miles), leaf-shaped tropical isle of almost 1,700,000 people, it is a prosperous country—on paper. It should be; it is the world's biggest exporter of bauxite, and still a major sugar exporter (some $25,000,000 worth a year).

Naturally, however, Jamaica's mines and ores are not Jamaican. They belong to ALCAN, Kaiser, Reynolds, or Alcoa—all North American enterprises. In 1961, for example, Kaiser Bauxite Company shipped 3,183,909 tons and Reynolds Jamaica Mines 1,810,299 tons of ore, and ALCAN 703,466 tons of alumina (refined), together worth some $200 million. Since Jamaica has many beautiful beaches and many swanky resort areas (Port Antonio, Ocho Rios, Montego Bay), plus colorful jungle streams and two jet airports, tourism is another major industry, which in 1961 gave Jamaica $40,000,000 from 500,000 visitors.

Despite these assets, Jamaicans are poor. The Negro masses live in shacks we would call slums, are exploited on sugar and banana plantations or in the mines. Unemployment is at more than 20 percent of the island's 700,000-man labor force. The government, currently in the hands of white-haired Prime Minister William Alexander Bustamante, seventy-nine, a bitter egomaniac and demagogue, is corrupt and inefficient. His only opposition comes from a cousin and former Premier (when Jamaica was not independent), Norman Washington Manley, sixty-nine, who is just as demagoguish, but more aloof.

During the April, 1962, elections, Premier Manley, who called himself "The Man with the Plan," claimed that "the opposition is made up of fools. They are crazy." Cousin Bustamante referred to Manley as "The Clot with the Plot." Both were probably right. One of Bustamante's first acts, once elected, was to prepare the independence ceremonies, inviting only the United States and its allies. The Kingston Daily Gleaner resented the matter: "We would have preferred if it could have been possible for Jamaica to open its house to all members of the United Nations." But "Busta" would have none of it. "There will be no neutrality from this day on!" he shouted; "I will go to the United States shortly to make a mutual defense treaty." Since it would seem highly improbable that Jamaica could efficiently defend the United States in war, Busta's statement could mean only that he would offer more concessions to United States industries and military missions in exchange for financial aid.

Jamaica needs aid. Indebted before independence by some $115,000,000, the new country, with new diplomacy (especially embassy) costs, will now go deeper into the red. But even if Jamaica gets plenty of Alliance dollars, chances are that its people (7 percent of whom earns more than $480 a year; the rest earn from that down to zero) will not profit. After all, more than $200 million in recent United States investment has not brought up the standard of living. Alliance money will, however, strengthen Busta's hold on Jamaica and, naturally, assure us that our companies will not be expropriated—until Jamaica, too, gets a nation-alistic revival.

Haiti, being a combination of Latin (French) culture and Negro tempo, is in immediate contrast to the British islands. It has life, zest, and plenty of art. It is also the hemisphere's poorest country, Of almost 4,000,000 people, it is made up of the western third of the island of Hispaniola and is the most consistently mountainous territory in the Caribbean.

Discovered by Columbus, settled and taken over by the French, populated by African slaves brought to work the fields, Haiti has had a turbulent history. The Negroes rebelled, a civil war ensued, and, after a dozen years of slaughter, Haiti became independent in 1804. Since most of the French were killed, it became a Negro nation. But since most Negroes were French-trained, French remained the official language and a Creole patois the common tongue.

From independence to the present, Haiti has been ruled either by Negro "emperors," dictators, or self-styled "presidents," or by the United States Marines—except for a short span of mulatto semi-democracy in the nineteenth century, when a caste system was instituted, the hated elite being whiter, richer, and more "cultural" than the Negro masses. As a result it has been fairly easy for Negro demagogues to seize power on anti-elite platforms. François Duvalier, the current President, has done just that.

A former country doctor elected for six years in 1955, he had himself declared reelected in 1961 (unconstitutional). A dictator whose ruthlessness is currently unmatched this side of Paraguay's Stroessner, Duvalier deposits $1,000,000 a year in foreign banks. His regime's graft is $6,000,000 a year—20 percent of impoverished Haiti's national budget. Every government institution is corrupt, as are its monopolies in cement, soap, matches, and tobacco. United States aid is another handy way to enrich Duvalier and his cronies, and so are loans from the World Bank (to repair Haiti's terrible pock-holed roads).

Peasants are encouraged to keep to their voodoo satis-factions; the press is cowed; opponents disappear; critics are beaten or tortured; critic's wives are raped and sexually mutilated or blinded. Haiti's motto, printed on official dai-lies, is "The Haitian who does not love President François Duvalier is a dangerous enemy of the country." To enforce this motto is the work of Duvalier's private army, 10,000 hoods known as the *Tonton Macoute* (Creole for bogeyman) backed by a 20,000-strong United States Marine-trained militia.

The Tonton Macoute terrorize all aspects of Haiti's life. For funds they shake down businessmen for "contribu-tions" as high as $40,000 apiece, and force them to "deduct" more contributions from their salaried employees. For silencing opposition they use Fort Dimanche, a yellow-brick fortress north of the capital, Port-au-Prince. There, for example, they tossed gasoline on the man who hid the brothers of former presidential candidate Clément Jumelle, then burned him to death. But they also use Haitian forests, where, for example, they raped, beat, and mutilated Yvonne Hakim-Rimpel, a newspaper editor. And the Tontons also have a run of the various prisons. The following is an account of Francis Brenton, a thirty-five-year-old British photographer, who landed at Jacmel, Haiti, from his yacht *Nengo* to pick up supplies. Arrested without charges, he was jailed for ten days:

During my detention at Jacmel, which covered five days, I was given only two meals—one on the second day and one on the fourth day. The cells were about 12 ft. by 14 ft., and the only furnishing was a reed mat. There were no blankets at night and no allowance for washing or toilet.

From Jacmel I was flown to Port-au-Prince and placed in the police-military headquarters at the Casernes François Duvalier. I was placed in an 8-ft. by 10-ft., blood-spattered cell in the interrogation section. To reach these I went through what I am certain is a courtroom. In the courtroom an officer sat behind a desk with 30 or 40 prisoners in front of him. A prisoner was on the floor being heavily beaten with sticks. The officer asked questions and made notes, and the prisoner answered, punctuated with a few sharp smacks of the sticks. For some of the prisoners, this was only a primary beating.

Opposite my cell was the beating cell. It was about 10 ft. by 10 ft., the wall painted a flat black, a broken chair in one corner. There were two women in the cell when I first arrived—one was lying on her side with her wrists tied behind her knees, the other was trying to protect herself as best she could. Two well-dressed civilians were beating her across the shoulders. She was hit 25 or 30 times. The other woman was left lying on the floor for 20 to 30 minutes and she was hit on the shoulders, legs and back more or less at random. The male prisoners went through the same treatment as the females, except the civilians (the *Tonton Macoutes*) also punched the males across the face. Of the 44 other prisoners, this was only a primary beating.

On Tuesday, Feb. 20, I was taken to the main jail. I was transferred to an isolated enclave where there were only political prisoners. One elderly prisoner was in a truly terrible state. All his body was white and scaly from bug bites, and he was mentally withdrawn into himself. I was told this was perfectly normal.

Thursday, Feb. 22, I was returned to the Casernes François Duvalier and taken to the office of Captain Tomas. There I was introduced to Mr. Denis Roper, the British Consul; he told me he was doing everything possible to get me out of jail. I stayed at the Casernes for three days and two nights. No food was offered to me and no furniture or bedding provided. Mr. Roper provided me with food and cigarettes for the last two days. On Saturday, Feb. 24 [1962], I was released.

To a European diplomat, Haiti is beyond understanding. "There must be a worse government somewhere, but if so, I am not acquainted with it." Another was shocked out of his slumber: "Slowly and against my preconceived notions, I have come to see this as a Nazi state. The Tonton Macoute and the militia are the storm troopers. The President hails himself as *le Leader*, which is bastard French for *der Führer*."

Who supports *der Führer*? Since Duvalier took over Haiti, Washington has given it $30 million *in grants;* in 1961 we added another $13,500,000—45 percent of the budget. Then we lent Duvalier $9,000,000 more. A United States Marine mission under Colonel Robert Debs Heinl, Jr., long trained Duvalier's "Presidential Guard," whose graduates thereupon trained the militias. Our military aid to Haiti has been about $300,000 a year until 1964. To Colonel Heinl "our job is 'nation-building.' " (Though he had temporary second thoughts when his own twelve-year-old Creole-speaking son Michael was arrested by the Tontons after he told a girl next to him in a taxibus, as it passed by a group of wretched peasants, "The poor people, they haven't had anything to eat.") The reason we have continued to support Duvalier,[8] making a mockery of the Alliance's insistence on reforms is, as *Time* magazine so ably and approvingly put it, "With Communist Cuba only 50 miles away, the U.S. cannot cut flat-broke Haiti off the dole without risking a Red takeover." A Nazi is a sure anti-Communist, after all.

On the other part of the island of Hispaniola live 3,000,000 people in the Dominican Republic. Their history has not been much happier than that of their Haitian neighbors.

Until 1916 the Dominican Republic was ruled by dictators who were corrupt, inefficient, and ruthless but who lasted usually for only short periods. Then, after we sent in our

---

[8] Early in 1962, we finally threatened to cut off all aid to Haiti because Duvalier had not paid a $1,000,000 bill to a Peoria, Illinois, construction firm. Relations deteriorated after that. Nevertheless, Haiti got $5,000,000 in AID aid and $1,000,000 in Food for Peace in 1963.

Marines, occupied the country until 1930, trained the constabulary and educated its chief, we departed, convinced things would change.

They did. The man we had educated was more corrupt, more ruthless, and more efficient than any previous dictator—so much more, in fact, that he lasted thirty-two long years. His name was Rafael Leonídas Trujillo y Molina.

It is impossible to detail Trujillo's numerous operations. He, his sons, cousins, uncles, nephews, and a few trusted pals ran the country as their private playpen. Trujillo's policy, like that of most Latin American dictators, was "Anti-Communism," a catchword he used so well that he caught numerous admirers in Washington, especially among State Department officials, senators, and congressmen. Under the anti-Communist slogan, Trujillo executed his opponents, an estimated 500,000 over the thirty-two years, counting the Dominican exiles his henchmen sought out and murdered in New York, Mexico, Caracas, and Paris.

Trujillo's first mass murders to shock the world occurred in October, 1937. Previously, Haitians had been invited to cross the border into the Dominican Republic to work the Dominicans' sugar plantations. When the price of sugar dropped, however, these poor Negroes became a burden upon the Dominican economy. *El Benefactor* opted for a quick solution. Journeying to a small outpost along the Haitian-Dominican border, Trujillo said to his flock from a local church pulpit: "I found that Dominicans would be happier if we got rid of Haitians. I will fix that. Yesterday 300 Haitians were killed. . . . This must continue." It did. Throughout that night of October 2nd and during the whole next day, Negroes were dragged out of their hovels and were literally hacked to pieces by the Dominican Army and farmers under its command. Between 12,000 and 25,000 Haitians died.

But Trujillo was not just a murderer. He was also a torturer *par excellence*. Among the country's scores of jails and dungeons were the infamous La Cuarenta, a jail on Fortieth Street of Santo Domingo (the capital, called Ciudad Trujillo then), and "Kilometer Nine," the luxurious air-force base nine miles out of the city. There, Trujillo's SIM (Military Intelligence Service) used slow-shocking electric chairs, or an electrified rod known as "The Cane," especially effective on genitals, or nail extractors, or whips, or the *Pulpo* (octopus), a many-armed electrical device screwed into the skull. Kilometer Nine also featured a water tank with bloodsucking leeches.

The incredible inhumanities perpetrated by Trujillo and his pals are too long and too ugly to describe. Suffice it to say that even Laura Bergquist, a *Look* senior editor, who went to the Dominican Republic to see for herself, could not refrain from writing about one monstrosity, despite the magazine's genteel "family" readership. "I still shudder," she wrote, "about Snowball, a dwarf—now jailed—whose specialty was biting off men's genitals."

But Trujillo was "anti-Communist," and thus was our friend. He had more apologists in Washington than any other strong man in the continent or even, except Formosa's Chang Kai-shek, in the world. One United States economist sent there later to help the Dominican Republic's finances, reacted: "Let's face it: this was a government of gangsters. And anyone who did business with them knew it." Yet plenty of businessmen did business with Trujillo, and so did our government, giving Trujillo millions of dollars with which he supported a huge lobby in Washington—to sell *his* sugar to our country's housewives.

According to Trujillo's secret papers, released in July, 1962, one of his friendly contacts in Washington was no less than Representative Harold D. Cooley, North Carolina Democrat, who was (and is at the time of this writing) Chairman of the House Agriculture Committee. Its job, among others, is to recommend sugar-quota regulations and legislation. According to Trujillo's informants, Cooley assured them he would firmly support Dominican sugar interests. These agents remained in contact with Cooley even after the United States followed OAS recommendations and broke relations with Trujillo, applying (in theory) economic sanctions. On January 7, 1961, Marcos A. Peña, Trujillo's consul general in the United States, wrote his boss that Cooley "reiterated to us his previous promise of working firmly in favor of our sugar." On February 15, 1961, Peña wired his Foreign Office that "Cooley let us know today that he held individual conversations yesterday with Bowles, Berle and Muñoz Marín, [and] said that it is urgent to send a person of the highest confidence of the Illustrious Superiority [Trujillo] to treat basic aspects of the work he [Cooley] is carrying out together with our friends."[4]

Because of mounting criticism, however, Washington finally decided that the Dominican regime had to change hands. On May 30, 1961, Dictator Trujillo was caught in a CIA-organized trap on a lonely road. Though both he and his bodyguard-chauffeur were armed, and the latter emptied his pistol before collapsing seriously but not mortally wounded, the tough Benefactor, Son of God, Saviour of Mankind, Generalissimo, Father of the Fatherland, and so on, shrank to the floor and lay there shaking until, wounded, he tried to run for safety—abandoning his .38 pistol unfired. He was run over a dozen times, sprayed with bullets, tossed into the trunk of another car and, his hand dangling, was abandoned on Santo Domingo's elegant seaside George Washington Avenue.

Lest the Dominican Republic take on a Leftist regime, Washington went into action, trying to ensure a "gradual process of change." We were ready to accept an old Trujillo puppet named Joaquín Balaguer or Trujillo's son Ramfis or a military junta "in the hope that [one of them] could bloodlessly 'democratize' Trujilloland," as our editorial writers put it. In other words, we still preferred some kind of Trujillo gangster than to risk a popular democracy that might turn to the Left.

But the Dominicans had had enough of killings, dictators, and benefactors. Despite army bullets that continued to fly for the first few weeks, they rallied and rioted, and when it became obvious that they would not settle for anything less than giving democracy a chance, we suddenly reversed ourselves, and placed a fleet of ships and 4,000 Marines in Santo Domingo's harbor. Then we told the Dominican Republic's army to lay off.

It was our first intervention in favor of democracy and, though it gained us no friends ("Had the United States not intervened in the first place, we would not have had Ramfis or Balaguer or even Trujillo," one Social Christian Party

[4] References are to Chester Bowles, Assistant Secretary of State; Adolf Berle, Jr., former head of President Kennedy's Task Force on Latin America, now special consultant to the Secretary of State; and Luis Muñoz Marín, Governor of Puerto Rico.

leader told me), still, it gained us no enemies. Though some resentment for our tardiness was to be expected, as one new politician, Dr. Luis Baquero of the very moderate and pro-United States *Unión Cívica* put it: United States officials "were always trying to get us to settle for less, a Balaguer, a military coup, or Ramfis. We knew that a process of 'slow democratization' was impossible. We knew our people; they didn't."

The Trujillos were gone—with the people's money. The new government, a seven-man Council that included one of Trujillo's assassins and was headed by President Rafael Bonnelly, was made up of ex-Trujillo collaborators; but after thirty-two years of rule it would have been miraculous to find any "name" with clean hands. The Council was weak. It could not get the air force's permission to investigate Kilometer Nine incinerators. It could not arrest the murderers in the armed forces because, as one Council official explained: "lots of military men are implicated. You know where we would end up if we pressed too hard." Only a handful of SIM agents were arrested; thousands went into exile, but most still walk the streets or even remain on the job.

The new regime promised elections, but first had to set up election committees, train poll watchers, registration clerks, and so on—after thirty-two years of tyranny, electoral processes could not be guaranteed overnight. The Council did pass a law (Number 5891) making voting compulsory for all citizens from 18 to 60, voluntary for those above 60 or those who are located 60 miles or more from the polls, and forbidden for members of the Armed Forces or police. Theoretically, all legal parties were allowed to wage election campaigns.

In deference to the United States, the Communist Party was kept illegal, but it need not have been, since its strength was and is weak. Otherwise, until November 1962, there was complete and total freedom. True, some Leftists were under indictment for disturbing the peace, caused when unemployed youth groups (known as *Los Tigres*) stoned stores and offices or burned cars of our officials. But the newspapers supporting these very same men were not banned. Neither were scores of other dailies, weeklies, semi-monthlies, and so on, whose opinions ranged from extreme Right to extreme Left. Freedom of speech was wider than in the United

States, since hundreds of Dominican politicians, agitators, or reformers publicly campaigned for revolutions, that is, the violent overthrow of the government. But in fact the extremes were weak. "Our trouble," a Communist told me, "is that we have no issues."

Ironically, the man responsible for both the freedom (at first) and the lack of issues was none other than the late dictator himself. Not that he planned it that way, of course. But Trujillo and his family were so greedy that they took over 71 percent of the country's arable land and 90 percent of all industries. Naturally, all this wealth, 85 percent of the Dominican Republic, was then taken over by the new government, which therefore became Socialistic. As a result Communists could not shout, "Expropriate the land!" Anti-Yankees could not raise the slogan "Expropriate U.S. monopolies."

There were and still are only three major United States corporations on the island: the South Portorican Sugar Company, United Fruit's Granada Company, and the usual ill-functioning Telephone Company. All others had been forced to sell out to Trujillo, and these three, except the phone company (which should be nationalized), had to compete hard to survive. South Portorican, for example, had a sugar mill, but the new government inherited thirteen. Furthermore, the middlemen were either the Dominican government or Dominican entrepreneurs.

Since most of the government-owned Trujillo corporations were (as their ex-boss had them) efficiently run, they made money. As a result, the Council was able to raise wages up to 40 percent, which satisfied workers. Never had a government had such an opportunity. It could launch an Agrarian Reform without facing the problem of payment. It could initiate cooperatives without having to start from scratch. It already possessed the basic ingredients: the cane, the bananas, the cattle, some machinery, the roads, the ports, and even the loaders. It could try industrial cooperatives without risking its economy. And with the huge *latifundios* that were used by the Trujillos for private shooting ranges, it could experiment on new crops, aiming at diversification. (Even the influence of the Church, which is discredited because it was pro-Trujillo until just before the end, was reduced to religious affairs.)

The Council did inherit a near bankrupt economy with

huge debts and little reserves. Having no oligarchy to fight against reforms, however, it could enact a graduated income tax without too much trouble. It did: Law 5911 (May 22, 1962) detailed all-inclusive though perhaps mild levies of up to 38 percent profit taxes and up to 40 percent income tax. It was a beginning.

The Council also promulgated an Agrarian Reform (Law 5879) which, though vague, committed the government to parcel and distribute its land, giving credit, forming cooperatives, establishing agricultural communities, and training farmers in modern agricultural technology. Unfortunately, however, the program did not amount to much more than words, though the first parcels of land were distributed (a modest eight acres each) and were well handled, thanks to loans to farmers totaling $500,000. Then, suddenly, progress stopped.

First, in order to attract United States investments (which the Dominican Republic did not need), it signed an investment-guarantee agreement that gave us the right to impose our will on all Dominican policies pertaining to such investment. Next, the Council indicated it would join the United States-conceived, Panama-proposed Anti-Castro Front.[5] And finally, it destroyed that great Freedom it had allowed at first. The Council gave orders that all "disturbing" Leftists be rounded up; literally hundreds were deported. The Dominican Republic had obviously "matured," as a USIA man told me. I suppose that also meant it was ready for elections.

By the end of 1962, the Dominican Republic had 18 or more legal parties of which three were major: The National Civic Union (UCN), the Democratic Revolutionary Party (PRD) and the 14 of June Movement (1J4). Top among the minor parties was the Social Democratic Alliance (ASD).

Oldest and best known was the UCN. But it was losing

[5] Officially proposed by Oligarch Gilberto Arias, Panama's Finance Minister, the Front was to be a "NATO-type military alliance for defensive as well as offensive purposes" (another invasion of Cuba?) and was to include: Guatemala, El Salvador, Nicaragua, and Haiti (dictatorships), Honduras, Panama, and Colombia (corrupt oligarchies), and Costa Rica and Venezuela. The Front never materialized as an official body.

its popular appeal because of the extreme reactionary tend-
encies of its leaders. The PRD, headed by Juan Bosch,
was considered within the Center. It had lost some of its
moderate Left following, and Bosch, who had been hailed
as a hero when he returned from exile, had slowly been
discredited in the eyes of university students. His strength
with peasants, however, had remained solid; he had been
the first to organize them. The 1J4 movement, once strong,
had been weakened considerably by the Castro issue: it
had split in two, the right wing being anti-Castro, the left
wing pro-Castro and now persecuted. The former currently
dominated the party machinery, but the latter (officially
ousted) had the adherence of the majority of members. As
a consequence the 1J4 right-wing leadership had announced
that the party would boycott the election, a way out without
losing face at the polls.

The ASD was moderate insofar as it did not want to
nationalize more industries or lands, and Left in so far
as it did not want to sell to private firms what the government owned. But it had yet to win the support of youths then
backing the more Leftist MPD (Dominican Popular Movement).

Just before the elections finally took place in December,
Dominican churchmen publicly accused Bosch of being
a Communist. Nothing could have helped Bosch's chances
more. He eloquently denied the charge, described himself
as the victim of a Rightist plot—and won. For the next
nine months, Bosch accomplished little, but talked a lot,
and what he said sounded much too radical to the army
and the rich. The professional anti-Communist agitators
in this country began to stir up trouble, and launched a
concerted campaign against him. What most irritated these
self-styled defenders of democracy was that Bosch was a
true democrat, that is, he refused to arrest or persecute Communists unless actually caught violating a law. "We have
not returned to this country to persecute," said Bosch who
had lived out most of Trujillo's 32-year dictatorship in
exile. That in itself must have seemed plenty of evidence
to a Miami news reporter, for example, who claimed that
"Communist penetration of the Dominican Republic is
progressing with incredible speed and efficiency." Naturally,
the reporter did not name a single Communist in the Bosch
government.

When the old gangsters both in the armed forces and in the oligarchy thought that "free world" opinion had finally swung against Bosch, they acted. In a lightning-fast, bloodless coup, they had him deposed, arrested, and shipped off to exile. Jails were then immediately filled with new inmates, and again the Dominican Republic was clamped under a rigid, vicious, repressive dictatorship—all in the glorious name of saving the country from Communism. But this time it was too callous, too phony and too brutal. Said *Newsweek*: "Democracy was being saved from Communism by getting rid of democracy."

PART IV: The Rebels

Not all Latin American governments are at the exclusive service of the oligarchies. Mexico, as we have seen, has had its revolution and has had its Cárdenas. Brazil is torn between the oligarchy and the Nationalists, and though the former rule through the Army now, the outcome is not certain. And there are three more countries where some or many social reforms have been instituted—as a result of revolution.

In all three cases that revolution has been corrupted, frustrated, or betrayed. In Costa Rica the betrayal has been so thorough that only one basic reform remains. In Uruguay, where the revolution was peaceful, progress has been turned into regression. In Bolivia, whose structural upheaval was both the purest and the most complete, progress seems to go hand-in-hand with corruption.

Nevertheless the revolutions have become part of the three countries' consciences. And the very existence of this conscience is enough to warrant hope—for a brighter future without strife.

Chapter 14

Costa Rica

Democracy has ruled Costa Rica for a long time. With only 1,200,000 inhabitants, of whom 90 percent are white, this small yet fertile agricultural country has suffered from little bloodshed, while achieving a good literacy ratio. It has felt almost no concern for its neighbors (whom it regards, even today, with contempt) and has exhibited no desire to join them in federations, unions, or regional treaties. And, unlike them, Costa Rica has seen many free elections and almost as many freely adhered-to governmental transitions.

However, Costa Rica has been, in the words of one historian, "the perfect oligarchical democracy." The free elections were always limited to the choice of one big name over another, and the people who were free to vote could not participate in the choosing.

Nevertheless, Costa Rica never became the land of two, ten, or twenty *latifundios*. Because the population was not made up of former slaves or defeated Indians but of immigrant settlers who resisted peonage, the country has been saved from overpowering land barons. Some exist, true. But most farmers work their own lands, not someone else's. This is not to imply that Costa Rica does not need an agrarian reform (it does: there are 47,286 farms; 44,674, or 94.5 percent, occupy only 38.8 percent of the land; 59.3 percent covers 6.7 percent of the land; and just 50, or 0.1 percent, of the farms take up 20.95 percent of the land). However, the land distribution is fairer in Costa Rica than in other Latin American countries.

And to the people of Costa Rica, one man was going to make it fairer still. He was José ("Pepé") Figueres, modern Costa Rica's greatest hope and biggest failure.

Figueres himself was a landowner, as were his parents, immigrants from Catalonia. Born in 1906, he studied in his home town, then at a *liceo* in San José, the capital, and finally in the United States, where he took courses at M.I.T. After he returned to Costa Rica in 1928, he bought a rundown plantation, called it La Lucha (The Struggle) and applying modern technology, developed it into a wealthy enterprise employing scores of hands. Interested in economics and politics, Figueres finally entered the public realm by attacking the regime of President Rafael Calderón Guardia in a violent speech on the radio in 1942. Jailed, then deported, he rallied other opponents, wrote numerous articles, formed the Social Democratic Party, and returned for the 1944 elections.

Perhaps a clue to his later position can be seen in the fact that he had no difficulty joining Otilio Ulate, the conservative publisher of *El Diario de Costa Rica,* to back conservative candidate León Cortés—who was defeated. But in 1948 the Ulate-Figueres alliance was on again, this time in support of Ulate himself.

Ulate won. But Calderón Guardia, who had lost in a comeback try, had himself proclaimed President by Congress. A civil war erupted. The regular national defense forces supported the government, but they were defeated by the Figueres forces. Pepé, thereupon, set up a revolutionary junta, headed by himself, and decreed a 10 percent tax on capital, nationalized the banks, and gained continent-wide admiration before turning over the Presidency to Ulate.

While Ulate did nothing until 1953, Figueres worked his farm, was divorced by his wife (a United States citizen), traveled to the United States, married another of our girls, dissolved the Social Democratic Party, and launched a newly formed National Liberation Party into the 1953 elections. Naturally, he was its presidential candidate. His opponent was one Mario Echandi Jiménez, a member of Ulate's Cabinet. Figueres won, and ruled Costa Rica until 1958.

All Latin America expected a reign of true social justice. All Latin America expected a national revolutionary evolution. Figueres was known to be anti-Communist and anti-imperialist, for industrialization by home capital or by state enterprises, and against foreign exploitation. As late as August 31, 1953 (two months before his inauguration as President), Pepé had written (in *New Leader*):

> Foreign ownership of a large segment of a country's economy or territory constitutes "economic occupation." This is no wild fancy, I know. I am a citizen of a "banana republic." I know how it feels to have a state within a state; to play host to a privileged business that does not abide by the law of the land, but by the terms of its own "concessions," by the terms of economic occupation.
> . . .
> Large ownership is . . . a means of limiting local authority, especially when it operates under "contract loans" or discriminatory "concessions" such as the colonial companies have exacted from the weak nations. It would be wise if the United States withdrew economic occupation.
> . . .

But instead of helping our withdrawal, Figueres assured us a long life in Costa Rica. For a mere 30 percent of profits, he signed a new contract with United Fruit. Jubilant, the company immediately pressed the other "banana republics" to do likewise, and thus, thanks to Figueres, it enhanced its position in Central America.

Figueres had once also told his United States audience to keep foreign investment out of Costa Rica: "Please do not offer us as a remedy the very grievances of which we complain!" Yet, as President, he not only kept us in Costa Rica but also increased our power by giving Standard Fruit Company a "concession" to establish plantations all over Costa Rica's Atlantic coast (which United Fruit had abandoned in the 1920's).

Figueres' betrayal cost him his popularity. In 1958 the National Liberation candidate, Francisco Orlich, one of Pepé's good friends and his Minister of Public Works, was defeated. Elected instead was the same Mario Echandi whom Figueres' PLN had beaten five years before. Echandi's reactionary regime managed to be even worse than Figueres'.

Thus, in 1962, Orlich was finally elected. Immediately, he set out to prove he could be even more reactionary than Echandi. He clamped down on Leftist opponents, banned the Communist newspaper *Adelante* which had operated freely (and without much success) under Echandi, and instead of enacting needed reforms, spent his time plotting Caribbean alliances to bring Castro down (and, naturally, appealed to the United States for dollars). Once again, Costa Ricans have little hope for a New Deal.

Through Orlich, Figueres is once again in power. But his interests are not at home, despite his formidable assets—a rum factory, a coffee plantation, and hefty reimbursement for "damages" in the 1948 revolution. His current political concern eyes, instead, the international front. He travels constantly, delivering lectures—especially in the United States. And under his patronage, plus the backing of Peru's APRA, Venezuela's AD, and New York's Institute of International Labor Research, financed by the Kaplan Fund,[1] the pleasant hills near San José gained a strange new "school," called the International Institute for Political Education. This *Instituto* has become the center of Latin American counter-revolutionary activity. It is directed by a priest, Benjamín Nuñez, who was the "chaplain" of Figueres' revolutionary forces in 1948, and is staffed by "anti-Communist" experts from the United States and Latin America. After a long close look and a longer hard talk with Nuñez, I began to understand why some Latin Americans refer to the institute as the "Capitalist Comintern," and to backers Figueres, Betancourt, and Haya de la Torre as the "Capitalist Politburo's messengers." It seemed to me as if the whole purpose of the school was not so much how to get reforms without revolutions—as it claims—but rather how to convince Latin Americans that the best road to development is more United States investment. It is indeed a strange form of reconquest being taught in San José's Institute for Political Education.

Figueres' and the PLN's current preoccupation not withstanding, there is still hope for Costa Rica. Its banks are nationalized. Its planning boards are respected and able.

[1] Millionaire Jacob M. Kaplan made some of his money in Batista's Cuba and Trujillo's Dominican Republic, but most of it with Welch juices.

Its Church influence, never directed too strongly against reforms, is nonpolitical. Its schools and teachers are sufficient for the population. And, most important of all, Costa Rica has no regular army; its civilian security corps is not an oligarchical tool. Now Costa Rica needs a leader whose only preoccupation will be the life and conditions of his people.

Chapter 15

Uruguay

"An economic and political Utopia," have said the experts about Uruguay for decades. Smaller than the state of Nebraska and sandwiched along the South Atlantic coast by Latin America's two giants, Brazil and Argentina, it is the world's first welfare state. It had the eight-hour day before the United States, government-owned monopolies before the Russian Revolution, and established democratic traditions before most other Latin American nations held a free election. Basically a middle-class country, Uruguay has few poor and virtually no illiterates. As early as 1885, one English writer described it as the "perfect Republic."

But Uruguay is most imperfect. Its economic ills—currently a big recession and heavy unemployment—are not temporary: the whole economic structure is sick. Its ineffective executive body is not the result of a bad election: the whole political machinery is crippled. Its way of life—characterized by *coima,* or bribes—is not a momentary lapse: the whole moral makeup is poisoned.

Legally part of Spain's Rio de la Plata viceroyalty, and separated from Argentina by the River Plate, Uruguay until the seventeenth century was inhabited only by the fierce and primitive Charrúa Indians, who made a sport out of hunting the white man. Then, in 1603, Hernando Arias, the colony's first *criollo* (locally born) governor, ordered one hundred head of cattle and one hundred horses and mares released across the river, and Argentina's landless gauchos soon followed to track them down. Swift and slippery, strong and stubborn, the gauchos pursued the Charrúas with unrelenting cruelty, drove them out of Uruguay, and then established a new nation.

War between England and Spain in 1807 brought English occupation troops to Montevideo, Uruguay's elegant capital at the mouth of the River Plate. It also brought British merchant ships, prosperity, and a feeling of independence from the rest of the colony. Thus, when Argentina overthrew Spanish domination in 1810, Montevideo's merchants refused to accept Buenos Aires as its new ruler. But to the poor gauchos of the interior, where Montevideo's wealth never filtered, Argentina was their country. They declared their allegiance to Buenos Aires and war to Montevideo.

The gauchos were led by José Gervasio Artigas. A hawk-nosed, fair-skinned *caudillo*, Artigas is one of the most noble heroes in Latin American history. Incorruptible and indefatigable, he was a self-taught idealist who spent weeks studying our Constitution, months working out Latin America's first agrarian reform, years fighting all oppressors. With bands of ill-equipped, ill-trained gauchos always vastly outnumbered, he lost every battle except his first, but won unswerving admiration from the very men he led to defeat. His only concrete achievement was the formation of the Liga Federal, a short-lived United States-style federal league of provinces. Still known as the Protector of the Free People, Artigas is Uruguay's national hero.

England finally gave Uruguayans their independence in 1828. Hoping to assure its markets in the Rio de la Plata, it forced both Brazil and Argentina to recognize Uruguay as a free buffer state of 60,000 inhabitants.

Independence, however, did not bring peace. Constantly under attack, Montevideo became, as the French writer Alexander Dumas put it, "the new Troy." In one such attack—a nine-year siege by the Argentine dictator Juan Manuel de Rosas—the Uruguayans fighting with Rosas identified themselves by wearing white emblems. Those defending Montevideo chose the color of an Italian exile, the Republican patriot Giuseppe Garibaldi. Thus were born Uruguay's two traditional parties: the Blancos and the Colorados.

Rosas lost. The Colorados ruled—badly until Uruguay's second great hero emerged: José Batlle y Ordóñez.

The son of a Colorado President, Batlle was born in 1856 in a bed of politics. As a young man strongly influenced by French positivism and German idealism and, later, by small doses of Marx brought secondhand by traveling Uruguayan university economists, Batlle founded and edited *El Día,* which rapidly became (and still is) Uruguay's Number One daily, using its columns to preach reforms. "There is great injustice in the enormous gap between the rich and the poor," he wrote. "The gap must be narrowed—and it is the duty of the state to attempt that task."

During his two presidencies (1903-1907; 1911-1915), Batlle practiced what he preached. He gave (or lived to influence the enactment of) much social legislation—the eight-hour day, a day of rest for every five of work, mandatory severance pay, minimum wages, unemployment compensation, old-age pensions, and paid vacations. He legalized divorces, abolished capital punishment and bullfighting, established a state mortgage bank, made education free through university. To finance government expenses he levied taxes on capital, real estate, insurance, sales, profits, horse racing, and luxury items, but not on incomes, which he felt would discourage personal initiative.

According to the Constitution of 1830, a President was not allowed to seek reelection for more than two terms. Batlle obeyed it voluntarily—a first in Uruguayan politics. But until his death in 1929, his influence remained unchallenged—and the drums of welfare statism continued to roll. Insurance, railway, electricity, and alcohol companies were nationalized. The state launched its own oil, cement, meat-packing, and fish-processing corporations and took over the principal banks. By 1919 Church was separated from the State so completely that even religious holidays were secularized; Christmas, for example, became "Family Day." Batlle also made the Supreme Court inviolable, outlawed arbitrary arrests, searches, and seizures, and weakened the executive by setting up a popularly elected Council of Government with power equal to that of the President.

To make sure that no Uruguayan wielded too much power, Batlle wanted to abolish the four-year presidency altogether. It wasn't until 1952, however, that his nephew, President Luís Batlle Berres, got such a reform enacted into law. Since then, Uruguay has been ruled by a nine-man National Council of Government. Because both the Blanco and the

Colorado parties are divided into scores of factions and subfactions, makeup of the Council was devised thus: six councilors from the majority faction of the winning party; two from the majority faction of the first minority party; and one from the second-place faction of that party. Thus the Council often has no representatives from the second faction of the winning party even though that faction may draw more votes than all factions of the minority party put together. For purely protocol purposes the first four leaders of the majority faction of the majority party rule one year each as Council presidents. But they exercise no more power than any of their colleagues.

With this power-weak executive body, Batlle's transformation of Uruguay became complete. As one Latin American expert has put it: "Neither Napoleon nor Hitler, Atatürk nor Gandhi influenced a single country as much or as variously as Batlle did his own." Indeed, Batlle was one of the world's truly great pioneer advocates of social reforms and social justice.

But what Batlle and his successors failed to realize was that their welfare state ultimately depended on the interior of the country for its success. Uruguay has no minerals, no petroleum, in fact, no natural wealth except its fields. Its only valuable exports are meat, hides, and wool. Industry is artificial, owing its existence to dollar-dear imports of foreign raw materials. But instead of focusing his attention on the interior, Batlle looked at his capital and stimulated local industry—centered in Montevideo—by setting up high tariff walls.

Even tariffs were not enough. So, in 1931, the Colorados put into effect an intricate system of multiple exchanges whereby exporters were compelled to turn their earned foreign currency to the government at one peso price while importers of raw materials bought them back at another. As Montevideo's industry swelled, more and more gauchos and farmhands abandoned the interior (the capital now holds one-third of Uruguay's 2,800,000 people). And as the interior's dollars ran shorter and shorter, farmers and ranchers stopped buying machinery or fertilizers, causing fields to deteriorate. Today, according to estimates of the United Nation's Food and Agriculture Organization, Uruguayan fields are producing only one-third of their potential.

Poor fields mean poor cattle. And because meat prices

to the domestic consumer were held low by price control, meatpacking plants became unprofitable. Result: meat exports, traditionally Uruguay's second, fell sharply while cattle contraband into Brazil intensified. In 1956 the government estimated that some 300,000 heads were being sneaked across the border illegally every year.

Nevertheless, because Batlle's party had given Uruguayans the highest standard of living (in real distributed terms) south of the Rio Grande, it seemed that few Uruguayans were willing to risk a change. "The welfare state is now a way of life in Uruguay," wrote Professor of Latin American History Lewis Hanke, "and no politician can hope to win votes by advocating austerity, hard work, and the sacrifices of benefits enjoyed for many years." It seemed as if the Colorados would continue to rule Uruguay for decades.

But when the returns were in, on a warm election day in November, 1958, even Montevideo had gone Blanco. After ninety-three long years, the Colorado reign was over. The new Blanco government freed the peso, abolished import quotas, regularized and standardized import duties (which Colorado governments previously levied arbitrarily or as political weapons), set up Uruguay's first (and very mild) income tax, and replaced old profit-tax regulations with new ones that are more liberal for reinvestment and that exempt new industry or new products for ten years and export industry forever.

However, the Blancos, led by the late demagogue Benito Nardone, an ex-Colorado and then radio announcer turned "defender" of the interior despite the fact he had been brought up in Montevideo, also ordered the army's structure revamped. Mostly made up of 10,000 ignorant unemployeds, the army had rarely meddled in Uruguayan politics. Now it was trained to cope with "civil disturbances" and educated to defend "democratic institutions." This new army was already visible by April, 1961, when the anti-Castro invasion of Cuba sparked one of the biggest anti-United States rallies in recent Uruguayan history. The army, out in full force, convinced the demonstrators to behave.

Nardone, incidentally, was also most instrumental in the organization of various "anti-Communist" shock troops. One is ALERTA, set up somewhat like our own minutemen —armed and briefed, trained and disciplined by army regulars, "off duty" of course. Another is MEDL (Student Movement

for the Defense of Liberty); its members throw stink bombs
into university meetings, beat up opposition leaders, and
in 1962 cut or burned swastikas in the flesh of numerous
"Communist" students, even on the breasts of two young
co-eds, one of whom was a Paraguayan exile whose only
"Communist crime" was to have talked against Dictator
Stroessner.

The United States has apparently been pleased with the
Blanco regime. By following the suggestions of the International Monetary Fund, Uruguay abandoned the import
quotas that the Colorados used to have. This meant that
our goods could go into Uruguay faster and in bigger
quantities than before. Furthermore, the large landowners
of Uruguay's interior were again making profits. Wool
exports went up, bringing in more money to launch pasture-
improvement projects that would eventually result in more
and better cattle.

But these measures in no way guarantee better living
conditions for Uruguay's peons; they work for masters
who spend half their time in Montevideo, and sometimes
the other half in Paris—proving that what is wrong with
Uruguay's welfare state is its incompleteness. Batlle y Ordóñez
was a city politician. He and his successors failed to realize
that reforms in the city are not reforms in the country. Where
reforms were applied, the results were almost always credit-
able. Uruguay's phones are state-owned, and they are cheaper
and work better than anywhere else in Latin America, despite
the shortages and waiting lists. Electricity is state-owned,
yet it benefits more people and its rates are cheaper. The
state-owned cement, alcohol, and sugar corporations were
efficient and profitable until 1962 when the ruling Blancos
packed them with featherbedders before the general elections,
and sank the corporations into the red. Even the mismanaged,
autonomous aviation company PLUNA, which like all
other airlines in the world runs at a deficit and must receive
subsidies, is Latin America's most pleasant airline, and the
only one on the continent with an absolutely perfect safety
record.

Uruguay's state-run or -owned corporations or bureaus
are not, however, free from corruption or immorality. On
the contrary, Batlle's suspicion of all politicians led them
to institute so many divisions of power that responsibility
is extremely hard to locate. This in turn has created a

system of patronage, influence peddling, and degenerate political practices that affects many Uruguayans directly.

One of the worst examples of total corruption is found in the Caja de Jubilaciones, the state Pension Funds Bureau. In theory, Uruguay's pension system is one of the world's most commendable. Financed by payroll deductions of 14 to 17 percent matched by the employer, a pension is available by law to any Uruguayan at the age of fifty-five after thirty years of work or at sixty after ten. The retired worker is entitled to his highest gross salary, adjusted periodically to the rise in the cost of living. But because 80,000 are having their applications processed at any one time and 15,000 more apply each year while at most only 1,000 are approved each month, the waiting list increases by at least 3,000 every year. Thus, just to reach the approval-possibility stage is a feat of endurance. Paper work takes a year. From there to approval can take up to ten years, depending on the size of the applicant's bribe offers.

I visited the Caja's huge, ever-crowded concrete quarters near Montevideo's downtown, and found wrinkled old men and frail aged women sitting on the long narrow rows of wooden benches, dreaming for years on end, of the day they would stop being a burden to their children. They came early, they left late, and they returned the next day. Some played cards. Others grumbled in bunches, sipping cold maté tea and munching toasted sugar-dipped peanuts, Uruguay's equivalent of popcorn. One former textile worker named Alfredo had been waiting since 1953. One lacemaker named Luisa had gone to the Caja every single workday since 1952. And there was even one white-haired old man the others affectionately called "El Negro," who had sold his watch, his two sets of cufflinks, his only horse, the stove he used to warm his one-room shack, and his only overcoat to raise enough money to bribe his way to his pension. Having got it in June, 1961, he found the habit of ten long years of waiting unshakable: he still goes to the Caja every day.

The politicians responsible for (that is, who profit from) the Caja's slowness—and such profiteers are found all the way up to the top—are criminals. They are members of both traditional parties, and hence are still in power, since in the general elections of November 1962, these parties were victorious—as expected. The Blancos won a majority in the Council (though Nardone's faction was trounced), the Colorados in Montevideo.

I would agree with Nationalists that these criminals should be jailed for decades, if not put against a wall and shot. But a few executions to modernize and especially to moralize Uruguay's welfare state is not the same thing as starting a new revolution. Uruguay has experienced decent, efficient governments. It went a long way toward its reconquest half a century ago. Now it needs to push on to the necessary conclusions.

Chapter 16

Bolivia

Early in 1952 the people of Bolivia—farmers, miners, intellectuals—revolted against the dictatorial regime of a military junta. With stones and spears, pistols and rifles, they fought against a German-trained army equipped with cannons and tanks. This was the famous revolt of the Movimiento Nacionalista Revolucionario (MNR), one of whose founders, Hernán Siles Suazo, stood proudly in the battles' front rank.

Another founder, Victor Paz Estenssoro, who had won the presidency in the previous year's election but had been prevented from taking it by the junta, rushed home from exile. By the time he arrived in La Paz, Bolivia's main city and government seat (Sucre is the official capital, and lies at an altitude of 12,130 feet in a canyon surrounded by snow-topped Andes peaks), the rebellion had ended, successfully.

Paz was proclaimed President, and from the balcony of Government Palace he committed himself and the new MNR regime to a profound social revolution—with democracy.

Today, Paz is again President; the MNR has ruled a dozen solid years; the social revolution has been carried out—democratically and with all possible vigor—and Bolivia is in a mess.

It would have taken a miracle for it to be otherwise. Twice the size of Spain, Bolivia is a landlocked nation, 75 percent of whose 3,500,000 inhabitants live in one-tenth of the

219

area—at 10,000 feet or more above sea level. Peaks of between 19,000 and 21,420 feet and a number of active volcanoes separate it from Chile, to which it lost its nitrate land and the Pacific port of Antofagasta during the War of the Pacific (1879-1883). On the *Altiplano,* a windswept, treeless 38,000-square-mile plateau 13,000 feet high, almost 1,000,000 Indians try to cheat death by raising sheep, potatoes, corn, and hot peppers in between frosts, or catch occasional salmon in hazardous Lake Titicaca. The lake is 100 miles long, 85 miles wide, and up to 1,500 feet deep—at 12,507 feet above sea level it is the world's highest navigable body of water.

It is on the lake's southern shore that the pre-Inca, Aymara-speaking Tiwanaku (*Tihuanaco* in Spanish) Indians flourished from 600 B.C. to around A.D. 900. Three hundred-odd years later, the Quechua-speaking Incas of Cuzco (Peru) conquered the lake area and eventually (by 1315) the rest of Bolivia. The Spaniards came next, and soon the excellent Inca communication and economic system disintegrated, but not the Indian's will to be free. Revolutions broke out in 1661, 1730, and from 1776 to 1780 (Indians even managed to capture La Paz for a few days in 1780). But not until 1825 was Bolivia proclaimed independent.

Independence, however, did not bring better living conditions for the Indians who still make up 75 percent of the population (and 60 percent of them speak only Aymara or Quechua). Working from sun to moon for scraps of food and a windowless one-room mud hut (they did not receive wages, and until 1952 were totally outside the money economy), the Indians were also forced to provide landlords, living in the cities (mainly La Paz), domestic help—and bed companions—from their own families. Both the army and police were the oligarchy's tool, and any complaints brought on vicious massacres of Indians, including their wives and children. Bolivia's rich tin mines (which account for up to 80 percent of the country's export earnings) were run like seventeenth century pits, and any miner's attempt at organization was punished with murder.

Nevertheless, the miners did organize, and rebel, as did the farmers. Understandably, then, the victorious MNR set about, almost at once, to correct their rank-and-file's living conditions. The bigger tin mines (producing 70 percent of the minerals) were nationalized, as were some others (copper, silver, gold) and some of the oil wells. Unions were recognized and allowed active participation in government mine policies. The vote was given to all Bolivians, literate or not. And, on August 2, 1953, land reform was decreed.

Perhaps because United States interests were not involved— most nationalized mines were either British or Bolivian—we decided to back the MNR. We started pouring in aid, and eventually even helped support Comibol, the newly formed government mine corporation. An International Co-operation Administration (ICA, now called AID) team dispensed technical advice, chipped in on the effort to modernize health, education, and transport conditions.

More important than all that, however, was what the MNR revolution signified to the Indian. Free to travel when and where he wished, a voting armed citizen, the owner of the land he tilled, he became, at long last, a Bolivian. Thus the MNR revolution has been dubbed the Indian Revolution, and this alone is enough to justify subsequent errors.

And errors came aplenty. Some were inevitable: peasants deserted their farms, flocked to the cities to become "white," remained unemployed, ideal receptors for extreme Right and Left rabble-rousers. Miners' unions became strong, tough, featherbedded, and many soon fell to the control of sharp Trotskylike agitators. Since neither President Paz nor his successor Siles wanted to restrict political or personal freedom, opportunists and demagogues abounded quickly. From the start, while most revolutionaries were frantically trying to put order in the chaos they had inherited, one Juan Lechín, an organizer who called himself a miner but whose main physical effort in life had been to play soccer, began to manipulate MNR forces until he became Bolivia's Vice President in 1960. He was outmaneuvered by Paz in 1964 and, together with Siles, was tossed out of the MNR for opposing Paz' reelection in 1964 (Paz won). Nevertheless, Lechín remains one of Bolivia's shrewdest and most powerful leaders; he claims to be a Leftist but is actually a Lechínist—and his forces are armed.

Meanwhile, Siles, appointed Ambassador to Uruguay when Paz succeeded him in 1960, began losing his grip on the MNR. To try to retighten it, to help clean out the vast corruption that had set in, to try to thwart the rising influence of MNR's younger militants whose impatience have pushed them closer to the extreme Left, and to try to break Lechín's hold on the miners' unions, Siles returned to Bolivia in April, 1962. He went back to Uruguay three weeks later, his mission a failure. That left Paz to go it almost alone.

After a dozen years Paz is a frustrated man who increasingly withdraws into mystical prophecies of "the course of history." Nevertheless, he is pushing on his reforms: land titles are being given to Indians at faster rates (3,400 in 1955, almost 45,000 in 1961 for a total 3,000,000 hectares distributed so far); roads are being built (some with AID funds) to help farmers market their produce; the new army is being put to work on public projects; and alphabetization and colonization of the fertile but until this year uninhabited eastern lowlands (500 families were settled there in 1962) are going forward.

Paz has also pressed forward with his plan to reform the oil industry, which now produces $15,000,000 a year after dipping from $14,700,000 in 1957 to $13,100,000 in 1959. He has tried to cut down on tin-mine featherbedding, one of the main reasons (another: a fall in world market prices) why mineral exports fell from $99,400,000 in 1956 to $69,000,000 in 1959, by relocating almost 10,000 miners from a total force of 36,000 mainly to a new sugar industry in Santa Cruz. Though it still costs Bolivia more than the world market price to produce a ton of tin, the government's Corporación de Fomento (development) is making some gains, from profits on new meat, sugar, cement, and rice industries.

The complete picture, nevertheless, is sad: Bolivia's economy remains at the near bankruptcy point. The overall production index continues to slip (106 in 1959, 105 in 1961). Manufactured goods are down from $55,700,000 in 1955 to $47,300,000 in 1960, to $42,900,000 in 1961, and to about $40,000,000 in 1962. One-fourth of Bolivia's imports (about $90,000,000 a year, 40 percent above exports) are for foodstuffs. Agriculture, despite the gains mentioned, continues downward, $132,600,000 in 1959, $118,700,000 in 1961. And on top of everything else, the mines are running out of minerals. "We can't do it alone," says Paz. "No matter how much we try, unless we get an opening on the sea—and a port—or unless we get massive aid, we cannot save Bolivia."

There are scores of tough young men who think they

can. The Nationalist Left (not Lechín) already controls key city MNR *comandos* (militia organizations) and they look to Castro for their ideas. "We can take over anytime," one such Leftist told me, "but we have to wait until a popular government comes to power in Chile, Peru, or Brazil—otherwise you can strangle us." The Right, too, is power-hungry and powerful. "The MNR will be destroyed in 1962—this I swear to you!" a fascist Falange Party leader told me, "—even if by civil war."

It was not, but it may still be. While top MNR leaders become accustomed to bourgeois comforts, the infighting of their lieutenants is destroying the party. Popular discontent (since 1956, the cost of living has gone up 60 percent, housing 2,452 percent) has almost put an end to the revolutionary myth. Gangsterism has become common in unions, fields, and political groups. And United States aid, higher per capita than anywhere else in the world, is badly directed into individual, often invisible projects, instead of for overall development through such sound organizations as the Corporación de Fomento (which has an all-encompassing, ambitious, but needed ten-year plan).

If the Alliance for Progress really wants to help push reforms, it should back the MNR still more. As one of our high embassy officials put it: "The MNR has carried out all the reforms the Alliance demands. Its Right is Fascist, its Left Communist. We should go all the way with it." With $1,000,000,000 limited to roads, electricity, and farm machinery, Bolivia could be totally self-sustaining in two years—even without a port. Whole fertile regions could be opened to life and industry.

Why do we not do it, as a propaganda showcase if nothing else? Is it possibly because, while we fear far-Right or far-Left takeover enough to send Bolivia some help, we are afraid that the MNR, a nationalistic popular movement, once solidly on its feet would become "independent"? It would. We could no longer pressure, demand, or expect. But, then, neither would Bolivia be our enemy. Bolivians would have simply reconquered Bolivia for themselves.

Chapter 17

—A Digression: United States—Latin American Inter-History

Latin America, as we have seen, is in deep need of reforms. Not just a new tax structure or an improved federal agency, not just putting the outs in and the ins out, is required. To toss out one oligarchy in favor of another will solve nothing, even if the new oligarchy is modern and progressive and willing to make less profits on its investments and ready to delegate some of its power to technicians. What is needed is a total rejuvenation, a change in attitude, habits, interests, and alliances, a change in philosophy and a change in practices.

"Self-help!" Adlai Stevenson told the Inter-American Press Association in an October, 1961, speech; "that is the key to much of our common concern." He added: "If it is lacking, no amount of money in outside aid will do much good" in Latin America. But what Stevenson failed to understand was that the peoples of Latin America are perfectly willing to help their countries—without outside aid. Those who are not are the ruling classes—who receive all the outside aid.

In that same month of October, sixty-six tax experts from Latin America (except Cuba, Haiti, and the Dominican Republic) met in Buenos Aires. They complained that the maximum tax on top-bracket Latin Americans is 37 percent (compared to 91 percent in the United States), that many countries do not even have profit, property, or income taxes, and that those that do lose $3 billion a year in delinquencies. No expert pointed out, however, that the reason most taxes do not get collected in Latin America is that the governments are run, directly or indirectly, by the richest, biggest, and the most corrupt tax dodgers around—that is, by the oligarchies.

The oligarchies, which Stevenson would have us help, are supported by the policies and the armies. These in turn, are trained, equipped, and oriented by the United States. We insist that private enterprise be safeguarded above all else. In Latin America the private enterprisers are the oligarchies. Thus, the circle is complete. There is no escape from it except to break it. Cuba, Bolivia, and Mexico tried to do so, more or less, and have had to rely upon force. Uruguay broke the circle long ago—without force but at a time when the free-enterprisers (mostly British) were not entrenched.

Many United States and some Latin American "Liberals," who see the vicious circle clearly enough, insist that Latin Americans are responsible for it. "If Latin Americans had any integrity," the liberals say, "they would not have let this circle clamp down on them." They ask: "Who is to blame when United Fruit obtains a giveaway concession? United Fruit, whose purpose is to make money, or the givers-away, whose purpose should be to protect their country's sovereignty?" Again: "Who is to blame, the United States, which sees danger wherever a Nationalist regime takes over a Latin American country and therefore tries to have it condemned, or the other Latin American countries that do condemn it and therefore help destroy it?" Once more: "Who is to blame, our pentagon, which thinks it is a good thing to arm Latin America, or Latin Americans who beg for and avidly accept the military aid with which they are dominated and repressed?"

The questions are loaded. True, the rulers of Latin America are *cipayos* ("sold out"), as Argentines call them. They are cowards, bigots, and swindlers. But they *are* the rulers precisely because they belong to the oligarchies that profit from the circle they impose upon their countries. Elections are meaningless; whenever popular candidates manage to win, the military tosses them out. Who have been the popular candidates in the last decades? Perón, the post-Perón Peronists, Vargas, Quadros, Alessandri *pére*, Velasco Ibarra, Arbenz— all forced out of office or prevented from taking it by military coups planned by and for the oligarchies. Even Haya de la Torre, forgetting whatever personal or financial interests may have guided him to compromise, is an excellent example: every time he has been allowed to campaign for election, he has won, and every time he has won, he has been deprived of power.

Never has any freely elected candidate from Right, Center, or Left who showed himself the least bit independent of our policies been able to last out his whole term. Always the forces that threw him out have been trained and equipped by and sometimes in the United States. The only exceptions have arisen when popular revolutions had previously destroyed these forces. Thus, the Latin American patriot, the Nationalist, the genuine reformer has had to buck us as well as local oligarchs. Today, if we are to understand him, we must not only accept this fact; we must also realize that to him all our aid, our treaties, our loans, and our military missions are evil.

The Latin American Nationalist has had too many examples of United States intervention in his continent during the last few years to let him forget the long list of our interventions in the past. Memories are short only when suffering is short. Latin Americans' memories are long because they are still suffering. And any policy that we may adopt, if it is aimed at reconquering Latin America as our friend, must be careful never to forget that such a long list exists. It goes back very far. Let us glance at it rapidly, starting only from the last century, in fact, from 1823 when the Monroe Doctrine was conceived.

To us, the Doctrine was and is virtuous because it warned non-hemisphere nations to stay out of the American continent. To Latin Americans it is despicable because it asserted no bar to our own ambitions.

One year later, in 1824, we made clear those ambitions in Cuba and Puerto Rico. Saying that the Monroe Doctrine "must not be interpreted as authorization for the weak to be insolent with the strong," our Secretary of State (later President) John Quincy Adams told Simón Bolívar, one of Latin America's great liberators, to stay out of (that is, not liberate) Cuba and Puerto Rico, which were still under the Spanish yoke. Bolívar, who was also miffed when we refused to attend the first Pan-American Conference called by him in Panama in 1826, said in 1829, "The United States appear to be destined by Providence to plague America with misery in the name of liberty."

In 1833 England invaded the Falkland Islands belonging to Argentina. Instead of invoking the Monroe Doctrine, we backed England, which still owns them today. Two years later England occupied the north coast of Honduras. Again we refused to remember the Doctrine. In 1836 England invaded Guatemala, tripling its Honduran territory, and in 1839 it took over the island of Roatán. Instead of moving against England, we moved against Mexico.

Hardly had Mexico gained its independence when United States landseekers swarmed over its borders, bringing Negro slaves with them despite the fact that slavery was outlawed in Mexico. When Mexico objected, the newcomers proclaimed their own republic, calling it Texas, and agitated against their hosts. When Mexico, understandably, tried to stamp out the rebels, we annexed Texas outright. In the war that ensued, we seized the whole region from Texas to the California coast. In its first generation, independent Mexico lost half its territory—and the richest part of it. Mexicans have never forgotten.

Nor did we let them forget. In the 1870's, for example, we complained that our residents in Mexico were being compelled to pay taxes—just like any Mexican. "Foreigners locating in a country accepted the mode of life of the people," retorted Mexico's President Porfirio Díaz. He added: "Foreigners should enjoy the same guarantees and the same legal protection as natives, but no more." Our President Hayes reacted by sending troops to the Rio Grande, and when Mexico protested, Hayes' Secretary of State scoffed at "the volatile and childish character of these people and their incapacity to treat a general question with calmness and without prejudice."

Mexicans are not the only Latin Americans to bear grudges. In 1853 former Secretary of State and then Senator John M. Clayton affiirmed that we "never can nor will want to recognize" the British Territory of Honduras; but three years later we did just that, by the Treaty of Dallas-Clarendon. Meanwhile, in 1854, we settled a minor argument with Nicaragua by sending a warship to bombard San Juan del Norte. Three years later, when one of our citizens was wounded there and President Buchanan levied a fine of $20,000, which Nicaragua could not pay, we repeated the operation, this time followed by a landing of our Marines, who proceeded to burn down whatever was still standing after the shelling. The next year we forced Nicaragua to sign the Cass-Irisarri Treaty, which gave us the right of free passage anywhere on Nicaraguan soil and the right to intervene in its affairs for whatever purpose we saw fit.

The period from 1840 to 1860 is also full of United States adventurers who tried (and often succeeded) to conquer parts of Latin America with private armies. They are known as "filibusters," the term which originally referred to the seventeenth century buccaneers who plundered the Spanish colonies and which in recent years has come to mean obstructionists in legislative assemblies. When Texas was still Mexican, United States filibusters were quite common. Two who were prominent there went on to gain ill-repute in Latin America.

One was John Anthony Quitman (1798-1858), a New York-born attorney who practiced law in Mississippi, then took part in the Texas Revolution, became a general, and served under Zachary Taylor in the Mexican War. Quitman later fought under General Winfield Scott at Veracruz, Puebla, and at the storming of Chapultepec, and was made governor of Mexico City during the 1847-1848 United States occupation. Returning to Mississippi, Quitman became governor and used the office to plan a filibuster expedition against Cuba, to be led by a Venezuelan adventurer named Narciso López (who had fought with Spain against Bolívar and in Spain against the Carlists). Indicted for violating the peace between Cuba (Spain) and the United States, Quitman resigned as governor but went unpunished. He was then elected to the House of Representatives, where he defended states' rights until his death.

Another, better known, filibuster was William Walker. Born in 1824 in Nashville, Tennessee, Walker was a qualified doctor, lawyer, and journalist by the age of twenty-four, but practiced none of these professions. A frail-looking—he weighed one hundred pounds—tight-lipped, restless egocentric, ascetic and puritan, he wandered about for a while, showing up in San Francisco in 1850 with an indestructible faith in America's "manifest destiny" (to run the world) and in his own destiny as America's prime mover. In 1853-1854 he led a private army into Lower California, was badly beaten, returned home, was tried for violating neutrality laws, and was acquitted by a sympathetic jury.

In 1855, better armed and with more men (financed by private United States corporations bent on exploiting Central America), Walker invaded Nicaragua, captured Granada and, though he failed to occupy Rivas, had himself "elected" President of Nicaragua in July, 1856. Though Guatemala's envoy to the United States, Antonio José de Irisarri, lodged a strong protest, President Franklin Pierce received Walker's messenger and toyed with the idea of recognizing Walker with the purpose of admitting Nicaragua to the Union as a slave state (Nicaragua had long outlawed slavery).

But Walker, whose main financial backers were competitors of Cornelius Vanderbilt's Accessory Transit Company, canceled Vanderbilt's concessions in Nicaragua. Vanderbilt thereupon threw his weight and power behind other Central American governments opposed to Walker. As a result he was defeated at Santa Rosa. He surrendered himself to the United States Navy at Rivas, and once again returned home a hero.

Again indicted for violating neutrality laws, he was again acquitted. In 1860 he invaded the Bay Islands, declared himself President of El Salvador and Honduras (where he decreed English to be the official language) as well as Nicaragua, "legalized" slavery (outlawed since 1823) and burned Granada to the ground. But once again he was defeated in battle and was forced to surrender, this time to the British Navy. Promptly turned over to Honduras, Walker was tried summarily and executed by a firing squad.

In detached retrospect, such filibusters as Quitman and Walker may appear colorful swashbucklers. But to Latin Americans there can be no detached retrospection. These men murdered, pillaged, and violated every law of the lands they invaded, and our government did not repudiate them. Worse still, we were on the point of profiting from their deeds, at least Walker's, and we considered them heroes. When one of our citizens, as we have seen, was molested by accident on Latin American soil, where he was neither welcome nor legally admitted, we exacted exorbitant compensations or carried out massacres as retribution. But when

Latin Americans suffered en masse because of our citizens, no payment was offered, no retribution dished out.

But let us return to our list. In 1860 we intervened in Honduras. In 1871 we occupied Samaná Bay in Santo Domingo. In 1881 we openly sided with Peru in its war against Chile in exchange for the port of Chimbote (for a United States naval base), nearby coal mines, and a railroad from the mines to the port. In 1885 our Senate's opposition to a Central American federation, because it might jeopardize an Atlantic-Pacific Canal owned by us, was enough to torpedo the project.

By then we were also intervening on the economic front through private individuals and corporations. In 1884-1885, a United States Government commercial commission toured Latin America, then reported: "Our countrymen easily lead in nearly every large town. . . . In every Republic will be found businessmen with wide circles of influence. . . . Moreover, resident merchants offer the best means to introduce and increase the use of our goods."

In 1895 President Cleveland forbade the British to deal directly with Venezuela in a border dispute between that country and Britain's recognized, pre-Monroe colony in Guiana. In 1897 (and again in 1899) we stopped federation attempts in Central America. Then, from 1898 on, we really got involved in the Caribbean.

After fabricating (with the agile aid of the Hearst press) a phony war with Spain, we annexed Puerto Rico and set up Cuba as a "republic" controlled by us through the Platt Amendment (1901). This amendment gave us the right to intervene in matters of "life, property, individual liberty" and "Cuban Independence"—that is, in everything. Our intentions were clear enough: in 1848 we had tried to buy Cuba for $100 million, and when that failed, the non-official but popular "Ostend Manifesto" asserted that "by every law, human and divine, the United States has the right to take it by force." In 1902, also, we "negotiated" the contract that gave us Guantánamo Bay as a naval base for $2,000 a year *for ever*. Until the 1934 abrogation of the Platt Amendment, we repeatedly intervened in Cuba with force of arms, fashioning the island republic into a United States protectorate. Cubans, as we have since learned, bear their grudge to the present.

Unfortunately, there are scores of such incidents. President

Theodore Roosevelt is known to every high-school student—in the United States as well as in Latin America. We are taught to respect him; Latin Americans do not need to be taught to loathe him. They know that in 1903 he fomented a revolution by the Province of Panama against Colombia, of which it was then part and where the Panama Canal was being built. T.R., who proudly proclaimed that "the United States does not have in the world—and does not need to have—more than one single friend, the United States," recognized Panama as an independent nation before fighting ended, leased and fortified the Canal Zone from the yet-to-be-established new government, turned Panama into a United States protectorate, and in 1911 boasted, "I took the Canal!"

Latin Americans can also read that in 1904 T.R. decreed that weakness or misbehavior by a Latin American government "which results in general loosening of the ties of civilized society . . . require intervention by some civilized nation." The Platt Amendment already limited "some civilized nation" to the United States, and to make our role clear T.R. further stated that we must assume the "duty" of intervention to safeguard the investments of the civilized world. His declaration became famous as the "Roosevelt Corollary to the Monroe Doctrine," and the Doctrine itself as "Dollar Diplomacy."

Armed with this Corollary, we intervened, before 1933, some sixty times in the affairs and territories of Latin America. Never, unfortunately, did we do so to bring a better life to our neighbors; always did we intervene for purely economic or territorial gain, or as the strong-arm agents for wealthy companies or high-class adventurers. One witness report has often been quoted in Latin America: "I helped make Mexico and especially Tampico safe for American oil interests in 1914. I helped make Haiti and Cuba a decent place for the National City Bank boys to collect revenue in. . . . I helped purify Nicaragua for the international banking house of Brown Brothers in 1909-1912. I brought light to the Dominican Republic for American sugar interest in 1916 [occupied officially until 1924, unofficially until 1934]. I helped make Honduras 'right' for American fruit companies in 1903. . . ." That harsh indictment was sired by a much-decorated United States patriot: Major General Smedley D. Butler of the United States Marine Corps.

The "American sugar interest" Butler mentions had by

then become powerful enough to intervene openly in Central American affairs. In Nicaragua in 1912, for example, United Fruit ships carried both men and supplies for rebel General Juan José Estrada. Another example follows. It is part of a letter supposedly written in 1920 but not published until 1949, though often reprinted since, including in the respected Mexican magazine *Cuadernos Americanos*, March-April, 1954). The letter is said to have been written by H. V. Rolston, who represented the United Fruit-owned Tela Railroad Company in Central America in 1912 when it obtained its major concession from the Honduran government. Tela later absorbed the Cortés Development Company, on whose stationery the letter was written, and later still obtained its best concessions as a consequence of the 1954 invasion of Guatemala (from Nicaraguan and Honduran bases). Addressed to the company's lawyer, the letter was sent by messenger who, it explains, also bears a gift for "Doña Anita," wife of Honduras' then President, General Rafael López Gutíerrez. It then lists ten "instructions" or steps of action that the lawyer must follow to increase company's power. Seven of these instructions are herewith quoted in full:

CORTES DEVELOPMENT COMPANY
Puerto Cortés, July 2, 1920

DR. LUIS MELARA
SAN PEDRO SULA

Dear Luis:
. . . .

3. We must obtain rigid contracts of such a nature that no one can compete against us, not even in the distant future, so that any enterprise that could establish and develop itself must be under our control and must adapt itself to our established principles.

4. We must obtain concessions, privileges, franchises, repeal of custom duties, freedom from all public liens, burdens and all those taxes and obligations which restrict our profits and those of our associates. We must erect a privileged situation in order to impose our commercial philosophy and our economic defense.

5. It is indispensable that we cultivate the imagination of these enslaved peoples [Central Americans], attracting them to the idea of our aggrandizement, and, in general, of the politicians and local bosses whom we have to use. Observation and careful study allow us to be certain that these, vilified by alcohol, are assimilable to our needs and directives; it is in our interest to concern ourselves with this privileged class, which we need at our exclusive benefit, so that it bows to our will; generally, these [the politicians and local bosses] as well as those [the enslaved peoples] have no convictions or character and still less patriotism, and they only crave for position and honors which, once obtained, we shall make appetizing.

6. These men must not act at their own initiative; they must act according to determining conditions, and under our direct control.

7. We must get rid of our friends who have been at our service [but] whom we consider vilified by their loyalty because sooner or later they will betray us, firing them without offending them and by treating them with some respect, but not using them any more. We do have a need for their country, for their natural resources, for their coasts and ports, which little by little we must acquire.

8. In general, all our words and thoughts must revolve around these words: power, material well-being, work camps, discipline and method. We must proceed with subtlety, without exposing ourselves to any idea which would indicate or justify [to others] our domineering pretensions. Summing up, no beneficial act or consideration or generous impulse. If our plans turn out badly, we would adopt a new course; we would become more modest, less demanding, more friendly and, maybe, good.

9. We must produce a disbowelment of the incipient economy of this country [Honduras], in order to increase and to help our aims. We have to prolong its tragic, tormented and revolutionary life; the wind must blow only on our sails and the water must only wet our keel.

. . . .

We'll be seeing you,
[signed] H. V. ROLSTON

Naturally, against such interventions, some local patriots

fought back. In Haiti, where our Marines landed in 1915 and stayed until 1934, two thousand "rebels" (called *Caco*) were killed before we "pacified" the island—after two disguised Marines sneaked into the jungle camp of *Caco* Chief Charlemagne Péralte and killed him.

In Nicaragua, however, one such "rebel" took much more than two soldiers to kill. On November 26, 1926, a Liberal Party revolt, headed by General Jóse María Moncada, overthrew the regime of President Emiliano Chamorro, a conservative general who had signed the 1916 Bryan-Chamorro Treaty giving us all ownership rights to a proposed Nicaragua Canal. That treaty ceded to us "in perpetuity and for all time" (Article I), "free from all taxation or other public charge, the exclusive proprietary rights necessary and convenient for the construction of a canal, *by way of any route over Nicaraguan territory*,"[1] for a price of $3,000,000 (Article III) that must remain in the United States against Nicaragua's debts or credits. The treaty, aside from being immoral, happened also to be illegal: Nicaragua's Constitution specifically forbade all public servants from signing any treaty unless authorized to do so by Congress (and Chamorro had not been so authorized).[2]

Elihu Root, a former United States Secretary of State who had conceived the Platt Amendment, reacted: "Can a treaty which is so serious for Nicaragua and in which perpetual rights are conceded in that territory, be celebrated with a President who, we have just cause to believe [he had been imposed on Nicaragua by us], does not represent more than one-fourth of those governed in the country, and who is kept in his position by our military forces and to whom, as a consequence of the treaty, we would pay a considerable sum of money so that he could dispose of it as President? It would cause me disgust to see the United States place itself in such a situation." (The Treaty was

[1] Italics mine.
[2] This provision was in Article 2 of the 1905 Constitution. To get around it, the government canceled it and convened a new Constitutional Congress. The article was reasserted; therefore a second Congress was convened and again the article was reaffirmed. A third Constitutional Congress was called, but once more the article was kept intact. The treaty remained illegal.

also declared illegal by the Court of Central American Justice in 1917).

Very unpopular, Chamorro had tried for the presidency in 1913 but, opposed by us then, he had failed. In 1917, however, he was backed by our cruisers *Chattanooga* and *San Diego,* and he succeeded. So in 1926 we opposed General Moncada, who wanted to overthrow Chamorro. To make sure this did not happen, Secretary of State Frank B. Kellog denounced Central America and Mexico as centers of Communist agitation, declared intervention in Nicaragua politically and militarily necessary, and dispatched our Marines in sixteen ships, commanded by Admiral Julian Latimer.

The Marines put down Moncada's rebellion and imposed a new election plan. But one of Moncada's men, a farmer and mining engineer named Augusto César Sandino, refused to accept it, and withdrew with his troops to a mountain town called El Ocotal. Marine Brigadier General Logan Feland thereupon ordered El Ocotal bombed and strafed, but Sandino escaped. When the news that three hundred Nicaraguans had been killed in the raid reached the United States, Illinois Governor Edward Dunne, among many others, protested our "indecency" (in an open letter to President Coolidge) and demanded that Feland be punished. Instead he was decorated, and El Ocotal was declared a "heroic victory."

Sandino, however, continued to fight, and we continued to bomb Nicaraguan villages—seventy in all (including Las Timas in Honduras by mistake). Finally, in 1933, our Marines were withdrawn, peace returned to Nicaragua, and General Sandino, never captured, retired to private life, launching a cooperative farm. Then, on February 21, 1934, he journeyed to the Presidential Palace for a conference. When he left he was caught in a trap set up by the new head of the National Guard—Anastasio Somoza. Sandino, his brother, and two of his generals were murdered. Soon afterward, Somoza seized the government and ruled with troops and terror for twenty-five years.

Not unnaturally Sandino has become the national hero of a Nicaragua still ruled by the Somoza clan. More damaging to us, however, he will remain for years to come Nicaragua's rallying cry against us. Even in his death, according to Latin Americans, we had a hand: he was killed on our orders.

This is their story, documented by their eyewitness reports:[3]

On February 21, 1934, Somoza called a "Great Council of Officials" of the National Guard at his house for "something very important." Present were sixteen officers, including two generals, a colonel, four majors, a captain, four first lieutenants and one second lieutenant. At 7:30 P.M. Somoza arrived (late) and said "I come from the United States ["*Norte-Americana*"] Embassy where I have just had a conference with Ambassador Arturo [Arthur] Bliss Lane, who has assured me that the government of Washington supports and recommends the elimination of Augusto César Sandino, for considering him a disturber to the peace of the country." Somoza thereupon explained the details of an ambush plan. Sandino left the palace shortly before 1:00 P.M. He was dead on the hour. Later that night, Guardsmen surrounded Sandino's cooperative farm Wiwilí and massacred three hundred unarmed men, women, and children. According to reports published at the time by San Salvador's *El Diario Latino*, the "elimination of Sandino's followers continued until May 5, 1934."

Despite these crimes, attributed to us, many Latin Americans began to think highly of Franklin Delano Roosevelt, who was then our President. His Good Neighbor Policy (announced on his very first official speech—his March 4, 1933, inauguration address) proved to have some substance. To the surprise of the 1933 Montevideo Inter-American Conference delegates, we voted in favor of a nonintervention pledge. F.D.R.'s Secretary of State Cordell Hull also promised Latin America tariff reductions and special trade agreements.

[3] Among them: Sofonías Salvatierra (a Cabinet minister at the time of Sandino's death). *Sandino o La Tragedia de un Pueblo* (Imprenta Europa, Madrid, 1934); Anastasio Somoza in *El Verdadero Sandino o El Calvario de las Segovias* (Tipografía Robelo, Managua, 1936) describes the events leading up to the murder, as well as the murder itself, in such a way that the other witnesses' accounts are verified; testimony of Lieutenant Abelardo Cuadra, one of the soldiers who fired on Sandino, published in pre-Castro Cuba's *Bohemia* (Year 41, No. 7, Feb. 13, 1949), in Costa Rica (in May, 1954), and in Buenos Aires (in a heavily documented biography of 800 pages in two volumes, *Sandino, General de Hombres Libres*, by Gregorio Selser, a reporter for *La Prensa*).

Though F.D.R. was trying to salvage our own depression-riddled economy, the Reciprocal Trade Act of June 12, 1934, was hailed by our neighboring businessmen, and was followed by Reciprocal Trade Agreements with Cuba, Haiti, Brazil, Colombia, Honduras, Nicaragua, Guatemala, Costa Rica, El Salvador, Ecuador, and Venezuela.

We were not yet good neighbors. Our navy again intervened in Cuba; said, correctly, its President Grau San Martín when he resigned in 1934, "I fell because Washington willed it." We continued to incense Haiti; and its delegate to the Montevideo Conference said, justifiably: the United States has brought "indescribable anguish" to Haiti. F.D.R. also invited Dictator Somoza to visit Washington in 1939, and we refused to abrogate the illegal Bryan-Chamorro Treaty. Wrote Luis Quintanilla, a pro-United States Mexican diplomat: "How could one speak of the inter-American solidarity, Pan Americanism, or Good Neighborliness when the stumbling block in the path of good relations was nothing less than the most powerful republic of the hemisphere? The situation could change only if and when the United States decided to abandon once and for all its imperialistic interventionism."

But we tried. Sumner Welles, F.D.R.'s Assistant Secretary of State admitted that "The effect of these [United States] interventions was to arouse widespread and bitter resentment against the United States." F.D.R. dumped the Platt Amendment, launched the Export-Import Banks (in 1934 and 1935), and ordered an end to Dollar Diplomacy. Furthermore, we reversed ourselves on the subject of our residents abroad. Welles said in 1935: "It is my belief that American capital invested abroad, in fact as well as in theory, be subordinate to the authority of the people of the country where it is located."

Latin Americans had a chance to test the sincerity of our new attitude in 1938 when Mexico's President Lázaro Cárdenas expropriated our oil companies. Cordell Hull was shocked. He dispatched strong notes urging Cárdenas to reconsider, then to guarantee prompt payment, and finally to abide to third-party arbitration. Relations were strained. But neither F.D.R. nor Hull ever questioned Mexico's right to expropriate property, and in the World War that soon followed, Mexico remained a firm ally. (Today, Latin Americans inevitably ask why did we not follow the same policy when Fidel Castro, then still not within the Communist camp, did in 1959 exactly what Cárdenas had done in 1938?)

In 1938, also, F.D.R. set up the Interdepartmental Committee of Cooperation with American Republics, which was, in effect, the precursor of today's Technical Aid Program of the Organization of American States (OAS). And during the war, the United States Department of Agriculture began helping Latin American nations to cope with soil-conservation problems; by June 2, 1945, ninety United States research teams were on the job in neighboring lands.

But under the cover of good neighborliness, F.D.R. encouraged an economic policy that has since become the major source of friction. Government and private interest, said F.D.R. early in 1940, should invest heavily in Latin America in order "to develop sources of raw materials needed in the United States." On September 26, 1940, he increased the Export-Import Bank's limitations from $100 million to $700 million, and by Pearl Harbor Day most Latin American nations had received "development" loans.[4] Neither the loans nor the investments, however, were aimed at helping Latin American nations cure their economic ills, which were mainly caused by reliance upon one crop or commodity productions. The loan's object, Roosevelt said, was to force those nations to become totally dependent, economically, on the United States.

That policy succeeded. When war began, we could demand (and received) valuable concessions, especially bases in the Caribbean. Latin America's economic dependency was further secured during the war through our Lend Lease program, which poured $262,762,000 worth of United States equipment into eighteen Latin American nations. The two excluded were Panama, virtually ours anyway, and Argentina.

Until World War II, F.D.R.'s hands-off Latin America policy applied to all twenty nations—whether governed by dictators, oligarchies, or popular governments. But during

---

[4] Some of the biggest: $45 million for Brazil's steel industry; $40 million for strategic Mexican highways; $30 million for Colombian, $25 million for Cuban, and $20 million for Chilean industrial needs.

most of the war, Argentina was ruled by neutralist (if not pro-Axis) generals, notably General Pedro Pabro Romírez. Though dictatorships, their regimes were ostensibly revolutionary and loudly nationalistic, which simply meant anti-imperialist, that is, anti-British and anti-United States.

In no condition to understand Argentina's problems, and naturally reluctant to help a potential enemy, F.D.R. gave it no aid, no Lend Lease and no letup from pressure. In 1943 it was excluded from the United Nations Conference on Food and Agriculture in Hot Springs, Virginia, and from the United Nations Reconstruction and Rehabilitation Administration Conference in Atlantic City, and in 1944 from the Bretton Woods Monetary and Banking Conference. Roosevelt cannot be criticized for his tough stand on Argentina; but even if only economically, he did steer us back onto the road he himself had abandoned—the road of United States intervention in Latin America.

President Harry Truman found the road to his liking. Late in 1945 he appointed as Assistant Secretary of State one Spruille Braden, up to then our Ambassador to Argentina, a vociferous advocate of help-only-your-servants policy. There was no doubting the significance of the appointment; Braden was chosen, said Secretary of State James F. Byrnes, for his "accurate interpretation of the policies of this government in its relations with the present government of Argentina."[5] To make certain no misunderstanding arose,

[5] To Latin Americans, Spruille Braden is a very familiar figure, the symbol of "imperialistic capitalism." Born in 1896 in Elkhorn, Montana, he is the son of William Braden, the founder of the Braden Copper Company (a subsidiary of Kennecott Copper Corporation since 1916) which, with Anaconda's Chile Exploration Co. and Andes Copper Mining Co., controls 90 percent of Chile's vast copper resources. In 1921 Spruille Braden was involved in the purchase of 3,145,000 hectares of Bolivian oilfields for Standard Oil of New Jersey (Rockefeller). This contract was widely criticized because of a 1916 law forbidding all new transfers of oil lands, but thanks to loopholes in the law and vested interests within the government, the transaction stood. Braden next appeared as a "peacemaker" in the Chaco "Petroleum War." After that, Braden became Ambassador to Colombia (where, later, his son served as president of Rockefeller's IBEC), then to Cuba (where he was accused

Secretary Byrnes further agreed, on November 27, 1945, to the Larreta Declaration, a note prepared by Uruguay's Foreign Minister Eduardo Rodríguez Larreta which justified occasional multilateral intervention in Latin America. No Latin American government, except Uruguay's, favored such intervention, and it was severely denounced then and since, but it was legally recognized by and incorporated into the Inter-American Treaty of Reciprocal Assistance Pact (Rio Treaty) signed in Rio de Janeiro in August, 1947. We convinced member hemisphere states to accept the intervention provision in exchange for the promise of military aid, which all Latin American militarists (in control of most governments) sought.

With multilateral intervention becoming an inherent part of Inter-American "cooperation," the OAS increased its strength and importance. To Latin Americans, however, multilateral intervention was just a fancy phrase for United States intervention, and the OAS came to represent a new institutional arm of the hated Monroe Doctrine. The OAS headquarters were in Washington, its operating funds mostly contributed by the United States, its delegates known as staunchly pro-United States. But if the OAS was discredited in Latin American eyes before President Eisenhower was inaugurated, it became dubbed a "tool for United States aggression" shortly thereafter.

For a while, Eisenhower and his Secretary of State, John Foster Dulles, exhibited little interest in Latin America. They were deaf to its problems and blind to its needs. Then, too late, they were shocked out of their slumber by events in Guatemala where United Fruit lands were to be expropriated for an Agrarian Reform. As Guatemala's regime

of interfering in financial circles to force the price of sugar to drop). In 1945 Braden spent six months in Argentina as United States Ambassador and was so outspokenly critical of the revolutionary regime that when Perón ran for President in 1946, his campaign slogan was "Braden or Perón?" (Perón won overwhelmingly—in a free election). Braden next irritated Latin Americans for his anti-Arbenz crusades (he was then United Fruit's public relations). More recently, Braden was a leader of our pro-Katanga Secession committees (and Union Minière, Katanga's huge mining corporation that has benefited most from secession, is partly owned by Rockefeller).

became more and more radical, our tactic was to smear it with the charge of Communism. Finally, in January, 1954, United States Ambassador to Guatemala John Peurifoy said: "Public opinion in the United States might force us to take some measures to prevent Guatemala from falling into the lap of international Communism."

To Latin Americans, that statement was already sheer interference. Then our motives were challenged when it was published that (1) Foster Dulles' law office had written the drafts of United Fruit Company's 1930 and 1936 agreements with Guatemala; (2) CIA Director Allen Dulles had been president of United Fruit; (3) John Moors Cabot (then Assistant Secretary of State for Inter-American Affairs and more recently United States ambassador to Brazil) and his family were United Fruit shareholders; and (4) Spruille Braden, then chief of United Fruit public relations, said in a Dartmouth College address on March 12, 1953, that to act with arms against a foreign country representing a Communist threat does not constitute intervention.

We did, of course, act with arms against Guatemala. Later, when its new ruler, Dictator Castillo Armas, was assassinated, Eisenhower called the death "a great loss to his own nation and to the entire free world. President Armas was a personal friend of mine." Ike then dispatched his brother Milton to represent him at the funeral.

Latin Americans were shocked. Everywhere, homage was paid to Romeo Vásquez Sánchez, the half-Indian Armas bodyguard who had shot down his boss. But the real damage had already been done: it is impossible to exaggerate the importance of our intervention in Guatemala in the shaping of Latin American public opinion; not one professor fails to mention it, not one student forgets to denounce it, not one popular politician misses the chance to brandish it as a warning to United States apologists.

As for the OAS, its chances of gaining respectability were permanently drowned at the 1954 Caracas conference, where we got Guatemala's radical regime branded Communist in what is termed in Latin America "the most infamous of victories." Unfortunately, the facts support the epithet: our partners, co-signers in the Caracas declaration, included Cuba's Fulgencio Batista, Nicaragua's Anastasio Somoza, Venezuela's Marcos Pérez Jiménez, Colombia's Gustavo Rojas Pinilla, Paraguay's Alfredo Stroessner, Peru's Manuel

Odría, Dominican Republic's Rafael Trujillo—some of the most vicious and bloody dictators Latin America has ever known.[6]

Is it strange, then, that Vice President Richard Nixon was hooted and heckled throughout his Latin American tour in the spring of 1958? When Nixon was stoned in Caracas, Venezuela's provisional President, Wolfgang Larrazábal, who had led the rebellion that ousted Dictator Pérez Jiménez, was asked why more precautions had not been taken. (Nixon had also been stoned in Peru.) Larrazábal was reported to have replied: "If I weren't an official and if I were younger, I would be in the streets too, to tell Nixon what we all think of United States complicity with Pérez Jiménez." It is ridiculous to blame Communists for the fiasco of Nixon's tour or, for that matter, of Eisenhower's own tour in 1960 which, despite our press reports to the contrary, was also a failure. Anti-Yankeeism was then the one characteristic common to most Latin American politicos, parties, and populations. Promising a new look at our Latin American policy, Washington acted as if it had understood the reasons—at long last.

Eisenhower had made the promise before, at the 1956 Panama meeting of the hemisphere's Chiefs of State. He had set up a Committee of Presidential Representatives that issued a few recommendations, appointed a few sub-committees, then quietly died. Now, after Nixon came home a new try was scheduled. Brazil's President Juscelino Kubitschek proposed an Operation Pan America to rebuild hemispheric solidarity, and in August, 1958, Dulles flew to Rio to give it our O.K. The hemisphere's Foreign Ministers assembled in Washington in September and called for a "Committee of 21" conference in December.

Experts from all twenty Latin American nations showed up on schedule; some, such as Brazil's Augusto Federico Schmidt, even had plans for raising Latin America's per capita income to $480 by 1980. But the delegate from Nation Number 21, United States Assistant Secretary for Economic Affairs Thomas Mann, passed off the plans ("the United States has never itself had any") as well as the conference, for he rarely attended, leaving as his substitute

---

[6] Only two nations abstained: Mexico and Argentina, both governed by mass-supported regimes.

an alternative ambassador to the OAS who was not even accredited to the "21."[7]

The conference collapsed. Said Chairman Alfonso López of Colombia: "Perhaps it is better that we go home and tell the truth. When the United States put on a 'new look' in Latin America, after the lamentable Nixon stonings, I had hopes, great expectations. I was mistaken."

To Latin Americans there was no "new look." True, we had softened our let's-be-friends-with-dictators policy, but, said our neighbors, only because of circumstances: Pérez Jiménez, Odría, and Rojas Pinilla were overthrown; Somoza, Sr., and Armas were dead; and Batista was having beard troubles.

And on Trujillo we had not changed, Latin Americans were convinced. It was not that our ambassadors in the Dominican Republic were overtly pro-Trujillo. That had been the case before when Ralph H. Ackerman praised Trujillo in a public speech as "your own illustrious President" and his bloody rule for "the great benefits he has already succeeded in bringing about." Nor was it because one or

[7] Our Latin American diplomats have been particularly bad. Under Truman and Eisenhower they were mostly business or political friends, and were taken by Latin Americans as proof of our disinterest. Arthur Gardner and Earl T. Smith, for example, did much to alienate Cubans before Castro ever came down from the Sierra Maestra. Edward J. Sparks, Kennedy's former envoy to Uruguay, was much too close to Dictator Castillo Armas when Sparks was Ike's ambassador to Guatemala. And in Nicaragua, Ambassador Thomas E. Whelan's chumminess with the Somozas during ten long years has done irreparable harm.

When Tom Whelan's good friend Tacho Somoza was shot in 1956, the former grain-and-potato warehouse owner from North Dakota became the trusted adviser of Tacho's two sons, President Luis and Guard Commander Tachito. "He has been almost like a father to me," Luis said before Whelan retired in 1961. Whelan, who managed not to learn one hundred Spanish words during ten years in Spanish-speaking Nicaragua, retorted, "Those boys are all right."

The boys used the Guard more than fifty times to keep in power. Tachito is a West Point graduate. Thanks to arrangements made by Whelan, the Guard's officers are mostly United-States-trained, and one-fourth of the enlisted men have been

two of our congressmen felt the same way. That, too, had happened when such undemocratic Democratic senators as James O. Eastland or Allen Ellender said, "I wish there were a Trujillo in every country of South and Central America."

In 1958, however, Latin America could point to our whole House of Representatives, which went on record as opposing unfavorable action toward Trujillo, and the whole House, after all, is almost the government.

What happened was this. After newspaper reports indicated fairly convincingly that an Oregon pilot named Gerald Lester Murphy, who worked for Trujillo, was involved in the kidnapping from New York of Columbia University History Teacher and Trujillo-critic Jesús de Galíndez and then himself disappeared, Oregon Representative Charles O. Porter tried to get the House to move against Trujillo. He suggested that we start "openly condemning dictatorial regimes and praising democratic ones, . . . giving wholehearted support to those . . . who are striving to liberate their countries . . . by democratic means." Specifically he proposed

schooled in our Panama Canal Zone schools. When Guardsmen shoot down Nicaraguan discontents, they use United States M-1 rifles, Browning automatics, and mortars. When they attack rioters or rebels, they use United States Mustangs, P-51's, and Sherman tanks. The Somozas have been Nicaragua's worst butchers in its history; but, said Whelan, "Nicaragua is our best friend in Latin America." To him, of course, Nicaragua was the Somozas. "They've never once voted against us at the United Nations," said Whelan to prove *his* point, which also proves mine.

Louisiana's late deLesseps Morrison, Kennedy's Ambassador to the OAS, was also a bad mistake. Deemed a racist who had a great softness toward Trujillo, Morrison was the source of much of Latin American delegates' irritation with our delegation at the first Punta del Este Conference. Perhaps the worst Kennedy appointment was old Adolf Berle, Jr., as head of the United States Task Force on Latin America, mainly because Berle's view of diplomacy is still stuck in the Roosevelt (F.D.R. and T.R.) eras. Extremely unpopular (and very undiplomatic) Kennedy ambassadors have included McClintock (to Argentina), James Loeb, Jr. (to Peru), and especially Thomas Mann (to Mexico), now President Johnson's Special Assistant on Latin America as well as Assistant Secretary of State for Inter-American Affairs.

two amendments to the bill authorizing "mutual-security" funds for the fiscal year of 1958: one would set up priorities for democratic regimes; the other would allow the State Department to cut out all aid to dictatorships.

Porter's opposition in the House was formidable. Pennsylvania Democrat Daniel J. Flood was against because "the Dominican Republic has been honored by that great enemy of Communism, Cardinal Spellman, for their [its] outstanding fight against this menace." New York Democrat Victor L. Anfuso, who also admitted being influenced by Cardinal Spellman, added: "I cannot overlook the fact that the Dominican Republic is an ally of the United States, that she is part of our Western Hemisphere defense, that we do business with her." Kentucky Republican John Marshall Robsion seemed to think that no United States ally should be criticized, no matter how evil: "The two nations cooperate in plans for hemisphere defense." As for George S. Long, one of Huey's brothers from Louisiana, he didn't believe Trujillo was bad at all, and even if he were, so long as he's anti-Communist, all crimes should be permitted him: "I have learned by experience not to be taken in by the word 'dictator.' . . . The Dominican Republic and its chief of the armed forces [Trujillo] . . . have always and unequivocably been on the side of God and Christianity. . . . They have been to us a vital and necessary bulwark against the encroachments of atheistic Communism." Even House Majority Leader John W. McCormack, Democrat from Massachusetts, was opposed, having already spoken of the "broad, humanitarian policies of Generalissimo Rafael Leonidas Trujillo Molina, L.L.D."

Other congressmen, less the defenders of Trujillo than of non-intervention, stressed United States pledges of never using economic means to intervene in Latin America. Others, in their heat to defend anti-Communist dictators, contradicted this by pointing out what good Guatemala Dictator Carlos Castillo Armas had done with the special favors (economic intervention) he had received ($30 million worth of gifts during 1956-1957). The result: both amendments were defeated 171-4 and 168-7.

But that was only the beginning of our trouble with dictators. In November, 1958, when Fidel Castro accused our ambassador of overfriendliness with Batista (both ambassadors Arthur Gardner and Earl Smith were, in fact, on excellent terms with the Cuban dictator), we roared in outrage. The New York *Mirror* told Castro to shut up or "he may talk himself into a restoration of the Platt Amendment," while the little Davenport (Iowa) *Times,* a sudden authority on history, forgot that the Platt Amendment ever existed and concluded that "the whole history of Cuba shows it has had the friendly assistance of the United States." Then, that same month, Washington sent Haiti a detachment of United States Marines (Dictator François Duvalier had barely escaped a revolt four month's earlier) and their presence was called "an act of friendship."

When Fidel Castro won, more disagreeable facts became public: our private companies in Cuba had long bought Batista's "cooperation" for $12 million worth of stocks; Batista had received another $34 million worth of stocks in foreign and joint United States-Cuban corporations; Batista's army, trained and armed by the United States, had been the center of government corruption; and Batista himself had fled Cuba with $250 million.

Castro's reaction is well known: he expropriated, confiscated, and executed, refused to pay off Batista's debts, and pushed his regime to the Left. Nevertheless, Castro first hoped to find help within the hemisphere. At the Buenos Aires meeting of the "21," in April, 1959, he pleaded that "$30 billion, spread over ten years, was required fully to develop Latin America." Nothing was done, however, except talk; in fact, the 21 talked 23 months.

Meanwhile, our self-criticism was mounting once again. The United State's "stop-and-start" Latin American diplomacy, said Indiana's Senator Homer Capehart, appoints "too many committees and fact-finding boards" that make reports "on which no action is ever taken." Finally, after another wave of Castro confiscations and his constant challenges to other Latin American countries to do the same, we announced our willingness to finance most of a $1 billion Inter-American Development Bank (IDB).[8]

Before the IDB began actual operations on October 1, 1960, we collected political returns—so, at least, complain Latin Americans. The payoffs came at the second of two meetings of Consultation of Foreign Ministers of the American

[8] Even *Time* called our new "aid to Latin America program" the "Castro Plan."

Republics under the Rio treaty held in San José, Costa Rica, during August, 1960. The first, called by Venezuela, condemned the Dominican Republic for plotting an assassination attempt against Venezuela's President Rómulo Betancourt. The ministers ordered mild sanctions imposed on the Trujillo regime, but the press, both here and in Latin America, reported that we had voted in favor of the sanctions only in order to set up precedents applicable to Castro's Cuba.

The second meeting, called officially by Peru but essentially by us, "condemns energetically the intervention or the threat of intervention, even when conditional, by an extracontinental power in the affairs of the American Republics. . . ." The San José Declaration, as the resolution is labeled, was aimed specifically at Cuba (which it did not name)[9] and at the Sino-Soviet powers (which it did). The "even when conditional" clause was directed at Russia, whose Premier Nikita Khruschev had warned that Russian rockets would come to the aid of Cuba *if and only if* the island were attacked by the United States.

That the San José Declaration was not "general in character," as Mexico hoped, but was specifically loaded against Cuba became clear to Latin Americans when they compared the scope of its full text to the narrowness of its application. Article 3 "reiterates that each state has the right to develop its cultural, political, and economic life freely," and Article 4 "reaffirms that the inter-American system is incompatible with any form of totalitarianism." The declaration, hence, should have applied to the dictatorship regimes of Ydígoras in Guatemala, Duvalier in Haiti, the Somoza brothers in Nicaragua, Stroessner in Paraguay, and so on. But we used it to justify our Cuban economic boycott and embargo, Cuba's non-participation in the Alliance and, finally, the United States-sponsored and supported Cuban exile invasion of Cuba. As that invasion shocked, anew, the hemisphere, Latin Americans inevitably saw the San José Declaration as just another Caracas 1954 infamy.

[9] The declaration, said Mexico's delegate, is "general in character," and "in no way is it a condemnation or threat against Cuba, whose aspirations for economic improvement and social justice have the deepest sympathy of the Government and the people of Mexico."

Within a month of San José, the Committee of 21 met again, in Bogotá, Colombia, and the United States offered to set up a $500 million Development Fund. To be handled by the IDB, the fund would be available for five basic Latin American needs: (1) rural development, (2) housing, (3) education, (4) public health, and (5) mobilization of domestic resources. The "Act of Bogotá" also called for a meeting of the Inter-American Economic and Social Council (IA-ECOSOC) in 1961—what turned out to be the Punta del Este Conference in Uruguay. Thus, before Kennedy had given it its name, even before Kennedy had won the election, the Alliance for Progress was born. What was new about it, in appearance at least, was our willingness to commit ourselves to help Latin America's social development.

The Alliance for Progress has become our main policy in Latin America. It is being proclaimed as the making of a new era. It is being hailed as the guarantee of social justice for all. Within ten years naked children will no longer die from leprosy, illiteracy will be wiped out, disease arrested, superstition routed, poverty ousted—all because of the *Alianza para el Progreso*.

PART V: The Alliance for Progress

Chapter 18

Birth Pangs

The Alliance for Progress was officially born at the Special Meeting of Inter-American Economic and Social Council (IA-ECOSOC) held in Punta del Este, Uruguay, from August 5 to 17, 1961.

That birth was deemed so important that the conference was at ministerial level, the hemisphere's twenty-one nations being represented by their economic ministers accompanied by dozens of financial and political experts. Our own delegation was headed by Secretary of the Treasury Douglas Dillon and included Ambassador to the OAS deLesseps Morrison, former Ambassador to Uruguay and then Assistant Secretary of State for Inter-American Affairs Robert F. Woodward, and Kennedy aides Morales Carrión, Arthur Schlesinger, Jr., Richard Goodwin, and so on. Officially, at least, it was expected that the Alliance would herald a new era in Latin America, though no Latin American quite knew what the Alliance would mean.

The Alliance for Progress, said Kennedy in his August 5, 1961, message to the delegates, "means full recognition of the right of all people to share fully in our progress. For there is no place in democratic life for institutions which benefit the few while denying the needs of the many." Added Dillon: "Latin America, if it takes the necessary internal measures, can reasonably expect its own efforts to be matched by an inflow of capital during the next decade amounting to at least twenty billion dollars." Dillon

251

defined these measures thus: "It will require a strengthening of tax systems. . . . It will require land reform so that underutilized soil is put to full use and so that farmers can own their own land. It will require lower interest rates on loans to small farmers and small business.[1] It will require greatly increased programs for education, housing and health. And for the United States it will require a clear acceptance of further responsibilities to aid our sister republics." That responsibility, said Kennedy, is "public assistance from the United States . . . (at) an annual rate of more than one billion dollars."

With the Alliance promising to encourage another $1 billion a year from private (mostly United States) investors, IA-ECOSOC ministers incorporated all of Dillon's suggestions into the final Charter of Punta del Este, signed August 17, 1961. The Charter calls for raising the per capita income of each Latin American country by 2.5 percent a year; for eliminating illiteracy by 1970; for significant increases in low-cost housing; for the stabilization of prices; for the purification of water supplies and the control of communicable diseases; and for the raising of life expectancy 70 percent among urban and 50 percent among rural populations. The Charter also encourages Latin American economic integrations (common markets), which had begun in a fashion before the conference, and it insists that Latin American governments speed up land reforms, diversify agriculture production, and meet once a year to review progress.

Officially, all delegates at Punta del Este, except Cuba's Minister of Industries Ernesto "Che" Guevara, praised the United States and the Alliance. "Finally a hope for our starving millions," said the conference's host, Eduardo Víctor Haedo, then President of Uruguay's National Council of Government. Most of Latin America's press editorials, from the Rio Grande to Patagonia, hailed our "genuine new look." Officially, both the governments and the press are still extolling Kennedy, the Alliance, and the Punta del Este Conference.

But, privately, all were at least skeptical. Latin America's

[1] No money is lent in Latin America at less than 10 percent a year, often reaches as high as 50 percent, and is always limited to just one year.

press is generally controlled by its governments, oligarchies or militarists; rarely do editorials coincide with or reflect public opinion. (Even the man in the street in Argentina, for example, says: "Oh, we get all the truth all right. We just take everything the press says and reverse it. And that is the truth.") Where not at the service of vested interests, press criticism of the Alliance has been harsh.

But even at the conference itself, most delegates voiced their reservations—in between highfalutin' phrases of diplomatic praise. Their gripes: our vagueness, our insistence upon reports, analyses, and expert sessions while the low ultimate results must await ten years, our own tariff walls, our practice of measuring progress in terms of exports, and our policy of hoarding world market demands.

The Latin delegates pointed out that their trade has been steadily dropping, that their total dollar earnings have dwindled from $4.3 billion in 1951 to $3.3 billion in 1959, that they now face increasing protectionism from the European Common Market, that their one-crop economies make them totally vulnerable to that crop's world market price fluctuation, and that they cannot industrialize because their dollar shortages cut them off from dollar-expensive equipment. They reminded us that if trade barriers and tariffs were eliminated, they would benefit more each year than they can from the Alliance. Argentina, for example, cannot sell its meat in the United States because we say it is contaminated by hoof-and-mouth disease—a phony[2] charge meant as an excuse in order to protect our own cattlemen, whose meat is 400 percent more expensive than Argentine meat delivered to our retailers.

"If there is a genuine desire to collaborate in the process of Latin American development," said Chile's Finance Minister Eduardo Figueroa, "the industrial countries must accept a system of preferences that would allow us to place our exportable surpluses on the world market." Added Uruguay's Finance Minister Juan Eduardo Azzini, the conference president, in a pointed attack on our policies: "International financial institutions insist, again and again, that in order to start development programs, the underdeveloped areas should try to increase their basic production. Otherwise they cannot possibly be counted on for effective and permanent

[2] Hoof-and-mouth bacteria are eliminated by freezing or boiling.

assistance. It is difficult to understand such contradictory aims. There are those who, on one hand, finance international organizations and then, on the other, obstruct the sales of the products obtained by the contributions from the same organizations. Latin America has been obliged to sell cheaply and buy dearly."

Mexico correctly insisted that internal development has nothing to do with exports. Panama accurately warned that dollars are not enough to stop revolutions. Argentina's Finance Minister Roberto Alemann asked that we commit ourselves "politically and economically" for ten years, which our government cannot do without prior congressional approval, and Congress, as everyone knew, was not about to give up its prerogative to review our year-by-year spending. In general, the consensus was that the Alliance promised too little, too late. "We are frankly fighting against time," said Figueroa. Added Haedo, "The changes that mark the great moments in the history of America have always come about through revolutions." "Latin America is boiling," said Azzini; "we cannot afford to waste time on theories or highly technical surveys."

I talked to at least one delegate from every country present at Punta del Este, to scores of Latin American correspondents, to scores more from the United States. Not one honestly believed that the Alliance would help push Latin America into the twentieth century—or that it was meant to. No delegate said so publicly, few correspondents wrote so for their papers, but all agreed with one high official from the OAS who told me: "The United States is trying to stop Castro, nothing more. That it may do; money and guns can stop a man. But it will never stop Castroism. True reforms require planning, state planning at all levels, not to mention expropriations and nationalizations, which is exactly what the United States hopes to avoid. That's why nothing will stop Castroism—except occupation armies, of course. Castroism means getting rid of all that junk that leads our countries. It means wholesale reforms. More than that, it means a new life, at least for those who have never seen a doctor, eaten a chicken, or been inside a school. You and I, we belong to the bourgeoisie, the unadaptable class. We shall not survive if Castroism wins, but the masses of Latin America will not really begin to live unless it does. And what makes

the difference today is that even the masses know it."
In his own sentimental way, Azzini said the same thing
when he told his fellow delegates, "It is necessary to reform
the hearts of men before attempting a reform in the economic
structure."

More criticism went unsaid—until up spoke "Che" Guevara, Cuba's Minister of Industries and chief of its delegation.
Already at Montevideo's Carrasco International Airport,
where about 2,000 *Fidelistas* awaited him patiently but
loudly, Che's arrival was upsetting. Dillon, and our delegation,
arrived first that warm, pleasant afternoon, and were immediately surrounded by the usual mobs of reporters, photog-
raphers, protocol men, and every other type of credential
holder. The long black limousines were waiting, but Dillon
decided to make a little arrival speech—and pulled out
his prepared text.

Just as he began to read, however, a whining roar muffled
his words. The crowd looked up to see a Cuban Airline
Britannia banking in. Dillon continued to read but no
one seemed to be listening. The youngsters up on the terminal
observation deck, by then shrieking frantically, would not
have let his words carry very far anyway. Then as Che's
plane taxied up to the terminal, Dillon found himself
alone with his aides, embassy staffers, and protocol men.
Even United States correspondents had abandoned him
to rush over to see Che. Dillon folded up his speech and
put it away.

As he did so, the new arrival was applauded, cheered,
hugged, even kissed as he tried to push his way to a small
pink Chevy waiting for him. Days before, the Cuban embassy
had tried to rent the usual diplomatic cars but were told
all cars had been rented. (Later, we—the *New York Times*
team covering the conference—had had no difficulty renting
a car.) Hundreds of Uruguayans volunteered to lend their
private cars, however, and thus, Che, after waving to
his fans on the deck, got into one of them and followed
Dillon up the west coast of Uruguay. After filing the arrival
story, we did too. And after everybody settled down in
smart hotels, country-club bungalows or rented houses
(that cost $1,200 or more each for the twelve-day con-
ference), the fun began.

My assignment, until I had to return to Montevideo
six days later to cover a pro-Castro riot, was "Che" Guevara.

"Stick with him, eat with him, sleep with him if necessary," I had been told. The Cuban delegation stayed at the most modest of the major hotels, called Playa (Beach), occupying two full floors. Off-duty bodyguards, delegate wives, Che's sister who had come over from Argentina for the occasion, and all the Cuban delegates ate together at two huge round tables at one end of the dining room, while the rest of us, a group made up mainly of Argentine and Chilean correspondents, plus Coffee Agreement public-relations men ate at the other. It did not take us long, however, to realize that Che was not a very warm fellow. His voice was high-pitched, his manner sometimes curt. But he was pleasant, greeting everyone who greeted him.

When he entered the delegates' lounge the next day, he was welcomed by applause—the only delegate to be so received. Always dressed in his fatigue guerrilla uniform with a small Cuban major's star on each collar, and with his somewhat motheaten black beard, Che was inevitably a standout. Women found him dashingly or fascinatingly handsome; men said he was intelligent with sensitive eyes (if Leftists), with devilish eyes (if Rightists). Cameras were trained on him at all times, even when others were speaking. His every move was described in full details over cable and phone lines.

Once, when Dillon had ended his first position-taking speech and Che got up and left the conference room (the main Punta del Este gambling casino converted, naturally, to suit the occasion), he was followed out by half the spectators, some rushing to their typewriters to dash off the "hot" story: Che walks out on Dillon. Unfortunately, no one filed the story before those who had pursued Che reported that he had gone only as far as—the Men's Room.

The Playa Hotel was only a short walk across a treeless park along Punta del Este's white beaches from the Casino (renamed Building of the Americas), and each time a session ended, Che and his entourage ambled leisurely through it. On one occasion, an unshaven, burly, local fisherman, riding a bike, spotted Che and speeded straight for him. One of Che's bodyguards, a bit itchy because known anti-Castro Cubans and MEDL hoodlums were all over the Punta del Este—with credentials from Uruguay's reactionary press—reached slowly for his pistol. But the fisherman arrived shouting *"Comandante!"* then grabbed both of Che's arms and said: "I want you to know that our government may be against you, the governments of all this hemisphere may be against you, but we the people, the poor, are with you. Don't let us down." Then he rushed off before Che, visibly moved, could stutter a thank you. It was Che's only moment of hesitation.

Those bodyguards turned out to be quite a conversation piece, too. There were eight or ten of them—all veterans of the Sierra Maestra days. One, fast and energetic, was no higher than four foot eight. But when anti-Castro Cuban exile Max Azicri-Levy, so called correspondent of *Avance* (the former Havana daily now operating out of Florida), shocked the conference by rushing Che, "Shorty" lunged at Azicri-Levy, a hefty six-footer, lugged him out of the conference, and pulverized him with lightning-fast jabs at chin and nose. Another Che bodyguard was an Amazonic Negro whom correspondents quickly nicknamed "Lumumba." Once, when I was standing toward the rear of the press section, I noticed Lumumba and Shorty staring my way. Then I realized why. Behind me, a Uruguayan sports writer (off duty) was listening to a speech, resting his left hand, Napoleon-style, in his right breast pocket. "I always keep my hand there," he insisted indignantly when I suggested he keep his hands to his side. Then I showed him Lumumba, who was pointing a .38 from between a newspaper, and Shorty, whose .45 could be seen peering out from under a raincoat folded over his arm. Both pistols were aimed straight at the sports writer, who quickly disappeared. I never saw him again.

In moments of relaxation, Che could be quite a talker. One night three Argentine correspondents and I sat up until 4:00 A.M. while he described his adventures in the Sierra Maestra. Through his "army experiences" talk, we detected a keen observer, extremely intense and in a great hurry. He gave us the impression that he was convinced he would soon die and that he must accomplish everything he can as fast as possible. It became obvious to us that Che was a Nationalist who had adopted Communist allies only because he had no other choice. "Without Russian aid we'd starve," he said frankly. In Washington late in 1962, I was glad to see that our so called Cuban experts had finally realized that Che was Marxist but certainly not Communist.[3]

"Every social revolution has to have its Stalinist phase," Che told us that night. "Let's hope ours lasts only a short time." He also apparently regretted the break with the United States. "We had to nationalize United States industry," he said. "And when we did, the United States cut us off. I'm sure if we really were Commies, we'd get along fine, just like Russia and the United States get along with tourism, plenty of trade, exchange students, and the rest. It's too bad, though; it will mean many shortages for us. We will run out of food. Our buses will stop. Everything will go down until we can raise the food we need and manufacture our own buses. If we can last until then, the United States is lost, because as soon as Latin America sees our economy going up, more revolutions will explode. That's why the United States must destroy us—before we recover completely, before we have rebuilt our economy."

Che's personal conviction came across during his conference speech, too. He began by pointing out, in his usual calm, unemotional, almost monotonous tone, that the only reason the Alliance was formulated is the Cuban Revolution—to stop it and to stop another one. He reminded his audience that no such Alliance was planned before the Castro regime took over Cuba. The delegates, of course, were aware of the Alliance's timing, which had been well publicized in Uruguay:

March 13, 1961: Kennedy announces the Alliance for Progress.

March 14, 1961: He requests $600 million for it from Congress.

March 22, 1961: He sends Congress another Latin American aid message.

April 17, 1961: United States-equipped, trained, and transported Cuban exiles invade Cuba's Bay of Pigs.

May 7, 1961: The OAS, without once taking up or referring

[3] Some two years earlier, when I was a *Time* editor in the Hemisphere Section, the writer's cover story on Che included this fact: When Che was in Arbenz' Guatemala he was offered a post in the Agrarian Reform Institute on the condition he join the Communist Party. Che refused. The *Time* senior editor in charge of Latin America cut that part out of the story.

to that invasion, accepts Kennedy's suggestions for an Alliance meeting, convoking the Punta del Este conference for August.

Che Guevara then read some documents that had been stolen by Venezuelan students during a riot the previous July 16th from the car of then Ambassador to Venezuela Teodoro Moscoso. Among the quoted passages was the following:[4] "The Alliance for Progress can stimulate radical reforms. But unless these projects [of the Alliance] are put into effect in such a way that quick positive results are achieved, they will not contain the increasing pressure of the Left. In the next few years, there will be a race between those who try to set those reforms by evolution and those who try to stir up the people in favor of a fundamental economic and social revolution. If the reformers do not hurry, they will soon see themselves deprived of popular support and cornered in an impossible position between the extreme Right and Left."

Che then asserted that Castro had carried out all the reforms the Alliance claims to want—agrarian, industrial, urban, housing, education, and so on, thanks to Russian and other Communist countries' help. "But where are America's millions?" he asked, and "where will they come from," he demanded. Quoting a Dean Rusk press conference, Che pointed out that the $20 billion promised by the United States is, in effect, public and private aid from the United States, Europe, and Japan, and from private foundations which together already contribute $1.6 billion a year, so that the increase aimed at is only for $.4 billion yearly.

Of the $20 billion total, Che went on, the United States is ready to put up half. The rest, Dillon said and Che repeated, must come from these other parties for which, Che insisted, Dillon cannot speak. If Japan is free it must commit itself, yet it has not done so. Either United States private companies are "free enterprises," and then Dillon cannot speak for them, or there is no free enterprise in the United States, in which case Cuba's system, which has no free enterprise either, is better: the reforms there exist already. Even public funds, Che continued, are not guaranteed. The United States Congress must

---

[4] I am retranslating from the official Spanish text released by the conference.

approve such funds. It might do so this year, and next, and in three years, but suddenly it might stop all Alliance funds and Dillon's word will not be worth anything. And if all these reforms are so easily attained, that is, just with money, "Do you think that Latin American governments would not have achieved them? If they did not do them before, why should they do them now?" They did not do them because reforms are not possible without revolution, said Che, and as proof he quoted another "Venezuelan document." It was a memo prepared by two Venezuelan United States Embassy staffers, Irving Tragen and Robert Cox, on June 12, 1961, and was addressed to Moscoso—confidential. It referred to Venezuela, and read in part:

> Reform of the administrative organism is an absolute necessity before trying to begin work as serious as an economic overhauling. Any plan that could be formulated, any program that could be established for the economic development of Venezuela, drawn by the Venezuelan government or by U.S. technicians, must inevitably go through the intermediary of Venezuelan administration. So long as this public administration is characterized by stupidity, indifference, inefficiency, formalism, party interests, corruption, duplicity and ill will, it will be practically impossible to make efficient and dynamic the development projects through such a bureaucracy. . . .
>
> The actual tax structure is a moral and economic detriment; not only is it unfair to ask the American middle class to pick up the tab while the Venezuelan oligarchy and the *nouveau riche* do not pay their share, but it is equally unrealistic to think that a modern industrial society could be built here on the basis of a medieval system of economic privileges.

Tragen and Cox went on to insist that the overhauling must come first and that "if the United States does not want to support such a program all the way, if it does not want to tell this country what it has to do and to contribute what this would suppose in terms of necessary aid, it would be better to do nothing. It would be preferable to buy time, preserving as much as possible and as long as possible the actual status quo. . . ."

These documents, undenied by United States (we couldn't;

they had all the official stamps), obviously stunned the delegates. The Venezuelans should have either recognized that what was described was true—and it is!—and resigned (since they were part of the system described), or they should have broken relations with the United States on the spot. Naturally they did neither—proof that we have able observers in our embassies but that Washington just does not listen to them.

Guevara ended his two-hour speech with: "We cannot promise that we will not export our example [the Cuban Revolution] as the United States asks us to because an example is a matter of spirit and a spiritual element can cross frontiers. But we will give our guarantee that no arms will be transported from Cuba to be used for fighting in any Latin American country."

Che's guarantee cannot be accepted; Cuba needs another Latin American social revolution to survive—or to bear the brunt of our attacks. But the first point of his final remark is obviously true; nothing can stop Castroism as a philosophy except thorough reforms, and these will never be accomplished, as our United States Embassy Venezuelan experts correctly pointed out, without an over-hauling of Latin America's structures.

The Charter of Punta del Este was approved 20 to 1, but the one—Cuba—carried the day.

Chapter 19

Concept and Application

On August 17, 1962, the Alliance for Progress was one year old. It was even older according to planning, since Kennedy had announced it almost six months before its Punta del Este signing. Whatever its official birthday, however, the Alliance was old enough to be evaluated, and all who did found it a dismal failure, prompting our government to defend it.

That task fell mainly to Teodoro Moscoso, now out of it but then its chief, a balding Puerto Rican with glasses, white moustache, and pockmarks on his face. A former Administrator of Economic Development in Puerto Rico, Moscoso directed "Operation Bootstrap" which, as we saw, is a highly successful private-enterprise venture but a total failure in social justice—as anyone who wanders through the island's numerous slums can tell at a glance. Moscoso was later Ambassador to Venezuela when the Tragen-Cox documents were stolen from his briefcase, and he had to be relieved from his post in Caracas. Brought to Washington, he became chief of the Latin American program of AID, the Agency for International Development created to coordinate all the various federal aid agencies into one central clearinghouse.

Shortly thereafter, too, our State Department tried to modernize and "efficiencize" our Latin American policy headquarters. Thomas Mann, Ike's last Assistant Secretary of State for Inter-American Affairs, an unimaginative former Texas lawyer who had been kept on by Kennedy, was sent to Mexico as Ambassador (where he quickly succeeded in gaining a reputation for being one of the worst in United States-Mexican history). Mann's replacement as policy-maker was Adolf Berle, the former F.D.R. aide and ambassador. One of the Cuban Invasion master-"minds," he was soon kicked upstairs to boss Latin American propaganda.

Robert Woodward, who was taken out of Uruguay where he had gained wide respect as United States Ambassador because of his refined, polite, British-style gentlemanliness, was the next Kennedy Assistant Secretary. But old-school diplomat Woodward could not adapt to the New Frontier high-pressure salesmanship; he constantly ran afoul of such Kennedy-clan Latin American experts as Richard Goodwin, the brash young (thirty) lawyer who thought up the Madison Avenue slogan "Alliance for Progress," or as Arthur Schlesinger, Jr., another Kennedy speechwriter, or as W. W. Rostow whose superficial economic brilliance is so anti-Soviet-tracked that he even managed to pronounce (at the second Punta del Este Conference) Latin names with a Russian accent. Goodwin, Schlesinger, and Rostow were eventually given new assignments to play with, but nevertheless, after eight months, Woodward was obviously considered unsalvageable and was shipped off to Spain as ambassador.

He was replaced by a career government economist named Edwin Martin who, knowing that the best way to get ahead in an area where every daring has led to failures, let his underlings take the initiative—and drown. Thus, Moscoso, who was under Martin, tried to float the Alliance almost alone and was immediately (while Kennedy was ultimately) responsible for its sinking in that first short year.

To Moscoso, naturally, the Alliance was not sinking at all. He admitted, however, that it had a slow launching: "We should have found out much sooner what the bottlenecks were and how to solve them. Here is just one example: After a decision has been made to send assistance to a country that requires engineering talent, it takes months even to get an engineer down there to examine the situation. It shouldn't take that long. Everyone tries to play it so very safe that the result is you just immobilize everyone."

Still, Moscoso insisted, the Alliance has done well. "By summer 1963," he said in summer 1962, "these results will have been achieved in the field of construction: 168,000 homes, 15,000 miles of roads, 620 water supply systems, 360 hospitals and health centers and 17,250 classrooms. In addition, some 17,000 technicians in the field of agriculture and 20,000 teachers and other educational specialists will have been trained and 27,000 agricultural loans affected. It is expected that approximately 35 million people in Latin America will have benefited from Alliance projects."

Moscoso also pointed out that Latin America received $866,000,000 and a committed pledge of $234,000,000 more, for a total of more than the $1 billion we promised at Punta del Este. He warned repeatedly that what the money is used for by the recipient Latin American countries must not be automatically attributed to us: "We cannot and shall not do for them what they can and must do for themselves." Or again: "This is a twenty-nation effort in which we are junior partners, and it cannot succeed unless all twenty nations put their shoulders to the wheel with a shared sense of responsibility for success." However, Moscoso would certainly have agreed with his boss Kennedy who said, when the Alliance was officially one year old, "measured against all that has to be done, I think we have to do much better."

And at least one important opinion-maker, the powerful head of the press, the *New York Times*, concluded that the Alliance was just fine: "What is wrong with the Alliance for Progress is not the concept, and certainly not the goals. On the contrary, the best minds and most experienced statesmen and economists in the hemisphere cannot come up with anything better or anything very different. The main trouble with the Alliance for Progress is that exaggerated hopes were raised in the first, enthusiastic flush of launching the program at Punta del Este."

If the *Times* insists on being blind to facts—and each of the three *Times* men covering the Punta del Este Conference were quite wide-eyedly aware of the harsh criticism the Alliance received—that was its affair. That "most experienced statesmen" are in favor of the Alliance was and is obviously true: most experienced statesmen belong to that class that profits most from the Alliance. That "the best minds" cannot come up with "anything better" was a definitional device used to con *Times* readers, whom the *Times* obviously wanted not to convince but to impress (and must, therefore, if we follow the logical application of its statement, consider them name-dropping pedants unable to think for themselves). The device goes like this: any mind that has anything but the Alliance to suggest is not among the "best minds"; therefore, the "best minds" have nothing better to suggest.

There are literally hundreds of other suggestions available, expounded by literally thousands of "minds" both here and in Latin America. Indeed, no respected Latin American academician considers the Alliance anything else but a fancy, propaganda-packed plan for keeping the old structure intact in Latin America.

One quick example: Brazil's Professor Josué de Castro, former President of the United Nations Food and Agriculture Organization (FAO), world-renowned anti-Communist economist and sociologist, author of *Geopolitics of Hunger*, *The Black-Book of Hunger*, and *Hunger and Peace*, considers the Alliance

a paternalistic concept of philanthropic humanism which has no authentic economic base whatsoever. . . . The injection of dollars does not help the people but governments whose interests are often opposed to the people's. What would help the people is the integration of their economies through the valorization of their work, of their production. . . . The plan of investing in isolated sectors of major returns does not help to develop Latin America economically; on the contrary, it aggravates certain social problems. . . . The Kennedy Plan, unfortunately, has been conceived more as a political plan than as an economic plan, and suffers from all the prejudices with which United States interests confuse foreign policy. . . . All of this is nothing but pure colonialism. . . . Colonialism is the only cause of hunger in Latin America.[1]

Here at home, to mention also only one, Professor Kalman Silvert of Dartmouth, by far the leading political scientist expert on Latin America, who has spent more than eight years in Latin America either on research fellow-

---

[1] *Mundo Economico*, Caracas.

ships or as a staff associate of the prestigious American
Universities Field Staff, had none of the *Times'* respect for
the Alliance which is based on the concept that dollars
to nondemocratic governments can save democracy. But,
wrote Silvert correctly, "Economically retarded countries
cannot, by definition, enjoy democratic politics."

The *Times,* in the same birthday editorial, stated that
the Alliance "is aimed at transforming the social and economic
structure of the twenty Latin-American nations, concentrating
on agrarian reform, housing, tax reforms, education and
industrialization." That may very well have been Kennedy's
intention—his motives are of no interest. What the Alliance
could or could not do, according to its carefully worked-out
definitions, principles, and project proposals, is very much
to our interest, however. Thus, let us analyze the Social
Progress Trust Fund that was suggested by the Act of
Bogotá and signed June 19, 1961, by President Kennedy.

The Fund is the basis of the Alliance, and furnishes
the rules by which the Alliance is administered. The Fund
was first limited to $500 million, divided into three parts.
One part, $6,000,000 was earmarked to (and then received
by) the OAS for institutional improvements. Another part,
$100,000,000, was to be distributed in grant form by the
International Cooperation Administration (ICA), now part
of AID. Neither of these parts is questionable since they
do not involve the "twenty-nation effort" that Moscoso
talked about. The third part, however, is very much an-
alyzable: it consisted of $394,000,000 to be administered
by the Inter-American Development Bank (IDB) in which
Latin Americans participate. The money was to be loaned,
on application, for housing, land, or sanitation reforms.
In reading its small print closely, we can find the Fund's
true makeup.

Section 1.04*a* specifies that the "resources of the Fund
shall not be used for the purchase of agricultural land."
This precludes all meaningful land reforms, since Latin
American governments cannot afford to buy the land—
unless, of course, they seize it *à la* Castro. Section 2.01*c*
insists that "loan requests shall be granted only for projects
or programs in which the applicant bears an appropriate
share of the total costs." This excludes practically all
public reforms; loans will be granted mostly to highly solvent
corporations which, continuing their past practices, will

enrich themselves further and carry out no publicly beneficial projects. It's the old story, say Latin American economists, of needing money to make money. IDB President Felipe Herrera complained of just such terms in a November 14, 1960 speech. Latin American countries, he said, "have found themselves in a vicious circle: their inability to increase and diversify their exports restricts their foreign credit, and restrictions on their foreign credit make it impossible for them to increase and diversify their exports."

Between sections 4.05 ("no part of the Fund shall be used for the purchase of goods or services originating in any [nonmember] country") and 4.06 ("funds . . . shall be used for the purchase of goods and services from the United States or . . . in the country where assistance is received"), the United States not only forbids aid-receiving nations from buying goods and services wherever they are cheaper (and they are usually much cheaper in Europe), but also makes sure its lent dollars rarely leave the United States. Section 4.07, which has been hailed as a precedent-shattering milestone because it made loans repayable in local currencies, kills the effect by specifying that "the payment is equivalent in value to the dollar denominated amount due," meaning that should we devaluate the dollar, repayment must be at the old rate—a clause that never applies if, on the contrary, the debtor devaluates his money.

Section 5.02 defines the role of the Administrator (the IDB) as the same as "its own affairs," which means (a) it charges interest and (b) it is controlled by the United States because loans must be approved by two-thirds of the vote. Each nation does not have one vote; each one's voting power is proportional to its financial contribution, and we ante in 40 percent. Section 6.02 states that the United States can terminate the Fund at worst within thirty days. Section 6.03 states that "any assets remaining in the Fund at the time of termination, including outstanding loans, shall revert to the United States." In sum, the Fund may have been "aimed" at stimulating reforms, but only in the same way as a mortgage at 6 percent allows me to buy a home if I have collateral, while the bank, of course, makes a profit. There is nothing dishonorable about this, but there is nothing honorable either. It is just sound, profitable business for the bank—the United States.

Nor is there anything new about such a policy. Throughout

all of Latin America's history, we have tried to lend money to its governments. In the past we have even helped local opponents overthrow those governments that refused to accept our loans, as in Nicaragua and Honduras. And we have always used our loan-giving as an index of our generosity. Yet there is nothing generous about lending money. Bankers do it everyday, and no one considers banks especially generous institutions. A man who earns $15,000 a year but has always paid cash for his TV's, cars, and suits will have difficulty establishing his credit when he suddenly seeks a charge-a-plate or credit card; a man who earns only $6,000 a year but has bought everything on time payments will have excellent credit, even if he has been consistently late or even occasionally delinquent in his payments. The rationale is simple. An indebted man is "hooked." An indebted country is equally hooked (unless it should suddenly adopt a revolutionary regime that disowns the country's previous debts).

When Betancourt took over Venezuela's government in 1958, he inherited so many debts to the United States that he had to pay them off at the rate of $50 million a month during his whole five-year term. Almost every year he had to beg us to reschedule his payments to avoid chaos. Under such conditions was it possible to conceive Betancourt voting against us? (Unless, of course, he had really balked and refused to pay his debts, nationalizing our corporations had we reacted by applying a boycott.) Castro may or may not have been a Communist; that is of no interest here. But what are the facts concerning his nationalization of United States corporations? After taking over Batista's governmental apparatus, he found that more than 60 percent of the whole economy was owned by the United States, that our sugar companies kept much more land uncultivated or rented out than it cultivated itself,[2] that in general our companies paid very minimal official taxes to the government but hefty bribes or "thank you" presents (including in one case a solid-gold telephone[3]) on the side, that the government was heavily indebted, and that the peasants were poor, shoeless, and homeless. Thus, Castro

[2] See *Latin American Issues*.
[3] See Samuel Shapiro's article, "Cuba, a Dissent," in *The New Republic*, Sept. 12, 1960.

enacted an agrarian reform and exchanged sugar for Russian oil. Perhaps Castro did it because he was a Communist, perhaps not. In any case any nationalistic government would have done the same and, furthermore, *must* do the same.

In Cuba in 1959-1960, any true nationalistic government would have realized how disadvantageous a one-sided economy is. That government would have tried to establish its economic independence at all cost. It could not continue, it would have realized, to send its sugar and tobacco to only one country, receive its oil from that same country, have it refined by companies on its soil belonging to that same country, and also have to depend on loans from that same country for its budgetary health. So Cuba sold sugar to Russia and received oil in exchange. That oil became Cuban oil, and the United States oil refineries in Cuba were under signed contract to refine all Cuban oil. The companies refused. Cuba nationalized the companies. Our government demanded compensation. Cuba could not afford cash but was willing to pay bonds for what the companies estimated their worth to be in their own tax statements. What ensued is history, and today Cuba is again dependent on just one side. The point remains: an underdeveloped country will never become developed if its economy *and* its debts are controlled by the same developed nation.

Yet the Alliance, which claims to want Latin America's development, insists that the only way to achieve this is by more loans and more debts, that is, by our obtaining more control over Latin American economies. As such, the Alliance does not differ from Eisenhower's policy. And despite the Madison Avenue glitter given to the Alliance, its loans are not so much more stupendous than those granted by Eisenhower. In 1959 and 1960, Latin America received an average of $504 million. From March, 1961, to August, 1962, that is, from the Alliance's announcement to its formal first birthday, the amount was $866 million, which is about a yearly average of $605 million, a boost of only 20 percent. In 1963, AID commitments to Latin America were only $549 million, plus $185 million under the Food for Peace program. For 1964, the projected total is $767 million. Surely from the fanfare one would have thought that the Alliance at least tripled Eisenhower's program.

For Latin America, it is fortunate that it has not done so. When you or I receive a personal loan from a bank,

V

we receive a check that we can use as we please. We can even deposit it in a competitive bank. But Alliance loans are not so free. Most are credits: X nation receives the right to buy machinery or fertilizer *in* the United States at United States retail prices. The tab is picked up by our Treasury, IDB, or some other lending institution, and X must pay it back at so many years' time plus so much interest—usually in dollars. The money never leaves the United States, while as the loan is paid back, new money enters the United States. If the loan is paid back in dollars, we have increased our dollar circulation total. If it is paid in X's currency, the money is used to buy X's exports; hence X does not increase its dollar reserve. When our economy is in bad straits, Washington orders a loosening up of credit—to stimulate spending and internal circulation. This is what the Alliance has done, by 20 percent. Washington is pushing foreign loans to increase our net income. The loans, however, may or may not strengthen the borrower's economy. This depends on their use. But loans always (unless unrepaid) strengthen the lender's economy.

Here's an example that documents the above and gets us to our next argument as well. On December 1, 1961, a State Department press officer read the following statement to reporters:

The first loan made by the United States Agency for International Development (AID) was signed on November 20 by Roberto Campos, Brazilian Ambassador to the United States, and Teodoro Moscoso, AID Regional Administrator for Latin America. The loan agreement makes available $50 million of a total of $100 million in credits earmarked for Brazil by AID. The purpose of the loan is to provide further assistance to the Brazilian Government's program of promoting economic and social progress under conditions of financial stability. These objectives are an essential part of the Alliance for Progress concept as expressed in the Charter of Punta del Este. . . . The proceeds of the loan will be used to help Brazil finance essential imports from the United States. In order to contribute most effectively to the objective of easing Brazil's foreign debt repayment obligations, particularly during the next few years, repayment of the loans will be made in 40 years without interest and with no payments during the first 10 years. Repayment will be in dollars. There will be a small credit fee of three-quarters of 1 per cent of the balance outstanding each year.

Across the United States and Latin America, on December 2, 1961, the press headlined: BRAZIL GETS 40 YEAR SOCIAL PROGRESS $50 MILLION LOAN AT NO INTEREST. The headline was technically correct, the implication absolutely false. Here's why:

1. Brazil did not get a loan; it got credit. The money is to be used for United States imports. No cash will leave the United States. The "loan" will eventually increase Brazil's dollar shortage.

(This is a general condition on almost all loans to Latin America. Herewith a quote from *The Vision Letter*, November 12, 1963, Special Supplement: "A study made by *Visión* to find out what actually happens to the dollars and credits supplied to Latin America under the Alliance indicates that as much as 86 percent of the money is spent for the purchase of U.S. products and services, and that those purchases represent between one-fifth and one-quarter of the total value of annual U.S. exports to Latin America.")

2. The "loan" is at no interest, but the "small credit fee" is actually the same thing as interest, though not exorbitant to be sure. For the first ten years that credit fee of "three-quarters of 1 percent" adds up to .0075 times $50 million, or $375,000 yearly, that is, $3,750,000 for ten years. And .0075 of the balance due for each year thereafter is equivalent to .0075 times $25,000,000 (half, or the average) times thirty years (the remaining allotted time), that is, $5,625,000. The total "small credit fee" ends up being $9,395,000—almost 20 percent or one-half of one percent a year, not high but profit nonetheless.

3. The "loan" is to promote "conditions of financial stability," not social progress. It *assumes* that stability leads to social progress. This is not fact. For twenty of Trujillo's thirty-two-year reign, the Dominican Republic was stable, politically, economically, and administratively. Nicaragua is stable today under the Somozas. So is Haiti under Duvalier.

In fact, the hemisphere's most economically unstable country—Bolivia—leads the hemisphere in social progress.

Furthermore, if the Alliance's reason for being is to "accelerate the economic and social development of the participating countries of Latin America, so that they may achieve maximum levels of well-being, with equal opportunities for all, in democratic societies," as the Charter of Punta del Este clearly states, why are we lending money for budget support ("financial stability") which serves no function except to keep a government in power? Moscoso has tried to answer this question various times:

> We say to a government coming to us with a development plan: "You have to reform or we'll give you nothing." . . . But suppose that a government says to us: "If you don't help us immediately, the Communists will take over." What do we do then? I think the United States, through the Agency for International Development, has been fairly cool and discriminating about such situations. In most cases—we have been insisting on reforms, but we cannot wait for *complete* reform. . . .

Or again:

> So far, we've disbursed about $1 billion. But most of that money, unfortunately, has been used to cover government deficits, support shaky currencies and keep countries from going bankrupt. We had to do it, to save those countries.

The first statement was published in the *New York Times* on August 12, 1962. The second, in *Look* dated August 28, 1962, was out on the stands only three or four days after the *Times*. In the *Times* Moscoso implied that the Alliance had not given in too often to budgetary loan requests; it had been "cool and discriminating." And in "most cases," he insisted, since the word "complete" was italicized by him, we got *some* reforms *first*. In the second article, Moscoso frankly admitted that most Alliance funds have gone to save economies and not to stimulate reforms. (Quite a discrepancy within the same week!) Indeed, the facts are that the Alliance loans earmarked for budget support have far, far outweighed any others.

Just before the 1962 elections that led to his undoing,

Argentina's Frondizi received a $150,000,000 loan for budgetary needs; Chile then received $120,000,000; Guatemala got $15,000,000; and so on. More than 60 percent of the loans are of this type, like the Brazil loan cited above. Argentina has received many such loans, some even after Frondizi was overthrown by the military. Always the pretext is the same—"If we don't help, the Communists will take over."

"Antikommunism" is a famous word in Latin America; spelled with a "k" it means the excuse used by tyrants to squash revolts, jail grumblers, impose censorship, rape constitutions, and get United States dollars that are then used for graft. That Communism will take over if he fell was the argument Trujillo used to get our support for thirty-two long years. So did Somoza *père*, so do Somoza *fils*. We helped Batista and we got Castro. Why do we have to "save those countries" at all? And how do stability loans save them anyway?

The answer has nothing to do with Communism. It has to do with business. What does "stability" mean? It means more or less frozen wages. It means more or less frozen prices. It means tight credit, a cutback in government spending, a slowdown on expansion. It means, therefore, a halt or a near halt in government-subsidized projects and industrialization. It means, finally, an economy propitious for investors with money—that is, foreign investors. Stability is a distinct advantage to United States corporations investing in the country and for United States buyers of the country's commodity exports. That is why the International Monetary Fund conditions its standby credit to stability or austerity measures. The budget may become balanced, the export-import trade may become favorable, the country's dollar and gold reserves may even increase. But the nation's resources have become tied more closely to United States capital. Actually, trade does not improve because inflation in manufacturing countries force Latin America's austerity-bound nations to pay more for their imports while receiving less for their commodities. And proof that the budget does not balance out under "austerity" is shown by the very fact that these austerity-bound countries are the first to ask for and receive budgetary-support loans.

Stability loans also improve, we think, a government's popularity. It is not accidental that Frondizi got $150

million just before the election. The loan's propaganda value
was well milked. Frondizi, his Cabinet ministers and economists, and the press that supported him spent two weeks
arguing on what to use the money. *La Prensa* was full
of suggestions, until it finally announced (Año XCIII,
Number 31,614, March 1, 1962) that a "coordinating
committee of economists" will consider "the various aspects"
possible. Why back Frondizi so hard? More than any other
Latin American government, Frondizi's encouraged United
States corporations to invest huge sums—on paper—for
extraordinary concessions throughout Argentina. The so-called
industrialization program, launched by Minister of Economy
Alvaro Alsogaray, included the denationalization of numerous
government-owned corporations, from steel mills to transportation lines to hydroelectric power plants. It brought
United States investment to its highest point, yet gave
Argentina a $500,000,000 deficit in 1961 alone and caused
more small businesses to file bankruptcy in 1958-1962
than in any other four-year period in Argentine history.
When Senator José Mario Guido became "President" late
in March, 1962, as the front for a military dictatorship,
the United States did not break relations or refuse to
recognize the new government (as we did in Peru); Argentina's
military were *"gorilas,"* that is pro-United States business
(while in Peru, the military junta that took over after the
1962 election tended to be nationalistic). Guido thereupon
reappointed Alsogaray, the symbol of the giveaways, and
we announced (June 6, 1962) a new $50,000,000 loan
for Argentina, then $200,000,000 more in credit. Another
$100,000,000 from the International Monetary Fund was
thus explained: under Guido, Argentina has returned to
policies of "strict monetary and fiscal discipline" (and
a foreign debt of $3 billion).

A deeper pattern is now becoming clear: The Alliance
for Progress, meant to or not, helps governments support
private enterprise through talk of reforms but with loans
that increase dependency on the United States. Are we
exaggerating this emphasis on private enterprise? Let us
see the stated record. The Subcommittee on Inter-American
Economic Relationships of the Joint Economic Congressional
Committee, (Number 7811, Washington, 1962):

A major effort of U.S. policy toward Latin America should

be to point up the merits of and assist these countries to develop a reliance on private enterprise and the processes of private investment decision-making. Everytime we encourage reliance on centralized planning we risk playing into Soviet hands, by showing a distrust of our own characteristic national method and encouraging the technique of our ideological competitors.

This is in direct contradiction to the Punta del Este Charter, which calls for "comprehensive and well-conceived national programs of economic and social development." And Moscoso himself gave away his free-enterprise outlook when he asked, to justify the slowness of Alliance-supported housing units, "Does the country under consideration have a sufficient number (indeed, any) private construction firms to undertake the job. . . ." Why must it be private? There are three main reasons:

1. As long as Latin America's industry remains in private hands, United States investment, which owns or controls almost half of the area's total worth, remains dominant.

2. As long as Latin America's industry and agriculture remain in private hands, vast equalizing and balancing programs cannot be undertaken, meaning that we shall continue to export our manufactured goods to Latin America—some $3.3 to 4.2 billion every year—and import our needed raw materials and commodities from Latin America—some $2.8 to 3.3 billion yearly. In point of fact, Latin America has had a deficit of more than $1 billion every year since 1956, and according to calculations by ECLA economists (Preparatory Report to the U.N. Conference on Trade and Development, Brasilia meeting, Jan. 1964), this deficit will average $2.3 billion by 1970, if current practices continue.

Attacking the problem from the other side, these statistics hide another harsh truth: Latin America could develop its own manufacturing industries but we cannot go on without Latin America's raw materials. Even Nelson Rockefeller has said: "North American industries everyday depend more and more on the raw materials of the Western Hemisphere. These sources are indispensable for the United States to maintain industrial production that amounts to more than half of the total goods manufactured in the free world." Another harsh truth: though Latin America owns not one of the companies that manufacture the goods it imports from us, we own about 85 percent of the companies producing the raw materials Latin America exports to us.

3. As long as Latin America's industry remains in private hands, our investments in Latin America will continue to bring us fat rewards. Investments abroad have always been less than remitted income. For example, in 1950 we invested, on a world basis, $0.7 billion; we brought home from our foreign investment $1.3 billion. In 1960 we invested $1.7 billion, remitted $2.5 billion. "Remitted income on private investment abroad," says a First National City Bank survey, "is actually the largest single item of our international receipts apart from merchandise exports."[4] This is especially true in Latin America. According to an official United Nations ECOSOC report: "In recent years the earnings of United States-controlled branch enterprises in Latin America have substantially exceeded the capital that the parent companies in the United States had put in."

Argument Number Two above also has an important corollary that explains our continuing relations with dictators —as long as they are anti-Communist. Aside from food (coffee, cacao, bananas) which we do not grow, we would suffer shortages in bauxite, tungsten, manganese ore, and tin if Latin America did not trade with us. In the Second World War we desperately needed, for military purposes: nickel, quartz crystal, quinine, tin, tungsten, rubber, antimony, chromium, ferrograde manganese, mercury, and mica—all produced in abundant quantities in Latin America. Even in the Korean War our investments in Latin America controlling the production or mining of strategic raw materials fed us copper, tin, zinc, lead, tungsten, vanadium, not to mention sugar, coffee, wool and vegetable fibers. As Edward Tomlinson has put it, "With [Latin America's] twenty republics solidly on our side, we could be almost invincible in time of war, even if they did not supply a single soldier to support us in battle."

To ensure such "invincibility" we have apparently decided to make pacts with the worst devils, covered up by fancy phrases. We are committed a million times over to oppose dictatorships and support democracies. Yet we have not only continued relations with dictatorships, we have even

---

[4] Which brought the following surpluses: in 1959—$0.9 billion; in 1960—$4.7 billion; in 1961—$5 billion.

supplied and trained their armies, and lent them money
to use for their personal indulgence. In 1961 alone, the
Inter-American Development Fund, restricted by the Act
of Bogotá to "assure the fullest measure of well-being to
the people of the Americas under conditions of freedom
and respect for the supreme dignity of the individual,"
and bound by the Social Progress Trust Fund Agreement
(the base of the Alliance) to make no loans except for
the "preservation and strengthening of free and democratic
institutions" and to "foster greater social progress," made
these loans to these dictatorships:

$5,300,000	to	Guatemala (Ydígoras)
3,500,000	to	Haiti (Duvalier)
2,750,000	to	Nicaragua (Somozas)
3,950,000	to	Paraguay (Stroessner)

Plus many other loans from other agencies, including grants
to finance the four dictators' armies.

In 1963, the figures were much worse:

$36,000,000	to	Ecuador (junta)
13,000,000	to	Guatemala (junta)
6,000,000	to	Haiti (Duvalier)
7,000,000	to	Nicaragua (Somozas)
9,000,000	to	Paraguay (Stroessner)

Moscoso, again, had an explanation: "Dictatorships have
given me more moral suffering than any others. I came
into this job with my mind made up to ignore them. But
I've changed my mind somewhat. You've got to keep
a flame alight in the hearts of their people." If the rationale
were really humanitarian principles—a flame alight in the
hearts of their people—we ought to lend money to Castro's

Cuba. Yet, after Cuba was hard hit by hurricane Flora in October 1963, and Casa Cuba, a New York social club, raised 50,000 lbs. of old clothes and shoes for relief, the U.S. refused to grant it an export license on the grounds that such shipment was "contrary to the national interest." Apparently, the more we analyze, the more the Alliance seems to be a sheer collection of words.

Moscoso was very good at words. In Colombia, where the Alliance has done its best work, as we shall see, President Guillermo León Valencia campaigned for the presidency as a great friend of the Alliance. Said Moscoso: "In Colombia, the political leadership understands the program." Said Valencia: "When the money comes in from the Alliance, I will take the check and hand it over to a committee, a fair committee made up equally not only of Liberals and Conservatives but also equally of men and women. Then you can be sure the committee will distribute it to you fairly." This is undoubtedly a very noble and fair concept of the Alliance, but is this what Moscoso means by "understanding?" In El Salvador, as we saw, Rivera, a military usurper of power, had himself elected—unopposed —after his party "won" all 54 seats on the national assembly in an election controlled by his army. The new dictator has committed his regime to the Alliance. Said Moscoso: "In El Salvador, the new President, Julio Rivera, and his people understand the program."

Calling the slumdwellers "the Voiceless Ones," Moscoso was quick to state that they "are the natural allies of freedom." He went on: "They are the natural, and potentially the truest, friends of the Alliance." And finally: "For our national interest happens to coincide with the interest of the peoples of Latin America to build strong economies and nations."

Without a doubt, this is what it should be. But Moscoso, who was a hard judge of others—"I do not care what a man says; I care what he does"—should be judged hard. "Most of the political leaders, I hope, will understand the unselfish motives we have," he said. But judged by what the Alliance *does*, not says, the Alliance backs only corrupt governments. It does not uphold democratic institutions, but helps dictatorships. It does not oppose military takeovers, but defends private enterprise. And when Moscoso was the boss it was not led by a man who did what he said, but who said he did what he should have done.

Moscoso personally wanted to be judged by what he did. Let us do so. The Cuban Invasion was organized by our Central Intelligence Agency. The CIA chose the Cuban exiles who were to participate, appointed their leaders, and trained both. It chose more than one hundred well-known followers of Dictator Fulgencio Batista, "including former police agents with criminal records—men hated by most Cubans, pro-Castro or anti-Castro," to quote Tad Szulc writing in *Look*. The CIA refused to back an underground leader named Manolo Ray because he was obnoxious to the pro-Batista men: Ray was anti-Castro but not anti-Cuba's social revolution. The CIA actually jailed on an isolated island in Guatemala seventeen anti-Communist but pro-reform anti-Castroites. Rather oversimplifyingly Szulc concluded: "With the decision to limit support to right-wing Cubans, the CIA assured the defeat of the planned anti-Castro invasion." Manolo Ray demanded that *Batistianos* be expelled from the invasion force. He explained that he opposed the return of expropriated property but would advocate adequate compensation and an end to both dictatorship and Communism. Although his group *inside* Cuba was the most effective and active underground unit, it was not enlisted. Obviously, the CIA's only goal was that after Castro's fall, Cuba be returned to its Batista conditions—totally dependent on the United States and 60 percent owned by the United States. The Cuban invasion tactics were masterminded by one Richard Bissell, then Number Three man in the CIA. After the invasion's failure, Bissell should have retired. Instead, in March, 1962, Moscoso appointed Bissell as his aide—to study how Alliance funds should be spent! It was also announced that Bissell would then go on to the Pentagon's Institute for Defense Analysis.

By what is done, not said, it seems inescapably clear that the Alliance for Progress was not aimed, during Moscoso's term, at his "Voiceless Ones" but at fostering "antikommunism" in Latin America.

Since then, such purpose has been made clearer. President Kennedy was assassinated. Martin was sent off as Ambassador to Argentina. Moscoso was made Ambassador to a newly formed Committee on the Alliance for Progress (CIAP). And President Johnson appointed as his "Mr. Latin America" that old Texan pal of his, Tom Mann, a pro-business, old-line hardliner who is known not to think much of CIAP, compromise, or conferences.

As Assistant Secretary for Inter-American Affairs during the Bay of Pigs, Mann favored using U.S. planes. As Ambassador to Mexico during López Mateos' switch to the Right, he pressured for repressions. As Assistant Secretary once again during the Panama crisis of 1964, he insisted that the U.S. not give in because the whole thing was caused by Communists and Castroites. There could be little doubt that under Mann, the Alliance would not be between the U.S. and Latin America, but between the U.S. and U.S. businesses in Latin America.

Chapter 20

Achievements

During the last ten years, Latin America has received more than $10 billion in public aid—the sum promised by the Alliance for Progress for the next ten. Not all of it has come from the United States Treasury, to be sure. Among the participants have been such charities as the Catholic Caritas, such Foundations as Ford and Rockefeller, a flock of United Nations agencies,[1] and other United States agencies such as AFL-CIO. Money has come from Public Law 480 (the lending of local currencies derived from the sale of our agricultural surpluses), food from our Food-for-Peace program, and labor from our Peace Corps program.

But 90 percent of this fabulous amount of money has been received by Latin Americans in loans, not grants. We have had a policy of keeping grants down to a minimum —in Latin America. That this policy is not motivated by our lack of financial strength is proved by the following facts: from 1945 to 1960, Latin America received a total of $625 million in nonrepayable grants, while the rest of the world received $31 billion; the Philippines alone got more grants than all twenty Latin American nations combined; most of our grants went to industrialized nations who needed them the least (and would not accept loans

[1] Among them: The International Finance Corporation, FAO, UNESCO, the UN Children's Fund, ILO (International Labor Organization), various Technical Assistance Missions.

that restrict their independence); one such independent nation, Yugoslavia, received almost three times ($1.5 billion) what Latin America's twenty received.

The biggest non-United States lending agency in Latin America is the International Bank for Reconstruction and Development, known as the World Bank. By June, 1961, it had lent a total of $1,252,970,000 to sixteen Latin American countries (and had recovered $1,200,196,000). As an international organization in which any United Nations member can share as stockholder and borrower, the World Bank has been able to make quite a few loans to non-private agencies, for example, $71,000,000 to Uruguay's public corporations. One of the best features of this bank is its policy of never lending money for balance-of-payment or budgetary support. Thus its loans have concentrated on development, namely:

Electric Power	52%
Transportation	34%
Agriculture	6%
Industry	5%
Communications	3%

The United States institution that has lent Latin America the most money is the Export-Import Bank, a government agency. This bank has loaned more than $3 billion to Latin America in the last ten years alone, but the greatest single purpose of its loans has been political, namely:

Balance of Payments	31%
Transportation	24%
Steel Mills	12%
Electric Power and Water	12%
Other Industries	9%
Mining	6%
Agricultural equipment	5%
Other	1%

Since 85 percent of steel mills and hydroelectric plants, 40 percent of transportation systems, 95 percent of mining, and 30 percent of all other industries are United States-owned, 70 percent of the Exim Bank's loans have not helped Latin America increase its capital.

However, since much of our balance-of-payment loans are used by Latin Americans to pay short-term debts due to European creditors, we are currently trying to toughen our loan policy. Other political loans—stability, United States credits, and so on—would continue, but loans used to pay off non-United States loans would be harder to obtain.

Most of today's political loans are handled by the International Monetary Fund. A worldwide organization open to all countries (currently seventy), the IMF is technically nonpolitical. But its philosophy and operations are guided by the old-fashioned concept that a steady boost in sound (undeflated) money increases the entrepreneur class, which in turn generates development—a concept that refuses to take into consideration the twentieth century pressure on social spending (which has caused British Economist Joan Robinson to dub economics a "branch of anthropology"). As a consequence, IMF, has become the main "political stabilizer" in Latin America. It conditions all loans to austerity measures, fiscal reforms, and tight credit restrictions. Furthermore the IMF has disproportionate powers because both our Exim Bank and the World Bank are now required to ask all prospective borrowers to get an IMF clearance first. This is very convenient for us: Latin American economies are pressured into being predisposed toward United States investments by an international organization that carries out the political pressure.

Some loans to Latin America have shown valuable results. Most countries boast new hospitals. Roads have been built in Uruguay, Paraguay, Bolivia, and Central America. Major housing projects, not all middle class, are up or going up in Rio de Janeiro, Bogotá, Cali, Lima, Caracas, and Santiago de Chile. Throughout the hemisphere signs stating "This project has been built with aid from the United States" can be seen at the entrance to hydroelectric and water purifying plants, experimental farms, factories, and so on.

In Bolivia, where Point IV (ICA, now AID) has been in operation since 1942 and where more United States-aid per capita has gone than to any other country in the world, we have set up an experimental farm in Cochabamba Valley, another near Lake Titicaca, a milk plant (with United Nations help) capable of turning out 40,000 liters of pasteurized milk daily, and various agricultural education centers.

We have given special instruction to 134 teachers, repaired 52 urban schools, and administered smallpox vaccine to 2,750,000 Bolivians. We have delivered 470 road-equipment units (worth $4,000,000), built or improved 2,500 miles of road, participated in the settlement of four self-sustaining agricultural units on virgin lands, and trained 230 officers in Panama, 25 engineers in the United States, and 99 public safety officers, 1,000 policemen, 55 public administrators, and 152 health officers on the job in Bolivia.

However, if the social problems that plague Latin America are as lethal as cancer—as both Latin American and United States reformers claim—the medicine that this aid is meant to be seems like an aspirin. In fact, such were the words used by one Latin American statesman, Uruguay's Eduardo Victor Haedo. The Alliance for Progress, Haedo complained when it was one year old, has sent many high-ranking representatives with advice and "good words" but has taken no action. He pointed out that Uruguay has submitted serious development plans under the Alliance program but that nothing had happened. "The Alliance for Progress has degenerated into a program of using aspirins to cure cancer," he concluded.

In the case of Uruguay, Haedo's argument is not totally justified. It is true that the United States has not acted on Uruguayan loan applications; but Uruguay's Parliament, which must approve all loans to the government, has refused to do so for more than a year. Actually, Uruguay's Parliament has been very wise to stall. Very little (if any) of the money we have lent Uruguay in the past has filtered down to its people.

This has been the case throughout Latin America. A four-lane highway has been built to Montevideo's airport, a farm to grow tomatoes in the middle of Haiti's sugar land has been proved efficient, a dock to accommodate foreign tankers to pick up Venezuela's foreign-owned oil has been constructed. But rarely has genuinely low-cost housing project been made available to the very poor.

Here's why—through an example. Uruguay wanted to put up low-cost housing units in various cities. It applied to the United States Embassy for guidance. The embassy's economic staffers investigated the needs, costs, and rents or prices askable in relation to salaries, the loss or profit margins this signified, and so on. These staffers, young, capable and hard-working, came up with a well-balanced, detailed report. The local work was done well—even without directives from Moscoso (one of whose first to-all-embassy-personnel messages was something like: "Hereafter work will not begin at nine or end at five, but will be considered continuous"—a message that did not change the lazy but insulted the dedicated). The staffers concluded that low-cost housing in Uruguay is badly needed. The propaganda value was considered well worth the risk (what risk? The Uruguayan Government was willing to guarantee the loans). Uruguay's Parliament was willing to vote in favor of the loan request. But it was never made.

Washington decided that because a thorough survey of Uruguay's long-range as well as emergency needs had not been prepared, because Uruguay's financing plans had not been made clear, because population growths, with urban-rural trends, migration and emigration projections, had not been traced, we could not make the loan. In other words, Uruguay was required to establish an overall national plan first. It would have to set up boards and committees, hire experts and train census men, stage the census, then plot tables and graphs, calculate equations, evaluate reports, and come up with a 300-page book, bound in colorful paper, with footnotes, a table of contents, and perhaps an index, entitled *Uruguay's Housing Needs, 1961-70* If this book were to get Washington's approval, another "Emergency Housing Development" committee would then have to work out a new plan for immediate housing needs.

Incredibly, Uruguay decided to try. It set up a planning commission, CIDE (*Comisión de Inversiones y Desarrollo*), with a budget, a capable staff, and offices. CIDE went on to sign contracts with the OAS, the Inter-American Development Bank, and ECLA (Economic Commission for Latin America) by which it would get a team of economists and technicians from these organizations to help it set up the overall plans.

Before anything else, however, CIDE's Uruguayan staffers had to be trained on how to collect and analyze data, how to use approved statistical and budgeting methods. They were so trained. Then, CIDE carried out an all-encompassing census. Now the staffers are in a position to work out an overall plan. When it is finished and if it is satisfactory to *us*, the Housing Department of CIDE will proceed to draw up particular housing-project plans. With luck and no new obstacles, Uruguay might finally build those low-cost units, except, of course, that by then the need will have doubled.

No one would deny that Uruguay needed a census, an overall plan, and a well-paid bureaucratic machinery to evaluate both. But no one that visits Uruguay's *Cantegriles* (slums) or overcrowded workers' tenements or rural waterless shacks could deny, either, that Uruguay needs emergency housing *now*.

And even if these plans *are* carried out, there is no guarantee that our loans will be approved any faster. Bolivia, Chile, Ecuador, and other Latin American countries have had overall plans for years, yet loans to them are just as slow. Everywhere in Latin America I heard complaints that loan applications were continuously being turned down, pending revisions. "A comma in the wrong place held up our loan two solid years," the director of Cali's light-and-phone company told me, an autonomous municipal-federal enterprise that has not lost money for ten years. The director of Costa Rica's Oficina de Planeamiento (Planning Board) replied to my question on how the Alliance was doing thus: "I don't understand the Alliance. The United States says it is for social and economic progress, but every time we apply for money, we are treated like corporation lawyers in front of bankers. Is it a banking mentality you want? If so, don't call it social progress. There has never been a banker in the history of the world who lent money for social progress."

In Colombia, where the Alliance has worked best, one of our friends, former Minister of Health and now Universidad del Valle Dean of Studies Dr. Alfonso Ocampo-Londoño, put the criticism this way:

> In this new program we cannot possibly fulfill the requisites of rigid banking policy or of detailed planning requirements for which we have not the preparation, the capacity, the money, or the time. It is a matter, therefore, of securing the highest possible efficiency with a maximum degree of flexibility. I believe that now is the time, at least in some instances, to trust ourselves.

In less diplomatic language, he simply meant that we should

decide what is important, our "success" in every loan
we make, or a chance for Latin America to save its own
people without bloodshed. If we want to help Latin America,
why must Latin Americans become Anglo-Saxons first,
adopting our style, our economics, or our standards? "Problems should not be adjusted to a system, but systems should
be adjusted to the solution of our problems," Ocampo-
Londoño said. "The Alliance for Progress was conceived
and born in order to make a strong initial impact and to
launch a long-term transformation of the economic and
social structures. In order to achieve these goals we must
act vigorously and not allow the program to be hidebound
by premature perfectionism and bureaucracy."

And if the Alliance's only goal is to make propaganda,
we seem to flub that too. In the small Chilean town of
José María Caro, Chile's Housing Corporation put up
a project of low-cost houses. The project, however, did
not include a pharmacy, post office, telephone, civil registry,
or health unit. Christian Democrat Senator Eduardo Frei
visited the area soon after people moved into their new
houses, and made a speech about hope—the Alliance for
Progress that would soon deliver $100,000,000 to help
the little people. A committee of Caro's new homeowners
thereupon went to Santiago to ask aid from AID. They
were told to make their request on paper in so many copies,
indicating who was their administrator, executor, trustee,
and so on.

The Russian Embassy got wind of the affair meanwhile,
and one month later, without prior warning, the new homeowners of Caro received two brand-new, fully equipped
ambulances. Within hours, Caro's new residents had organized
a schedule whereby each adult male driver would contribute
three hours a week, enough to assure two drivers on duty
twenty-four hours a day. Next, a nurse-training course
was organized for some 150 young men and women. They
learned how to use the emergency equipment, and divided
their time so at least one nurse would be available at
all times. "When I went back there," Senator Frei told
me, "the people knew all about the Alliance. They would
tell me: 'Dollars are for the governments, not for the people.'
Unfortunately, I could not show them proof of the contrary.
In Chile, United States aid does not filter to the people."
In the 1961 municipal elections, a majority of Caro's

population voted for the Left, naturally.

Much of our aid, to press the point, is not even necessary. Bolivia does not need experimental farms in Cochabamba Valley, which is so fertile that it can grow its own experimenters by the bushels. But Bolivia does need 10,000 miles of roads leading into the lush but uninhabited lowlands of Caranavi, Alto Beni, and Santa Cruz. Our missions have always insisted on quick and not very costly results—something showy, near enough to La Paz so that all visiting firemen can be sure to see it. We have built roads to Cochabamba, to airports, and to military installations. Landlocked Bolivia needs some kind of exit to the sea; until Peru or Chile allows it one on the Pacific, Bolivia must make the most of what it has on the Atlantic. To get to that ocean, it must rely on river transportation. The rivers are not very navigable, but enough so to let a heavy barge traffic filter down to the River Plate, then out to sea. Why is there not a network of roads connecting Bolivia's rivers to its population centers?

Bolivia's Corporación de Fomento (Development Corporation) is government-run, efficient, well-staffed with engineers, economists, and agronomists. It has successfully put whole battalions of Bolivia's armed militia to the task of clearing virgin lands, building colonization cooperatives and temporary housing. Fomento has already proved its worth by launching successful industries in many parts of Bolivia that, as late as 1960, were unchartered and unconquered. Yet our Point IV missions have refused to use Fomento engineers, technicians, or economists. Dr. Adolfo Linares, president of the corporation, reviewed the Bolivian-Alliance situation for me thus: "Up to now (1962), the United States has helped us a great deal—on paper. It is true that it has given us more aid per capita than to any other country. But except for budget support, which we have asked for, most of the United States help went for projects that your mission people thought we needed. Sometimes I could not find out what they were doing and often I discovered some other aspect of Point IV that I had no idea was even planned. My country is very grateful for all this aid, but now is the time to start planning ahead. We will not grow into a healthy nation with ten miles of roads here, twenty there, with a school here, a clinic there, with a cattle farm here and a sugar farm there—

especially when we ourselves are launching a whole sugar industry elsewhere. We do not need many little projects. We need one overall massive, co-ordinated project.

"We have one," Linares continued. "It was worked out in such a way so as to guarantee that within ten years Bolivia can be strong enough never to have to borrow again from the outside. Our plan is detailed, accurate, carefully thought out. It was prepared with the help of the United Nations, ECLA, and FAO. It establishes our aims, lists our potentials, describes our methods of exploiting them, and evaluates our chances. We have the technicians capable of handling it. They are not all graduates of United States universities. But they are able just the same. May I point out that not one of the industries that our corporation has started has been considered less than very worthwhile even by your own people. Why does the Alliance refuse to help us on this plan? Our main task is threefold: roads, electric power, redistribution of population. We have proved we can do it alone when we have money. We built the Cochabamba-Santa Cruz highway. We cleared the land, set up irrigation, put up the houses, provided the tools, and are maintaining medical assistance for the first ten thousand families settled in the virgin lands of Alto Beni, Caranavi, and Santa Cruz. Now we need more money, not only to continue what we started but also to prepare the tiny, specific, step-by-step plans that your Point IV people want."

Concluded Linares: "I know we should be very grateful for the Alliance, but gratitude will not feed our people, and more than half are still on the edge of starvation. They need help fast. If it does not come from the United States, we will have to find another way of saving them. But our methods may not be to your liking. Bread comes before elections."

A day or so later, I had a long session with political staffers of our Bolivian Embassy. I tried to find out exactly what our Point IV program was. I had already seen the AID people—but was only handed booklets. Some were very nicely arranged with tables and graphs in color and a romantic painting of a llama. But none gave me a clear picture of where the millions of dollars went. I did not have the time to check every item on the list because I had been much more interested in Bolivia's truly impressive agrarian reform and colonization projects.

Our embassy people could not help me either: they too were having a hard time finding out. One did point out that after Bolivia's university students had launched a literacy campaign, got plenty of volunteers to fan out throughout the country to teach the alphabet to peasants, and asked for help from everyone, our AID mission had sent them one man who quit after three weeks. The Russians, however, came through with so much material that not one volunteer has ever run short of pencils, paper, visual aids, or books. "There's nothing so depressing," one United States Embassy political staffer told me, "than to try to find out what the hell our foreign dollars are doing here."

At that point I could not help remembering that in 1961 a United States Senate Investigating Committee uncovered the following facts: millions had been lost in theft and spoilage of food in transit to Bolivia, in mislocation of irrigation projects and industrial plants, and in donations to wealthy Bolivians and wealthier Americans; among the United States beneficiaries of our foreign aid had been the holders of $57 million in defaulted Bolivian bonds issued in the 1920's.

Mismanagement can be corrected. But preaching seems to have become an unshakable habit. In Rio's *favelas* live hundreds of thousands of Brazilians who earn so little that they cannot afford even a dime for rent. Thus they use the waterless, electricity-less, sanitation-less hills of Rio (or São Paulo or Bahia or Santos or Anytown) to put up ten stolen or discarded planks, cover them with corrugated tin or paper, and call the result "home." It's free. Then, with much fanfare, the Alliance was announced. Rio's Governor Carlos Lacerda thereupon launched a slum clearance project. We sent him $2,500,000 worth of aid. Vila Alianza, a housing project in a workers' district, was begun. Actually, it was started with a rush just before Kennedy was supposed to visit Brazil in July, 1962, presumably so he could visit it and make a speech there (the visit was later postponed). When completed, Vila Alianza is to have 2,500 units of one room, one bath, and one kitchen each, and will be rented at 15 percent of the minimum salary (about $35 monthly).

But those who live in the *favelas* are generally the unemployed. Even if they do earn the minimum, their actual take-home pay is less than 20,000 cruzeiros a month, while 15 percent of the gross minimum is 4,000—a hard bite when a quart of milk costs 400 and a pound of Grade B meat as much as 1,000. Still, assuming that one family could afford the 4,000 and would move into one of these units— father, mother, and seven children in one room—that family must necessarily add a few rooms and build a fence to keep the tots from getting onto the nearby highways. But by contract all construction must be in keeping with the established style; for example, all fences must be made of bricks. One *favela* dweller was perfectly right to react: "I cannot afford brick, and if there is no fence my three children will run loose while I'm at work."

To Moscoso who visited the project in August, 1962, and who made a speech to the nearby dwellers of Bom Jesus (Good Jesus) "favelatown," all these regulations seemed normal. He said that the families who would move in would be ready to "assume new responsibilities," that they would be under the "obligation of maintaining solid individual credit," and cooperating with others "so that this will be an example and incentive to others." Moscoso's preachings stopped him from seeing that *favela* dwellers are far more cooperative than probably his Washington neighbors: the ones at the site he visited—and to whom he lectured in such lordly fashion—had, long before hearing of the Alliance, formed a community association and had themselves built a school and health center from planks, tin, and stones. But Democrat Lacerda had not been interested. As one *favela* dweller said: "We never received any help; the state did not send a teacher or a doctor."

Insensitive preoccupation with private enterprise has rendered much of our aid useless. We have sent hundreds of millions of dollars into Brazil to help increase its electric power. Almost all of that country's power units, distributors, and sale companies are United States-owned, mostly by American & Foreign Power Company of New York, a subsidiary of Electric Bond and Share, which is the largest investor in electric utilities thoughout Latin America. Argentina, too, has received many loans to improve its electricity production. Yet what are the results, in both cases? Argentina produced 646 million kilowatts per month in 1959; Brazil, 1,759 million. By 1962, Argentina was producing 630 million and Brazil, 1,356 million.

That private enterprise comes first in our AID-thinking is most obvious in the banana republics. New AID-financed roads inevitably lead to United Fruit or Standard Fruit or some other major private plantation, while the vegetable-growing small farmers are forced to lug their products over stretches that the best imagination would not call roads. In Guatemala, where I traveled extensively, the best paved highways are all along the coast and to the ports; the worst unpaved paths lead to farming centers of the interior—where the majority of Guatemala's Indians live.

Perhaps the Alliance's failure, caused by its unending allegiance to private enterprise, can be explained simply by the fact that neither Moscoso nor Kennedy, neither Mann nor Johnson nor any other of our Latin American policy-makers in Washington understands that most United States businessmen, operating in lands without business law or in lands where they can control the law enforcers, are out for only one thing: to milk the lands dry of all their wealth. As now operating, free enterprise is Latin America's worst enemy. Unless we understand this, and adapt the Alliance accordingly—instead of passing the 1963 Foreign Aid bill with the proviso that aid be cut off from countries expropriating our property, as our Congress has done—we shall eventually lose all of Latin America. As Professor Kalman Silvert has written, "The ultimate measure of the worth of a Latin American government should not be whether or not it is a paradise for foreign capital."

Then, perhaps, we shall reconsider our Alliance loan policies. Almost all of Latin America's big mines, for example, are owned by United States corporations. Almost all have received United States loans, which, as in the case of the Southern Peru Copper Corporation (Guggenheim), are used to claim a higher investment so as to make profits seem proportionately smaller. Naturally, not one of these mines ever runs short of the water it needs for its operations.

But in Peru's Comas region, four or five children die every day just from lack of water.

Chapter 21

Commodities and Common Markets

One of the most persistent arguments against the Alliance, heard from Latin American businessmen, politicians, economists, and labor leaders, is that no amount of aid or grants can offset what Latin America loses every year through falling prices on its commodities. Latin America is forced to sell cheap and buy dear. A drop of one cent per pound of coffee in one year can literally wipe out all gains from Alliance loans and grants, private foreign investment, and reinvested native earnings combined in Brazil, Colombia, and El Salvador. A drop of 10¢ a pound in wool prices can mean a loss to Uruguay equal to its whole budget. A drop of one cent per pound on Chilean copper can mean a loss of $11,000,000. On the other hand an increase of one dollar per television set costs Latin America about $15,000,000, and an increase of $100 per imported car costs about $50,000,000. And our TV sets and cars do keep going up while Latin American coffee, wool, and copper prices do keep falling.

As I said in Chapter 1, however, this gripe—though statistically accurate—seems to me invalid. If Latin America sold its coffee, wool, and copper to whom it pleased, it could get out of the vise. For example, Russia has repeatedly offered Uruguay oil for wool on a straight barter deal. Anti-Communists immediately complained that barter deals are unfair; they restrict free trade, eliminate cash earnings, and involve government interference (using its local oil distribution earnings to pay sheep raisers). This is true enough. But such a deal would eliminate paying dollars for our oil imports and might knock out the local competition of Shell and Texaco whose cash earnings are converted into dollars and sent back to the United States. Furthermore, a Latin American government might refuse all imports of TV sets, might exchange meat exports for a factory to make its own TV sets. Latin America must accept the fact that it is underdeveloped, that it needs industrialization, and that, until it can stand on its own two feet, it must stop its luxury imports.

This last policy is supposedly part of IMF "austerity" recommendations, but IMF also recommends the abandoning of all import-export restrictions. Development cannot be achieved, in the twentieth century, with halfway measures. If there's a coffee surplus and a meat shortage, there's only one way to solve both: force coffee growers to cut their production and raise cattle instead. If they refuse, expropriate. If there's an oil shortage and a power shortage, exchange whatever surpluses available for oil and the financing and building of electrification projects—until electricity is so plentiful and therefore so cheap that every factory, every home, every train can run on electric power, and oil imports can be sharply reduced.

Uruguay, for example, has enough rivers and water sources to feed enough hydroelectric plants to furnish enough power to run 100 times the number of factories now operating. Naturally, such hydroelectric projects would cost billions of dollars. But, fortunately for Uruguay, the cold war rivalry between Russia and the United States is fought on commercial as well as other levels. If one side is unwilling to barter oil and hydroelectric plants for, say, twenty years of wool, the other will. Such deals need not be so extreme, however. One hydroelectric plant for one wool clip. Once built, the plant's earnings from the sale of electricity can finance another. And so on. This presupposes, of course, that a country owns its own electric power. Uruguay does. But in Latin America as a whole, nine out of every ten utilities are owned by foreign corporations, almost always ours. (And in every such case, the utilities, be they electricity, telephones, gas, or transportation, are expensive and of extremely inferior quality and service.)

Latin Americans must learn to fight for their development. No one is going to help them: The old cliché that no one gives anything away for nothing applies to nations as well. Certainly, as we have seen, the Alliance is no giveaway. Most of the Latin American critics who praise our "generosity" as a people but condemn our businessmen for forcing prices to fall on their commodities and to rise on our manufactured goods are missing the point. They are fuzzy thinkers who mix sentimentalism (in philosophy) with patriotism (in economics). Here are some samples:

Enrique Caballero Escovar, a very anti-Communist, Castro-hating Colombian senator, lawyer and businessman, a former president of ANDI (Asociación Nacional de Industriales) which is equivalent to our Association of Manufacturers, told me:

> The Alliance ends up as just words unless coffee prices are returned to a fair level. We have lost, in the first year of the Alliance, almost twice as much as we have gained from the Alliance. Our raw materials control our whole economy. The World Coffee Agreement is a subterfuge. There is no reason why North Americans have to come and tell us that the American housewife does not want the coffee prices to go up and on the other hand make us appear like beggars. When coffee was sold at $1 a kilo we had $53,000,000 a month for our essential imports. Now, we have more coffee to sell, but the price is 41¢ and we have only $33,000,000 a month for more imports at higher prices. Pay us good prices for our coffee or—God help us all—the masses will become one great Marxist revolutionary army that will sweep us all into the sea.

Guillermo Bedregal, president of Comibol, Bolivia's government-owned mining corporation, an efficient, dynamic anti-neutralist, and pro-United States Nationalist, who has done much to improve the country's tin mines, fire their feather-bedders, and modernize their operations but still cannot avoid a monthly deficit of up to $500,000:

> The United States has been very generous with Bolivia. But we can never achieve a solid development just on

grants and gifts. We have to earn our development. And our only earner is tin. Many of our problems, I say, most, would be solved overnight if our tin was bought at higher prices.

Zelmar Michelini, a Uruguayan deputy for the liberal, welfare-statist Colorado Party, long one of Colorado Chief Luis Batlle Berres' "young Turks" and his personal friend, now independent (but within the Colorado Party) because among other reasons he opposes the Alliance (which Batlle does not) but is anti-Marxist ("I cannot be in favor of Fidel Castro") and has a fair nationwide popularity:

I think the Alliance for Progress is a mistake. The continent needs no charity in dollars, but stability in the price of its raw materials and fair prices for the industrialized articles we need to buy.

And so on. This most common of all anti-Alliance arguments really asks: "Why should the United States want to help us on one hand and hurt us on the other." But such an argument is based on a set of errors. First, that our government is the same as our coffee, copper, wool importers; second, that the Alliance wants to help Latin America's economic independence; and third, that the people of the United States would tolerate controls on fluctuation of commodities just as easily as we have accepted the fact that our taxed dollars are being distributed in Latin America.

What leads these neighbors of ours to such confused assumptions is their naïveté: they are anti-Communists and pro-United States; therefore, they assume that they are our friends, and thus think that our joint political philosophy should have its corollary in a joint economic philosophy. That this is in error we have seen already many times, by the fact that our government tries to stop Latin American countries from trading with Communist countries, while our own businessmen or our European allies continue to do so; by the fact that we forbid the sale of "strategic raw materials" to the Reds by our Latin American Military and Mutual Assistance Pacts but then resell Latin America's strategic raw materials ourselves to the Reds; and by the fact that our economy, needing Latin America's markets for our surplus production of manufactured goods, and Latin America's raw materials to fill our own shortages, is dependent—we erroneously insist—on Latin America remaining in a state of total or semiunderdevelopment. For all these reasons, plus the fact that as long as we sell high and buy low we help our own dollar shortage, we will not try (except superficially for appearances' sake) to stop the fluctuation of Latin American commodity prices.

Many of these fluctuations are deliberately created by our businessmen and even by our government. For example, early in September, 1961, just a couple of weeks after the Punta del Este Conference where we promised that we would try to favor Latin American commodity sales, we announced our intention to put on the world market huge quantities of our tin reserves in order to stop prices from rising. As expected, Bolivia was outraged. On September 14th an editorial in *Presencia*, a Catholic, pro-United States La Paz daily, wailed, "A policy that leads to such a situation cannot call itself constructive, nor will it be in accord with the spirit of the Plan for the Alliance for Progress." On September 18th Bolivian President Victor Paz Estenssoro, usually reluctant to criticize the United States publicly, sent a telegram to Kennedy (reprinted in the official daily *La Nación* on September 19th) expressing his "deep shock and alarm" at "the United States government announcement." Added Paz Estenssoro: "I must remind your illustrious government of its oft-repeated promises to take into account Bolivia's interests concerning the problem of tin. . . . (United States dumping) does not coincide with the intentions proclaimed in the Punta del Este Charter."

A year later, in September, 1962, Paz Estenssoro canceled his trip to the United States because of our announcement that we would sell 50,000 tons of our surplus tin on the world market. Such dumping depresses the world tin price, and Bolivia is badly hurt every time. (A *New York Times* editorial reminded its readers of our vast aid-to-Bolivia programs, concluding: "It is not sensible of Bolivia to kill a goose laying such badly needed golden eggs. Anti-Yankeeism will hurt Bolivia more than the United States." Not so, if it led Bolivia to nationalize United States holdings and to sell its raw materials to Russia.)

But our businessmen or government can also create fluctuations in other commodities besides tin. The world's copper prices, for example, are set by just a handful of British and United States copper dealers. Controlling copper production in Chile, Peru, Katanga, and in the United States, and smelters here or in England, they have forced copper prices on mined tin to drop consistently, though they often resell it to iron-curtain countries at a huge markup; this happened in February, 1956, for example, when Latin Americans learned that Chilean copper had been resold by England to Russia with our official governmental approval. Coffee prices are also manipulated by us to a great extent, as are wool, cotton, lead, and zinc prices.

But in our defense, it must be clearly and unequivocally stated that most of these commodities' prices would fluctuate (and generally fall) almost as much as they now do, if left to the mercy of free competition—unless, of course, Latin America's producers joined forces and coordinated their selling *and buying* (as an economic blackmail weapon) policies, using Russia's barter offers as an additional bargaining lever. Without such tactics, commodity fluctuations are bound to continue.

One of their causes is the purely seasonal price change (mainly for agriculture products); since 1901, for example, the average annual fluctuation in the mean price of cacao, coffee, cotton, wool, and sugar has been 27 percent. Two other causes—cyclical change (variations in demand) and secular trends (changes in consumer tastes) are hard to differentiate, though it is the former that has helped force lead and zinc (on which the United States has import quotas) to vary 18 percent a year, copper 15 percent, and wool 17 percent, while the second helped force tin, cotton, maize, and meat production and exports to fall 11 to 41 percent. Other factors that affect exports are technological change (coffee exports were hard hit by the invention and public acceptance of instant coffee) and the development of new producing areas (Africa, for example, in recent years).

Various restrictive measures have been tried on a world or regional basis. Three are now in operation: the export quota (coffee); the buffer stock agreement (tin); and the multilateral contract (wheat). None is really sound. The quota system restrains the free play of market forces, cannot hit a fair proportion between high-cost and low-cost producers, and encourages international smuggling (very high in coffee) by new or oversupplied producers. The buffer stock system is useful for temporary imbalances of supply and demand, since what it calls for is the storing of excesses that are released when demand finally surpasses supply. But signers must be rich enough to live off savings while demand catches up on their stockpiles, and this, in turn, prohibits them from using savings for expansion. The multilateral contract, finally, requires that importers sign minimum purchase and minimum price agreements before production begins and requires that exporters sign maximum release and maximum price agreements before production ends. Such contracts might help avoid fluctuation of prices on certain commodities only if all the world's buyers and sellers joined in the agreements—a most unlikely possibility. There are other international resources available, but they involve self-regulations and self-controls, as well as international cooperation and goodwill. As long as economic warfare is a valid weapon of the cold war, international cooperation is out of the question. As for self-regulations from Latin America's side, an attempt is now supposedly being tried out.

The attempt is the economic integration of Latin America, which has two sections: CAFTA (Central American Free Trade Association) and LAFTA (Latin American Free Trade Association). CAFTA, for all practical purposes, is insignificant, but both are being highly encouraged by the United States, the Organization of American States, and the United Nations. The Alliance for Progress insists on the "importance" of their success, especially LAFTA's, and is pressuring members to hurry up paper work and start actual integration measures.

The inspiration, of course, comes from Europe's Common Market, whose success becomes more phenomenal every day. In the first four years of operation, the Common Market has turned into the fastest growing economic unit in the world. In 1960, for example, Common Market industrial production jumped an unbelievable 12 percent and the members' GNP 7 percent (while our GNP went up 4½ percent). Such are the hopes and goals of Latin America's integrationists.

Thus, in 1958, Guatemala, Costa Rica, El Salvador, Honduras, and Nicaragua signed an agreement to integrate their customs, and in December, 1960, they further committed themselves (Costa Rica in 1962) to a Common Market, establishing in June, 1961, the Central American Bank for Economic Integration.

Much more important, though, is LAFTA, which was born in June, 1961, when Argentina, Brazil, Chile, Peru, Paraguay, and Mexico agreed to do the same (Ecuador and Colombia joined later in 1961 and 1962).

According to the LAFTA Treaty, a free-trade area is to be established gradually during twelve years. The removal of import duties will proceed through annual negotiations based on the principle of reciprocal benefits. The goal is to get rid of all restrictions on three-fourths of common trade by the end of those twelve years. Members are supposed to coordinate policies not only in respect to industrialization and marketing of farm products but also in respect to foreign investments. Each must set up a National List of products they want free-traded at a reduction rate of 8 percent per year. Then, at triennial meetings (the first one to be in 1964), they will place products on a Common List on which tariffs are to be removed 25 percent every three years.

Neither CAFTA nor LAFTA has a serious chance of success. First, as even the OAS special study group reported, "There is strong resistance to integration on the part of those with vested interest. . . . [Other difficulties are] differences in population pressure, size of the economy, income levels, degree of complementarity of the economies, entrepreneurship, and so on, as well as divergent social trends and political orientation." Because of such difficulties the treaties permit members to withdraw products from either list at any time.

In Europe's Common Market a multilateral payment scheme, credit arrangement, and currency convertibility help smooth operations (and creator Jean Monet is now trying to work out a single currency for all six members); in Latin America such a system is impossible because mutual exchange of goods represents only a tiny percentage of overall trade and is confined to a few unimportant products. The seven original LAFTA members' exports to the world: in 1948, $3,867 million; in 1959, $3,985 million. Intra-LAFTA trade: in 1948, $406.6 million; in 1959, $301.3 million, a sizable drop (and less than 10 percent of total trade). Overall industrial production by the seven in 1960 was $10 billion. Trade of manufactured goods among themselves: a mere $10 million. The exact reverse is true in Europe.

In any case, such a system would work only if all member nations stabilized their currencies and coordinated their financial policies. The latter, in turn, is impossible since LAFTA (and CAFTA) members' industries compete with rather than complement one another and are not strong enough to support heavy industry. To make industry complementary, the inbuilt "cooperation" snafus are formidable: one nation is supposed to trade off its right to produce a specific item (say, tractor wheels) in return for an agreement to supply another (say, tractor gears). But since any member can withdraw a product from the list at any time, the whole apparatus can come to a sudden stop (gearless or wheelless tractors).

Furthermore, Latin America's integrating nations are not at the same development stage, and their trade is unsurmountably disproportionate:

	Intra-LAFTA Exports		LAFTA World Exports
Argentina	45.6%	almost ¾	25.3%
Brazil	24.8		32.2
Chile	11.5		12.5
Mexico	1.1		18.9
Paraguay	2.4		0.8
Peru	13.8		7.8
Uruguay	0.8		2.5
	100 %		100 %

Also, LAFTA (and CAFTA) members do not form a "natural economic region." All 170 million people of Europe's Common Market area live in an area smaller than Peru, with excellent transportation facilities, diversity, and distribution of buying power. Whereas just transportation problems in Latin America are enough to kill off most intertrade; to ship steel, for example, from Buenos Aires to Santiago de Chile, which must be done by sea since roads or railways are impossible or nonexistent, is more costly than to ship it from Buenos Aires to Lisbon. Mexico is nearer Paris, London, or even Hamburg than it is to Buenos Aires. To trade with Peru, Brazilian ships must pay high Panama Canal tolls. In sum, until each Latin American country goes through its industrial revolution and develops its transportation facilities, a Latin American Common Market is bound to fail.

LAFTA's headquarters during its first, crucial year was at Montevideo's red-brick, rectangular Victoria Plaza Hotel, known to all as the VP. Indeed, only very important persons go there, since it is Uruguay's most luxurious—and expensive —tourist home, facing the Government Palace on Independence Square. Most of the delegates, their aides, and secretaries, observers, and staffers naturally resided at the VP, and LAFTA itself rented two full floors for $1,200 a month for its offices. In these offices the delegates from the original seven, then nine, signers talked hours on end, each trying to get the other to admit products of his country into one, two, or all of the others with lower custom rates. The bargaining was sometimes pleasant, oftentimes dull, all the time serious—for the bargainer. There was no unitarian philosophy behind it, no united-we-are-stronger atmosphere. Each delegate was there to get what he could for his country, not for Latin America. Not one officially expressed the thought that unless they all rose together, Latin America would never be in a good bargaining power in the world. Chile has copper but needs oil. Peru has oil but needs meat. Uruguay has meat but needs copper. They can take only a little from each other. But united they can withhold outside pressure. Chile can dump its surplus if it gets what it needs from the others. Uruguay can dump its meat if it gets oil from Argentina. United, Latin America could put up a fight.

But even united, Latin America would still not be self-sufficient—not yet. It could nevertheless hold its own against the big international market men. It could force prices on its exports up slightly, since without them many United States, British, German, even Russian industries would suffer. But the delegates were interested in only one thing: using LAFTA to make a few dollars more for their own big corporations.

In that, the delegates succeeded. They got some 2,000 items accepted among themselves at reduced custom rates. Now Argentine meat will go into Chile at a faster clip since, presumably, it will be cheaper on the Chilean market. But Argentine meat will still be taxed high in Uruguay, a meat producer. The whole first-year agreement, which weighs ten pounds in paper, is no more than a series of bilateral agreements. Except for very few, a handful at the most, all the items are already traded among the member countries; they are noncompetitive products. Where they are competitive, the importing country does not produce enough—and the exporting country could not sell enough abroad—for either to get hurt. And no item will help an importer accelerate its industrialization program.

It couldn't, even if all ten members decided to withdraw all restrictions on all their products: a nonindustrial country cannot help another nonindustrial country to industrialize. For this, what is needed is electric power, roads, trains, refined and not just crude oil, commercial steel and not iron ore or even ingots, shipyards, not ships; factories, not assembly plants for foreign parts; electronic machinery, computers, pipelines. Which Latin American country can export such items? Which even produces them? At best LAFTA and CAFTA could have formed a sellers' trust, a sort of federation for bargaining abroad. That it did not even succeed in this is proof that the delegates' governments are not peoples' governments.

Officially the delegates insisted they were optimistic. Mexico's Mario Espinosa de los Reyes said: "The first year has convinced us that we can look forward toward the second." Argentina's René E. Ortuño, whose government tried to show its interest by giving him Cabinet status, concluded: "We have proved this year that we can sit down at a table, exchange views and, most importantly, actually agree on specific products, no matter how unimportant they may be."

But the delegates were not blind. Off the record they had their doubts—on two levels. First, they agreed that even a huge increase, say by 100 percent, of Intra-LAFTA trade will amount only to an increase of $300 million or so. In view of the fact that Argentina alone has yearly trade deficits of $500,000,000 or more, such overall trade boosts are rather insignificant. And besides, as one delegate put it, "We need dollars to import heavy machinery if we are to industrialize, not pesos that can buy only more coffee or more meat. And dollars we won't get unless the United States buys more from us."

The delegates' second doubt was even more to the point.

In the words of one delegate: "Why should the United States insist on being a member, in fact the leader of the OAS, the Pan American Union, and everything else that is political? Is the United States Latin? Does it owe its heritage to Iberia? Is it a mulatto or mestizo nation? When we wanted to set up our own Latin American bank [as proposed by Chile at the 1954 Caracas Conference] the United States refused to join, insisted such a bank could not work, and told us to wait for the United States to create a better one, an Inter-American Bank which it dominates. And now that we finally need United States participation, when a hemispheric free trade zone which includes the United States would give us all bigger and better markets, when the United States itself insists on such a Free Zone,[1] then, oh, no!, the United States suddenly remembers it is not Latin."

Another delegate, who had been listening and nodding his head, then took out his nation's list of products presented at LAFTA. "Look at this list," he said. "This item is produced in my country by a United States corporation; so is this one, and this; in fact, look at it closely, and 63 percent are theirs. You know who benefits from LAFTA? United States businessmen."

---

[1] The Charter of Punta del Este says:

"The American republics consider the broadening of present national markets in Latin America is essential to accelerate the process of economic development in the hemisphere."

If the United States was a "partner" in the Alliance, as Moscoso claims, the wording should be: "The American republics consider that the broadening of present national markets *in the hemisphere* is . . ." Ask any Latin American producer where markets should be "broadened" most, his answer will be: in the United States. That the text reads "in Latin America" is another proof, say Latin Americans, that the Alliance is *not* meant to "accelerate the process of economic development" in Latin America.

Chapter 22

Military Aid

Military aid to Latin America is not technically part of the Alliance for Progress. But because the two go hand in hand, an evaluation of the latter cannot be complete without a close look at the former.

For many years Latin America has been receiving both monetary and logistic support for its Armed Forces. This practice, which is apparently to continue, was begun during World War II as part of our Lend Lease program. In addition, F.D.R. gave Brazil arms and instructors in 1944 to convince Vargas to place "two or three divisions near the Argentine border" to impress, as Cordell Hull put it in his memoirs, the "military gang in control of Argentina."

Because of the success of wartime hemispheric cooperation, President Truman was naturally reluctant to abandon it after the war. Though Congress refused to pass "military aid to Latin America" bills in 1946 and 1947, he got Latin American nations to join us in an Inter-American alliance (the Rio Treaty) in 1947.

Military aid was opposed by Spruille Braden (who resigned from the State Department in 1947) and Dean Acheson, then Under Secretary of State (in a March 19, 1947, memo to the War and Navy departments), as a policy detrimental to Latin America's economic development. But Secretary of War Robert Patterson insisted that unless we give such aid, we would lose our armament monopoly, enjoyed since the Lend Lease. Secretary of State George C. Marshall agreed with the Pentagon, and Congress finally began appropriating money for military aid.

By the end of fiscal 1959, 12 Latin American nations had received a total of $317 million in grants for military aid and 19 countries had received another $140 million worth of equipment. In 1960 military grants and equipment reached $96 million.

In theory, military aid is aimed at fortifying Latin American Armed Forces against extracontinental, that is, Communist, attack, and assuring us of their support in case of conflict. Are these aims achieved? Obviously not: no Latin American armed force has received enough aid to stop a Russian invasion, in the unlikely event one occurred, and only one nation—Colombia—has ever supported us in conflict, by contributing token forces to the United Nations command in Korea. What, then, is our purpose?

The first is to stop Communist *influence* within Latin America. That is why Kennedy, who had promised a cut in military aid during his campaign, reversed his position as President. In 1961 we sent Latin America's armies $91,600,000 in grants alone. In 1962 the total was cut back to below $70,000,000. But in 1963 military assistance to Latin America went over the $80,000,000 mark, as it was scheduled to do during 1964. Wrote James Reston in an August, 1962, column: "Nobody even talks about hemispheric defense now. It is conceded that subversion is the problem, that our arms are now intended to maintain internal order, that President Kennedy has formally authorized their use in this way."

But subversion by whom? According to a Senate investigating subcommittee report (which found Communists where others would find only Marxists), the Communist menace, in its 1958 numerical strength (see list, page 307) cannot be considered serious.

The maximum number of Communists in Latin America is still only slightly above one-tenth of 1 percent (.001). Thus, there is no chance whatsoever that Communists can ever win power through honest elections anywhere on the continent. Nor could they forcibly seize power alone. They can and do take over certain unions or even union federations. They can and do infiltrate student movements.

If there were secrets worth uncovering in Latin American defense ministries, they could easily find them and send them to Russia or to China. But by themselves, Latin American Communists are harmless.

Argentina	70,000 to 80,000
Bolivia	4,000
Brazil	50,000
Chile	20,000 to 25,000
Colombia	5,000
Costa Rica	300
Cuba	12,000
Dominican Republic	negligible
Ecuador	1,000
El Salvador	500
Guatemala	1,000
Haiti	negligible
Honduras	500
Mexico	5,000
Nicaragua	200
Panama	500
Paraguay	500
Peru	6,000
Uruguay	3,000
Venezuela	30,000 to 35,000
TOTAL	229,000

In conjunction with another party or movement, however, Latin America's Communists can and have reached power. The "Popular Front" has won elections in Chile and in Guatemala. And if Communists have not joined Popular Fronts more often, it is because in Latin America they have preferred to join the extreme Right, as we shall see, rather than the not-extreme Left. The point, however, is not that Communists can or cannot join forces with Socialists, Nationalists, or oddballists, but that the Socialists, Nationalists, and oddballs should *want* the Communists as allies.

This implies that conditions are so unfavorable for the nonconforming non-Communists that they are "pushed" into such alliances. And the conditions are so unfavorable because Latin America's militarists usually persecute all oppositionists as "Communists." Our arms, then, are used not against Communists but against Left-wingers and Nationalists.

In Frondizi's Argentina, Communism was officially outlawed and its press banned; all other parties (except Peronists) and all other presses were permitted. Yet such known Communist leaders as Luis Codovilla and Rodolfo Ghioldi were free to travel, talk, and even plot, and their newspapers and magazines were readily available (*Principios* was even legally published), while hundreds of non-Communist Left-wingers or Nationalists were constantly pursued. Scores of their magazines were banned, confiscated, and burned, including the famed *Che* and *Voz Popular* on the Left and *Alianza* on the Right.

Thus, as a "defense against subversion" we arm and aid Latin America's armies and as "defense against subversion" these armies persecute not just Communists but also all who oppose our policies. Costa Rica has no army, yet it is under no more danger of Communist takeover than any other Latin American country, in fact, much less so than most. On the other hand, Haiti has no Communists, yet its army has received plenty of aid, equipment, and United States Marines to train it.

"The objectives of United States military programs in Latin America are primarily political, although it has seemed wiser to express them in military than in political terms," wrote Edwin Lieuwen. He added:

Washington cannot and does not ignore the obvious fact that (Latin American) armed forces play key political roles in most of the republics. Nor can it ignore their seemingly insatiable desire for arms. Thus military training and assistance are provided to secure—and ensure—political cooperation. The arms supplied help keep the armed forces friendly; the missions provide a means for cementing political as well as professional relationships. Political gains are expected to flow from military programs: well-disposed governments, support for United States policies in international organizations and assurance of access to military bases and strategic raw materials in Latin America.

In 1957, Assistant Secretary of State for Inter-American

affairs Roy Rubottom[1] said frankly that our military aid
to Latin America is designed "to help develop the friendliest
possible relationship between ourselves and our neighbors
. . . and to encourage and bring about support of United
States policies"—and, of course, as Secretary Patterson
said and Professor Lieuwen repeats, "in cornering the
Latin American armaments market."

The purely profit-motive aspect of our military aid program
is made only too clear, unfortunately, upon close reading
of the bilateral military-assistance agreements between Latin
American countries and the United States. All of the agreements are about the same. (See Appendix B and Appendix
C for full texts of two that are typical.) The one with
Honduras, for example, specifies in Article I, Paragraph
3, that all of our equipment is to "be returned to the Government which furnished such assistance" if no longer used.
Unless Honduras keeps buying United States parts and
replacements, the aid-arms fall into disuse, and hence are
taken back. Paragraphs 4 and 5 stipulate that Honduras
cannot dispose of the aid in any way whatsoever except
as we decide. Yet in exchange for our "aid" (which remains
ours) we are entitled to sidestep all Honduran laws, duties,
and obligations concerning imports and exports (Article
V, Paragraph 3) and *regulate and control Honduras' trade*
(Article VIII). Furthermore, "to furnish assistance to each
other," we are entitled to *demand and receive* "raw and
semi-processed materials required by the United States
of America as a result of deficiencies or potential deficiencies
in its own resources" (Article VII). In other words, for
some puny military equipment that Honduras does not
need, we are entitled to import and export what we feel
like at no cost, inspection, or regulation, to dictate what
can be traded with whom, and to suck out of Honduras
whatever we need or think we might need from its only
source of wealth, raw materials.

---

[1] Appointed United States Ambassador to Argentina, Rubottom
in the few months before he "resigned" last October, made
himself—and the United States—almost as unpopular as Braden
had in 1945, and according to undenied Argentine press reports,
he was recalled after Frondizi was forced to ask Kennedy to
remove him.

Our arms and such nondefense policies have encouraged Latin American armies to rule, violating constitutions, denying elections, and making a mockery of democratic process. Their success has fortified the officer corps. Latin American officers oppose reforms; they come either from the oligarchy itself or from the oligarchy-emulating middle class. "Genuine agrarian reform in Latin America," concluded Lieuwen, "was impossible without the destruction of the officer corps." This is still generally true.

In Brazil, governments have always existed only as long as the dominant faction of the officer corps tolerated them. With 107,000 men in uniform topped by no less than 3,700 generals, Brazil's army can violate the constitution at will. Most of these generals have never respected democracy; most have never cared about public opinion or public needs; most have been at the service of the oligarchies and the powerful corporations.

General João Punaro Bley, for example, commanded an infantry division in Belo Horizonte in December, 1961, when the weekly *O Binómio* reminded readers that during World War II "he was closely connected with Naziism and Fascism, created the ill-famed Guaiamum German-style concentration camp for political prisoners, arrested most individuals who publicly condemned dictatorship and Fascism, dismissed Espírito Santo police chiefs who dared stop *Integralistas'* tumultuous demonstrations, apprehended books, newspapers, and pamphlets that attacked him, and was responsible for political murders." Bley thereupon sent troops to smash the weekly's offices, its machines, cameras, toilets (by bursts of machine-gun fire), and rough up and arrest its owner (later freed on order from Goulart).

But with so many generals, some are bound to be patriots. In fact, all it takes is one to set a precedent. Generals overthrew Vargas, Quadros, and, finally, Goulart. But then one general was loyal—Machado Lopes. His example was enough to force the officer corps to split wide open. As a result Goulart was able to surround himself with some patriotic generals. Had he not succeeded in this, he would long before he actually was have been overthrown by the group loyal to Lacerda. Goulart's generals have since been dubbed "the people's generals."

General Nelson de Melo, then Goulart's War Minister, helped create this impression by issuing a statement in

August, 1962, that "only a manifestation of popular will, freely expressed in the ballot boxes, will give the political and institutional stability necessary for constructive work." Another general, Commander of Army Schools Landario Pereira Telles, told Goulart, "We await your voice of command in the battle of national restoration." A few days earlier, Goulart's Premier Francisco Brochado da Rocha had made it clear that national restoration would be impossible without smashing Brazil's "voracious oligarchy that keeps the profits for itself and socializes misery." Obviously, some nationalistic generals—in Brazil—had finally realized that the time had come to "stand with the people." But they were too few still, and even many of them were eventually alienated by Goulart's wishy-washy self-interest. Thus Goulart was overthrown. But the true culprit is still our military-aid policy, which encourages Latin American governments to spend $2 billion a year—double what the Alliance lends them—on its armed services.

Those Brazilian militarists who tried to bring about Brazil's national restoration were denounced by the Lacerdas, by our businessmen, and by the Moscosos. These "democrats" who did not denounce the militarists when they overthrew Vargas or Quadros (because Vargas and Quadros were "independent") were suddenly outraged that United States-trained, equipped, and aided Brazilian soldiers dared to intervene in nonmilitary matters. An ironic moment in our military aid policy.

When Peru's militarists dumped our friend President Prado and canceled an election "won" by our friend Haya de la Torre, we immediately suspended relations (and when we renewed them, once the militarists made it clear they were not extreme Nationalists, we still did not resume military aid). We were suddenly "outraged" that Colonel Gonzalo Briceno, who led the attack on Prado at Pizarro Palace, had been trained at the United States Ranger School at Fort Benning, Georgia, and that the palace's iron gates were smashed open by a United States Sherman Tank. Similar scenes had occurred hundreds of times before. But we had never so protested—the militarists had always acted so as to preserve our interests.

Such examples of Latin American militarists behaving as Latin American patriots are still few. That they exist at all is extremely significant—for what will happen in the future. Ultimately, our policy of military aid to Latin America will have boomeranged against us. Sooner or later Nasser-type officers or, if we don't wake up in time, officers like Laos Neutralist Captain Kong Le will spring up all over Latin America. Meanwhile, because our Pentagon thinks (correctly still) that the militarists in most Latin American countries are strongly "pro-United States," our military aid continues.

Argentina's "pro-United States" militarists are still our Pentagon's best justification, despite the mess they cause. Argentina's army includes 147,500 men. Of these, 15,000 are upper-rank (from colonel to full general) officers. There are 30,000 more in retirement at full pay and benefits, and with only one diversion—plotting. Untried since it defeated (with difficulty and the help of our oilmen's advice and maps) neighboring Paraguay in 1870, Argentina's army gets only 20 percent of the national budget by law, but more than 40 percent in practice. In addition the army earns millions of dollars more as the nation's Number One industrial power, employing 20,000 civilian workers in twenty-odd plants producing everything from foodstuffs to planes, from TV sets and scooters to plows and tractors.

During Frondizi's rule, military men staged no less than thirty-eight coups or rebellions without punishment. They failed to overthrow him for four years only because he was always making deals with at least one important military faction, obeying that faction's dictates. In so doing, Frondizi eliminated almost all civil liberties. But when his policies finally backfired—Peronists won 9 out of 14 provincial elections—all military factions united to toss him out.

Because the new "rulers" were neither Nationalists nor Leftists, we had no trouble adapting ourselves to their new regime. There was no break in relations, no stopping of military aid, no public outcry. "There is very little difference of the Argentine military coup toward Peronists and of the Peruvian armed forces toward the APRA party, although the image of these two parties is very different in the United States," the *New York Times* admitted. The Peronists "are linked to the figure of an exiled dictator who was anti-American, the APRA party . . . is militantly anti-Communist." There was a difference in the outgoing regimes, too. Peru's Prado had ordered his representatives to support us at the second Punta del Este Conference, which tossed Castro out of the OAS; Frondizi had abstained.

Argentina's militarists are too ambitious to let independent elected officials alone, or even allow puppet presidents follow orders quietly. Thus they are constantly fomenting trouble over rules, laws, appointments, and policies. From April until December, 1962, not one day passed without some military squabble. Since Illia's inauguration, they have argued over promotions. Sooner or later, one general will impose his will. Sooner or later, future elections notwithstanding, a one-man military dictatorship will return to Argentina.

We are hoping it will be a *gorila*, one of those brass-heavy frontmen who, under the phrase "democratic transition," ends up allowing the plunder of Argentina by its oligarchy and our corporations but who proves his "democratic genuineness" by jailing "Communists" (not Codovilla or Ghioldi, naturally), by breaking relations with all Communist countries and by selling all of Argentina's exports to the West (which then may resell them to the East).

The Communists are hoping for a "Fascist," one of those old-fashioned *caudillos* who gets sentimental at the sound "corporative state," an iron-fisted man with iron-lensed eyesight who will destroy Argentina's value to us by stimulating constant friction, yet be so anti-Communist that we would never dare to send a battalion of Argentine exiles across the River Plate from Montevideo to unseat him.

And the people are hoping for a Nasser-type Nationalist who will listen to both sides, sell to both sides, and keep both sides from interfering in Argentina's affairs, a man who is neither Red nor Black, neither Democrat nor Plutocrat, but simply an Argentine—who will lead Argentines into the long-delayed Reconquest of Argentina.

Chances are we will have our way—for a while longer. Historical trends never change rapidly. Latin America's military, with only the exceptions noted, have always been anti-Latin America. And they have always been strong enough to defeat the Latin Americans.

From 1930 to 1957, for example, fifty-six military men held power for one year or more in Latin America. In Argentina, in the same period, eight out of ten "Presidents" were generals or colonels. Today, the army (or National Guard) dominates politics outright or from behind the scenes in all Latin American countries except Costa Rica,

Mexico, Bolivia, Chile, and Uruguay.

In Chile the 1964 election can reincarnate the army. In Bolivia, a new army can reappear anytime, especially if the feud between President Paz Estenssoro and former Vice President Juan Lechín continues. And in Uruguay, where we have helped modernize it, the traditionally nonpolitical army is gaining new ambitions.

The late demagogue former Government Councillor Benito Nardone who classified all his opponents, including the Catholic Unión Cívica (now Christian Democratic Party) as Communist when I was there, once called for military rule. When I complained about this to one of our Military Mission chiefs there, he told me: "But it's all right, don't worry. The new Uruguayan Army has been well indoctrinated, especially the officers. Whatever they do, even if they do seize power, they'll be with us. When I first came here, I was very depressed about the army. The boys looked like a bunch of bums, and they didn't give a damn about what the government was doing. Now they care enough to keep it in line. If they see it go wrong, they'll throw it out all right—I hope. That's my doing, in part at least. I consider their new army the greatest accomplishment in my career."

In 1937 when Sumner Welles suggested sending warships to Latin America, Eduardo Santos, leader of Colombia's reactionary Liberal Party, wrote: "Don't do this evil thing to us. The use of armaments is like the vice of morphine. Once begun, the cure is almost impossible. You will ruin us with cruisers and create for us new problems. . . because there is always someone with the desire to try out the armaments and obtain from them some advantage." In 1946, when the Inter-American Military Cooperation bill was submitted to our Congress, Chile's President-Elect González Videla said: "I don't like any idea that means an increase in our spending on armaments. . . . We're too poor to bear the load and need the money to raise the public standard of living."

But we did, and the arms race ensued, renewing old rivalries (between Ecuador and Peru), accentuating spending (Latin American armies cost $2 billion a year, more than all our aid, Alliance, private foundation grants, and so on, combined), and stimulating dictatorship-prone militarists (as in Colombia, where in 1953, after the military had been out of power for half a century, the receipt of aid gave fuel to a military rebellion, followed by a military rule).

After the Venezuelan army overthrew AD and set up a dictatorship run by Colonel Pérez Jiménez, Truman wrote to the AD leader and famous novelist Rómulo Gallegos (1948): "I believe that the use of force to effect political change is not only deplorable, but contrary to the ideals of the American peoples." Nevertheless, we proceeded to pour aid and advice (eighty United States officers and men in 1957) to Pérez Jiménez.

United States military equipment has been used to crush strikes and smash protest rallies by Chile's Ibañez, Colombia's Rojas Pinilla, Cuba's Batista, Peru's Odría, and by most of today's "anti-Communist" presidents or premiers. In Nicaragua, not only do the Somozas use our material to squash all opposition, but our missions there have come to represent both United States complicity and United States corruption. The agreement (see Appendix C for complete text) setting up those missions, signed November 19, 1953, specify, for example, that their members shall be immune from civil jurisdiction of Nicaraguan courts (Article 12), shall not be subject to any tax or assessment (Article 14), shall have all their goods, baggage, and automobiles transported by and at the expense of Nicaragua (Article 15), and can import what they wish without inspection, tax, or restriction (Article 20). Such agreements profit from extraterritorial rights unknown in nonoccupied lands since Commodore Perry's fleet bullied "trade agreements" out of the Japanese Government in 1853.

No wonder, then, that "much of the available evidence seems to indicate that the military aspects of United States foreign policy have been appreciated and supported by scarcely anyone in Latin America save the armed forces," as Professor Lieuwen says. "The great majority of civilians, whose experience leads them to fear their own Armed Forces far more than they do the Russians, are opposed to these military programs."

As long as our military aid continues to flow south, Latin Americans continue to think that there is only one way to defeat their armies—by arming the people. Mexico's revolutionaries did just that in 1914, and even there a

whole generation had to pass before the outcome—a basically nonpolitical army—was created.[2] Bolivia armed its
miners and peasants in the 1952 revolution, and Cuba's
barbudos, after routing Batista's United States-trained and
equipped regulars on the battlefield, replaced the professional
army with peasant militias.

Significantly, only three wide-scale agrarian reforms have
been seriously tried in Latin America (excluding Arbenz'
attempt which was quickly nullified by Dictator Armas'
army): in Mexico, Bolivia, and Cuba—the only three nations
where the people defeated the armies.

Armies are led by officers, and officers are like oligarchs:
they live too well to know suffering, too restrictedly to
understand other classes, too standardly to ignore intrigues,
and too superficially to reject all propositions of con-
spiracies. If democracy has caused corruption, immorality,
fraud, and exploitation to become ingrained in Latin America, only people's militias can wipe the slate clean; only
a movement in which the masses feel direct participation
can overturn the structure.

There is no logical argument that proves these militias
or this movement must be run by Communist elites; on
the contrary, most Communist "revolutions" in Europe
have been Communist coups, aided by Russian tanks, and
the people were never armed. Nor is it necessary that
the leading elite not be military; on the contrary, most
Nationalist movements are usually strongly influenced at
the top by military members of such movements. But
the revolutionary Nationalists, be they military or civilian,
must be able to overturn the very institutions from which
they have come. And the best way to overturn the armies
of Latin America—the only way that has been successful
so far—is to arm the people.

[2] Mexico wisely refused to sign the Mutual Defense Assistance
Pact, has kept military budgets low (12 percent), officer corps
small (3,500) and promotion within the army (limited to 50,000)
only on merit and examination.

Chapter 23

Case History: Colombia

Nowhere in Latin America has the Alliance for Progress done so much or so much good as in Colombia.

Actually, we have been providing this country aid for a long time. In 1943 we began helping its health and sanitary programs, in 1954, its agriculture, and in 1958 its education. This was supplemented in recent years by special assistance in malaria eradication, and since 1961 in housing.

But except for these Special Assistance programs, all of our aid mission's work has been in the training of Colombian technicians, either by arranging for our experts to go to Colombia or by sending Colombians to the United States or by stimulating joint programs by United States and Colombian universities. Until June, 1961, we had spent a total of only $16,000,000 in Colombia. Therefore all our major visible accomplishments in Colombia today are the direct result of the Alliance for Progress.

In Colombia, the Alliance has concentrated on a few specific, top-priority target areas that are related to Colombia's ten-year economic and social development plan. Colombia is another in the small group of Latin American nations that have worked out such a plan, and the only one whose plan we have approved.

Adopted in 1958, Colombia's Plan called for specialized studies (on customs, postal service, the ports agencies, and so on), an Agrarian Reform Institute, and regional development authorities. A government Planning Department was set up to screen all requests of foreign assistance, remaining in constant liaison with AID, ECLA, OAS, CARE, Rockefeller, the United Nations, and other aid-dispensing institutions. In December, 1960, Colombia enacted new tax legislation giving incentive writeoffs or concessions for "industrializing" ventures on the one hand, and creating graduated taxes on incomes on the other. On June 19, 1961, an IMF report praised Colombia's public revenues representing "one-fifth of national income, which is a fairly high rate of taxation for an underdeveloped country" (though tax collection has been and still is very lax, especially on the agricultural sector where it borders the zero mark).

The 101 articles of the Agrarian Reform Law, which the Institute administers, is basically a colonization program, though some reforms are contemplated: the expropriation of unused lands and of huge extensions detrimental to sound economics, and the redistribution of land in such a manner as to avoid uneconomic parcelization. The articles are general enough so that either a wide-scale or a meaningless reform can be the outcome, except for one stipulation: expropriated lands will be bought at market values and the buyer must pay for it on credit at interest. These clauses, which we insist upon as part of "self-help" provisions, mean that the mass of agricultural workers who live outside the money economy on a barter-for-goods basis, and hence have zero credit, will not be able to acquire expropriated lands.

Whatever the ultimate fate of the Land Reform project, absolutely no reforms have yet been undertaken in the social field. Exploitation, peonage, and even old-fashioned slavery (illegal) are still practiced just as they were before the Institute went into operations. No expropriations have taken place, one reason being of course that the government does not have the money to pay for them.

A few agricultural projects, called "reforms," *are* under way, and the United States is helping turn them into successes. Ten land-reclamation projects, for example, are being planned for the next seven or eight years, costing some $100,000,000. One, in Subachoque near Bogotá, will cost about $20 million of which half will come from the United States. The project will include a dam and irrigation canals. Another project on the Río Sinú on the Atlantic coast will render 100,000 hectares fertile, costing $7,000,000 for the first, reclamation stage. Another project for flood control is to begin soon in the Magdalena Valley.

A project of major importance in terms of its significance is a survey to be run by the Agustín Codazzi Institute, an autonomous (nonpolitical) government geographic agency that will photograph, map, test, and evaluate Colombia's soil, a fundamental first step for any vast-scale agricultural program. The United States has correctly accorded this project top priority, contributing $1,500,000 in grants (partly) to support contracts, equipment, and the training of Colombian technicians by thirteen United States experts.

Because 90 percent of Colombia's 30 million agricultural hectares are grass—natural or unimproved—while Colombia is still a meat importer, the Alliance is also lending $100,000 to the Agrarian Reform Institute for the development of a credit program to help boost the rate of beef production, cutting the current five-year cycle (or more) to eighteen months. The objective is to turn Colombia into a meat exporter with a 1970 foreign earning goal of $70 million from meat alone. In this connection we are supporting a national program of artificial insemination of cattle, having brought in 15,000 ampoules of frozen semen from the United States in 1961-1962 which were crossed with native cattle and "took" on 70 percent of the cases (United States average is never more than 75 percent). All cattle expansion programs are being handled by private corporations helped by the Institute.

Our AID mission is also interested in helping lower-class co-operatives on a voluntary basis and is considering both technical aid and a dollar loan for cooperative credits to the Caja Agraria. But the program is being stalled, our agricultural people insist, because of the lack of potential managers. Another program being investigated is for the diversification of agriculture through the raising of (1) crops now imported (vegetables producing oils, jute, or kenaf, a good substitute, and sheep, cacao, and perhaps rubber) and (2) cash crops (bananas,[1] and yucca, which is good for starch and paper industries and is cheaper than corn).

AID assistance for schools, mainly primary schools,

[1] See page 171.

is also new—and impressive. The Project Agreement, including $3,770,000 in Alliance funds matched by Colombia, was signed on December 12, 1961. Yet by June, 1962, thirteen schools were already in operation. The schools are not fancy, but comfortable, well lighted, airy and gay. The one President Kennedy visited during his March, 1962, visit to Colombia is in a district called La Perseverancia (perseverance), once an area in which no policeman dared walk alone, even with a submachine gun. In 1962 it was safe enough, since my wife and I wandered carelessly all through it. At the school itself—we arrived just during a play break—we were welcomed by about sixty-five tots, each of whom insisted we inspect *his* classroom. Perhaps the Kennedy visit had made them realize that they were among the lucky; whatever the reason, there was no doubt that these children, born and bred in slums, were proud of their school.

Our AID Colombia mission has also launched a series of teacher-training centers, and is currently training administrative personnel not only to handle schools but also to prepare, produce, and distribute teaching and school materials. One such center, in Palmira in the Pacific Cauca Valley, had developed some amazing visual aids, with just a few strips of color cartoons, attractive enough to make mathematics a game rather than a chore.

Early in 1962, the educational achievements of the Alliance were temporarily clouded by a bit of tactless no-yes-ism. Pressured by Protestant lobbyists, Washington toyed with the possibility of sending future aid to Colombia only on the proviso that the aid be dispensed without religious discrimination. This would, of course, create a nasty problem, since Catholicism is the state religion in Colombia, and all state schools are compelled by law to teach religious (Catholic) education and to require allegiance to Catholicism. Though it is unfortunate that such provisos must come about as a result of Protestant pressure, it seems to me that the no-discrimination clause is perfectly justified: the Alliance's stated motive, after all, is to help develop social progress under democratic evolution, and neither democracy nor social progress is possible in countries where Catholic dogma is federalized and officialized.

It seems to me a glaring contradiction to help precisely those institutions which most force dogma into innocent minds, namely, primary schools. And Colombia's schools certainly do uphold such dogma; every one I visited was crowded with statues, paintings, and inscriptions revering Christ, the Virgin, almost every saint imaginable, confession, communion, and so on.

In any case, when the news of such possible antidiscrimination aid clauses hit Colombia—via a UPI article signed by Martin P. Houseman—then-President Lleras Camargo immediately issued an official communiqué stating that Colombia would categorically refuse all aid so conditioned—and *we* said no more about it. The UPI report was interpreted by officials as interference in the domestic affairs of Colombia, which it would have been if carried out, and our abandoning the issue was interpreted by progressives as our unwillingness to risk offending Colombia for the sake of democratic principles, which it was.

By far our best showing in Colombia has been in the field of housing. True, Colombia was ready for housing aid through its Instituto de Crédito Territorial, or ICT (Land Credit Institute). Formed as a result of a 1938 law (Number 224) to alleviate the housing shortage already serious then, ICT was at first no more than a union of mortgage banks. By 1942, however, it was lending money for housing developments to municipalities and cooperatives, and by 1946 the ICT policy of helping low-income families was made clear by its self-imposed restriction of lending money only to families whose personal holdings were less than 30,000 pesos (then about $8,000). ICT's funds were raised through bonds, at 6 percent to mature in thirty years, in which savings banks were forced by law to invest 25 percent of their deposits. And when rural housing developments were passed on to the Caja Agraria in 1956, ICT became an autonomous federalized agency dedicated exclusively to urban housing.

Despite ICT's emphasis on lower-income housing, its projects inevitably attracted mostly the middle class. Thus, in 1959, ICT lowered production costs—and loans—to 15,000 pesos (only about $3,000 by then) and has tried to keep to that scale ever since (which, because of inflation, is now at 25,000 pesos, still about $3,000). It has added higher-cost projects for middle-income buyers, as well.

"Self-help," which we keep insisting on, has been part of ICT's programs for years. The Institute has various kinds

of projects, all of which require the active participation
of the prospective tenant. In some cases he is given land,
a house shell with plumbing and sanitation, and a loan
for additional material which, under ICT supervision, he
must use to furnish his house in one out of five or six possible styles. In other cases, a buyer receives his house completed and pays off part of the loan by working so many
hours free a week for so many months or years on the
other project houses. In still other cases, the prospective
owner receives only the land and installed plumbing, and
must build the whole house and also pay off the loan for
the land and material by helping lay the area's roads and
build its schools, health, and community centers.

From the builder's angle, there exist many forms of
financing. In some cases, the owner is required to put up
one-third; the builder finances one-third at 10 percent,
guaranteed by ICT, and ICT puts up the remaining third.
In other cases, employers pick up the first third, deducting
it from the employees' paychecks. In most of its projects,
ICT puts up a little more than half of the money and we
put up the rest. On the average, a completed house for
a buyer who will work off some of his mortgage (either
on his own or on someone else's house) costs no more than
5,000 to 6,000 pesos, that is $600 or $700.

All ICT projects are meant to include the guidance of
social workers, who help the new owners organize their
living, washing, eating, and garden areas in such a way as
to assure them maximum space distribution (for minimum
tensions) and maximum functionality (for maximum health).
Unfortunately, ICT is short of such social workers and
has requested, backed by our embassy housing experts,
trained Peace Corpsmen to fill the gap.

As part of the Alliance, we gave ICT $500,000 in May,
1961 (Special Assistance grant), $12,000,000 in June, 1961
(DLF loan), and $15,200,000 in February, 1962 (IDB
loan), with the promise of more. In 1961, 10,000 homes
were completed. In 1962 the goal of 40,000 more was almost
realized on a total ICT expenditure of 509,000,000 pesos
(about $56,570,000) of which 227,000,000 pesos (about
$25,220,00) were contributed (loaned) by AID or other
United States agencies.

One particular housing project, inaugurated in March,
1961, by the visiting Kennedys is going up on Bogotá's

old airport called El Techo (the roof), an area of 308 hectares. Completed, it will have 12,000 one-family houses (about 84,000 inhabitants) and will have cost 200,000,000 pesos of which 81,000,000 (about $9,000,000) were loaned by AID. A bus hour or so out of town, El Techo currently appears extremely disorganized. Because the houses are going up by groups, some are already lived in, others are up but without interiors, others still are just beginning to sprout out of the ground. On weekdays, after 6:00 or 7:00 P.M., on Saturdays and Sundays, thousands of future dwellers, perhaps helped by a few friends, can be seen hard at work on their own or their neighbors' houses or on El Techo's various centers and schools. Sewer pipes are being laid, streets are being marked off, gardens are being leveled. Most of the houses, of white bricks and white clay-tile roofs, have two rooms, with loft-type cutoffs on top for the extra children, a kitchen, a bathroom, and enough surrounding space for a vegetable garden or additional rooms or both. Each completed house I saw seemed perfectly comfortable, a house that might cost about $5,000 or $6,000 here at home. There, each house's cost of $1,625 includes, pro-rated, expenses incurred for erecting schools and community health centers.

AID has undoubtedly done well in Colombia.[2] It is not surprising that Kennedy was greeted there with tumultuous ovations. I was not in Colombia when he went there, but all my correspondent friends who accompanied him later told me that as much as his Venezuelan welcome was phony, too well organized, and "assured" by government bayonets, his Colombian reception was genuinely spontaneous and warmly popular. Even the extreme Leftists admitted to me later that attempts at keeping Colombia's reception for

[2] Credit for which, in passing, should also be directed in part toward our Ambassador Fulton Freeman (who then replaced Tom Mann in Mexico). Milton Drexler, USAID's housing adviser, is a former house builder and construction-company owner who may not be a refined diplomat but, much more importantly, knows how to get houses built well and gets his satisfaction from seeing them go up in Colombia; in fact, the whole AID team seemed, if not more capable than usual, at least more enthusiastic—with reason, of course.

Kennedy cool were dismal failures.

Yet, for all its accomplishments, AID has not forced meaningful reforms in Colombia. Perhaps as many as 300,000 people will live in new homes by the end of 1964. Perhaps as much as 300,000 hectares fallow today will be cultivated tomorrow. Perhaps Colombia's export trade will increase by as much as 20 percent in the next four years. These are *gains*, but not *changes*.

The vast majority of Colombia's people are held in semifeudal bondage, chained to the land of others through peonage, unable to escape either physically (they are stopped by the police, army, guerrillas, or bandits) or economically (they receive no cash for their labor). Most of the Alliance showplace projects are in the cities—out of reach of the rural masses. There is a shortage of 400,000 houses in Colombia today, and that figure is augmented by 40,000 to 50,000 more every year.

A country as large as Texas, Oklahoma, and New Mexico combined, it has only 2,065 miles of railroad and 18,613 miles of roads, of which less than one-sixth are paved. It has only three hospital beds per 1,000 inhabitants (11 in the United States), and almost 3,000 inhabitants per doctor (780 in the United States), 80 percent of whom are in the big cities despite the fact that more than 50 percent of the population lives in the fields. Almost 50 percent of its people have never been inside a school; only 6.5 percent finish primary school. About 92 percent of the land is owned by 12 percent of the people and 65 percent by 3.5 percent. More than 70 percent of Colombia's agricultural export dollars (mostly from coffee) are earned by 90 individuals, and 56 percent of all local capital is owned by 320 individuals. That means that 410 individuals (actually much less, since the agricultural exporters are also the city capitalists) earn more than $7,000,000 *each*, while the average per capita income is $300. And 50 percent of the population lives outside the money economy.

United States direct investment in Colombia is about $400,000,000. Private United States holdings are worth about $2,000,000,000—in oil, power and light, shipping, rubber, chemicals, textiles, construction, mining, auto products, and machinery. Colombia has an investment guarantee treaty with the United States, meaning that any expropriation must be paid for at satisfactory (to the United

States) prices. It also has a Military Assistance pact with us, meaning that it spends some 800 million pesos (almost $100,000,000) on arms and armies yearly. About that much was taken out of the country in 1961 as profits of United States-owned corporations. Another $100,000,000 was shipped out of the country by Colombia's oligarchs to be deposited in United States, Swiss, or West German banks.

By Colombia's law only two parties can present candidates—the Liberals and the Conservatives. Both are run and controlled by, and at the service of the oligarchy. Socialists, Agrarians, Nationalists, or any type of "nonconformists" have no electoral voice or representation. All governmental offices, institutions, services, and so on, are (by law) run fifty-fifty by Liberals and Conservatives. Even if one of the two parties fell into the hands of modernists, all actions must be approved by two-thirds of the directorates (or Congress), which are split fifty-fifty. Under such conditions how can meaningful reforms ever be enacted? Those who would be hurt by them control all legal and structural power.

Who benefits from the Alliance in Colombia? In some cases, the not well off, certainly. But not the 50 percent of the population that has no money whatsoever. And of the rest, can any man who has a job afford an Alliance-ICT built house? The average Colombian worker (meaning *not* the lowest paid) earns $100 a month in metals and textiles, $80 in foodstuffs and tobacco, and $70 in furniture and shoes—for an average week of 51.6 hours. Milk costs him 10¢, each egg 5 or 6¢, a pound of beef 45¢, cheap meat 30¢, poor quality blue jeans $2, a wool suit $35, a small desk radio $25, a television $300. It averages out that a frugal worker's needs (not a tourist's) are about one-third the United States equivalent, meaning that the average skilled worker earns, in United States-cost scale, at most $300 a month.

Many $300-a-month workers could afford a home in El Techo, undoubtedly. But in El Tejar, another "low-class" project where houses are sold outright, the monthly payment of $15 ($45 to our $300-a-month worker's standards) is reasonable, but the $3,000 down payment is not. El Techo withstanding, 80 percent of Colombia's "low-cost" housing is financially beyond the reach of all but a handful of skilled workers. One reason is that ICT does not build the houses; it contracts for them, and private construction firms must make profits. This is the way we do housing in the United States, and this is the way we want it done in Colombia. This is definitely economic progress but it is not social progress. Only a social-minded government can carry out social progress—by building 500,000 minimum-space houses (or furnishing land, materials, and supervision) and *giving* them to the needy. When we wanted to defend our friend, Costa Rican President José Figueres, from a possible invasion-revolution, we sold him fighter planes at $1 each. Why have we never sold houses at $1 each?

"Self-help," says Moscoso, that is what we want to develop. (In Bolivia, once peasants got their land, the right to go where they wanted and do what they wanted, they began building schools. Angel Gemio Ergineta, Director of Bolivia's National Agrarian Reform Council, showed me a file that contained hundreds of applications for teachers by peasants who had built, on their own and without Bolivian or United States aid, hundreds of schools. "Once a peasant is assured a minimally decent living for his whole family," Gemio Ergineta said, "he automatically begins to want to better his condition. As long as he feels himself a slave, he will hope only for liquor.")

In Colombia, there are 7,000,000 people who feel themselves slaves, and not one of our Alliance projects will reach them until they own their land, until they have a few pesos to spend on toys for their children, and until they have the freedom to say "The hell with all this; let's go to the city." Social progress and exorbitant private profits do not go together in underdeveloped nations. It is not by pressing for tax reforms that the latter are cut down and the former financed. A lopsided, worm-eaten, sinking house cannot be salvaged by a new paint job. It must be repaired and, added to new material, a new house must be built.

A nationalistic, socialistic, authoritarian government can build such a house. But enough of the results desired can perhaps be brought about through a nationalistic, non-socialistic, and nonauthoritarian government. If such a government is not at the service of vested interests, it can create the incentives needed to accelerate the voluntary building of the new house. One such incentive plan has been proposed in Colombia. It was thought out by an economist and farmer named Lauchlin Currie, a former Roosevelt Brain Truster, who settled in Colombia shortly after F.D.R.'s death, became a Colombian citizen, and has since prospered as a consultant to Colombian industrialists. His plan, known as Operation Colombia, is fundamentally very simple: mechanize agriculture, reduce its working force, increase industrialization in the cities, and increase exports of both agriculture and industry as a result.

Operation Colombia is based on some hard economic facts:

1. Any social-minded agrarian reform, even if it eliminates many of the tiny holdings of *minifundios,* increases agricultural competition by creating overproduction, which results in a fall in prices and a general dissatisfaction, if not economic chaos in the country.

2. In all underdeveloped countries, such as Colombia, the land is generally in the hands of absentee owners who get enough of a return from their peons' labor to forgo capital investment. The peons are tied to the land, which makes them incapable of flocking to the urban centers to demand jobs. Thus, as in Colombia, more than half of the population is rural. The peons' cheapness, as far as capital is concerned, prohibits progressive farmers from mechanizing because the colonial-style farm products can undersell those produced on farms needing large investments in machinery—at least at first.

3. The huge rural population forces governments to spend more money, per capita, for rural roads, electricity lines, schools, transportation, and so on, than in urban areas where the population is concentrated. This rural expenditure prohibits poor (underdeveloped) governments from raising vast urban development projects.

4. The lack of constantly expanding urban labor forces and their own consumer needs keeps urban industries from incorporating steady expansion programs within their structures. That lack of industrial expansion creates unemployment as the industries adopt automation methods, and the unemployment frightens away those rural workers who might have come to the cities.

5. These rural workers remain in such strength that their labor force is inexhaustible, hence stays very cheap,

which in turn keeps owners from mechanizing, letting one of the most important revolutions of modern times—technology—bypass the country.[3]

(In the United States, technology has so speeded up that even the high mobility of rural workers has not been enough to force a cutdown on agricultural production. Thus, our government has been compelled to maintain a gigantic price-support policy—a deliberate policy of foregoing some of the benefits of technology and of maintaining what is in reality an excessive number of workers in agriculture. We, apparently, can afford such luxury.)

Nevertheless, Colombia's rural workers are so badly paid or live so poorly that on the least incentive they could be led to desert the farms for the cities. What Operation Colombia proposes, then, is the following:

1. A government policy of guaranteeing rural workers the right to travel.

2. A government policy of using most of the money now earmarked for rural development to finance loans (on future, not immediate, repayment) to farmers and peons migrating to the cities for their urban relocations. These relocation projects can be planned so as to direct urban growth to where industrialization is most capable of handling the flood. The projects themselves (demolition, urban redistricting, construction, and so on) would create a vast number of jobs for unskilled labor.

3. A government policy of rural loans only for machinery on economically sized farm units, creating incentive for mechanization. Marginal farmers, unable to compete, would sell out or abandon their farms, thus allowing the bigger farmers to expand. The rapid depletion of colonial-style *latifundio* labor force (wooed to the cities through the above loans and, if possible, grants) would also compel the owners of such *latifundios* to mechanize.

4. A government policy of building roads only to the large agricultural producers, again forcing the marginal farmers to abandon their farms.

5. A government employment and relocation bureau to help the rural worker find lodging and jobs in the city, perhaps even a system by which a whole community of

[3] See Appendix D for Currie's quick look at what technology could do to some crops.

marginal farmers could move into the same city suburb development, guaranteeing their children schooling which they now lack in their rural areas.

6. A government policy of aiding industries to expand through tax concessions, loans, and so on, carefully encouraging those that would increase production of export goods so as to expand Colombia's capital intake.

The government should then use its agrarian reform tools to ensure a curtailing, *not an increasing*, of agriculture competition, keeping prices high enough to be profitable (by limiting land reclamation projects) but reasonable enough to be acceptable (by launching just enough of such projects to keep production equal to demand). On the rest of its reclaimed land, the government could start export-crop farms whose profits would be used to keep the cycle going—until 30 percent of Colombia's rural families are resettled and working in the cities.

Currie's Operation Colombia, carefully researched, tested, and detailed by a whole battery of economists and the staffers of the Foundation for the Progress of Colombia, shows that Colombia's GNP can jump 20 percent in just two years from the date of inception. (In the 1953-1962 decade, Colombia's GNP increased 2 percent yearly while population went up 2.9 percent yearly.)

If well managed, the Operation would assure social progress by giving rural families a chance to have their children educated, a chance to use city doctors, a chance to a better life, and a chance to the personal freedom and dignity that come with belonging to the economy rather than being its outcast.

Operation Colombia, finally, is not even Socialistic. On the contrary, it not only defends free enterprise; it also helps it become stronger. It encourages big farms, big industry, big productions. Yet Colombia's oligarchy is opposed. Why?

First, because it is the oligarchy that owns the big colonial-style *latifundios*. Second, because the industrial oligarchy is afraid that a huge, surely soon unionized, labor force would demand better pay, better conditions, unemployment compensation, health insurance, and all sorts of other rights that would cut down the oligarchy's disproportionate profits. Third, because "education leads to ideas" and ideas are dangerous; they may include such "Communist" concepts as justice, equality, and religious tolerance. (The Church, a major landholder in Colombia, is opposed to Operation Colombia.) Fourth, industrialization, even if the oligarchy profits from it (as it would), can lead to a bigger middle class, and the middle class inevitably ends by demanding political power. The whole political structure of Colombia might collapse. The middle class may also become industrially wealthy, setting up its own corporations, which would create competition. Fifth, the militarists fear that strong labor would force them to stop meddling in politics. And finally, United States private investment is opposed to Operation Colombia because 20 percent jumps in GNP can create enough capital to give them competition too, leading to restrictions on the commerce and trade they now practice without controls.

Operation Colombia is unacceptable to the rich, be they Colombians or Americans, because, though it defends free enterprise, it would modernize the country enough to bring about a change in structure. To the rich, all changes are dangerous. But why is our embassy and the Alliance for Progress officially opposed to Operation Colombia?

That the Alliance is not aimed at people so much as at projects can be seen from the history of USAID's aid to Colombia's health needs. From September, 1961, to December, 1962, we maintained a small health crew in Colombia: Dr. William Cope, a general physician working in the Foreign Service for fifteen years; an expert in hospital administration; and a veterinary. There were others on a temporary basis, to fight a particular disease or crop pest. But these three men made up the basic service.

Their total yearly expense to us was $46,000 for their salaries, travel, supplies, and stationery, and $75,000 (their budget) for fieldwork. Colombia added another $350,000, and with this sum, just 1 percent of our total Colombia aid costs, these three men brought medical help to no less than 250,000 Colombians.

Cope himself organized sixty-six health centers in the backwood towns of Colombia. The people built the centers; sometimes foundations or the local church or prominent local men chipped in with money. A doctor, medical equipment, and a nurse were always sent by Colombia to the centers once they were completed. Cope and Housing Adviser Milton Drexler taught the local people how to run water lines, how to read plans, and how to build the centers.

Cope supervised until the center began functioning.

The centers were always voluntary enterprises. For example, after the people of an Ibaque neighborhood asked for one, Cope and Drexler helped them to get it started. The people built it. Colombia's government staffed it. After a while the neighborhood decided to call itself Barrio Kennedy. President Lleras Camargo praised it. And the center still works fine.

They all work. People who had never seen a doctor now get medical attention. They pay nothing or what they can afford. Amazingly, all try to afford something, even if only a chicken.

But no more such centers are to be built. The Alliance for Progress laid down a new policy. The Health Service was discontinued as of January 1, 1963. Thereafter we lent money to build hospitals. But no more grants.

Thousands of Colombians wrote letters: "Keep the service." President Lleras Camargo personally asked that the service continue. To no avail. Said one United States Embassy staffer, "We have converted health into a loan program." Added another: "I'm not opposed to lending money for hospitals, God knows, on the contrary. If we can't afford to give Colombia hospitals, then we must lend them the money to build them, by all means. But why stop the service? I don't understand. Perhaps the health centers are not showy or big or modern or fancy. But they work."

Before word reached Colombia that the *servicio* would be discontinued, a handout by the embassy singled it out thus: "This project demonstrates very effectively that the government of Colombia and the United States are interested in those who wish to help themselves. . . ."

Very effectively.

Chapter 24

Political Considerations

The meeting of the hemisphere's Foreign Affairs Ministers that took place at Punta del Este, Uruguay, from January 22 to 31, 1962, and which is commonly referred to as the second Punta del Este Conference, had technically nothing to do with the Alliance for Progress. The Council of the Organization of American States (OAS) had convoked the meeting on December 4, 1961, under provisions for such matters in the Inter-American Treaty of Reciprocal Assistance. The twenty-one ministers met "to consider the threats to the peace and to the political independence of the American States that might arise from the intervention of extracontinental powers directed toward breaking American solidarity."

Insofar as "American solidarity" means, as we have unfortunately amply seen, Latin America's solidarity with the United States, Cuba's revolutionary regime is very definitely a break. Under the treaty's clauses, there is no doubt that the meeting was justified. But the ministers had theoretically no right to take up matters pertaining to the Alliance.

Nevertheless, since the Alliance is a political tool used by us to combat Castro's appeal in Latin America, it would have been impossible to stick to the letter of the OAS resolution calling for the meeting. So the Alliance became a dominant behind-the-scenes influence in the meeting's proceedings. The ministers even agreed (twenty for, Cuba against) in Resolution V to reaffirm their hope and faith in the Alliance for Progress. Secretary of State Dean

Rusk, in a report to the nation on February 2, 1962, put it this way:

> The foreign ministers unanimously recognized that the struggle against communism in this hemisphere is not merely a question of defense against subversion but of positive measures as well—economic, social, and political reforms and development, to meet the legitimate aspirations of our peoples. In this spirit the governments committed themselves anew to the great constructive tasks of the Alliance for Progress.

The legal "justification" for the meeting—Rusk himself said so on February 2nd—was Castro's "I am Marxist-Leninist" speech, delivered December 1, 1961, which *proved* that the hemisphere was faced with a Communist conspiracy. In point of fact, however, Castro's Marxist-Leninist speech came after much of the pressure for the meeting had already been operating.

That pressure had begun under the official auspices of Colombia, but at our suggestion. What we hoped to achieve was to get all hemisphere nations to cut off trade and perhaps even diplomatic relations with Cuba. These goals were based on two assumptions: (1) that Cuba's economy cannot hold up with aid and trade only from Communist countries, and (2) that Leftist revolutionary movements in Latin America would be greatly curtailed without a Cuban embassy nearby to egg them on with money, propaganda, advice, and invitations.[1] Our purpose was to isolate Cuba. And it was hoped, as Rusk himself said in a Punta del Este mid-conference briefing, that our NATO allies would join the plot.

[1] By September, 1962, about 100,000 non-Communist Latin Americans had been invited to see the Cuban Revolution at work. For every traveler returning disillusioned, one had remained in Cuba to offer his services and ten had returned enthusiastic supporters. Ariel Collazo, for example, was a rightist (Blanco) deputy in Uruguay's Parliament, interested only in a "brilliant career," as he said himself, before he visited Cuba in 1960; since his return he has abandoned his old party, ruined his political chances to launch a pro-Cuba revolutionary movement for which he speaks every single day. Another example is

To achieve that purpose we launched a concerted campaign against Cuba. Not only did we attack it for its alliance to Communist nations (which is fact), and for its executions (which were also facts), but we began also to say that Castro's revolution was really a Russian invasion, an "armed attack," which is willful distortion of facts. Writing in *Reporter* (November 23, 1961), Kennedy's Latin America policy-maker Adolf Berle, Jr., so defined armed attack as to include "a rebellion or internal seizure of power organized, armed, or fomented by an outside power," then stated categorically that "precisely this type of armed attack . . . has taken place through the Russian operations in Cuba." Not satisfied with this distortion, Berle went on to accuse Cuba of trying to start such revolutions elsewhere as "Cuban documents brought to light in Ecuador, Peru, and Argentina make it abundantly clear."

Perhaps Cuba did try to launch revolutions. Do we need a half-truth to "prove this?" The half-truth, in this case, is that those so-called Cuban documents were forgeries. Suffice to quote parts of two letters to the *Reporter* (printed January 4, 1962) to set the facts straight:

From Brian B. McDermott, New York:

> It should be pointed out to Mr. Berle that in the 1950's it was not from the shores and airbases of Russia that the small boats and planes carrying men and munitions set out for Cuba [to launch the Revolution that Berle labels Russian-organized, armed, and fomented], but from Florida. Also from the U.S.A. came dollars and considerable

conservative Argentine Radical Party deputy Agustín Rodríguez Araya, still conservative but nevertheless publicly "impressed with what has been accomplished in Cuba." Another was Jánio Quadros who visited Cuba before his election, said Brazil should do what Cuba has done but, he hoped, through democratic means. More examples can be found in Peru, where a whole flock of anti-Communist Social Progressists became staunch pro-Castroites; in Mexico, where deputies, General Cárdenas, writers and non-Communist labor men became Castro fans; and, in fact, in every other country. (Such conversions led Peru's "democratic" Prado regime to outlaw free travel, threatening jail terms to anyone who left the country without permission or visited any country not listed in his original application.)

moral support via the press. It was also not until late in the revolution that Communists gave any support to Castro—a point Mr. Berle himself makes. Lastly, it was not until the latter part of 1960, after the U.S. oil companies had refused to refine [Cuban purchased] Soviet oil and cut off the remaining U.S. supply, and the Cuban sugar quota was cut, that Cuba began turning to Russia for economic support.

From C. Frank Glass, Los Angeles:

Cuba's foreign minister pointed out that the signatures, the numbering, and the way the documents were prepared showed clearly that they were fakes. He offered to open the files of his ministry to the Argentine government in order to prove the falsity of the documents. Perhaps Mr. Berle will contend that Cuba's denial is worthless. But surely he knows that the Argentine government backed Cuba's denial and issued an official statement declaring that the documents were forgeries.

One more point on Berle should be made—since he is still considered one of the United States' top-ranking big shot experts on Latin America. He said that "Communists have regularly supported the dictators" in Latin America, which is true (as it is for us). But to prove his point he wrote: "The Argentine Communist leader Americo Ghioldi recognized Perón for the fascist he was. Communists were supposed to oppose fascists; Ghioldi decided he would do so. He was promptly called to order by the then director of operations for Latin America, Jacques Duclos. I happened to see the correspondence." First, Perón was not a Fascist (and we too supported him under Ike), but let us allow all interpretations. Second, did Berle find such crucial correspondence in a waste-paper basket or did he win the confidence of Duclos or what? But let us assume he has special connections somewhere. Third, Americo Ghioldi is and has always been a leader of Argentina's moderate, extremely pro-United States Socialists; his brother Rodolfo is the Communist leader. Can we assume a careless slip? Or was it all part of a hurried propaganda plan meant to whip up hysteria against Cuba? If so, why? Were we planning another invasion?

The propaganda, the pressure, and the back-door deals did not convince all Latin American governments. At the OAS Council meeting calling for the second Punta del Este conference, unanimity (excluding Cuba) was not achieved: six countries refused to follow our lead. Mexico voted No, and Argentina, Bolivia, Brazil, Chile, and Ecuador abstained. Nevertheless, the required two-thirds (14 out of 21) voted in favor, and the conference was scheduled. Almost immediately difficulties began.

First, no country seemed willing to have the conference on its territory—until Uruguay finally offered Punta del Este a resort free of workers, slums, unemployed, and potential trouble. More serious were our difficulties in getting Latin America to vote in favor of economic and political sanctions. After many caucuses, long-distance phone calls, and hush-hush haggling, it became clear that no more than fourteen nations would follow our lead—and perhaps not even fourteen. Uruguay was the crucial country. Its delegate to the OAS had voted in favor of the conference. But in Uruguay even members of the Government Council claimed that his vote represented a double cross, his instructions having been to abstain.

Finally, the New Frontier decided to abandon its demands for sanctions but not without a bit of shrewdly sophisticated diplomacy. Our strategy seemed airtight, and the State Department was sure nothing would go wrong. Officially we would insist on full sanctions, the hard line. We, or preferably one of our sure votes, would introduce resolutions calling for just such sanctions. Debate would follow. Those countries which have serious pro-Castro strength to contend with at home would argue against sanctions. Their theme would be "nonintervention," a slogan neutral enough to be palatable to the six's Right-wing elements and valid enough to satisfy Left-wingers. Then, after much heat, harangues, and publicity—proving the six's "independence"—a compromise would be reached: a seemingly softer resolution kicking Cuba out of the OAS but not demanding bilateral diplomatic ruptures from each country. Trade relations would not be suspended, but by then we had decided that such trade was too small to bother with anyway (a mere $27,000,000 yearly from all twenty nations). Besides, the "compromise" plan was to include a recommendation that an OAS committee "review" Latin American-Cuban trade.

There were other justifications for the strategy: First

we suddenly realized that if all nations broke diplomatic relations, Castro would be cut off from the hemisphere all right, but we would also be cut off from Cuba. Refugees and underground men could no longer use embassy asylums to escape, and embassy staffers could no longer serve as our eyes and ears, or even as our agents, for slipping arms, money, and instructions to anti-Castro rebels.

Then it also dawned on us that, should we try to oust Castro through a multilateral or unilateral invasion of Cuba, the fact that Cuba would be out of the OAS, hence not defendable from a hemispheric solidarity point of view, would be just as good as if all nations had broken diplomatic relations. And kicking Castro out of the OAS but having some countries retain relations with him would be less a rallying cry; Castro would come out less a martyr. Finally, we knew that sanctions would never get twenty votes, but a United States "retreat" to a "softer" expulsion order would —we thought.

The strategy had its unquestionable appeal. History might even conclude, a century from now, that it had "charm"—so long as it worked, of course. The *New Republic* concluded that the Latins would appreciate it: "The strategy wore a new and sophisticated look that astonished and delighted those strategically-placed Latin Americans who were privy to the plan. Latin delegates could inveigh against the US proposals and go back to their people with nationalist colors flying, while the US would get what it really had in mind all along."

The whole plan, and now in retrospect, our pre-conference propaganda efforts (Berle's franticness), the amount and—to Kennedy's eyes—the quality of our delegates (Rusk, Woodward, Morales Carrión, Rostow, Goodwin, Schlesinger, Senators Wayne Morse and Bourke Hickenlooper and Representatives Armistead Selden and Chester Merrow)[2] makes one wonder if we were not indeed planning a new invasion of Cuba. Most observers so concluded. That it was canceled was because our plan failed.

[2] The four congressmen were obviously not "in" on our strategy since, aside from a few statements that the "diplomats" contradicted, they seemed to be limited to standing around in the lobbies, telling reporters they were "100 percent in agreement" with each other—"probably the first time in history that Morse and Hickenlooper have been in 100 percent agreement about

And the reason it failed is that its crucial pawn, too weak to keep his pledge, though too brave to obey his own army's orders, betrayed us. That pawn was Argentina's Frondizi, who had promised Kennedy at their December 24, 1961, talks in Palm Beach that he could swing the rest of the six.

Knowing that his Armed Forces might try a coup should his representative not vote against Cuba, but also knowing that his standing in Latin America would sink should Brazil be the only nation to refuse to vote for expulsion, Frondizi tried desperately to convince Goulart to go along.

Goulart could not risk losing the support of Brazil's Leftists. Still shaky in his amputated throne, not yet in control of the army, opposed by most congressmen, Goulart's only strength was his popular support. Without it he would not last a day. And the people of Brazil, more pro-Castro than against, were at least solidly in favor of abstention. Thus Goulart refused to give in.

As it turned out, Mexico would not give in either. Not only was popular opinion against expulsion (in fact, against any anti-Cuba measure), but also General Cárdenas, Mexico's most respected citizen, had publicly warned the government not to bend to United States pressure, even if Mexico should stand alone.

Bolivia, too, could not afford to go along with us. Paz Estenssoro himself might be "persuaded." But his armed MNR commandos were led by pro-Castroites, and an anti-Cuba vote by Paz might provoke a revolt, which could upset his government, especially since ambitious then Vice President Juan Lechín would view himself in a position to profit from it. Thus, Paz ordered Bolivia to abstain.

Ecuador's Arosemena ruled a divided country; the people were pro-Castro while the army was against. But the brass, involved only too recently in a coup, did not yet seem strong enough to be able to deal with a revolution if one

anything," as John Crosby reported to the *Herald Tribune*. The four represented the United States aspect of the "ghost of public opinion," a catch phrase invented by an AP correspondent to characterize the tremendous importance of public opinion at the conference, all delegates talking especially for hometown consumption.

erupted. (When the army later consolidated its strength, it handed Arosemena an ultimatum ordering him to break relations with Cuba; but by then the conference had ended.)

As for the Conservatives who ran Chile, they could no more think of voting for expulsion than letting the illiterate peasants vote. As it was, the Left had become the strongest vote getter, and rumors were already flying (surely as far as Alessandri's ears) that the government would undoubtedly "resign" before the end of its term. Alessandri was in no mood to hurry up his own "resignation."

Thus, abandoned by the other five, faced with the possibility of a military coup or Latin American disgrace, Frondizi had to re-evaluate his own situation. He called in his military aides, explained his dilemma, and decided that at worst he would have to break relations with Cuba later, if he voted against expulsion now. Hence, he ordered his delegate to resist United States pressure.

That pressure was enormous. The conference was held at the swank, château-shaped San Rafael Hotel, two sand-duned miles from the casino where the first conference had been held. The San Rafael also has a gambling room, and it was there that the delegates hashed out their comedy. But it was in private rooms, in isolated villas rented for the occasion, and even in cars that the pressure was exerted.

It did not take our "diplomats" long to give up on Brazil. Its Foreign Minister San Thiago Dantas talked about "pacific coexistence," "nonintervention," and "autodetermination" too often and too publicly for a possible change of mind. Still, with nineteen votes, we would be satisfied. We kept trying.

José Fellman Velarde, Bolivia's Foreign Minister, was collared once too often. In a moment of undiplomatic exasperation, he suddenly exploded in front of five or six reporters (myself among them): "What's the matter with those *Yankis*, can't they understand that if Bolivia votes against them, it's because we have no choice. We know damn well what could happen to us. Without United States aid we're all finished. And we know that we *are* risking getting cut off. But what do they expect us to do, vote for another revolution?"

Argentina's Miguel Angel Cárcano, an old, bald, wrinkled aristocrat, whose long years of government service have involved many controversial deals, was repeatedly seen entering off-limit rooms and offices with one or more of

our "diplomats." After I spotted him coming out of one
such meeting, I caught him and, as politely as possible,
tried to insist he at least hint at what had transpired. Smiling
weakly at last, he said: "I will tell you only this: Never in
my life have I been under so much pressure, and never
in my life did I think it possible that these kinds of discussions
could become known as diplomacy."

Perhaps the biggest shock came from Haiti, considered
a "safe" vote. On January 25th its Foreign Minister René
Chalmers suddenly began speaking at length about "nonintervention" and his country's long-proved neutrality in Caribbean
entanglements. Haiti's people, he said, "will have the auda-
ciousness not to renounce to this vocation, to refuse to
take sides." After an hour, he concluded: "As for the Cuban
case, [Haiti] is rather prone—though it will still consider
with great care the various projects of resolution presented
to this assembly—to objectively seek with the other members
of the Organization of American States an efficient formula
to establish the conditions for a fruitful dialogue with Cuba
on the basis of mutual respect, peaceful coexistence, and
within the framework of a national philosophy and the
humanism of the United States of America's assistance for
Latin America."

Sitting in front of me in the press section, the tall blond
correspondent from Russia's TASS news agency leaned over
toward one of our columnists and quipped, unable to withhold
a slight grin, "There goes your fourteenth vote."

A few days later, the following story—told by a Haitian
delegate—made the rounds: One of our "diplomats" cornered
Chalmers, threatened to cut off all United States aid on
the one hand or increase our aid on the other, and asked
him what was Haiti's price. He was told: a 1,500-bed hospital,
a jet airport, a road to the airport, and $15,000,000. Our
diplomat was said to have agreed. Later still, reporters claimed
that another of our diplomats, when asked what Haiti's
vote had cost, retorted, "Cheaper than expected."

True or not, the story *could* have happened. Haiti voted
with us, and Pan American Airways then announced it
would build a jet airport in Haiti. In any case, our prestige
was badly hurt. As one United States columnist wrote:
"Though the economy of Haiti is dependent on a US
subsidy, the Duvalier dictatorship was able to humiliate

the US in Latin eyes by upping the ante on Alliance aid
before giving Secretary Rusk one of the badly needed floating
votes which assured a bare two-thirds majority."

No speech at Punta del Este was meant to influence votes.
That task was handled behind closed doors. But all speeches
were meant to influence peoples, and as such, the one delivered
by Osvaldo Dorticós Torrado, Cuba's President and (temporary) Minister of Foreign Affairs, was especially effective.
Extremely demagogic, furious and fiery, it held Latin listeners
spellbound for almost three hours (Anglo-Saxons can never
seem to take more than an hour). Speaking extemporaneously,
except to read off statistics now and then, Dorticós was
obviously aware that most Uruguayans were glued to their
radios. Thus he made sure to tell them everything the Cuban
Revolution had accomplished for the Cuban people. Dorticós
also must have known that his speech would be reprinted
hundreds of times (some places legally, most places illegally)
across Latin America. Indeed, even in Nicaragua months
later, I found an accountant who had a copy.

Dorticós stuck to our sore points. Because so many correspondents were present, one of his remarks was especially
clever. To us it was amusing; to Latin Americans, for whom
it was really meant, it discredited all of us. The remark was
based on the then recent news that riots had broken out
in Venezuela and that Caracas' opposition newspapers had
been raided, that their equipment had been smashed, and
that they had been closed down by Betancourt's police.
Dorticós, armed with a wire copy obviously passed on to
him by a Cuban supporter in the wire room, said:

A U.S. journalist who has a side job—not a professional
one, to be sure—and who I believe is listening to me,
Mr. Jules Dubois, sent this cable to New York only
a few days, hours ago, which, translated, can be seen
by all of you gentlemen. The cable said: "It is imperative
that you do not transmit any statement referring to closing
of newspapers by Betancourt in Caracas." This is the
freedom of the press exercised by the champions of
the freedom of the press.

(Dubois, present as Dorticós had said, represented the Chicago
Tribune. But he was also then, and still is at this writing,

president of the Inter-American Press Association's Freedom of the Press Committee.)[3]

Dorticós' speech hit hardest when he said:

> The Ministers of Foreign Affairs know this, those who voted in favor of the convocation and those who promoted this meeting know it, he who proposed it knows it, and so do those Ministers of Foreign Affairs who abstained or voted against the meeting. Some may not be able to say it in public, but they may well repeat it daily in private. This meeting was promoted to prepare a favorable climate in the Hemisphere for a new physical and military aggression against my country, and as such I denounce it.
>
> I know my words will be denied. Our words were denied, gentlemen—please recollect—when we announced before the Playa Girón events (the Bay of Pigs invasion), that we would be invaded by a military force prepared by the Government of the United States, and history proved us right.

Nevertheless his speech changed no votes, nor was it meant to. The big six, representing 75 percent of Latin America's area and 140 million of its 200 million people, abstained. Cuba voted No. We and our followers voted Yes. Cuba was booted out of the OAS.

Without unanimity, our invasion (if indeed that had been in the wind) was off. It was a temporary victory for Cuba. And in losing, we had laid bare the Alliance for Progress. As John Crosby summed up the conference:

> The congressmen were not part of the hard bargaining

[3] Mr. Dubois, who saw a pre-publication copy of this book, has supplied the full and accurate text of his telegram: STRONGLY URGE THAT NO REPEAT NO STATEMENT ABOUT CLOSURE NEWSPAPERS CARACAS BE ISSUED BECAUSE THEY WERE OPENLY INCITING TO A COMMUNIST REVOLUTION. REGARDS.

Presumably, under Mr. Dubois' definition of Freedom of the Press, it is not only acceptable to close down newspapers *he* thinks are Communist, but also desirable for non-Communist newspapers not to report such closures.

team which hammered out the agreement. Still they helped (if that's the word for it) by collaring hapless Latin American delegates and (as they said) "Letting our views be known." The views were quite simple: If you're not with us, you're against us. If you're against us, Congress is going to take a very cold view of any foreign aid toward your country. . . .

There was only the mildest splatter of applause for Rusk. "This is not our finest hour," muttered a correspondent to me. We achieved our aims, if indeed we have achieved them, by the toughest cracking of skulls, reminiscent of the days of the big stick. The Alliance for Progress is the new-style dollar diplomacy. . . .

PART VI: Free Enterprise vs. Free Choice

Chapter 25

Dollars and Sense

Much has been said so far, directly or indirectly, about the nefarious effect of "private enterprise" in Latin America. It is time, therefore, to document such contentions more fully.

I have no intention of evaluating the ultimate values of capitalism or Socialism. But I do insist that though capitalism may be the best way to push a fully developed industrial power into world market competition—West Germany being an excellent example of this—in underdeveloped countries trying to compress centuries into decades or even years, unregulated capitalism does not work.

The reason is simple. On international levels, capitalism works in trusts or huge groups whose various holdings are meant to complement each other, not compete. Katanga's mines are meant to help feed Rockefeller's home-ground manufacturing interests. It is to Rockefeller's financial interest to keep Katanga exporting its raw materials—instead of developing its own manufacturing industry, which might then compete in the world market with Rockefeller's products.

Once a nation is fully developed, huge concentration of wealth in the hands of a few may be ethically unfair, but it does not necessarily retard social progress. The trusts can set up lobbies, finance elections, buy newspapers and radios to support their candidates. There is no doubt that big money can bulldoze through its candidate over others not so wealthy—as T. H. White's *The Making of a President,*

1960 clearly shows. But big money alone is not enough to win all the time—or to maintain an arrogant state of mind. In a developed nation there is always enough small money that can be added up so that *its* candidate can be heard. Once heard, the people are more apt to make up their minds without the trusts' welfare at heart. Big money, for example, supported Tom Dewey in 1944 and in 1948, yet F.D.R. and Truman came out the victors.

In the case of Truman, the example is especially acute. Almost 99 percent of our press supported Dewey. So did the financiers, the manipulators, the so-called taste-makers. But Truman found enough support in the labor unions, small businessmen, professionals, and marginals to be able to finance one of the most successful campaigns ever staged— the to-the-people campaign. And to the astonishment of the "big shots," who even stated flatly just a bit too soon on election night that Dewey had won, Truman was the victor.

In Latin America such campaigns are impossible. Even assuming, which is rarely the case, that one of the traditional parties nominated a Nationalist as their candidate, his campaign would seldom be able to get off the ground. Labor unions that are not at the service of their employers are too poor to support anything but their own activity. Workers are much too underpaid to keep up even with their dues. In fact, nongovernmental unions are lucky if 10 percent of their membership pay their dues regularly. Salary deductions for dues are unheard of in 99 percent of the cases. Few unions would consider such regulations a reasonable demand: the workers themselves, often too poor to buy enough food, would vote against automatic checkoff clauses.

Small businessmen can afford political contributions, but their strength is very limited. In Uruguay, Argentina, Chile, parts of Brazil and Mexico, the middle class is strong enough to demand a role in politics. That is why traditional parties there (except Mexico, where patterns were changed by the revolution) have become increasingly more nationalistic. The Peronists' election landslide early in 1962 would have been impossible without middle-class support. In Chile, even the Christian Democrats, a middle-class party, demand the "Chileanization" of copper mines. In Uruguay, the Colorado Party has long been a middle-class party, and if it lost in 1958 after ninety-three years of rule, the reason was not because the middle class became weak but because the Colorados had bungled their chances too long. The opposition Blancos, always claiming to be Nationalists, made the most of it *without* criticizing the principles of the Colorado's welfare statism. In Brazil, middle-class support for the nationalism of Brizola and Goulart, and even Vargas before them, is almost as potent as the people's support.

But in Latin America the people do not vote. Most nations have a residence-proof requirement for voting eligibility. Thus, floating laborers and squatters (one-third or more of every major city) are not legally anywhere, hence cannot vote. Furthermore, Latin American countries (Bolivia is an exception, Mexico another) prohibit illiterates from voting. That means that at least 50 percent of the adults are eliminated. In such developed countries as our own, where literacy is almost 95 percent, literacy restrictions are not too meaningful (except in the South, where Negroes would elect Negro candidates if allowed their own political decision-making). But in underdeveloped countries a literacy test for voting is undemocratic. Not one nation that has such restrictions can be considered a democracy, no matter how much the argument is twisted.

Under such conditions, capital naturally controls the electoral processes. This means not only that presidents and governors and mayors are generally representative of capital, but that so are congressmen and city councilmen and water inspectors. Labor legislation or unfair-practices investigations cannot normally be expected. They do happen, almost by accident, when a candidate backed by capital suddenly develops a conscience. But even where labor legislation is on the books, rarely is it applied. Chile, for example, has a decent labor code, but not one *latifundista* that I met, not one that I read about, not one that ECLA's investigating teams investigated, complied with the code. Big capital rules, and naturally it rules for its own interests.

Big capital, lumping together United States, British, and native holdings, is even more centralized in Latin America than it is in the United States. Here at home, the F.D.R. Trust Committee found the following statistics:

254 industrial corporations control 66.5 percent of all production, 96.7 percent of metallurgical production, 88.9 percent of naval construction, 78.1 percent of aeronautical industry, and 76.1 percent of mechanical industry.

These 254 corporations received 78 percent of all war-production contracts and put up 78 percent of all military installations.

Later our Congress' Temporary National Economic Committee came up with these statistics:

0.1 percent (.001) of our industrial corporations control 32 percent of all United States capital, employ 40 percent of our labor force, receive 50 percent of all profits. And in 1945, exactly 63 corporations had a liquid capital of $10,000,000,000 enough to buy 71,700 medium or small corporations, which amounted to 49 percent of all existing corporations in the United States. That is to say, 63 companies could have owned one-half of our country.

By 1947, the Federal Trade Commission estimated that 113 corporations owned 46 percent of the United States' manufacturing assets. By 1951, Prof. M. A. Adelman of the Massachusetts Institute of Technology was calculating ("The Measurement of Industrial Concentration," *Review of Economics and Statistics*) that 135 corporations owned 45 percent of industrial assets of the United States and almost one-fourth of the manufacturing volume of the entire world. And more recent estimates have figured out that 200 corporations own two-thirds of the United States industrial worth.[1]

Be it 63, 113, 135 or 200, these corporations, it turns out, are in turn in the hands of eight "groups": Morgan, Kuhn-Loeb, Rockefeller, Du Pont de Nemours, Mellon, and three regional trusts known as the Chicago, the Boston, and the Cleveland groups. Each of these groups are interlocked with the others through their companies' boards. Thus five families (the majority of the eight) could materially influence the fate of the United States by owning half of its total value.

They could—but they don't. Why? There are two and only two reasons, one fallacious, one real. The first is that the corporations themselves belong to what everyday public relations men like to call "people's capitalism." That means that the stocks, being sold on the market, belong

[1] See: Robert J. Lampman's *The Share of Top Wealth-Holders in National Wealth 1922-1956* (Princeton: National Bureau of Economic Research, Princeton University Press, 1962).

to the millions of stockholders—the people of the United States. This argument is false because no people hold the voting majority of the stock, control remaining with the real owners, the five families; although 17 million Americans are shareholders, 1.6 percent of stockholders own 80 percent of the stock while, contrarily, 98.4 percent of these "17 million Americans" together own only 20 percent.

The second reason, valid this time, is that our laws prohibit the acquisition of so much value. As we saw, the economics of over-developed countries produce enough of a monetary surplus so that even the funds of a limited minority can be used to help candidates opposed to Big Business. The candidates, guaranteed free access to the people (the right to travel, to talk, to campaign, and so on), can and do win in sufficient strength so that *all* elected officials are forced to keep public opinion in mind for their own interests (their reelection). "People's laws" can and do pass through Congress and *are* applied. Thus we have antitrust Laws, anti-price-fixing laws, anticollusion laws, and so forth. Big Business can be big in the United States, but it cannot control the whole economy. But no matter how hard it tried, our Big Business cannot destroy our Constitution, assassinate our presidents, organize, finance, and arm revolution, or give our land, factories, trade, and reserves to a foreign power. In Latin America, Big Business can do all these things—and it has, many, many times.

In Latin America, a corporation or company whose stock is listed on the market is called a Sociedad Anónima (S.A.). Table IX is based on all S.A.'s—United States, British, or native—operating in Latin America. That table shows that the most economically democratic country is Uruguay, where 2,740 individuals control 50 percent or more of the 23 percent of corporations that control 50 percent of Uruguay's capital, which in turn is responsible for 66 percent of the country's Gross National Product, and earn 68 percent of all earnings, whether in salaries, interest, or profits. Brazil comes next, but the jump is already significant, since 1,590 individuals control 71 percent of such a rich country's capital, which in turn is responsible for 86 percent of the Gross National Product; but because Brazil's working force is stronger, larger, and earns more, Brazil's capital brings in only 51 percent. Big Business earns only 49 percent of Argentina's cash income (though its overall worth is 90 percent of the Gross National Product), but 78 percent

Table IX

Latin America's Concentration of Economic Power

1 Countries	2 % of S.A.'s	3 2 controls this % of all S.A. capital	4 3 is worth this % of GNP	5 3 earns this % of national income	6 No. of groups controlling over 50% of 2	7 How many individuals control 6
Argentina	32	78	90	49	10	1,000
Bolivia	(major industry and mines nationalized)					
Brazil	35	71	86	51	12	1,590
Chile	22	71	91	57	3	120
Colombia	5	56	70	60	—	320
Costa Rica	29	80	60	76	6	40
Dominican Republic	(85% of industries, farms, etc., having been Trujillo-owned, are now government-owned)					
Ecuador	25	72	65	71	—	108
El Salvador	45	91	89	82	14	70
Guatemala	12	69	66	50	1	50
Haiti	21	95	89	96	1	20
Honduras	16	90	80	90	—	12
Mexico	20	77	85	60	4	—
Nicaragua	50	99	99	99	Somozas and Friends	
Panama	29	80	80	90	—	20
Paraguay	10	90	85	92	Stroessner and Friends (U.S. included)	
Peru	33	85	80	80	1	100
Uruguay	23	50	66	68	—	2,740
Venezuela	10 (count. Oil)	99	92	94	U.S. Corporations (and Royal-Dutch Shell)	
Average	25	80	81	74		

of those big businessmen include only 1,000 individuals,
and these 1,000 individuals control 70 percent (78 percent

of 90 percent) of the country's Gross National Product. Once past Argentina, the figures become ludicrous. In Honduras, 12 individuals receive 81 percent (90 percent of 90 percent) of all the earned money. In Haiti, 20 receive (95 percent of 96 percent) 89 percent.

In Venezuela, United States corporations, mostly in oil and mining, earn 94 percent of the money. These corporations do pay taxes, or at least are supposed to; nevertheless, statistics show that the 6 percent left from the money available is distributed among all the people employed in anything except oil, mining, and government (since government employees are paid with the taxes derived from oil and mining). These particular industries account for the following manpower: 3 percent in oil, 1 percent in other mines, 18 percent in government. So, while 22 percent of the labor force is paid from 94 percent of Venezuela's income (the earnings of oil and mines), 78 percent of the labor force must share a bare 6 percent of the income.

Latin America's Gross National Product is about $60 billion. United States private investment in Latin America is slightly over $10 billion—on paper. These investments currently control 40 percent of Latin America's Gross National Product, that is $24 billion—more than all Latin American budgets put together.

Our interests invade every possible phase of Latin America's economy, specialize in mining and raw materials and, on a secondary level of earning importance, in public services. Said Tomlinson in 1959:

> United States mining operations in Latin America are endless. In addition to the great copper mines and smelters in Chile and Peru, zinc and lead mines and smelters in Mexico, the new iron mines in Venezuela and others, there are now the manganese mines in Brazil, tungsten mines in Bolivia, and dozens of such properties from Mexico to Chile, which dig out of the earth everything from gold and silver to the vitally important new alloys necessary to all the metal and metallurgical industries in the United States.

Even on paper, our investments make disproportionate profits. Officially, we get a return of 14 percent to 20 percent on investment, and contrary to endless assertions that we reinvest in Latin America more than we take out every year, the reverse is true. Here are a few examples from reports of the First National Bank, which has a branch in most Latin American countries:

In Chile in 1959, United States profits were $77 million, remitted income $71 million. Nine years before, United States profits had been $41 million, all shipped home. In Venezuela in 1959, our profits were $425 million, of which $370 million went back to the United States. In Peru in 1960, we earned $26 million, remitted $23 million. In Mexico in 1957, our profits were $54 million, our shipment home $42 million; in 1959 we earned $52 million, brought $35 million back across the Rio Grande.

From 1946 to 1951, our investments in Latin America earned $3 billion in remitted income *plus* $1.3 billion in reinvested profits. In fact, Latin America is where our investments make their greatest profits—and take home the most too. A 1961 British survey showed that United States companies in England made an average profit of almost 17 percent on their investment. That was already 50 percent more than our investment averages in the United States. But in Latin America, average earnings soar beyond reason, as Table X, an official United States Department of Commerce 1961 release, clearly shows.

Since 1958, United States businessmen have been investing less in Latin America than in Western Europe, but have always taken out more. In Latin America they take out more than they bring in. In 1960 our investments in Europe reached $1,322 million and our earnings were less than $500 million. That year our investments in Latin America were $267 million, almost five times less than in Europe. But our take-home earnings were $641 million, almost one and one-third more than we had taken out of Europe. In 1961 we took out of Latin America about one and a half times what we shipped home from Europe, but on an investment one-third the size.

And these are official figures—numbers the companies themselves admit and put down on paper. A little investigation, however, will discover other, unofficial, earnings. They come home via gimmicks.

One is very simple, and works like this: Suppose I earn $100,000 a year and am allowed by my government to claim bad debts as losses and I lend $50,000 to my wife, who is abroad and does not pay taxes on income earned here. Then I claim that my net income was only $50,000, and I pay taxes on only $50,000. Such juggling in the United States with income earned in the United States is illegal.

But juggling from Latin America to the United States is perfectly legal.

Many of our companies send back money as loans which, when "defaulted," are considered losses. We saw how Rio Grande do Sul's I.T.&T. subsidiary did just that. And since 99.9 percent of our operations in Latin America are subsidiaries of United States corporations here at home, the loan-loss claim is very widespread. The "loan" never shows up as profit on the books; yet as far as Latin America is concerned, it has not only lost currency (the loan amount taken out) but taxes on the loan (remitted profit) itself.

Table X

*United States Investments and Income
A Comparative Study*
(in millions of dollars)

Year	Investment *Includes new capital and earnings not returned*		Income *Earnings returned to the U.S.*	
	Western Europe	Latin America	Western Europe	Latin America
1956	516	826	280	800
1957	631	800	311	915
1958	422	317	325	653
1959	750	347	393	600
1960	1,322	267	497	641
1961 (est.)*	1,500	500	525	770

*Note: 1961 estimates are from *U.S. News & World Report Economic Unit.*

"Loans" can also work advantageously the other way. It is impractical in terms of public relations for a company to claim $100,000 investment and $500,000 annual profit. So another gimmick is used. The parent corporation in the United States "lends" the subsidiary money—on paper. The money is never brought into the country, but the local "capital" includes it, thus making it appear that the profits in relation to the investment are not so disproportionate.

There are other gimmicks—and we'll analyze a few as we look at individual corporations operating in specific countries—to prove that Latin America's worst liability in its goal for self-development is foreign investment.

Chapter 26

Paper Capital and Cash Profits

Guggenheim's Southern Peru Copper Corporation (at Toquepala, Peru) claimed an official 1961 investment of $283,465,-237.56. Its net official profit that year was $9,197,639, on which it paid $5,758,398 in taxes. Very reasonable indeed! But of the $283,465,237.56 investment:

$ 20,130,396.69	were reserves (depreciation)
7,465,617.13	short-term loans
198,229,445.74	long-term loans
6,701,595.00	depletion
9,140,544.00	Peruvian State loan
9,197,639.00	undispensed share profit

Leaving a mere $32,600,000 of actual direct capital. The profits meanwhile were calculated thus:

$ 39,037,945	gross profit
19,225,371	depreciation
6,701,595	depletion

1. The Peruvian State loan was for machinery tax deferment. Why should there be such deferment? The company is in business to make money; it brings in machinery to do so; if there are import duties, it should pay them.

2. What are depreciation and depletion? The mine has 1,000,000,000 tons of reserves, good for 100 years at

357

the current production rate of 10,000,000 tons a year. Perhaps as much as 3 percent or 5 percent rakeoff is justified for depletion and another 5 percent for depreciation. But certainly not 17 percent for the former and 49 percent for the latter!

3. In most cases, undispensed share profit is paid as soon as the next fiscal year begins; in other words, it is money held over only for its added capital effect.

4. And the loans? More than $198 million! Part comes from the Export-Import Bank, part from the parent organization, American Smelting. Paper loans?

It certainly seems as if Southern Peru makes 100 percent on its investment each year and pays less than 25 percent on taxes. Even a butcher or a garage mechanic pays more than that in the United States.

Big business in Latin America is also favored by government laws—passed by governments controlled by Big Business.

One such law, in Peru, was to permit companies to forego reserves (depreciation). This law was passed in 1955 by Dictator Odría. What were the results? Until 1955 our Cerro de Pasco Corporation in Peru listed its reserves as follows: $53,910,359.07 in 1951; $56,538,812.30 from 1952 to 1955. Then, in 1956, its reserves disappeared. Were $56,538,812.30 taken out of Peru tax free? From 1955 on, Cerro began a wide-range buying spree in the United States: Circle Wire & Cable Corporation on December 1, 1955; Fairmont Aluminum Company in 1956; Levin-Mathes in 1957; Titan Metal Manufacturing Company and Rockbestos Products Corporation in 1958; and so on. Cerro's worldwide assets, meanwhile, rose as follows:

$175,481,861 in 1955
202,754,934   1956
209,232,712   1957
212,099,958   1958
229,572,082   1959

The jump is more than $27 million from 1955 to 1956, but only about $6.5 million in 1957, less than $3 million in 1958, and though about $17.5 million in 1959, Cerro had accrued that year Rio Blanco Copper Development Project in Chile and oil and gas holdings in Texas, Louisiana, Illinois, New Mexico, Utah, Wyoming, and Canada.

Another anomaly is as follows: because Cerro has no funds, its reserves having disappeared into assets, Cerro in Peru must borrow money on which it pays interest—to the United States, not to Peru. This interest is a profit loss, naturally, even if it is paid to Cerro in the United States. Cerro Peru has always had some loans and paid some interest —$655,767.17 in 1956, $630,000 in 1955 and 1954, $395,-321.92 in 1953, and so on—but in 1957 its interest on loans paid to the States (on which, naturally, no taxes are paid in Peru) jumped to $2,000,000.

One more anomaly. In 1950 another giveaway law (Number 11357, Article 54) passed by Peru's "democratic" regime, allowed 50 percent (later 33.3 percent) for depletion; that is to say that half, then one-third, of profits could escape from Peru as "depletion" tax free. Thus, Cerro's profits are not quite what they seem, as indicated below:

	1955	1959	1960
Real profits	20,049,334.91	10,052,949.80	11,101,432.20
Listed profits	15,356,033.70	6,600,272.57	7,178,324.20
Taxes	6,307,896.12	3,166,453.90	3,895,516.02

So, even if Cerro uses no gimmick to ship undisclosed profits home, it pays less than one-third its earnings in taxes to Peru. No wonder that Peru's Gross National Product cannot increase more than 2.2 percent a year while its population jumps 3.5 percent.

Most United States companies in Latin America sell to their own United States parent companies Latin America's raw materials, which they then put to manufacture in their United States plants. Such companies are not worried by a fall in the world market prices on raw materials. The difference can always be added on at the manufacturing end.

For example, a standard sheet of zinc less than one-tenth of an inch thick cost (in 1957 dollar values): 17.556 cents in 1924 but 31.270 cents in 1957. This was the manufactured United States price. But Peru received 11.597 cents in 1924 and 11.399 cents in 1957. We had added only 5.597 cents, or one-third, onto the raw material in 1924, but 19.871, or 65 percent, onto the commercial product in 1957. By not raising the Peruvian price (actually lowering it), "profits" in Peru were kept low, hence taxes remained low. The profits were made up in the United States.

Despite all these manipulations, some United States corporations' profits in Peru, or anywhere else in Latin America, can still be disproportionately high. Marcona Mining Company, for example, on a capital investment of $500,000 in 1954, made the following profits *by the books* (and paid the subsequent taxes):

1954 (its first year)	*1955*	*1956*
$4,913,654.81	$1,657,137.00	$5,411,036.52
(1,440,768.83)	(770,337.00)	(1,551,381.48)

1957	*1958*	*1959*
$11,680,387.12	$6,051,557.69	$4,624,362.35
(3,097,238.11)	(1,711,163.22)	(1,464,422.83)

1960
$8,409,270.56
(2,335,825.08)

In just six years Marcona made more than $30,000,000 net (after taxes) on $500,000 investment—a return of no less than 6,000 percent.

Chapter 27

The Lost Value of Copper

Exorbitantly high profits are not standard, to be sure. Chile provides an excellent example where profits, though high, are well balanced by taxes.

Almost 70 percent of Chile's Gross National Product and export earnings come from copper, and just three companies mine and sell 90 percent of Chile's copper. These are: Braden Copper Company, a subsidiary of Kennecott Copper Company; Chile Exploration Company (Chilex), a subsidiary of Anaconda Copper Mining Company; and Andes Copper Mining Company, also a subsidiary of Anaconda. As foreign corporations they represent in Chile what would be the case here at home if General Motors, General Electric, General Foods, Ford, all the banks, aviation, mines, mills, electronics, construction, and a thousand more companies were owned, say, by two British corporations.

Braden, Chilex, and Andes ship their net profits home. Their paper investments (in 1959):

	Material and Parts	Assets	Land	Total
Braden	$12,319,000	$ 69,559,000	$ 6,979,000	$ 88,857,000
Chilex	27,036,000	247,036,000	5,743,000	280,293,000
Andes	25,000,000	120,000,000	25,000,000	170,000,000
				$539,150,000

Their profits (shipped home), reserves (really also profit but remaining in Chile), and taxes, in millions of dollars:

	Shipped Home	Reserves	Taxes
1955	54.4	10.4	156.0
1956	75.4	13.5	126.6
1957	35.9	16.6	74.5
1958	27.4	17.0	52.5
1959	57.3	23.7	84.7
1960	52.2	33.0	88.2
1961 (est.)	45.0	34.0	70.0

The sharp drop in taxes paid to Chile after 1956 was the result of Law 11,828, May 5, 1955, which regularized (and obviously liberalized) accounting proceedings. Still, the tax amounts to about 50 percent of overall profits, which is fair by our standards and very high by Latin American standards. Technically, the companies can claim that their taxable earnings were $140.4 million in 1960, on which they paid $88.2 million, or 62+ percent in taxes. This is false, since profits laid aside as reserves are still profits, though, it is true, not to the parent corporations in the United States, since reserves are not brought home.

At this point, to be fair, we must point out that, unlike most other United States corporations in Latin America, Chile's Big Three maintain excellent working and living conditions. The companies are somewhat paternalistic, but they pay better, house better, and take better care of their employees than native corporations do.

The Chilex mine at Chuquicamata, 240 rail kilometers northeast of Antofagasta and at some 9,000 feet above sea level, is perhaps the best (though its wages are not) of the three, but the others are not far behind. During my visit there, I talked at length with both management and union, and was surprised to find the latters' gripes limited to benefits and not to wages, hours, or work conditions. The town of "Chuqui," which is mine property, has about 25,000 people, of whom 5,000 work in the mine. There are about 1,200 more workers, and their families, who live in Calama, about ten miles away, and they are transported free to and from the pit. The more fortunate ones who live in Chuqui are given company housing, some of which is on a par with that in Levittown, Long Island. The workers are not given appliances, yet in almost every house I visited, from the old-style corrugated tin shacks to the modern brick homes, I saw refrigerators and electric or gas stoves.

The company is building new houses regularly, but not so fast as the union would like. By mid-1962 there were 156 of one story (living room, two bedrooms, kitchen, and bath), 80 of two stories, more luxurious and larger; and 40 of varying types, for a total of 276 which housed about 600 workers and their families (more than one worker coming from each). The rest lived in shacks, which would be considered tenement slums in the United States, but are above average for workers in Chile. It was not for them, but for the 1,200 workers living in Calama that the union complained.

The union also wanted more schools. Currently, there are three, staffed by teachers paid by the company and by the government. But even at two shifts (morning and afternoon) they are insufficient. The union owns its company-built, modern hall, complete with a 2,500-seat auditorium. Union dues are compulsory (on automatic checkoffs) for workers, voluntary for staffers. There is a sleek glass-and-slab hospital with 240 beds, up-to-date equipment imported from the United States, and an efficient Chilean staff that includes 14 doctors. Costing about $250,000 a year to run, and available free to all Chuqui residents as well as to anyone else connected with the mine, the hospital surely plays a leading role in keeping infant mortality down to 73.2 per 1,000, when that part of the country's normal rate is 116.

The company's social-welfare expenditures, which by Chilean law, must be at least 1 percent of profits, was in 1961 $1,769,236.31, or more than 2 percent of remitted income plus reserves. The five union officers (one Communist, three Socialists, one Radical, that is, four members of the anti-United States Popular Front) told me that they never mixed politics with union-company affairs, had refused to strike for political reasons, and were mainly concerned with social benefits. I asked them if they felt that there was any discrimination in favor of United States or non-Chilean employees (35 percent); they all agreed there was none.

But as much as we should like to congratulate such conditions by wishing the United States Big Three copper companies a long life in Chile, the case is otherwise. When

Chile's budget, its development, its whole path toward progress, rely on copper exports, sentiment cannot erase facts. And the facts are that Chile loses beyond reason by not owning its copper. The companies' capital, some $539 million, has been returned to the United States almost three times in declared profits alone, thus:

1928-1950	$300 million
1950-1959	1,014
1960-1961-1962 (est.)	150
Total profits	$1,464 million

In addition, from 1928 to the present, some $100 million more have been lost to Chile in commissions, interests, and office expenses in New York and in other United States administrative centers (just for Chilean copper) and for storage while Chilean copper awaited refining. Chile also lost about $500 million during World War II when copper prices were frozen by the United States. Had Chile been free to sell where and when it pleased, we would not have frozen it out of our markets. Finally, there are the following disbursements that would have remained in Chile if it refined, insured, and shipped its copper on its own fleet since 1950, the year Chile was physically capable of doing all three:

	Refinery charges	Shipment and Insurances
	(in millions of dollars)	
1950	2.	3.6
1951	1.8	3.2
1952	2.4	1.3
1953	5.0	.2
1954	5.7	7.2
1955	6.9	6.2
1956	9.3	6.2
1957	9.9	8.8
1958	8.8	8.4
1959	10.0	10.1
1960	11.4	11.0
1961	13.8	12.7
1962 (est.)	14.5	14.5
	101.5	93.5 = $195

Adding it all up:

$1,464 million in	profits
100	administration charges
500	wartime freeze losses
195	refinery, shipment, and insurance charges

$2,259 millions

It seems not unreasonable to assume that a few hundred million more filtered back to the United States through some of the gimmicks described in the previous chapter. Thus, if Chile had nationalized its copper in 1928, it would be as much as $3 billion richer. And certainly more than $2 billion richer if it had nationalized it in 1950. Even if it had paid Kennecott and Anaconda their full book-value investment, Chile would be about $1.5 billion ahead—more than its trade-deficit accumulation. Today Chile would not need to borrow money, or have debts outstanding.

Furthermore it is generally estimated that capital (assets plus earnings) increases itself by 20 percent a year, meaning that the $1.5 billion remaining in Chile would have become in twelve years as follows:

1950	$1.5 billion
1951	1.8
1952	2.16
1953	2.592
1954	3.110
1955	3.932
1956	4.718
1957	5.662
1958	6.694
1959	8.033
1960	9.640
1961	11.568
1962	13.882

Naturally, such speculations are neither accurate nor even reasonable. But perhaps the $1.5 billion could have grown into $3 billion, enough to build Chile's 700,000 underfed and ill-housed families (3,800,000 people) a $3,000 house and give them $1,000 worth of food as well. Even if I'm still stretching the point by as much as an extra zero, can there be doubt that Chile would not be much, much better off owning its own copper?

Chapter 28

Black Gold and Private Banks

Venezuela is Latin America's biggest stage for our international companies. Their play is a drama, and the ending
is sad.

With 6.7 percent of the world's oil reserves (about half of
what we have below the ground in the United States), and
9 percent of the non-Communist nations' reserves, Venezuela
is not only a major petroleum producer but also a very
rich country—or it should be.

Yet its people are extremely poor. Its budget runs about
$1.5 billion a year, of which almost $800 million comes
from oil taxes and royalties; not very much when one considers that even at today's artificially depressed oil prices
(at point of export) Venezuelan oil could earn $3.084
billion yearly. How does Venezuela lose the difference?

Oil rests below the ground in hidden lakes. A tap at
one end can eventually pump out the whole lake. It
is estimated that 46.21 percent of Venezuela is over such
oil lakes but that only one-seventh of the area is actually
tapped or exploited. The one-seventh accounts for 6,180,896
hectares, or roughly 16,000 square miles, about the size
of New Jersey and Massachusetts combined.

At the rate of current production, Venezuela has enough
reserves for only sixteen years. After that, theoretically,
the underground lakes will be dry and Venezuela will
be broke—unless, of course, it either slows down its production or develops an industrial complex capable of leading

a transition to other earners, or both. Meanwhile, production increases steadily:

1950	1,497,988 barrels daily
1952	1,803,915
1954	1,895,309
1956	2,456,785
1958	2,604,840
1959	2,771,012
1960	2,846,107

Among the major five underdeveloped countries producing oil for export, Venezuela's rate is the highest:

Country	Reserves 1960	Production 1960	% of Production over Reserves
	(in millions of barrels)		
Kuwait	62,000	601	1.0
Saudi Arabia	50,000	456	0.9
Iran	35,000	385	1.1
Iraq	27,000	356	1.3
Venezuela	17,300	1,042	6.0

Venezuela has less reserves than any of the others, yet produces more. Already one conclusion can be made: whoever is exploiting Venezuela's oilfields is not doing so with Venezuela's future needs in view. On the contrary, such exploitation is against Venezuela's interest.

Who *is* carrying out the exploitation? There are three main groups, one United States, one Dutch-British, one Venezuelan. This is the way they share the land concessions:

United States	4,568,918 hectares	73.9%
Dutch-British	1,568,712 "	25.4%
Venezuelan	42,266 "	0.7%

Among the United States group are two big operators:
1. The Rockefellers whose Standard Oil Company owns 93.12 percent of Creole Petroleum Corporation and 17 percent of Socony-Vacuum, known to United States car drivers as Mobil. (Standard Oil also owns: 83.58 percent of International Petroleum Company, which operates in Colombia, another oil exporter, in Peru, and in other Latin

American countries; 100 percent of Esso Standard Oil Company of Ecuador; and, through International Petroleum, 100 percent of Tropical Oil Company, which has 26 subsidiaries in Latin America.)

2. The Mellons who own 45 percent of Gulf Oil Corporation, which owns 100 percent of Venezuela Gulf Oil Company and 100 percent of the shares of Mene Grande Oil ("Meneg") Company (though both Shell and Standard have an interest in Meneg's actual production and property).

The British-Dutch group is Royal-Dutch Shell, a mammoth outfit operating in the whole world (including operations in the United States), and owned mostly by British and Dutch entrepreneurs.

3. The Venezuelan group is the government-owned Corporación Venezolana del Petroleo (CVP).

Four foreign companies own almost 90 percent of Venezuela's total oil production and sales:

Creole	41.12%
Shell	26.16
Meneg	14.93
Mobil	4.90
Total	87.11%

All others (including Texas, Sinclair, Phillips, Superior, Atlantic, and so on) own and produce 12.73 percent. Venezuela does not yet produce even .2 percent (.002) of its oil.

Of these companies Creole is by far the most important, and the Rockefellers (Creole, part of Mobil and Meneg) by far the biggest dealers.

Since Venezuela's CVP has yet to earn one cent of profit, 100 percent of Venezuela's oil income is controlled by the foreign corporations, 73.84 percent United States and 26.16 percent British-Dutch. Since 92 percent of Venezuela's foreign exchange and 63 percent of its budget rely on oil revenue, our corporations control Venezuela by 68 percent (73.84 of 92) of its foreign exchange and 47 percent (73.84 of 63) of its budget.

In the years up to 1958, the oil companies' net profits (see Table XI) ranged from 26 to 33 percent of gross revenue and from 47 to 50 percent of taxable income. In 1958

the transitional revolutionary junta decreed the so-called
60-40 split; since then, profits have dropped to 18 percent
of gross and 34 percent of income. Total profits taken back
to the United States or Europe (see Table XII) during that
decade were about one-third more than their total all-time
investment. Despite this, Creole President Harold Haight
had the effrontery to characterize the so-called 60-40 decree
as "completely disregarding acquired rights and ignoring
the moral, if not legal, obligation to negotiate."[1]

Table XII also shows that in the 1951-1960 decade the
oil corporations made at least $5 billion profits and took
all of it home except a piddling $600 million—on paper
investment under $3 billion. Had Venezuela nationalized
its oil in 1950 (and a boycott not been organized by the
international trusts that control transportation, distribution,
refineries, and so on), the country could have paid the corporations' former owners the full book-value investment in
five years—in cash.

Furthermore, the country as a whole would have benefitted
from local oil expenses. (In every Latin American country
I came across this kind of operation: United States companies, hailed for "investing millions of dollars in Latin
America," actually deposited their "investment" in United
States banks in the United States, then took out the equivalent
in local currencies from the bank's Latin American branches.
Such "investments" are perfectly normal, but they add
nothing to Latin American economies except for small
interest charges if the local currencies are taken out as
loans.)

Our oil corporations also indulge in other manipulations
to avoid paying Venezuela its due. Here's an example:
though both production and taxes have been going up
steadily over the last few years, and our retail prices on
gasoline, kerosene, diesel oil, heating oil, asphalt, or lubricants
have certainly not been going down, Venezuela has actually

---

[1] Creole also reacted to the 60-40 split by cutting down its
Venezuelan cash outlay: In 1957 Creole spent $75 million in
explorations, in 1960, $3 million; Creole also transferred 70
of its top technicians to Libya, and once bustling Maracaibo
soon began to look as if there were more pumps than people
(1958 population: 450,000; in 1961, while all other cities increased
by 20 percent or more, Maracaibo lost 30,000 inhabitants).

Table XI

Venezuelan Oil Corporations' Costs, Profits, and Taxes, in Millions of Bolivars, and Percentage
($=3.3 Bolivars on average 1951-1960)

	1951		1952		1953		1954		1955		1956		1957		1958		1959		1960	
	Bols	%	Bols	%	Bols	%	Bols	%	Bols	%	Bols	%	Bols	%	Bols	%	Bols	%	Bols	%
Costs	1,411	32	1,516	33	1,516	33	1,678	34	1,711	29	1,854	27	2,100	25	2,270	30	2,286	32	2,409	33
Depreciation / Depletion	495	11	530	11	558	11	613	12	732	11	812	9	836	11	939	11	938	13	948	13
Taxes	1,298	30	1,369	29	1,395	29	1,545	29	1,774	30	2,128	31	2,777	33	2,938	38	2,724	37	2,631	36
Profits (net)	1,201	27	1,262	27	1,261	26	1,412	26	1,710	29	2,115	31	2,774	33	1,616	21	1,335	18	1,282	18
Gross Revenue	4,405		4,677		4,892		5,337		5,875		6,829		8,463		7,660		7,284		7,270	

been receiving less money from taxes: 2,938 million bolivars in 1958; 2,724 million in 1959; 2,631 million in 1960, and so on. The profits are simply "placed" where taxes are less.

Table XII

Venezuelan Oil Corporations' Investments
(Accrued and New)
And Return in Millions of Bolivars
($=3.3 on average 1951-1960)

	1 Investment	2 Profits	% ½	Reinvest.	Taken Home
1951	6,016	1,201	20	239	962
1952	6,237	1,262	20	445	817
1953	6,647	1,261	19	463	798
1954	6,896	1,412	21	232	1,180
1955	6,887	1,710	25	—106	1,816
1956	7,300	2,115	29	505	1,610
1957	8,690	2,774	32	692	2,082
1958	9,606	1,616	17	—762	2,378
1959	10,194	1,335	13	290	1,045
1960	10,584	1,282	12	—75	1,357

Ten-year Total 15,968 (average: 21) 1,923   14,045

The big oil corporations can juggle profits quite easily because they own the oil's tankers, refineries, and distribution systems. The simplest method of bringing down profits in Venezuela is to hike tanker costs charged to the Venezuelan subsidiaries but paid to shipping lines registered in Panama, Liberia, or wherever shipping taxes are lowest. This is the main reason why so many private United States ships fly non-United States flags.

(Juggling profits is common among all our companies involved in foreign commerce. For example, one United States company with plants in seven European nations has overseas sales headquarters in Geneva, Switzerland. Profits from products manufactured in West Germany and sold there, as well as in Denmark, Belgium, and Holland, go to the Geneva sales office. The reason: profits are taxed

20 percent in Switzerland but 51 percent in West Germany, 47 percent in Holland, almost 54 percent in Britain, 50 percent in France, and 52 percent in the United States.)

The possibility of profit manipulation is enough to render all tax reforms meaningless as far as Latin America's big earners—United States companies—are concerned. Hence, the international trusts did not offer too many objections when the Alliance for Progress began to clamor for such reforms from Latin America's governments. Stiff profit taxes hit only local companies earning local currencies from local sales. This is why Mexico's constitutional amendment (enacted in September, 1962) authorizing a special government committee to force all concerns (Mexican or foreign) to share their profits with workers did not worry our big subsidiaries there too much. They will simply juggle sale revenues (as well as their "loans") to reduce or cancel out their Mexican profits.

To counteract all these manipulations, evasions, and dispensations, Betancourt officially set up a three-point oil policy of merit:

1. No more concessions to foreign enterprises.

2. A national corporation to produce Venezuela's own oil—the CVP.

3. Firm support for OPEC—the Organization of Petroleum Exporting Countries.

In practice, however, that policy does not hurt the oil companies. As far as concessions are concerned, no more are needed. Most of Venezuela has been explored, and its oil content fairly completely analyzed. Besides, since oil rests in lake-type underground deposits, more wells can only accelerate production and depletion, not increase the country's reserves. As we have seen, production is already much too high. And yet Betancourt is actually helping to increase it even more.

In the past, a concession meant the right to explore 10,000 hectares for three years. Once oil was found, the exploring company selected half of the area (5,000 hectares), got a new contract for 40 or 90 years or forever, and the other half returned to the state as national reserves. Naturally, when the company started pumping its half, the nation's half was sucked out too, but at a slower rate. To keep this rate to a minimum, the exploitation contracts included provisos whereby the company's wells should be at least so many meters away from the borderline of the nation's half. (The further a pump is from the center of the oil lake, the slower the oil comes up.)

Under Dictator Pérez Jiménez that distance was 1,200 meters. But on October 7, 1961, the official weekly newsletter published by Betancourt's Ministry of Mines and Hydrocarbons, which applies his oil policy, announced that hereafter the distance limitation was abolished. Thus, Betancourt has perhaps not given new concessions, but he certainly has given foreign companies new production facilities, letting them advance 1,200 meters all along their halves—a potential production boost of 10 percent.

The CVP, despite its energetic President Juan Pablo Pérez Alfonzo, is not much more than a farce. Its budget has been set at 2,500,000 bolivars a year, which, at the 1962 exchange (one bolivar = $.2985), is about $750,000. With this lowly sum, CVP must pay all its salaries and all its machinery. It is a credit to its boss that it nevertheless began drilling operations in the spring of 1961 and had managed to put down 405 wells by the winter of 1962, producing 4,000 to 5,000 barrels a day. But the corporation was meant to compete with the foreign companies, which by then were producing more than 3 million barrels a day. (Venezuela consumes about 50,000 barrels a day.)

With only $750,000 a year, CVP can barely pay its staff of sixty and keep them in paper clips. It is forced to make contracts with the foreign companies for its own concessions. Thus the oil claimed to be Venezuelan is actually pumped on national property by the foreign companies CVP was meant to compete with. Why is CVP so handicapped? Is it that the Betancourt-Leoni regime does not want to ruin or even restrict the foreign corporations' sinecure?

OPEC's principle is laudable. So is its driving force: Pérez Alfonzo, the egg-bald (he shaves his head like Yul Brynner), tough, old-time AD man now nearing sixty, who is nationalistic-minded, yet remained on friendly terms with Betancourt until 1964, when he resigned his posts in the AD government. As Minister of Mines and Hydrocarbons, he was responsible for Venezuela's oil-policy applications, though naturally restricted by Betancourt's orders—and his lack of funds.

The members of OPEC include Kuwait, Iran, Iraq, Saudi

Arabia, and Venezuela, which together export 90 percent of the world's oil needs. Its main objective is to keep prices up, but unless all member countries decide as one to stop all exports of oil below a certain minimum price, the organization cannot succeed.

As it is, one or more members are constantly giving in. Kuwait does as Britain orders. Saudi Arabia, frightened of Nasserist nationalism, will do anything to keep its United States support. And even if all five stood firm, how long could they last out a boycott? It is possible for the big British-Dutch and United States buyers to hold out for weeks, perhaps months; and they control all but Italy's and Communist countries' markets and refineries. The United States itself produces enough oil to weather a freeze-out for a long time. The Italians cannot refine or distribute enough oil to the noncommitted nations to help for long. Russia is an oil exporter, but its surplus is constantly being squeezed out of the world markets by our trusts and our foreign policy.

Venezuela could survive a United States-British-Dutch boycott, however, if all Latin American countries bought its oil, transported by Russian, Greek, and Latin American fleets. (If Italy, Austria, Greece, all of Africa and all of Asia bought Middle East oil, those producers, too, could survive.) But is it conceivable that we would let a Somoza, a Valencia, a Figueres, Argentina's militarists, even an Alessandri, break our boycott? Besides, if pressure were put upon Saudi Arabia, Kuwait, and Iran, the feudal systems there could collapse in forty-eight hours. Certainly King Saud of Saudi Arabia, whose personal spending money is still $100 million a year even with falling prices, has no interest in balking at Standard-Vacuum's edicts.

Pérez Alfonzo, whose national interests seemingly out-weighed any of his desires for personal gain, tried to break the stranglehold. OPEC, after all, was his creation. But his buyers, who are also his producers and his refiners and his transporters, told him that "free competition" in Venezuela meant "our price or nothing." Since Alliance for Progress aid could be stopped anytime, Pérez Alfonzo accepted the fact that he had no choice. Is this why Venezuela gets so much Alliance help—and such praise from Washington?

United States corporations—especially those belonging to the Rockefeller family—are also powerful in Venezuela in fields other than oil. (We have already seen how Bethlehem

Steel and United States Steel control Venezuela's iron production.) The Rockefellers own Venezuela's supermarkets (C. A. Automercados and MiniMax), banks (Banco Mercantil y Agrícola), textiles (Telares Amana), and much more. The Rockefeller International Basic Economy Corporation (IBEC) has its finger in almost every pie available. And one such pie is INSA, a corporation whose main purpose seems to be to help importers avoid Venezuelan import taxes.

Hard hit by deficits, Venezuela has been forced to protect its lack of dollars by placing restrictions on imports. To get around them, United States importers must make (that is, *assemble*) their products in Venezuela. If a company is big enough and sells enough of its products in Venezuela, it can set up a "plant." Such putting-together shops exist all over Latin America, and are not enjoyed exclusively by the United States. In Uruguay, for example, France's Renault gets around import duties on new cars that range up to 150 percent by shipping its bodies and motors separately, which, as parts, come into the country on 10 percent duty; Renault then has them "built in Uruguay by Uruguayans" in three hours flat. In Venezuela, Ford has such a plant. So have other big-selling corporations. On the other hand, Rhode Island's Fram Corporation (oil, gas, and air filters) or RCA Whirlpool (refrigerators, washing machines, and gas ranges) simply do not sell enough in Venezuela to justify a plant. Together, however, many such smaller importers can profit from a single huge assembling plant—INSA.

Begun by one Roberto Salas Capriles,[2] INSA is partly owned and controlled by the Rockefellers (who put in 30 percent of its original $2,250,000 capital). It has received a $1,500,000 loan from our Export-Import Bank and, incredibly, $534,000 from the Venezuelan Government itself—too poor to increase CVP's funds.

[2] The Capriles family, old Betancourt friends, own most of Venezuela's press, including the dailies El Universal, La Esfera, Ultimas Noticias, and El Mundo; the magazines Elite, Páginas, and Venezuela Gráfica, all of which, naturally, support Betancourt-Leoni's AD regime. (The independent, world-renowned daily El Nacional, which does not support it, is under constant advertising blackmail and has very few ads despite the fact that its circulation is higher than that of all other dailies combined.)

Only in a country where foreign corporations can command its economic policies completely would the government waste its small amount of revenue available to help out foreign importers of luxury instead of its own basic industry. And only in a country where the foreign corporations completely dominate the economy would such commands be obeyed.

Yet even in Mexico, which does not blindly obey the dictates of foreign companies, we seem to hold such domination. In Mexico this is much more tragic since the country has had its great social revolution. Nevertheless, so far-reaching has been our penetration of the economy since the Cárdenas administration, that some Nationalists are already talking of the need for a second revolution to break our hold.

That hold is formidable. There are 2,100 corporations (Sociedades Anónimas) in Mexico. They control 85 percent of all money invested (capital). Of these 2,100, just 400 hold 77 percent. The 400, then, dominate the economy, and they break down thus:

168 are foreign (mainly U.S.)	36%	of the capital
17 are mixed (mainly U.S.-controlled)	19%	" " "
Total U.S. control:	55%	of the capital
38 are owned by the Mexican govt.	25%	
127 are Mexican (private)	20%	
Total Mexican:	45%	of the capital

When one controls 55 percent of capital invested in the pace-setting corporations and 42 percent (55 percent of 77 percent) of all corporations and 32 percent (42 percent of 85 percent) of all money whatsoever invested in Mexico, then one does almost control the country itself.

Furthermore, United States corporations control a good part of Mexico's fluid money as well, since 43 percent of all deposits are in United States-owned banks, meaning that we hold power over 43 percent of all loans within the

Before supporting Betancourt, however, Capriles' dailies were at the service of the Left when the Larrazábal junta was in power and, before that, at the service of Pérez Jiménez during his dictatorship.

country. It is understandable, therefore, that impatient Nationalists are talking of another revolution.

My own impression is that, as bad as is our monopolistic hold on Mexico's economy, the political structure is such that a Nationalistic president can still reorient the country onto its abandoned road of Reconquest.

A second Cárdenas, for example, if elected within the framework of the dictatorial PRI, could find that road. Backed by the overpowering PRI machinery, its police and armed forces, he could enforce reconquest measures. Still, with or without Cárdenas, sooner or later something or someone will erupt to break our companies' hold on Mexican economic life. If we adopt a policy of Reconquest ourselves, that inevitable economic break will not cause us to lose a good friend.

Chapter 29

Development and Foreign Investment

What has our vast amount of capital done for Latin America?

We have already amply seen the disastrous social effect—higher unemployment every year; a faster rate of increase in food, housing, and clothing prices than in wages; less social mobility; and so on. But what about the economic effects?

From 1948 to 1960, Latin America's per capita Gross National Product stayed about the same, while the world's GNP soared 40 percent. From 1948 to 1960, Latin America's exports went up 22 percent if Venezuelan oil is included, 4 percent if not; while ours increased by 45 percent, the world's by 88 percent, Asia's by 94 percent, the Middle East's by 128 percent, and Western Europe's by 184 percent.

Latin America's agricultural production, down severely after World War II, rose to its prewar level in 1956-1957 and is now 5 percent lower. Latin America's general production, up during the early 1950's, has dropped steadily for the last five years. Chilean coal is down from 169,000 metric tons per month in 1954 to 81,000 in 1960. In the same period, Peruvian coal sank from 21,300 metric tons to 14,500. Argentine meat tumbled from 145,000 metric tons per month in 1956 to 87,000 in 1960. Venezuela's milk and brick, Panama's manufactured gas, Chile's cement, Mexico's lead productions all slipped in 1960 and again in 1961.

Pushing hard for a boost in steel output, Argentina managed to produce 23,100 metric tons of crude steel per month in 1960, compared to 312,000 in Australia, a country of about the same characteristics and potential as Argentina but only half its population. (Even tiny Denmark, where milk and cheese mean more than all of Argentina's "World Power" declarations, turns out 26,500 metric tons a month.) Argentina's per capita steel production has dropped sharply from 157 kilograms in 1909 to 117 kilograms in 1929 to today's 80½ kilograms.

Investments have not led to the improvement of living conditions in any country as a unit. As Adolf Berle, Jr., himself put it, before he began to help create precisely those policies that contradict him: "Preachments about the value of private enterprise and investment, and the usefulness of foreign capital were, to most students of the situation, a little silly. . . . Foreign and/or private investment may industrialize, may even increase production, and still leave the masses in as bad a shape as ever."

Private enterprise and especially the huge trusts coming into Latin America with millions or billions of dollars are perhaps not to blame for profiting from conditions that favor them. Of course, they perpetuate such conditions through bribes, boycotts, and the financing of political parties, coups d'état, and even revolutions. Their aim is always the "cornering of a market."

Since competition is non-existent or very small, the big corporations set up operations in such a way as to develop huge particular industries without regard to the country's needs or its internal balance. Many companies may assemble cars, but not one will ever build a factory capable of turning out cars from brute steel up. Others may produce steel but not turn it into commercial bars or structures. Others may suck oil from the ground but not refine it on the ground. The big corporations are interested in profits, not development.

It is not their duty to care about development. But in Latin America they actively, willfully, determinedly use their wealth to prohibit development and an integrated economy. "Private enterprise," Kalman Silvert has written, "when operating within a system in which the checks and balances of government and other competing groups are impossible, simply cannot be trusted to be moderate, unselfish, and farseeing. To ask an angelic role of American direct investors abroad without control is not only to plead for the impossible, but is also an unwarranted cession of the making of American foreign policy."

Every time a Latin American cries out against Wall Street, we call him a Communist. Every time he boos or spits at one of our representatives (or a Vice-President), we say he is a Red agitator. Every time he praises Russia or demands the right to trade with Communist countries (which we ourselves do), we brand him a Moscow agent. And even when he simply asks his country to nationalize United States property, we call him a demagogue, a rabble-rouser, a "far-Leftist."

Usually that Latin American is simply an educated Latin American. He knows that Russia, underdeveloped and in the hands of a powerful oligarchy (there called nobility) only one generation ago, has become the world's second (and sometimes first) power. Meanwhile, he has seen Latin America, allied to the world's greatest democracy, floundering and withering and regressing. It is only normal that he be at least curious about other than democratic methods. Chances are he will never become Communist. Chances are he will never abandon his heritage or even his religion. These are closer to ours than to Russia's. But why must we insist on imposing our way and our vision on his?

In July, 1962, a group of Brazilian students had an interview with President Kennedy. These students had been carefully screened by the sponsoring United States-Brazilian organization. They were not Communists. They were not even anti-United States. Then they began asking questions: "Mr. President, what would be the reaction of the United States Government in the event we were to socialize the means of production in our country as a way to wage more effectively the battle against underdevelopment?" "Mr. President, how do you reconcile the fact that in spite of all the talk of peace that you say that your country advocates, the youth of this country, at least, is being prepared for war through all types of aggressive war propaganda?" and so on.

The Brazilian students were honest. They had seen our TV and our motion pictures, heard our talk of fallout shelters, and about our draft calls. Kennedy answered the questions. He explained our need for security, our commitments, and so on. As our President speaking to foreigners, he had to defend us, even where we are wrong. His answers are not criticizable. But our press reaction certainly is.

Most papers that referred to the incident saw in the students provocateurs, agitators, or obvious undercover Reds. Even the *New York Times* fumed that "we are still being attacked as if 'dollar diplomacy,' the intervention by American marines and the Platt Amendment giving us the right to intervene in Cuba still existed. President Kennedy was rightly indignant that the students should consider us the equivalent of war-mongers today."

Kennedy was; he had to be. But the *Times*, which claims to be objective, did not have to be. It knows better. True, we do not use marines today. But our high finances bring in the same results. True, we do not have Platt amendments. But our Mutual Assistance pacts are just as bad. True, we do not take over Latin America's customs bureaus. But our corporations take over 40 percent of its whole economy. True, we do not maintain "dollar diplomacy." But we keep the Alliance for Progress keyed to our dollars.

To Latin Americans, we *are* warmongers. We arm their repressive armies, train their political generals, and blackmail their foreign ministers. And we justify all this on the pretense of a Communist menace. Latin Americans have very seldom suffered from Communism, but very often from capitalism.

Chapter 30

The Sieve for Dollars and Pesos

Latin America's capitalists are just as unpreoccupied with its development as are ours.

One of the democrats' major arguments against socialization is that Latin America does not have enough capital to develop itself; hence, they say, it needs ours—both private and public.

The argument is false. In Latin America, native businessmen earn almost as much as ours do (and they are just a few). Since World War II, Latin American capitalist-oligarchs have exported to other areas at least $25 billion. In European banks alone, current Latin American deposit accounts hold $10 billion. Venezuela loses $100 million or more every single year. So do Brazil and Argentina. In 1960-1961 in El Salvador exportable dollars were so much in demand that buyers had to go on waiting lists of up to ten days.

In May, 1962, *U.S. News & World Report* quoted an American official who said: "Yes, it is about right that when the U.S. puts a billion dollars into Latin America, a billion leaks out at the other end into hideaway accounts in Switzerland or New York." According to ECLA, flight capital now amounts to $1.5 billion every year. Latin America does not need our dollars—either private or public. It simply needs its own.

Actually, as we have amply seen by now, neither our private nor our public dollars are sent to Latin America because of its needs. The former are invested in order to make our investors richer; the latter are loaned in order to make Latin America more dependent on us. The only Latin Americans who hope that we will invest or lend them more—with the structure as it is now—are those who profit from either or both: our corporations' Latin American oligarchic partners and Latin America's corrupted governments (run, for the most part, by the same oligarchs).

When he retired from the presidency of the International Finance Corporation, Robert Gardner, a former vice-president of the World Bank, said: "To most of the recipient countries, the amounts (of aid) are never sufficient. They never can be, because money alone accomplishes nothing. It is only a tool. The effective spending of large funds requires experience, competence, honesty, and organization. Lacking any of these factors, large injections of capital into developing countries can cause more harm than good."

All of these factors are missing in Latin America. Military dictatorships or army juntas are inevitably corrupt. Professor Lieuwen estimates that Perón stole $700 million, Pérez Jiménez and Batista $250 million each. But Democrats are no better. In Mexico, Miguel Alemán, once a small grocer's son, retired from the presidency (1946-1952) as owner of Mexico City's $4,000,000 Continental Hilton Hotel, a lime-and-grapefruit plantation, $5,000,000 Levittown-like Satellite City, controlling interests in the $25 million Tubos de Acero de Mexico S.A., and in the Celulosa de Chihuahua. In all, PRI democracy helped Alemán and his associates reap, according to Lieuwen, an $800 million fortune.

In Peru former Premier Pedro Beltrán was constantly hailed in the United States press as a great reformer, anti-Communist, and patriotic Peruvian. But the facts are these: Beltrán is a multimillionaire *latifundista* (and owner of Lima's important daily *La Prensa*) who in 1960 proposed a mild agrarian reform, to be financed by 3 percent of Peru's budget ($337.5 million in 1961) with so many conditions that neither his own lands nor those belonging to the Sociedad Agraria (a powerful club of big landowners whose leader is Beltrán himself) would be expropriated. Beltrán got much aid from President Eisenhower and more from Kennedy. One United States loan, $7.5 million from our Development Loan Fund, now part of AID, was to help create low-cost housing. The money went at 3 percent interest to a loan-and-savings association called Mutual de Vivienda Perú. Mutual then lent the money at 12 percent a year. The major stockholder of Mutual de Vivienda was, of course, Beltrán himself. (The deal was questioned in Parliament but was approved when Haya de la Torre's "reform-minded" Apristas voted to support Beltrán—and his boss Prado. The payoff, we have seen, was Prado's election "cooperation.")

In Brazil, government corruption has been so enormous it would require an encyclopedia to list it. During President Kubitschek's regime, which, said Rio's *Diario de Noticias*, seemed to be "sitting on a blanket of rottenness," fraud, shakedowns, and kickbacks were standard in every federal agency. Among the worst (or among the most-exposed ones) were: COFAP, Brazil's price-control agency; IBGE, the Institute of Geography and Statistics; SAPS, the social-security institute; NOVOCAP, the agency that built Brasília and sold choice lots for $900 to friends who resold them immediately for up to $11,000 (the government lost $800,000 here alone); SNAPP, the federal transportation agency in the Amazon; DNOCS, the relief agency in Brazil's starvation-ridden northeast (22 percent of its $70 million 1956-1960 funds disappeared); SPVEA, Brazil's biggest development agency (Amazon, roads, virgin lands), which had scores of newsmen, a senator, and a deputy on its payroll; the Mail Service, where $4,000,000 worth of packages are stolen each year and 30 percent of letters are undelivered (local delivery in Rio takes up to a month); most provincial politicians (one Paraná State governor, Moysés Willy Lupion de Troya, and his pals, accused of embezzling more than $100 million, officially fled to Switzerland before being apprehended, but actually hid out in a Sáo Paulo *Fazenda*, and now enjoys official protection); and many federal senators and deputies. (Just before its 1960 session adjourned, Kubitschek's Congress, with Brazil almost bankrupt and tight-money Quadros sure to use his veto in the next session, voted laws permitting deputies to double their own living expenses and to have four all-expenses-paid round trips to Rio every month.)

Corruption also plagues Argentina's "democracy," from government officials to customs men. One Ulises Pologna, whose long title as Frondizi's Presidential Delegate for Austerity and Reason in Public Administration meant simply that he was responsible for the morality of government employees, was fired in 1959 when it turned out that his own firms were chock-full of crooked deals. *Correo de la Tarde* said, "The teacher of morals is more rotten than any of his pupils."

Worse still was a $2,000,000-a-year baby-stealing racket uncovered in 1960. In Argentina, where divorce is outlawed and adoption too complicated (a father may reclaim his child at any time), public hospital officials told poor-ward mothers that their babies had died, then sold them for up to $3,000 apiece.

Even the champion of "Christian Democracy" was involved in shady deals. Frondizi and his aide Rogelio Frigerio were tied up with a smallish construction firm that, since the 1958 election, mushroomed into a multimillion-dollar venture (another member was Buenos Aires' equivalent of mayor). Frondizi's Minister of Services and Public Works was connected to Republic Steel Corporation and to Thyssen Corporation, which handled the costliest of government projects. Frigerio's successor in Frondizi's important Secretariat of Social Economic Relations was one Nestor Grancelli Chá, who simultaneously represented a flock of foreign companies in Argentina.

One deal was a dandy. Because of Argentina's lack of pipelines, much of Patagonia's natural gas gets lost (29 percent in 1950, 64 percent, or about $100 million a year, since 1959). To lay the necessary lines to Buenos Aires would cost about $200 million. Under Frondizi there were only two bids "accepted" for consideration for the pipelines' construction. One was presented by Gasodar S.A. (which would supposedly receive a $110 million Export-Import Bank loan). Frondizi's (and again Guido's) Finance Minister Alvaro Alsogaray had interests in Gasodar at the time the bid was placed; two of its board members were associated with one Carlos A. Juní who was then Secretary of Energy, and as such had to choose what bids to consider. The other bid was presented by Saipem, a subsidiary of the Italian Petroleum Consortium ENI. In Saipem were active Walter Prosperetti who is a Frondizi relative, Grancelli Chá (once again), and Adalberto Krieger Vasena, then Frondizi's commercial mission head to the United States. By the time the "bids" were judged, Alsogaray had been booted out by Frondizi. Thus, Saipem won. Its bid:

$410,000,000—105 percent profit. But such deals are legal, hence are not counted in usual graft estimates.

These estimates, conservatively calculated, show that more than $1.5 billion of public funds are stolen from Latin America's treasuries every year. This is 50 percent more than the Alliance promises at its best. In Latin America, private investments retard its development and deplete its resources. But public loans, granted according to our current policies, serve mostly to enrich the rich and to corrupt on a larger scale those already corrupted—another reason why many Nationalists turned toward Fidel Castro for their inspiration.

PART VII: Castro vs. The United States

Chapter 31

The Battlefronts and the Forces

Since Bolívar and San Martín led Latin America's fight for independence, no general, politician, *caudillo*, or statesman has had so much significance or created so many repercussions as Fidel Castro. He is better known than Stalin or Khrushchev, Roosevelt or Kennedy. His name plasters every city's walls from Patagonia to Monterey. Hundreds of songs praise or condemn him. In Uruguay, Cuba's revolutionary anthem (*Adelante Cubanos . . .*) is almost as well known as its own (*Orientales, La Patria o La Tumba . . .*). In Venezuela, the Committee for the Defense of the Cuban Revolution has 100,000 members pledged, theoretically, to rush to Cuba's defense as part of the would-be International Brigades should the next invasion get a foothold. And in Haiti, even a voodoo performer got into the act by sticking a pin into "Kastroh."

To us, Castro is either a Communist threat or a danger to free enterprise. To Cubans, he is either a savior or a tyrant. To Latin Americans everywhere else, he is a rallying cry, good or bad. As such he cannot be defeated by slogans, dollars, or invasions. And as long as the conditions he rebelled against exist elsewhere in the hemisphere, there will be new Castros.

This, and not Fidel, is what scares our policy-makers. A Communist Cuba even ninety or nine miles away from Florida is not a threat, just as a capitalist Iran zero miles from Russia is no threat to Moscow. But a rebellious Latin America, whence comes our copper and our oil, our bananas and our coffee, our tungsten and our tin, is very much a danger. And an independent Latin America whose big industry can eventually compete with our Big Business on the world markets is even more frightening—to many of our important citizens. If the ability of our trusts to make $10 billion a year instead of $8 billion *is* the policy of the United States, no more need be said. But if our foreign policy is to defend our system for ourselves, to guarantee our safety and to assure ourselves of a decent livelihood for *all* our citizens (and not a disproportionately high income just for a few), then we must make the effort to understand just why Castro became and remains a symbol of hope for many Latin Americans.

We have seen how underdeveloped Latin America is in a stranglehold. Its oligarchies, foreign companies and, except in a few cases, its churchmen and its Armed Forces are allied to keep that hold just as tight for just as long as possible. We have also seen how in underdeveloped countries money talks, as the saying goes. It does more than talk: it orders. Even if the press were free and independent, which it rarely is, and even if elections were honest, which they almost never are, political democracy cannot and does not succeed in economic undemocracy, that is, in underdeveloped countries.

"Underdeveloped" is not synonomous with "poor"; a country can be poor, yet its potential can be fully and *equitably* exploited. If so, it is developed. Switzerland, Denmark, Austria, New Zealand are poor countries, especially in comparison to the United States or even to France, Germany, and England. But the former are well balanced. There are few beggars. There are no deaths from starvation and there is enough distributed wealth so that competition can allow social mobility. Small farms in Denmark are solvent because there are not so many huge ones as to be able to crush all others. Nor is Denmark—or any European country, New Zealand, or Australia—owned 40 percent by corporations from just one foreign power and 51 percent by corporations of three allied foreign powers.

There are only two ways to develop and equitably industrialize a nation: through tough competition or through efficient government planning. For there to be competition, a country must have a great deal of capital distributed among many people, enough so that self-defeating duplication can be avoided only by creating many industrial centers throughout the country. Industrialization is not accomplished by raising one huge plant such as Venezuela's INSA costing

$5,000,000, but by numerous smaller ones costing $500,000 each in ten different sections of the country. (These expand, reinvest profits, attract local services, and only then begin interconnecting into trusts.)

Latin America does not have such capital. It has only the big kind, the kind that raises mammoth plants—and ships its profits either to parent corporations in the United States or to banks in Europe and New York. Now it is too late. Competitive industrialization takes time, as well as cheap labor to start. Latin America has plenty of cheap labor but no time. In the 1960's, when world communications make contacts, comparisons, and envy unavoidable, Latin Americans are not willing to sit back and "be rich next century."

Yet that is precisely what most Latin American Nationalists were forced to say—until Castro. They could not hope that our corporations would change their practices or that social revolutions could ever succeed. They knew that should United States corporations be nationalized, Washington would immediately resort to economic boycotts (if not marines.)

True, Mexico had had a revolution and subsequently nationalized its oil. But it did not dare push its social reforms all the way. As a result a new oligarchy, new United States corporations, and new economic repressions became standard. Sad but factual. As one character in *La región más transparente* (by Carlos Fuentes, perhaps Mexico's best young writer) says: "I cannot bring myself to think that the only concrete result of the Mexican revolution is the formation of a new privileged class, the economic hegemony of the United States, and the paralysis of all domestic politic life."

True also, Bolivia had had a revolution and subsequently nationalized its tin. But it too has seen its revolution stalled, not so much by adherence to nonrevolutionary economic policies per se, but by allowing democratic process to lead its revolution before development was completed. Until a country is developed, democracy is impossible. In extra-underdeveloped Bolivia the immediate return of democracy meant government hesitation and corruption and the upsurge of new crops of monopolistic industrialists.

Thus, Latin American Nationalists had lost hope. They talked of revolution, but did nothing. One group of intellectuals from each Latin American country became permanent expatriots. Another, mainly journalists, worked hard at whatever job paid best for two years in order then to spend a third in Paris. There they planned and replanned the revolutions they never really believed were possible. Some, it is true, went to Guatemala in the early 1950's. But Arbenz was either a phony or a coward, or both. He did not arm the people—an absolutely necessary move, since it was inevitable, as he must have known, that the minute he expropriated United Fruit property we would intervene by force of arms to bring him down. We did, in 1954.

Then came Fidel Castro. Until he launched his Agrarian Reform and nationalized our oil companies' refineries, Latin America's Nationalists supported Castro only because they were anti-Batista. Afterward, however, their whole lives were changed. Castro armed the people, destroyed the oligarchy and curbed the bourgeoisie, launched literacy campaigns, drafted what doctors did not flee to serve in the fields, giving medicine, care, and inoculations to the masses.

The intellectuals, the Nationalists, and the reformers *had* to back Castro. They poured into Cuba, helped set up people's universities, took over the alphabetization program, and launched Castro's Prensa Latina wire service, which became, objectively speaking, one of the best in the world in terms of depth, and the only one in Latin America that sent facts instead of propaganda. These Latin Americans were the technicians of Castro's revolution.

And then the inevitable happened: Cuba's Communists moved in. It was inevitable for two reasons. The first was our policy. When Castro began nationalizing our companies, which he had to do, we not only branded the whole regime Red but also cut off the sugar quota, instituted an embargo, and pressured all our allies and followers to do the same. Castro needed help, badly. Cuba's buses, phones, tractors, machines, elevators, roller skates, cameras, pencil sharpeners, meat cutters, freezers, lipsticks—in fact everything from food itself to airplanes—were United States imported. The embargo would have brought any leader to his knees. Castro called for help.

Russian diplomats were no fools. They knew that Castro would fall sooner or later from some United States intervention. Russia was unwilling and/or unable to wage a world war to defend him; and to help out economically until his fall was deemed too expensive and too useless a sacrifice. Thus Russia agreed to a few barter deals but not to massive aid. Castro wanted Russia not only to import buses but also to help Cuba set up its own bus industry, not only to import elevators but also to help set up Cuba's elevator industry, not only to import pencil sharpeners but also to . . . Russia refused. It had too many much-closer allies still far from being on their own feet to get involved with tiny Cuba halfway around the world, on which a United States base (Guantánamo) could not be removed without risking war.

Barter deals would not save Cuba, and Castro knew it. Hence, he had to force Russia to come through with more. Castro calculated, and rightly, that if Cuba identified itself as a member of the Socialist camp, Russia would lose immeasurable propaganda points if it let Cuba down. So Castro officially declared Cuba a People's Socialist Republic and Khrushchev was stuck. Russian aid began to pour in—too slow in 1961, faster in 1962. But Castro had to pay a stiff price: he opened his office doors to Communist Party regulars.

He probably would have done so anyway. Reason Number Two: Castro needed an efficient, financially uncorruptible, obedient organization to run his reform programs. The Latin American technicians could plan them. But Cubans had to put them into practice. Since his revolution was so radical, uprooting tradition, overturning habits, destroying old institutions, he felt unable to trust the non-Communist, educated men around him. In most countries of the world, certainly in all underdeveloped countries, to be educated means to be well off, either a bourgeois or an oligarch. The bourgeoisie and oligarchy were naturally hostile to Castro's reforms. The only other "safe" educated class was the Communist elite.

Though Cuban Communists follow the orders of Russia, not Cuba, Castro decided that since Russia would be stuck with Cuba, it must be in its interests to develop Cuba's economy. A strong, economically independent Cuba would do more to destroy United States propaganda in Latin America than a thousand Sputniks playing tag over it. Thus Castro thought Cuba's Communists would work hard for his revolution while his own men, the Sierra Maestra veterans sticking by him, would train their own cadres eventually to take over from the Reds.

Communists may be dogmatically tied to such world-shaking events as the polemic between Bernstein and Kautsky, but they do know the value of being in charge of training centers. Hence, they rapidly took them over. Suddenly Communists were so powerful and their influence so spread out that Castro decided it was imperative to strike back. That is the reason for his well-known December 1, 1961, "I am a Marxist-Leninist" speech which, while denying that he was a Russian-type Communist,[1] was meant to regain the backing of the militias, trained by the Communist regulars. Next Castro attacked the Cuban Communist Party itself, booting out of Cuba Red leader Aníbal Escalante (who is now in Prague). Finally, "Che" Guevara followed through with a Castro-approved attack on the Communist economic mastermind Carlos Rafael Rodríguez.

But as threats of a new invasion faced Castro anew, as the country shook to armed attacks from Cuban exile boats havened in Florida, and as our congressmen clamored for United States unilateral intervention in Cuba, Castro was again forced to beg Russia for more arms, more military instructors, more massive aid—and, discovered later, missiles. This provoked many of our congressmen to demand an immediate United States Marine attack upon Cuba.

President Kennedy reacted calmly. He insisted that no such intervention would be contemplated so long as the Castro regime did not acquire an "offensive capability." However, after such previous promises had been followed by the Bay of Pigs invasion, Castro obviously could not take us at our word. Furthermore, the Voice of America, a propaganda arm of our State Department, immediately broadcast that "the government of the United States threatens no nation and no people," which, as we have seen, is unfortunately false and which implied that it was Cuba that was doing the threatening. And many of our leading statesmen continued to demand an invasion to "stop Cuba's aggressive intentions." Anyone who can claim that tiny Cuba had or has such intentions when our Guantánamo base stares down its throat and when we have made it amply clear that we are anxiously awaiting an excuse to wipe Cuba

[1] Many anti-Communist Marxists are Leninists: all Trotskyites, for example, who hated Stalin earlier and longer and harder than even our most sincere Crusader.

clear of all Castroites is either insane or a liar. But then
lies did get us to invade Cuba once before, in 1898.

In this atmosphere, then, Castro was perfectly justified
to ask Russia for missiles, even with nuclear warheads.
If you are convinced that your enemy is going to try to
kill you, you are going to do your best to kill him too.
Cuba will be destroyed by the *Yankis*, Castro could say,
but maybe Cuba can get a shot at Washington too. And
so Russian missiles were installed 90 miles from the United
States—to protect Cuba.

The fallacy, of course, was that the missiles were Russian,
controlled by Russians and at the service of Russia—not
Cuba. As such, they did represent a threat to us. Objectively,
one can point out that Russia was only giving us back some
of our own medicine, since we have long pointed missiles
at Russia from 35 bases in foreign countries. Nevertheless,
Kennedy was perfectly right to denounce this as a breach
in the balance of power, even if our definition of "balance"
is plenty of United States bases around Russia, no Russian
base around the United States.

So we got tough. Aside from the nonsense about our
bases being "defensive" and theirs "offensive"—ours "good,"
theirs "bad," as Cuba's United Nations ambassador remarked
sarcastically—our justification for the Cuban blockade and
the ensuing risk of mass destruction was simply that we
thought we would have our way, and we did. Russia, unwilling to fight a war over a reluctant and costly ally, capitulated.
Cuba's genuine and fully justified fear of United States aggression had been used by Russia as a Cold War weapon, and
like most modern weapons, it had become obsolete before
it was even fired.

After that, of course, Russia and the United States began
to relax. Ironically, Kennedy's showdown and war risking,
which, granted, was unavoidable, turned out to be the first
step in a détente in the Cold War. It was as if both sides
learned that they were not willing to start the shooting,
hence could drop their guard. But the showdown also
benefitted Cuba, curiously enough. First of all, to save
face, Russia had demanded and received from us the promise
that we would not invade Cuba. Secondly, Russia's capitula-
tion widened the Russo-Chinese split, and Cuba began to
take advantage of it.

Without signing the Nuclear Test-Ban Treaty, which has

become Khrushchev's pet achievement, Castro found himself in the advantageous position of being able to exact more and more Russian aid, yet curb the influence of Communist regulars in Cuba. Thus he slashed Rodriguez' power, kicked upstairs Fabio Grobart, fired Juan Marinello from the rectorship of Havana University. Back in the top circle appeared such old Sierra fighters as Faustino Pérez, Pedro Miret, Efigenio Almejeiras, Sergio delValle, William Gálvez—anti-Communists all. But these men, as Castro himself, are not anti-Communists because they are moderate. On the contrary, they are revolutionaries who are convinced that Russian Communism is no longer revolutionary. Meanwhile, however —to go back to 1961—what was the outcome in Latin America when it did appear that Cuba had been taken over by Communists?

The Nationalists working for Castro until 1961 were not Communists. Most were not even Socialists. All, of course, realized that nationalizations are necessary in order to let Latin Americans recapture their own fates. They knew that they must reconquer Latin America in order to think, feel, and act like Latin Americans, in order to make it possible for Latin Americans, not foreigners, to make the decisions concerning Latin America. In the admirable book *Latin American Issues*, published by the Twentieth Century Fund, Editor (and Economist) Albert O. Hirschman put it this way:

> The aim of economic development is far more than an increase in per capita income: it is also, and more importantly, this "conquest of decision centers," which were previously in foreign hands, and a new ability to strike out on one's own, economically, politically and intellectually. For this reason, the quest for development is also a quest for self-discovery and self-affirmation and thus comes to be indissolubly tied to a new nationalism which is so noticeable a feature of the intellectual scene in Latin America.

The intellectual Latin American technicians of the Cuban Revolution were in a quandary: Stay and be bossed by Communists or return home but remain pro-Castro, since, in view of the United States position, Cuba's revolution is the only type possible.

For a while they managed to hold their ground. There were about 50,000 of them, and though none, except Che Guevara, was a decision-maker, they had acquired some strength. In January, 1961, the Argentines directing Prensa Latina went to Castro himself and got his permission to purge all Communists out of the service. They got Havana's university closed, reopened, closed again, but held on. In the fields, the doctors and engineers and agronomists had less trouble keeping Communists out. Then came the Bay of Pigs invasion. No act of ours could have helped the Communists more. As in any war, a national emergency was proclaimed, and under its cover the Communist militia heads moved in faster. The Argentines in Prensa Latina were first to go, then the university policy center fell, and finally there began a general exodus. But not all left. And with the new arrivals plus some who returned, the number of Latin Americans in Cuba is again about 50,000.

Those who did leave, including almost all the journalists (Prensa Latina quickly degenerated into a very poor propaganda service), were changed men. They were disillusioned, perhaps even feeling cheated or betrayed. But they could no longer resume their old habits. They now knew that social revolutions were possible. Communist or not, the Cuban Revolution did break the stranglehold of foreign and native capitalists. It did give shoes to peasants, medicine to the sick, education to all. According to all reports, whether from British journalists, pro-United States visitors, or Latin American returnees, Cuba completely wiped out illiteracy in three short years. That Cubans can now read only a controlled press, censored books, and propaganda posters is not apropros. They *can* read them; that is an achievement that no other Latin American political system has been able to do in three, thirty, or three hundred years.

Thus the returnees have remained publicly silent about their disillusionment. Committed to revolution, they are today the leaders of the national liberation movements that have sprouted across the continent. Not only do the returned journalists no longer earn fat salaries working for the *La Prensas*, the *El Commercios*, or the *El Mundos*, but they write the kind of article that gets them persecuted, beaten, jailed, or even, in the case of Argentina's novelist-essayist Ismael Viñas, bombed.

The dedication of these Nationalists is romantic, naïve, and misguided to our embassy staffers everywhere in Latin America. "They are the willing or duped pawns of the Communists," is a remark I often heard. Perhaps. The Nationalists, of course, feel otherwise. As one in Barranquilla told me: "During World War II we were with the Allies. That did not make us democrats. Today we are with Cuba, and that does not make us Communists. It is simply that we have learned that nothing is easy or perfect or pure and that we must fight hard and long and sometimes with people not too pleasant for the sake of our countries. The United States fought with Russia in World War II. Did the United States become Communist? Was it its pawn?"

At first, these Nationalists thought that direct action and/or participation in elections were both possible and advantageous. In Chile the Socialists may indeed win legally in the next election. The oligarchy might then try a coup to stop them. But this time the Socialists will be ready. They are armed and are being trained in peasants' and workers' leagues. As one Christian Democrat said: "Force to stop the Socialists, if they win—and they might—will only serve them. They will have legality on their side, and can wage a real revolution under the pretense of stopping the oligarchy from usurping power. I'm sure they are actually hoping that the Right tries a coup. And I'll tell you this: if it does, we'll fight with the Socialists."

The disastrous result of putting too much faith on winning power through elections and "democratic process" was shockingly visible in Brazil in 1964. There, the Nationalists were well on their way to power legally: Brizola trounced the candidates of Lacerda in Lacerda's hometown of Rio in a contest for a Congressional seat; Francisco Julião, head of the northeast's Peasant Leagues, won another such seat; Recife Mayor Miguel Arraes got himself elected Governor of Pernambuco and was becoming a very likely candidate for Vice President in the 1965 elections. But then, of course, the Lacerdas, the right-wing militarists and the U.S. got worried for many reasons: Goulart was already quite independent but the Nationalists would be even more so; U.S. corporations would surely get nationalized; and perhaps most important of all, Goulart wanted to buy oil from the Soviet Union instead of from Venezuela, whose reserves are owned by Standard Oil (a fact that was not reported in any

U.S. newspapers). Whether the CIA actually fomented the coup is hard to say, although we do know—from the highly documented *The Invisible Government* by David Wise and Thomas Ross as well as from Allen Dulles' own *The Craft of Intelligence*—that the CIA fabricates phony Communist "documents" and has plotted against popular regimes everywhere from Iran and Laos to Guatemala and Ecuador.

In any case, the Nationalists now know that winning power through elections is useless. In most cases, a revolution is also out of the question. They must therefore try to find or create or mold Latin American Ben Bellas or Nassers. Perhaps they have finally learned their revolutionary lesson, the same lesson taught by Che Guevara who warned that popular rebellions are doomed to failure in countries where the regimes maintain at least some semblance of democratic process. Perhaps, it was the failure of the Venezuelan Nationalists to overthrow Betancourt and stop Leoni's election that served as their eye-opener. In any case, Latin America's Nationalists appear calmer today because they are seeking stronger, firmer, sounder bases from which to operate. From these bases, they will be much more capable to taking power, and fashioning a revolutionary state. Precisely for this reason, too, they have lost the support of the traditional Communists.

Actually, it was Castro himself who frightened the Communists. Russia could never afford a whole bunch of Castros in Latin America. A Communist takeover of Paraguay or Bolivia or Haiti would drain Russia's funds like quicksand, and the resulting fiasco could only hurt Russia's prestige. Many of our brighter embassy staffers often say, off the record, that the best way to defeat Communism in Latin America is to let the Communists take over Paraguay. Within three years, every Latin American Communist Party would be changing its name.

It takes decades, not years, to rebuild an economy. Every day, despite all of Russia's aid, Cuba is finding it harder to feed its people, run its transportation, increase its production. Wages are cut, prices frozen, holidays eliminated, penalties applied. True, once the new structure is rebuilt on firmly balanced foundations, the Gross National Product can jump 20 percent a year. But meanwhile Russia's tab is huge. Khrushchev cannot afford a dozen Cubas; therefore, all Communist parties in Latin America have been given the order to create trouble, unrest, flareups, and instability but prevent the real social revolutionaries from taking power. This was made even more clear in September, 1962, when Russia's ideological magazine *Kommunist* said: "Neglect of general democratic problems and undue haste may narrow the popular basis of Socialist revolution and compromise the noble idea of Socialism in the eyes of the masses. That is why Communist and workers' parties warn the masses and politicians against unjustified overzeal in the use of Socialist slogans." Translation: If a Communist revolutionary regime cannot show quick results don't try it. Khrushchev also canceled an announced tax cut—foreign-aid costs being too high. Conclusion: Russia cannot afford, hence its parties must stall, revolutionary governments.

In fact, however, this has been Russia's Latin American policy for a long time: To keep Latin America capitalistic— and a headache for Washington. Once we realize this, we can readily understand Latin American Communists' tactics. Communists have often supported dictators, always opposed Nationalists, and inevitably formed alliances with the extreme Right to bring down centrist governments whose programs included mild reforms. In the past, Latin America's Communist parties have been our best allies.

Brazilian Communists fought Vargas until 1949, enduring years of jail and persecution, and reversed themselves only toward his end, by which time it was clear that his reforms were less important than his career. When Perón had mass support and the backing of all Nationalists, when his program was one of reform and social restructuring, Communists opposed him; when he began to falter because he did not carry out those reforms, when he did not take over the land and the big corporations, when Nationalists plotted against him, Communists supported him, as they do now.

When Quadros ran against Marshall Lott, an honest but traditional army man, Communists supported Lott. When Quadros fell and the country was on the verge of a civil war that would have been won by the Nationalists, Communists talked of avoiding bloodshed and saving lives. When Colombia's guerrillas began to acquire political consciousness, Communists backed the phony revolutionary oligarch López Michelsen. When Ecuador's Velasco found himself forced to be one of the leaders opposed to United States intervention in Cuba, Communists joined the far Rightists to bring him down. When we sent Cuban exiles to invade Cuba and Castro wired Russia for help or at least for open solidarity, Moscow ignored him until Castro's militias had definitely beaten the invaders. When Kennedy told Russia to get its missiles out of Cuba and Castro pleaded that they remain, Russia got them out.

In Bolivia, Communists oppose the MNR. In Brazil they opposed Julião, Brizola, Arraes. In Argentina they officially back Viñas' MLN but actually try to handcuff its activities. In Peru they refused to support the Social Progressists, voting instead for their own weak candidate or for Odría, the traditional Rightist military man. Today, they back Belaunde, not because he is a Nationalist but because he may nationalize U.S. holdings *without* appealing to Russia for aid. In Chile, at first glance, the theory is false: Communists and Socialists are united in FRAP. But a closer look reveals a different picture.

Chile's Communists make much ado about the *Vía Pacífica*. Theoretically, this means peaceful co-existence. Actually, it means no revolutions. The Socialists, stronger and more popular, are perfectly willing to wage a revolution if necessary to assure them of power. The Communists are not. In case Socialist candidate Allende won the presidential elections of 1964, the Communists, who supported him, indicated they would not participate in his government. They would "support" him in Parliament, they had said, but would retain their "independence." This so-called independence would let them criticize the reforms enacted by the Socialists as too mild, and their agitation would keep Chile from becoming a People's Socialist Republic that would require Russian aid. Such tactics were another reason the Socialists hoped that the Right tried a coup to stop them from taking elective power. "A Rightist coup would force the Communists to fight," one Chilean Socialist told me, "committing them to our revolution."

In our Uruguayan Embassy one day, a sharp observer said: "I have become absolutely convinced not only here in Uruguay but in Argentina and Honduras, where I have spent time, and elsewhere too, that the strongest counter-revolutionary party in Latin America is the Communist Party." Just a few weeks later, at the Punta del Este conference, Che Guevara greeted a delegation of Argentine Communists

thus: "¿Che, por qué están aquí? Para empezar la contra
revolución?" (Hey, you, why are you here? To start the
counterrevolution?)

I found only one Latin American Communist Party honest
enough to admit that it does not want power—in Venezuela.
"Do you realize what would happen if we took over?"
one Communist deputy told me. "We'd either be invaded
by your Marines, which would not be too bad from an
international cold-war point of view, or we would have
to nationalize the oil. But who the hell could we sell it
to? To Cuba and Chile, perhaps, but that's all. We'd go
broke. We can't eat oil and Russia cannot afford to feed
us." Later an official from Rockefeller's Creole told me:
"We're not afraid of the Communists. If they take over,
they'd raise our taxes a little, but they'd sell to us just
as always. But these goddam MIR bastards, they want
to nationalize the oil. They'd rather starve than compromise
their idiotic sense of dignity or whatever they call their
stupidity!"

The MIR represents one of the best examples of a National
movement allied to Communists. Having split away from
AD but only after Betancourt refused to nationalize or
control United States companies, the MIR soon realized
that only through violence could Venezuela break the vise
that we held on the country. Thus, it became progressively
more extreme until today it is openly acknowledged as
much more revolutionary than the Communists who, in
Venezuela, tend to be pro-Castro and pro-China. It is the
MIR, not the Reds, which launched FALN, the terrorist
outfit called Armed Forces of National Liberation, though
the Communists support it. Right now, this Alliance between
Communists and Nationalists is not producing the results
it desires. For one thing, it suffered a major setback in
the last election. For another, it is heavily persecuted; the
Machado brothers who head the Communist Party and Domingo Alberto Rangel, MIR's chief, are in AD jails. Nevertheless terrorism is bound to continue in Venezuela.

In Mexico, one Nationalist explained his alliance with
Communists this way: "Your propaganda is so consistently
limited to anti-Communism that you have fooled yourself.
You believe it. Instead of realizing that Communists have
one tactic for Europe and one for us, you lump everything
into the same bag. You look at Latin America just as you

look at Berlin or Hungary. You forget that Russian tanks and armored divisions cannot get here so easily. That makes quite a difference. Latin American Communists, like all Communists, talk about nationalizations and expropriations and agrarian reforms. If we do those things, how can they refuse to back us? They're stuck with us. And if they're stuck, Russia is stuck. Do you remember France after the war? The Communist Party was the biggest party, so it was asked to form the new government. It refused. No Communist Party wants power unless its country has frontiers with Russia. You say we are tools of the Communists. That's what your capitalists say because they are more afraid of us than of Communists. I say the Communists have become our tools."

If this statement is true, and if our Latin American policy is to defend the interest of our big companies, then our attack against Castro makes sense. He is a symbol to Latin American Nationalists, not to Communists. He is opposed to our investments, to our capital, and to our pressure. And what makes him even more dangerous, he does not even obey Moscow's orders. What if other Nationalists did the same?

Other Nationalists are hoping to do exactly the same in every country of Latin America. They are not Communists, whether we call them so or not. But they are committed to the very same reforms Castro has put into effect in Cuba. To these Nationalists, Castro gave not only the will to fight but the determination to do so even in failure.

"Castro may have disillusioned us, and I for one left Cuba a very bitter man, but he also gave us back the right to our own dignity," one former Chilean technician in Cuba said. "Now we have to earn it. We will."

Chapter 32

Motives and Principles

Before we draw our conclusions recommending specific policies in Latin America, we must first agree upon the overall goals of our general foreign policy. That is, we must establish the criteria for analyzing any policy at all.

I suggest that we have only one goal—the defense of our interests. Few politicians or statesmen ever put it so bluntly, but all act according to it once in power. Of course, debate will immediately start when we try to define just what our interests are. Perhaps, with some clear thinking, we can reach common ground.

Secretary of State John Foster Dulles may have been totally mistaken about what our interests were, but he came closest to being honest enough as to our goal. Not for one minute, he told Indiana Democratic Representative Winfield K. Denton back in June, 1957, during subcommittee hearings on the budget, do I consider the purpose of the State Department to be to make friends, but to take care of the interests of the United States. Referring specifically to foreign aid, Dulles went on: If the granting of these loans saves from Communism one country, one people, or one area whose delivery to Communism would have been harmful for the United States, I am not interested whether they like us or hate us. . . . We would have accomplished our purpose.

Under Dulles, our basic foreign policy was neither moral nor guided by altruistic principles. We were out to maintain our interest the best way Dulles thought possible. He had the courage not to care what other nations or other people felt about us or our government, and did in fact alienate many of our friends.

His reasoning, however, was not always consistent. For example, he opposed aid to Latin America on two counts:

> In the case of the Americas . . . they are now in the main able to meet their increased demands through private loans and Export-Import Bank loans and World Bank loans.

and

> If you . . . get into the practice of legislating in terms of special countries, that is going to lead increasingly to the development by every country beneficiary of this plan of . . . a lobby designed to promote aid to it. There is going to be pulling and hauling and I don't think it is a dignified or proper procedure. . . . You are going to destroy your flexibility entirely.

The first argument, that Latin America does not need aid, is inconsistent with our self-interest so far as it is immaterial. The second, that it is inconvenient for us to grant such aid, is very apt.

(Senators George Smathers and Spessard Holland of Florida, both of whom voted for aid to Latin America, obviously interpreted self-interest to mean *their* own interest, since in explaining their vote Holland admitted that their state was full of Latin Americans who could vote: "Senator Smathers and myself . . . have many people of the various Latin-American races who have become our good citizens.")

Whatever the diplomatic phrases to couch our foreign-policy goal, all our federal leaders have always interpreted it to be self-interest. Behind F.D.R.'s Good Neighbor Policy was the desire to corner Latin American raw-material production for ourselves; Kennedy's Alliance for Progress was to stop other Castros; Teddy Roosevelt's dollar diplomacy was to get the Canal; and Dulles' aid was to keep a nation "free," meaning pro-United States. Said Dulles: "A free country is a country which is not dominated by international

Communism." Nothing could be more blunt: If a nation freely votes itself a Communist regime, it is not free; but if a nation suffers a vicious non-Communist dictator, such as Trujillo or Stroessner, it is free.

Whether we agree or not that the United States is threatened by international Communism, as each of our Secretaries of State from Dean Acheson to Dean Rusk has claimed, we could all certainly agree that our first and foremost self-interest in the maintaining of our American way of life. That means our freedoms, our separation of powers, our checks and balances, our states' rights, our free enterprise, and our personal safety. Some of us may not feel like defending one or more of these "ways." A Socialist, for example, will want to destroy free enterprise; a states'-righter will want to destroy the division of powers; a John Bircher will want to eliminate most of our freedoms. But by and large the vast majority of the people of the United States will want to stick by what they have—free-enterprising democracy.

And to them, therefore, our self-interest is the defense of *our* free enterprising democracy. It is not, or should not be, the defense of someone else's free or unfree democracy, Socialism, or anything else, except insofar as such defense is crucial to our self-interest. Those among us who feel compassion or perhaps even responsibility for the well-being of all other peoples will want *also* to help the others. But when the ways of others are in conflict with our own ways, few of us insist that we prejudice ours to help theirs.

Thus, assuming that most of us consider Communism a danger to our ways, few of us would like our foreign policy to encourage the spread of Communism. Should Communism win out, not only our free enterprise would be eradicated but also our freedoms, our political structure, our rights, and our personal safety. In this context, then, do any of us feel that we should risk our form of democracy to safeguard our free enterprisers' "ways" not here at home but abroad, in someone else's country?

Let us be consequential. What comes first? The "ways" of the people of the United States or the "ways" of a handful of United States citizens? Do we wage wars to help the few or defend democracy for us all? Unquestionably, our past governments have waged many wars for the profit of the few, but that is not the question. What is, is whether the people, you and I and all our neighbors, *want* to risk death for the profit of just one of our neighbors.

When only one nation is strong in the world, it can impose its will and its "ways" on all the rest. But when two are strong, each can impose its ways on some countries, but neither can impose its ways on all. The in-betweeners, those neither black nor white, the "neutrals," become the world's Third Force. They are actually lucky that one nation is not overpowerful. This gives them the opportunity to choose their own "ways," as best suited for themselves. Our form of democracy may be viewed as perfect for our citizens (fortunately, for the sake of our progress, it is not). Russia's form of Communism may be viewed as perfect for Russia's citizens (fortunately, for the sake of their progress, it is not). But all the little countries of the world may view both ours and Russia's as very imperfect indeed.

There is absolutely no doubt that Latin Americans, whose government and "ways" have so far been fashioned, mostly by us, in our image and too often for our profit, do not want our form of democracy. The world was so divided, the spheres of influence were so erected, and the geographic realities were so arranged that, until only a few years ago, Spain, then England, and then the United States, could shape Latin America at will. If things went "wrong," our marines set them "right." It was as simple as that.

Today, nothing is so simple. Every local war is a potential mass execution. We have to be sure of what we are risking and for what gain, both immediate and long-range. Thus our means must be reevaluated in terms of our ends.

All of us have seen enough war movies (if not participated in wars) to know that the ends do justify the means. When a mother disciplines her child, when she spanks him for touching the electric socket, no one will say that the means-in-itself (the spanking) is good, yet no one will question that the end (saving the child from future electrocution) is good. The end justifies the means. We hear an awful lot of nonsense about "man is an end in himself." This argument is generally posited by weak minds who cannot seem to find any other argument to combat Marxist or Communist ideology. If that is our only argument against Marxism, then we have already lost. Actually, some ends justify some means most of the time and all means some of the time.

In war, if the end is to stop the killing, all means to that end are justified including, paradoxically, killing (but torture of the innocent, not a means to the end of stopping killing, is not justified). The true argument should always be based on an empirical evaluation of what means for what ends.

Ever since we became a world power, we have assumed that the defense of our way of life was to increase the value of our country not only at home but also abroad. We have been convinced that we would fare better if our moral prestige were greater, or if our material gains increased, or if our armed occupation of other people's territories were extended. Except for our propaganda to others as well as to ourselves, the fundamental question was never whether such policies were morally good or not. It was always whether the means we used (do-gooding, economic intervention, armed conquest) led to the desired end (increasing the worth or strength of the United States).

Today, because the balance of power is so precarious and because the other power is so attuned to take advantage of our mistakes, we are forced to add another factor to our empirical evaluation of our means: What does the third fellow think?

Our tactics at the second Punta del Este Conference, though defeated, exhibited such concern. Had we threatened armed intervention in every country not voting with us, we would have won unanimity. But the result would have been at least five revolutions, and six violently anti-United States governments. Then had we intervened and Russia not countermoved (except to take Berlin while China grabbed Formosa, South Vietnam, and Laos), we would have perhaps "set right" Latin America—and lost India, Indonesia, Burma, Ceylon, and many more Asian or African nations that would quickly have signed mutual-assistance pacts with Russia in order to save themselves from us. Thus, today, we must not only evaluate our means but also Latin America's end.

That end is the Reconquest of Itself: its economic independence, its balanced development, its industrialization, its capacity of making its own moral, political, and economic decisions—in sum, its need to limit our power in Latin America.

How does such Reconquest conflict with the available

or possible means for our own end, which is to obtain as much advantage as possible against the Communist world? We have five means available:

1. To gain more and firmer allies through armed intervention or the threat thereof.

2. To gain more and firmer allies through economic intervention or the threat thereof.

3. To gain more and better allies through economic manipulations such as controlling trade, financing armies, salvaging the budgets of pro-United States governments and /or accelerating our loans, that is, through the forcing of the allies' economic dependency on us.

4. To gain more and better allies through bribery, the acceleration and increase of our gifts and grants, commonly called the buying of friendship.

5. To gain more and better friends, though perhaps not allies, by encouraging them in their aims and aspirations.

Dulles believed in Means Number 1, tried to bully everyone with his threats of "serious reevaluations," and earned no new or firmer ally except (temporarily) Guatemala, where force crushed an elected regime. Furthermore, Dulles had to fall back upon Means Number 2 and Means Number 3. Aid was continued, in some cases increased. Dulles justified it in *Foreign Affairs*, October, 1957, thus: "Every government has a primary duty to serve its own people. But usually that service can be best rendered by finding ways which help others also, or which at least do not hurt others." That this was not a statement of moral principle is made clear by his very next sentence: "Occasionally, and happily only rarely, situations arise which cannot be resolved by this formula."

Not very happily, in Latin America these situations arose quite often, and Dulles relied on the other "formulas." These included not only the outright intervention noted but also economic blackmail, or, as he put it: "The United States market, which dependably offers so much that others want, and which dependably buys so much that others would sell, is the great stabilizer of the free world." What Dulles meant by "free" this time was not non-Communist, but any nation that follows the United States. To Dulles, neutrals were not free because they were not "interdependent," that is, dependent upon the United States. As he put it: "It [the United States market] helps to combat Communism and the self-centered nationalisms which are alike in rejecting the concept of interdependence."

In the very same issue of *Foreign Affairs*,[1] in fact, in the very next article, then Senator John F. Kennedy, disputed each of Dulles' contentions:

> Reassessment is urgently required for those American aid programs which have reflected an ill-conceived and ill-concealed disdain for the "neutralists" and "socialists" who—in a nation such as India—represent the free world's strongest bulwarks to the seductive appeal of Peking and Moscow. . . . We must see that our actions stimulate the healthy development of the new states even if they are neutral; that we do not encourage the prolongation of Western colonialism where it is stagnant, that the position we take against Soviet imperialism in Eastern Europe is not weakened by Western "imperialism."

Continued Kennedy: "There is an opportunity for the idealistic initiative of our people and the self-interest of the nation to intersect." This did not mean, of course, that idealism should be the guiding principle of foreign policy; the statement obviously implies that no matter how idealistic "our people" are, if, in his judgment, the "self-interest of the nation" should contradict idealism, it would be his duty,

---

[1] The Dulles article preceded another article in the same magazine (July, 1957) with which he must have been familiar (his CIA brother Allen is a member of its editorial board), one written by Habib Bourguiba, President of Tunisia, the United States's best ally among the Arab nations. Under the title *Nationalism: Antidote to Communism*, Bourguiba made the point that Nationalism and Communism are contradictory because the former is "inspired by concern for the interests of the nation as a whole," while the latter "is predicated on a class struggle designed to divide the nation rather than to bind it together." Bourguiba went on to analyze countries that have nationalistic governments, where, naturally, both East and West compete for major influence, and concluded that though none has become the unquestioning ally of the United States, "neither has there been any decisive result from the considerable efforts of the Communists to bring this part of the world under their sway, particularly by the clever tactic of exploiting nationalist feeling."

as President, to go against "our people" in favor of that self-interest. And in this, since most of us are agreed on our general aims, most of us concur.

As a presidential candidate, Kennedy raised Latin American hopes. He made some unpopular remarks about Cuba, but on the whole it was felt that he would adhere to Means Number 5 in his foreign policies. Often he seemed to promise just that. One example:

> Old liberal bromides have no appeal to nations which seek a quick transition to industrialization and who admire the disciplined attack which Communism seems to make upon the problems of economic modernization and redistribution.

His solution was

> to make a small number of investments through aid and loans, selected with an eye to their likelihood for success. There is no real need for us to be neutral as to the objectives which it [assistance] should serve. Successful foreign aid must be selective; otherwise a large amount of aid goes into projects designed to enhance the prestige of the receiving government and into military panoply which may only perpetuate feudalism.

His election was therefore hailed throughout Latin America as a great victory for modernism. Those who still hoped that Latin America could be brought into the twentieth century without violence, saw in Kennedy their last chance. He represented the end of aid to all Latin American armies and to all Latin American dictators, and the beginning of small, selective aid programs, designed to strengthen modernists in their uneven fight against medievalists. Thus, Latin Americans believed, not only would aid to the dictators Stroessner, Ydígoras, Duvalier, Luis and Tachito Somoza be stopped, but so would aid to the oligarchs of Peru, El Salvador, Ecuador, Chile, Argentina, Panama, and Colombia. Every modernist began to hope that now would come a flow of dollars to those sectors of Latin American universities where free thought is carried out by freethinking, secular-minded empiricists.

Once elected, Kennedy retreated. First came Means Number

3: a massive promise of aid, indiscriminately dished out to democrats, dictators, crooks, frauds, and loudmouthed "anti-Communists." True, the Alliance for Progress insisted on reforms. But who got the money? Such non-reformers as Frondizi and such phony reformers as Betancourt, not to mention such anti-reformers as Beltrán and Somoza. Then Kennedy fell back to Means Number 2: economic coercion, even an economic blockade against the people of Cuba against whom (no matter what we thought of the government) we could not bear any hatred. And, finally, failing anyway, Kennedy resorted to Means Number 1—force. Cuba was invaded. What followed—missiles, "quarantine," the threat of war—was unavoidable.

Fortunately, it did not end in war itself. Kennedy then, slowly, began to realize that for the masses of Latin America, Castro-style regimes may not be so monstrous after all. Though for political reasons at home he could not admit it publicly, he finally realized that coexistence with Castro's Cuba was not only feasible but, perhaps, desirable. One of the very last steps he took was to try to find out—through the highly respected French newspaperman Jean Daniel—what Castro thought of such coexistence. And then, he was shot dead.

President Johnson would have none of it. With hard-liner Tom Mann as his Latin American "expert," he swung the pendulum the other way, tightened the economic blockade of Cuba, cut off even our best allies from U.S. military aid for trading with Castro, and made a laughing stock of our State Department by permitting it to accuse Castro of a plot when four Cuban fishing trawlers were caught within our territorial waters. Naturally, we finally admitted our mistake and the fishermen were released, but Johnson then condemned his critics for "bellyaching" and made it quite clear that from then on, whether in Panama or Guantánamo, in the Organization of American States or the United Nations, our policy would be tough. A new deal was certainly not dawning for Latin America.

Conclusion:

A Policy for Reconquest

Friends are always better than unwilling allies.

Sooner or later an unwilling ally will find the opportunity to avenge himself. Sooner or later, all blackmailers must either quit or be killed. Sooner or later, all exploited men, no matter how low their fall or how hard their servitude, must stand up and say No.

If our interest is the interests of all of us, if we want to survive with our freedoms and our dignity, if we are concerned more with our unalienable rights—life, liberty, and the pursuit of happiness—than with the extra billions of dollars of a few selfish men, then we must realize that sooner or later the peoples of Latin America will demand the very same rights.

That time has come. They are demanding. Soon they will take. They will be fully justified in doing so. As Jefferson said, "it is the right of the people to alter or abolish" that which denies them their unalienable rights.

Latin America will have its social, nationalistic revolution, one way or another. There is still time for us to help rather than to hinder. Today we have no true friends among the peoples of Latin America. Tomorrow, we can gain many. Not allies, but friends. How? By encouraging them in their aims and aspirations.

By this time, we should all be agreed on what those aims and aspirations are. How can we encourage them? What we are doing now is wrong. Of that, simple observation

415

can leave no doubt. What should we do? Here, arguments can be endless.

Naturally, I have come to my own conclusions. Until now I have done almost nothing but criticize. The time has come to go out on a limb. Hence follows a list of policies for the Reconquest of Latin America as a friend of the United States.

Many of these policies are unrealistic. Taken as a whole, they are certainly unrealizable. They represent, however, the ideal toward which we should strive. And any approximation would lead us that much closer to our goal of safeguarding our way of life by helping Latin America choose and defend its own.

I. Diplomatic Policy.

a) Recognize any government whatsoever, no matter what the method of its coming to power, as soon as it is "in control of the administrative machinery of the state." If this is consistently applied, recognition will be thought of as neither reward nor interference.

b) Withdraw from the Organization of American States. Let Latin Americans set up their own regional organization, if they desire, in the Latin American site they choose. [Since we are unwilling and/or unable to join Latin American countries in other regional organizations, especially economic (for example, common markets), we should not participate in this highly political regional entity.]

c) Abrogate all *ad infinitum* treaties. Nothing is or must be for ever. A treaty that has no ending, no possibility of revisions from either end, and no cancellation clause is not only immoral; it is the physical domination of he-who-gets over he-who-cedes. Renegotiate all treaties to insert time limitations. The Panama Canal Treaty can be extended for thirty years [though its return to Panama on condition no ships of any nation would ever be barred and on condition we would run it in case of war would be far better.] All military-bases treaties should be cancelable or renewable every ten years or less if possible.

d) Exert no pressure whatsoever upon Latin American governments to get them to institute particular policies, especially concerning noncontinental countries whose interests in Latin America do not threaten the safety of the United States (safety being defined so as to exclude losses to private United States corporations in Latin America).

e) Never offer our services in the settling of any dispute between one Latin American country and another.

f) Revise the Monroe Doctrine so as to offer temporary military aid in cases of extracontinental invasions only at the request of the invaded country, except when the invader threatens our own physical security. Though

g) Having warned Latin America as well as our enemies, publicly and unequivocably, that all armed invasions by our enemies will be taken as acts of aggression against our security, intervene by force of arms, unilaterally if necessary, whenever such invasions do occur. But

h) Never construe requests by a Latin American country for aid from our enemies, whether military or otherwise, as an act of aggression, nor define invasion in such terms as to include unrest, instability, revolution, or subversion.

i) Drastically alter and reorganize the United States Information Service so that its function will be at all times to publicize to Latin Americans United States-sponsored projects in Latin America, to publicize all United States resources available to Latin Americans desiring to better their proficiency or trades, and to publicize and explain United States-Latin American policies. USIS must be forbidden to enter into the field of foreign policies not restricted to Latin America or to publicize life and conditions in the United States except insofar as it is explained that these conditions are available to Latin Americans in the immediate future if they are willing to undergo specific training. Eliminate all cold-war propaganda from USIS functions.

j) Appoint no ambassador to Latin America who does not speak the designated country's language fluently and has not had at least some substantial grounding in its history, culture, traditions, and current socioeconomic conditions. Forbid him to make any public statement on the country's current developments, whether favorable or not. Reinstitute the old-style diplomacy of silent, smiling decorum with maneuvers limited to closed-room sessions, by intermediaries whenever possible. Instruct all ambassadors to reply to all verbal attacks, denunciations, and defamatory campaigns with a smile and "no comment," and certainly never to write open letters, especially not to local university students.[1]

k) Try to appoint all embassy personnel for a period of at least three years, on a staggered system, so that at all times one man in each section, if possible, has been residing in the country for at least two years. Send such personnel to Latin America only after language and, if possible, socioeconomic training.

II. Military Policy

a) Abrogate all military-assistance pacts. No underdeveloped nation is morally, politically, or economically entitled to sign such pacts. Once a Latin American country has achieved development, proved its political and economic independence and its capacity for being represented by leaders who embody the will of the people, then it can sign its own liquidation, but not until then. Since it is impossible to judge when such conditions exist, the following arbitrary criterion should be used at all times: a nation is free, developed, and independent when it has achieved 90 percent literacy, when 80 percent of its adult population has completed primary education, and 70 percent the equivalent of high school.

b) Provide no loans, gifts, grants, surplus equipment, or material of any kind to Latin American armed forces, police, *carabineros,* or governments. Allow them to buy at regular, competitive prices the type of small arms used by United States law-enforcement services [but not by National Guards] from private manufacturers anywhere. Offer no grants, loans, or scholarships, not even for travel purposes, to any Latin American military personnel, but allow qualified Latin American officers or men [according to our own standards for our own military] to attend whatever war college, training course, or program is normally open to foreigners as paying students. Stick to this policy, even if Latin Americans buy arms elsewhere or convert nonmilitary material, vehicles, ships, or crafts into military equivalents.

c) Eliminate all United States military missions in Latin America except the usual attaché in each service branch. Allow him no budget beyond the normal sums allowed all civilian attachés for the conduct of his business, which is to be strictly reportorial, as are the tasks of civilian attachés.

---

[1] As our former Ambassador to Peru James Loeb did in 1961.

III. Foreign-Aid Policy

a) Make no loans to governments under any condition, whether for budget support, reform programs, administrative modernization, or any other reason whatsoever except as provided below. Stick to this policy even if the governments apply for and receive such loans from European countries.

b) Make no loans to private companies, firms, or enterprises in Latin America whether Latin American, United States, or others, even if such enterprises are subcontracted to the governments. Do not, however, prohibit in any way (but neither stimulate) loans from private banks to such enterprises.

c) Concentrate all United States grant money resources for the development of Latin American educational institutions, whether primary or secondary or higher, but always with the criteria that such institutions be state-owned and state-run and that they require no religious, political, or other eliminatory oaths. For selective purposes, especially at the university level, the criteria should be: Whether the recipient institution fosters empirical, impersonal research without discrimination either in its personnel or in its program; Whether the program benefits the nation; Whether the graduates' learning applies to all classes of the population. Agronomy, economics, public administration, engineering, medicine, and so on, are so qualified; while law, languages, business administration, history, art, music, and so on, are not. Recognize the value of the creative fields, but insist that, until a country is developed enough to provide all citizens with their basic, unalienable rights, the creative fields are a luxury. Encourage private foundations to help these fields if they so desire.

d) Send additional grants to nongovernment, nonprofit organizations for relief work. These organizations may be religious, political, or social, but must dispense their relief without discrimination and must be willing to open their books and show their work to any inspector sent to investigate. [Experience teaches that no true charitable or relief agency will ever be ashamed of inspection, or consider it intervention.]

e) Continue to send Peace Corpsmen to any requesting Latin American nation, province, city, or state for purposes of helping the country's development with the following provisos: no Corpsman can be used on work that would normally be handled by available Latin Americans; no Corpsman can work on a project that is not public; and no Corpsman can go into an area if he does not speak the local language or the local dialect where the area's dwellers do not uniformly speak the language the Corpsman has mastered [It serves no purposes to send a Corpsman fluent in Spanish to areas where residents speak mostly Aymara, Guaraní, Quechua, and so on.]

f) Accept by renting, lending, or supporting any request for United States technicians in any field whatsoever with the proviso that the services of those technicians be used only on public projects.

g) Invite on discounts, fellowships, scholarships, or grants as many qualified Latin Americans as possible for technical training in United States institutions with the proviso that these technicians immediately upon completing their United States training return to Latin America and work two years for every one spent in the United States on public projects, or, if not available, that these technicians put themselves at the call of our embassies in the technicians' home country, advising our embassies to look for public projects where these technicians might usefully serve.

Exceptions

A. Loans or grants for specific projects in countries where the social reforms listed below are not executed can be made under the following conditions: that the projects are public and benefit the public [building a hydroelectric plant where a private company owns and/or distributes electricity is unacceptable]; that the projects be built by United States technicians responsible to the United States Government; that the United States be responsible for the project to the contracting Latin American federal, provincial, or municipal authorities; that the United States Government be entitled to subcontract whomever or whatever company it deems fit for such projects, but neither the companies nor the individuals, on the job, can represent themselves as anything but representatives of the people of the United States serving the people of Latin America.

B. Make as many loans or grants as requested or as possible for any purpose whatsoever, including budgetary support, to any Latin American government or province that has undertaken a social, nationalistic revolution whether peacefully or violently. The criteria for judging whether such a revolution has taken place must include:

1. the nationalization of all public utilities and large mines of any and all types;

2. an Agrarian Reform: Where all large holdings are redistributed so as to include either large farms for cooperatives or small but economically efficient farms for individuals, Where the recipient farmers are either given the land or receive it on loans (at no or minute interest) whose repayment schedule does not begin for two or more years, Where the farmers receive technical aid and are loaned necessary machinery (if available) on the same financial principles, Where the government launches intensive projects of farm-to-city road building irrigation, electrification, and rural school building, and Where displaced peasants for whom land is not available are found jobs either in the cities or on the projects;

3. an extensive tax reform that includes such gradation that the top 1 percent is taxed proportionally to its earnings [if it receives 80 percent of the income available, it must pay 80 percent of the taxes];

4. an educational reform, which guarantees at least half-a-day schooling for all children under sixteen within two years and at least one hour of schooling a day for all adults under fifty, if they so desire;

5. a sanitation reform, whereby health teams are sent to every section of the country, those teams being made up of all the doctors, nurses, and medical students in the country or province, drafted for specified periods every year;

6. a housing project that provides all families at least the minimum space of one room, bath, and kitchen, with its financing calculated on a graduated scale so that all dwellers can first buy enough food to furnish each family member the subsistency level of 2,400 calories' worth of food;

7. an extensive all-aspect ten-year development program.

Before loans and grants to such a government are made, United States investigators must be satisfied that such a social revolution is under way through visible achievements. Naturally, without outside help, these achievements will be small at first. A good guide is whether the major land, public-utility, and mining holdings are nationalized. Another guide is the existence of a sound payment plan for nationalized property. Any underdeveloped country that pays cash is ruining its economy and depriving its people of needed project money. Governments should be encouraged to pay in 20-year or more bonds at interest rates covering devaluations and perhaps a small profit, though owners of expropriated corporations who have consistently taken out their profits and/or failed to pay taxes and/or lied in their official records so as to pay less taxes, should be penalized for it in their payments.

8. Stop selling surplus tobacco under the Food for Peace program; in fact, stop selling anything under this program. Either give it away, or change the program's name which, as it stands, does more harm than good.

IV. *Internal Policy*

a) Never appoint as State Department deskman an individual who has not spent at least three years in the country he must now deal with.

b) Pressure our private companies to sell out all their public-utility holdings in Latin America, be it electricity, telephone, or transportation, as well as all major raw-material holdings, especially where such raw materials bring in the bulk of the country's income, such as copper in Chile, bananas in Central America, oil in Venezuela, and so on. This pressure can be achieved negatively (constant investigation of profits, revision of tax statements, and so on) and positively (offering to subsidize part or all of their losses wherever such losses are unjustified).

c) If possible, enact and enforce anticartel laws, prosecuting those companies that handle a product from its source to its retail sale and those that form international price-fixing combines. [It *is* possible; namely, the Cease-and-Desist 1956 order against United Fruit Company.]

d) Eliminate, if possible, all corporation tax credits for profit taxes paid abroad, while granting special tax credits for profits reinvested abroad.

e) Eliminate all import quotas and fixed-price policies on sugar or any other product.

f) Eliminate all import duties on noncompetitive products [for example, coffee] and greatly reduce all duties on any product whatsoever originating in Latin America if such product is grown or produced by Latin Americans or by corporations owned and controlled 51 percent or more by Latin Americans, and reduce duties still more if the product is grown or produced by public Latin American corporations.

These policies are tough. As I said, not all are feasible, either for us or for Latin Americans.

The cancellation of sugar quotas and fixed prices, for example, will force many Latin American economies to fall so sharply that only immediate, vast diversification programs might save them from total collapse. Such diversifications, however, are best handled under an agrarian reform, which is the end desired.

In general, all Latin-American governments will be under overpowering pressure to carry out reforms. Thus, armies may stage coups to take over control, but then they, too, will have to modernize. Furthermore, such reforms will demand strong, tough executives, leading perhaps to the advent of numerous dictatorships. If these dictatorships carry out the reforms, they would be backed by the masses.

Democracy would not be drowned out, however. In six countries—Venezuela, Chile, Uruguay, Costa Rica, Peru, and Brazil—the enunciation of such a new "Alliance" on our part would immediately bring on popular democratic regimes willing to and capable of coping with the oligarchies and of assuring the realization of the needed reforms. In Mexico and Bolivia, that enunciation would be enough to set the current governments back onto the path of social revolution from which they are presently wandering. In Paraguay, the Dominican Republic, Honduras and Guatemala, it would be enough to topple present regimes without gunfire.

Violence may not be completely avoidable. The oligarchies will fight hard. Big business will spend millions of dollars to destroy our new friends in Latin America. But as conditions and policies now stand, violence will eventually erupt in most Latin American countries anyway (besides we should get used to the fact that the current situation, in which thousands suffer and die from lack of food, water or medical attention, *is* violent). With the policy detailed above, violence can be kept to a minimum.

Finally, even if only a few of the above policy measures

are adopted by us in the near future, they will be enough not only to help Latin Americans' long-overdue but inescapable Reconquest of Latin America but also to allow us to reconquer Latin America—this time with the arms of a new and lasting friendship.

GETULIO VARGAS' SUICIDE NOTE

(Written in lieu of a letter of resignation on August 24, 1954)

Once more the forces and interests against the people are newly coordinated and raised against me. They do not accuse me, they insult me; they do not fight me, they slander me and give me no right of defense. They need to drown my voice and halt my actions so that I no longer continue to defend, as I always have defended, the people and principally the humble.

I follow the destiny that is imposed on me. After years of domination and looting by international economic and financial groups, I made myself chief of an unconquerable revolution. I began the work of liberation and I instituted a regime of social liberty. I had to resign. I returned to govern on the arms of the people.

A subterranean campaign of international groups joined with national groups revolting against the regime of workers' guarantees. The law of excess profits was stopped in Congress. Hatreds were unchained against the justice of a revision of minimum wages.

I wished to create liberty by developing our riches through Petrobras, and a wave of sedition clouded its beginnings. Electrobras was hindered almost to despair. They do not wish the workers to be free. They do not wish the people to be independent.

I assumed the Government during an inflationary spiral that was destroying the value of work. Profits of foreign enterprises reached 500 percent yearly. In declarations of goods that we import there existed frauds of more than $100,000,000.

I saw the coffee crisis increase the value of our principal product. We attempted to defend its price, and the reply was a violent pressure upon our economy to the point of being obliged to surrender.

I have fought month to month, day to day, hour to hour, resisting a constant aggression, unceasingly bearing it all in silence, forgetting all and renouncing myself to defend the people that now fall abandoned. I cannot give you more than my blood. If the birds of prey wish the blood of anybody, they wish to continue sucking that of the Brazilian people.

I offer my life in the holocaust. I choose this means to be with you always. When they humiliate you, you will feel my soul suffering at your side. When hunger beats at your door, you will feel in your chests the energy for the fight for yourselves and your children. When they humiliate you, you will feel in my grief the force for reaction.

My sacrifice will maintain you united, and my name will be your battle flag. Each drop of my blood will be an immortal call to your conscience and will maintain a holy vibration for resistance.

To hatred, I respond with pardon. And to those who think they have defeated me, I reply with my victory. I was the slave of the people, and today I free myself for eternal life. But this people to which I was a slave no longer will be a slave to anyone. My sacrifice will remain forever in your soul, and my blood will be the price of your ransom.

I fought against the looting of Brazil, I fought against the looting of the people. I have fought bare-breasted. The hatred, infamy, and calumny did not beat down my spirit. I gave you my life. Now I offer my death. Nothing remains. Serenely I take the first step on the road to eternity, and leave life to enter history.

AGREEMENT BETWEEN THE
UNITED STATES OF AMERICA AND HONDURAS

*Signed at Tegucigalpa May 20, 1954—Entered into force
May 20, 1954*

Bilaterial Military Assistance Agreement between the Government of the United States of America and the Government
of Honduras

The Governments of the United States of America and
of Honduras:

Conscious of their pledges under the Inter-American Treaty
of Reciprocal Assistance and other international instruments
to assist any American State subjected to an armed attack
and to act together for the common defense and for the
maintenance of peace and security of the Western Hemisphere;

Desiring to foster international peace and security within
the framework of the Charter of the United Nations through
measures which will further the ability of nations dedicated
to the purposes and principles of the Charter to participate
effectively in arrangements for individual and collective
self-defense in support of those purposes and principles;

Reaffirming their determination to give their full cooperation to the efforts to provide the United Nations with armed
forces as contemplated by the Charter and to obtain agreement
on universal regulation and reduction of armaments under
adequate guarantee against violation;

Taking into consideration the support that the Government of the United States of America has brought to these principles by enacting legislation which provides for the furnishing of military assistance to nations which have joined with it in collective security arrangements;

Desiring to set forth the conditions which will govern the furnishing of such assistance by one government to the other;

Have agreed as follows:

Article I

1. Each Government will make or continue to make available to the other, and to such additional governments as the parties hereto may in each case agree upon, such equipment, materials, services, or other military assistance as the Government furnishing such assistance may authorize and in accordance with such terms and conditions as may be agreed. The furnishing of any such assistance as may be authorized by either party hereto shall be consistent with the Charter of the United Nations. Such assistance shall be so designated as to promote the defense of the Western Hemisphere and be in accordance with defense plans under which both Governments will participate in missions important to the defense of the Western Hemisphere. Assistance made available by the Government of the United States of America pursuant to this Agreement will be furnished under the provisions, and subject to all the terms, conditions and termination provisions of applicable United States legislation. The two Governments will from time to time, negotiate detailed arrangements necessary to carry out the provisions of this paragraph.

2. The Government of Honduras undertakes to make effective use of assistance received from the Government of the United States of America pursuant to this Agreement for the purpose of implementing defense plans, accepted by the two Governments, under which the two Governments will participate in missions important to the defense of the Western Hemisphere, and will not, without the prior agreement of the Government of the United States of America, devote such assistance to purposes other than those for which it was furnished.

3. Arrangements will be entered into under which equip-

ment and materials furnished pursuant to this Agreement and no longer required for the purposes for which it was originally made available (except equipment and materials furnished under the terms requiring reimbursement) will be returned to the Government which furnished such assistance for appropriate disposition.

4. In the common security interest of both Governments the Government of Honduras undertakes not to transfer to any person not an officer or agent of such Government, or to any other Government, title to or possession of any equipment, materials, or services furnished to it by the Government of the United States of America under this Agreement, without the prior agreement of the Government of the United States of America.

5. The two Governments will establish procedures whereby the Government of Honduras will so deposit, segregate, or assure title to all funds allocated to or derived from any program of Assistance undertaken by the Government of the United States of America so that such funds shall not be subject to garnishment, attachment, seizure or other legal process by any person, firm, agency, corporation, organization or government, when in the opinion of the Government of the United States of America any such legal process would interfere with the attainment of the objectives of the said program of assistance.

6. Each Government will take such security measures as may be agreed in each case between the two Governments in order to prevent the disclosure or compromise of classified military articles; services or information furnished by the other Government pursuant to this Agreement.

Article II

Each Government will take appropriate measures consistent with security to keep the public informed of operations under this Agreement.

Article III

The two Governments will, upon request of either of them, negociate appropriate arrangements relating to the exchange of patent rights and technical information for defense in order to expedite such exchanges and at the same time to protect private interests and maintain security safeguards.

Article IV

1. The Government of Honduras will make available to the Government of the United States of America Lempiras in an amount to be agreed for the use of the latter Government for its administrative and operating expenditures in connection with carrying out the purposes of this Agreement.

The two Governments will forthwith initiate discussions with a view to determining the amount of such Lempiras and to agreeing upon arrangements for the furnishing of such Lempiras.

2. The Government of Honduras will, except as otherwise agreed, grant duty-free treatment and exemption from internal taxation upon importation or exportation to products, property, materials or equipment imported into its territory in connection with this Agreement or any similar agreement between the United States of America and any other country receiving military assistance.

3. The operations and expenditures effected in Honduras by or on behalf of the Government of the United States of America for the common defense effort including those carried out as a consequence of any other foreign aid program will be relieved from all taxation. To this end the Government of Honduras will prescribe pertinent procedures satisfactory to both Governments.

Article V

1. Each Government agrees to receive personnel of the other Government who will discharge responsibilities of the other Government in connection with the implementation of this Agreement. Such personnel will be accorded facilities to observe the progress of assistance furnished pursuant to this Agreement. Such personnel who are nationals of that other country, including personnel temporarily assigned, will, in their relations with the Government of the country to which they are assigned, operate as a part of the Embassy under the direction and control of the Chief of the Diplomatic Mission of the Government of the sending country, and shall be accorded all privileges and immunities conferred

by international custom to Embassy personnel of corresponding rank. Privileges and courtesies incident to diplomatic status, such as diplomatic automobile license plates, inclusion on the "diplomatic list," and social courtesies may be waived by the sending Government for its personnel other than the senior military member and the senior Army, Navy and Air Force officer and their respective immediate deputies.

2. The two Governments will negociate arrangements for classification of personnel and for appropriate notification thereof to the host Government.

3. The Government of Honduras will grant exemption from import and export duties on articles imported for the personal use of such personnel and of members of their families and will take adequate administrative measures to facilitate and expedite the importation and exportation of the personal property of such individuals and their families.

Article VI

Existing arrangements relating to Armed Forces missions of the United States of America established under other instruments are not affected by this Agreement and will remain in full force.

Article VII

In conformity with the principle of mutual aid, under which the two Governments have agreed as provided in Article I, to furnish assistance to each other, the Government of Honduras agrees to facilitate the production and transfer to the Government of the United States of America for such period of time, in such quantities and upon such terms and conditions as may be agreed upon, of raw and semi-processed materials required by the United States of America as a result of deficiencies or potential deficiencies in its own resources, and which may be available in Honduras and in territories under its sovereignty. Arrangements for such transfers shall give due regard to reasonable requirements for domestic use and commercial export of Honduras.

Article VIII

In the interest of their mutual security, the Government

of Honduras will cooperate with the Government of the United States of America in measures designed to control trade with nations which threaten the security of the Western Hemisphere.

Article IX

The two Governments reaffirm their determination to join in promoting international understanding and goodwill and maintaining world peace, to proceed as may be mutually agreed upon to eliminate causes of international tension, and to fulfill the military obligations assumed under multilateral or bilateral agreements and treaties to which both are parties. The Government of Honduras will make the full contribution permitted by its manpower, resources, facilities and general economic condition to the development and maintenance of its defensive strength as well as that of the free world, and will take all reasonable measures which may be needed to develop its defense capacities.

Article X

Whereas this Agreement, having been negotiated and concluded on the basis that the Government of the United States of America will extend to the other party thereto the benefits of any provision in a similar agreement concluded by the Government of the United States of America with any other American Republic, it is understood that the Government of the United States of America will interpose no objection to amending this Agreement in order that its provisions may conform, in whole or in part, to the corresponding provisions of any similar Military Assistance Agreement, or agreements amendatory thereto, concluded with an American Republic.

Article XI

1. This Agreement shall enter into force on the date of signature, and shall continue in force until one year after the receipt by either party of written notice of the intention of the other party to terminate it, except that the provisions of Article I, paragraphs 2 and 4 and arrangements made pursuant to the provisions of Article I, paragraphs

3, 5 and 6 and of Article III shall remain in force unless otherwise agreed by the two Governments.

2. The two Governments shall, upon the request of either of them, consult regarding any matter relating to the application or amendment of this Agreement.

3. This Agreement shall be registered with the Secretary General of the United Nations.

DONE in duplicate, in the English and Spanish languages, at Tegucigalpa, D.C., on the twentieth day of May, nineteen hundred and fifty four.

AGREEMENT BETWEEN THE GOVERNMENT OF
THE UNITED STATES OF AMERICA AND THE
GOVERNMENT OF THE REPUBLIC OF NICARAGUA

*Signed at Managua November 19, 1953—Entered into
force November 19, 1953*

In conformity with the request of the Government of the
Republic of Nicaragua to the Government of the United
States of America, the President of the United States of
America has authorized the appointment of officers and
non-commissioned officers to constitute a United States
Army Mission, hereinafter referred to as Mission, to the
Republic of Nicaragua under the conditions specified below:

Title I—Purpose and Duration

Article 1. The purpose of this Mission is to cooperate
with the Ministry of War, Navy and Aviation of the Republic
of Nicaragua and officials of the Nicaraguan National Guard,
and to enhance the efficiency of the Nicaraguan National
Guard in matters of training, organization and administration.
The members of the Mission are, in the exercise of their
functions, obliged to use the Spanish language.

Article 2. This Agreement shall enter into effect on
the date of signing thereof by the accredited representatives
of the Government of the United States of America and
the Government of the Republic of Nicaragua.

Article 3. This Agreement may be terminated in the following manner:

(*a*) By either of the Governments, subject to three months' written notice to the other Government;

(*b*) By recall of the entire personnel of the Mission by the Government of the United States of America or at the request of the Government of the Republic of Nicaragua, in the public interest of either country, without necessity of compliance with provision (*a*) of this Article.

Article 4. This Agreement is subject to cancellation upon the initiative of either the Government of the United States of America or the Government of the Republic of Nicaragua in case either country becomes involved in foreign or domestic hostilities.

Ttile II—Composition and Personnel

Article 5. This Mission shall consist of a Chief of Mission and such other personnel of the United States Army as may be agreed upon by the Department of the Army of the United States of America and by the Ministry of War, Navy and Aviation of the Republic of Nicaragua. The individuals to be assigned to the Mission shall be those agreed upon by the Ministry of War, Navy and Aviation of the Republic of Nicaragua or its authorized representative and by the Department of the Army of the United States of America or its authorized representative.

Article 6. Any member of the Mission may be recalled at any time by the Government of the United States of America provided a replacement with equivalent qualifications is furnished unless it is mutually agreed between the Department of the Army of the United States of America and the Ministry of War, Navy and Aviation of the Republic of Nicaragua that no replacement is required.

Title III—Duties, Rank and Precedence

Article 7. The personnel of the Mission shall perform such duties as may be agreed upon between the Minister of War, Navy and Aviation of the Republic of Nicaragua and the Chief of Mission, except they shall not have command functions.

Article 8. In carrying out their duties, the members of the Mission shall be responsible to the Minister of War, Navy and Aviation of the Republic of Nicaragua and this responsibility shall be enforced through the Chief of Mission.

Article 9. Each member of the Mission shall serve on the Mission in the rank he holds in the United States Army, and shall wear the uniform and insignia of the United States Army, but shall have precedence over all Nicaraguan officers of the same rank, except the Commander of the Nicaraguan National Guard.

Article 10. Each member of the Mission shall be entitled to all benefits and privileges which the laws and regulations of the Nicaraguan National Guard provide for Nicaraguan officers and noncommissioned officers of corresponding rank.

Title IV—Privileges and Immunities

Article 11. Members of the Mission and their dependents, while stationed in Nicaragua, shall have the right to import, export, possess and use the currency of the United States of America and to possess and use the currency of the Republic of Nicaragua.

Article 12. Mission members shall be immune from the civil jurisdiction of Nicaraguan courts for acts or omissions arising out of the performance of their official duties. Claims of residents of the Republic of Nicaragua arising out of acts or omissions of members of the Mission shall be submitted to the Chief of Mission for appropriate disposition. Settlements of such claims by the Government of the United States of America shall operate as a complete release to both the Government of the United States of America and the Mission member concerned from liability for damages arising out of such acts or omissions. Determination as to whether an act or omission arose out of the performance of official duties shall be made by the Chief of Mission.

Article 13. The personnel of the Mission and the members of their families shall be governed by the disciplinary regulations of the United States Army.

Article 14. Mission members, whether they be credited or nonaccredited, or on temporary duty, shall not be subject to any tax or assessments now or hereafter in effect, of the Government of the Republic of Nicaragua or of any of its political or administrative subdivisions.

Title V—Compensation and Perquisites

Article 15. The members of the Mission shall receive from the Government of the Republic of Nicaragua such net annual compensation, expressed in the United States currency, as may be established by agreement between the Government of the United States of America and the Government of the Republic of Nicaragua for each member of the Mission.

This compensation shall be paid in twelve (12) equal monthly installments, payable within the first five days of the month following the day it is due. Payments may be made in Nicaraguan national currency and when so made shall be computed at the rate of exchange in Managua most favorable to the Mission member on the date on which due.

The compensation provided herein, and any which the members of the Mission may receive from the Government of the United States of America, shall not be subject to any tax now or hereafter in effect, of the Government of the Republic of Nicaragua or of any of its political or administrative subdivisions. Should, there, however, at present or while this Agreement is in effect, be any taxes that might affect this compensation, such taxes shall be borne by the Government of the Republic of Nicaragua in order to comply with the provision of this Article that the compensation shall be net.

Article 16. The compensation agreed upon as indicated in the preceding Article shall commence upon the date of departure from the United States of America of each member of the Mission and, except as otherwise expressly provided in this Agreement, shall continue, following the termination of duty with the Mission, for the return trip to the United States of America. Compensation shall be paid for unused accrued leave at time of termination of duty and prior to departure from Nicaragua.

Article 17. The compensation due for the period of the return trip shall be paid to a detached member of the Mission before his departure from the Republic of Nicaragua and such payment shall be computed for travel by the shortest usually travelled route, regardless of the route and method of travel used by the member of the Mission.

Article 18. Each member of the Mission and his family shall be furnished by the Government of the Republic of

Nicaragua with first class accommodations for travel, via the shortest usual travelled route, required and performed under this Agreement, between the port of embarkation in the United States of America and his official residence in Nicaragua, both for the outward and for the return trip. The Government of the Republic of Nicaragua shall also pay all expenses of shipment of household goods, baggage and automobile of each member of the Mission between the port of embarkation in the United States of America and his official residence in Nicaragua as well as all expenses incidental to the transportation of such household goods, baggage and automobile from Nicaragua to the port of entry in the United States of America. Transportation of such household goods, baggage and automobile shall be effected in one shipment, and all subsequent shipments shall be at the expense of the respective member of the Mission, except as otherwise provided in this Agreement or when such shipments are necessitated by circumstances beyond his control. Payment of expenses for the transportation of families, household goods and automobiles in the case of personnel who may join the Mission for temporary duty at the request of the Minister of War, Navy and Aviation of the Republic of Nicaragua shall be determined by negotiations between the Department of the Army of the United States of America, or its authorized representative, and the Ministry of War, Navy and Aviation of the Republic of Nicaragua or its authorized representative, as such time as the detail of personnel for such temporary duty may be agreed upon.

Article 19. Should the services of any member of the Mission be terminated by the Government of the United States of America for any reason whatsoever prior to completion of two years of service as a member of the Mission, the cost of the return to the United States of America of such member, his family, baggage, household goods and automobile shall not be borne by the Government of the Republic of Nicaragua, nor shall the expenses connected with transporting the replacing member to his station in Nicaragua, except the cost of shipment of his automobile, be borne by the Government of the Republic of Nicaragua.

Article 20. The personal and household goods, baggage and automobiles of members of the Mission, as well as articles imported by the members of the Mission for their personal use and for the use of members of their families or for official use of the Mission, shall be exempt from import taxes, custom duties, inspections and restrictions of any kind by the Government of the Republic of Nicaragua and allowed free entry and egress upon request of the Chief of Mission. This provision is applicable to all personnel of the Mission whether they be accredited or non-accredited members, or on temporary duty. The rights and privileges accorded under this Article shall in general be the same as those accorded diplomatic personnel of the United States Embassy in Nicaragua.

Article 21. Compensation for transportation and travel expenses incurred during travel performed on official business of the Government of the Republic of Nicaragua shall be provided by the Government of the Republic of Nicaragua.

Article 22. The Ministry of War, Navy and Aviation of the Republic of Nicaragua shall provide the Chief of Mission with a suitable automobile, with chauffeur, for use on official business. Suitable motor transportation, with chauffeur, shall, on call of the Chief of Mission, be made available by the Government of the Republic of Nicaragua for use by the members of the Mission for the conduct of the official business of the Mission.

Article 23. The Ministry of War, Navy and Aviation of the Republic of Nicaragua shall provide suitable office space and facilities for the use of the members of the Mission.

Article 24. If any member of the Mission, or any of his family should die in the Republic of Nicaragua, the Government of the Republic of Nicaragua shall bear the cost of transporting the body to such place in the United States of America as the surviving members of the family may decide, but the cost to the Government of the Republic of Nicaragua shall not exceed the cost of transporting the remains from the place of decease to New York City. United States military authorities shall remove and dispose of the remains in accordance with the regulations of the Department of the Army of the United States of America. Should the deceased be a member of the Mission, his services with the Government of the Republic of Nicaragua shall be considered to have terminated fifteen (15) days after his death. Return transportation to New York City for the family of the deceased member and for their baggage, household goods and automobile shall be provided as prescribed in Article 18. All compensation due the deceased member, including salary for fifteen (15) days subsequent to his death, and reimbursement for expenses and transportation due the deceased member for travel performed on official business of the Government of the Republic of Nicaragua, but excluding compensation for accrued leave and not taken by the deceased, shall be paid direct to such person as may be authorized or prescribed by United States Military Law for appropriate disposition. All compensation due the deceased under the provisions of this Article shall be paid within fifteen (15) days of the decease of the said member.

Title VI—Requisites and Conditions

Article 25. So long as this Agreement is in effect, the Government of the Republic of Nicaragua shall not engage or accept the services of any personnel of any other foreign government nor of any individual who is not a citizen of Nicaragua, for duties of any nature connected with the Nicaraguan National Guard except by prior mutual agreement between the Government of the United States of America and the Government of the Republic of Nicaragua.

Article 26. Each member of the Mission shall agree not to divulge or in any way disclose any classified information of which he may become cognizant in his capacity as a member of the Mission. This requirement shall continue in force after the termination of service with the Mission and after the cancellation of this Agreement.

Article 27. Throughout this Agreement, the term "family" is limited to mean wife and dependent children.

Article 28. Each member of the Mission shall be entitled to one month's annual leave with pay, or to a proportional part thereof with pay for any fractional part of a year. Unused portions of said leave shall be cumulative from year to year during service as a member of the Mission.

Article 29. The leave specified in the preceding Article may be spent in the Republic of Nicaragua, in the United States of America, or in any other country, but the expense of travel and transportation not otherwise provided for in this Agreement shall be borne by the member of the Mission taking such leave. All travel time shall count as leave and shall not be in addition to the time authorized in the preceding Article.

Article 30. The Republic of Nicaragua agrees to grant the leave specified in Article 28 upon receipt of written application, approved by the Chief of Mission with due consideration for the convenience of the Government of the Republic of Nicaragua.

Article 31. Members of the Mission who may be replaced shall terminate their services only upon the arrival of their replacements, except when otherwise mutually agreed upon in advance as provided in Article 5.

Article 32. The Government of the Republic of Nicaragua shall provide suitable medical and dental care to members of the Mission and their families. In case a member of the Mission becomes ill or suffers injury, he shall be placed in such hospital or receive the attention of such doctors as the Chief of Mission deems suitable. Such doctors and hospitals shall normally be chosen from doctors, hospitals and pharmacies, all acceptable to the Chief of Mission which shall have been designated in advance for regular use by the Ministry of War, Navy and Aviation of the Republic of Nicaragua in consultation with the Chief of Mission. All expenses incurred as the result of such illness or injury while the patient is a member of the Mission and remains in Nicaragua shall be paid by the Government of the Republic of Nicaragua. If the hospitalized member is a commissioned officer, he shall pay his cost of subsistence, but if he is an enlisted man, the cost of subsistence shall be paid by the Government of the Republic of Nicaragua. Families shall enjoy the same privileges agreed upon in this Article for members of the Mission, except that a member of the Mission shall in all cases pay the cost of subsistence incident to hospitalization of a member of his family.

Article 33. Any member of the Mission unable to perform his duties with the Mission by reason of long-continued physical disability shall be replaced.

Article 34. It is understood that the personnel of the United States Army, to be stationed within the territory of the Republic of Nicaragua under this Agreement, do not and will not comprise any combat forces.

IN WITNESS WHEREOF the undersigned, Thomas E. Whelan, Ambassador of the United States of America to Nicaragua, and Oscar Sevilla Sacasa, Minister of Foreign Affairs of the Republic of Nicaragua, duly authorized thereto, have signed this Agreement in duplicate, in the English and Spanish languages, in Managua, this nineteenth day of November, one thousand nine hundred and fifty three.

AGRICULTURE AND TECHNOLOGY

Part of a paper written by Lauchlin Currie in March, 1962, in defense of Operation Colombia

Paradoxical as it may appear, the Agrarian Reform, *without* Operation Colombia, is a program to benefit consumers (mostly urban dwellers) because of its tendency to increase agricultural production beyond demand and force prices down; Operation Colombia is primarily a program to raise the real income of countrymen by (*a*) providing new job opportunities for them, (*b*) by increasing demand for agricultural products and (*c*) diminishing competition in agriculture.

The tremendous possibilities of modern machinery and technique in agriculture are still not appreciated in Colombia. Agrarian Reform is being discussed as it would have been 40 years ago before the advent of the agricultural revolution. Hence, some quantitative illustrations follow to bring home the extreme gravity of the problem and the consequences of the adoption of the last alternative [increasing cultivation without Operation Colombia].

Let us take, for example, rice.

The crop in 1960 was placed by the Federation at 430,000 tons. Cultivation ranged from small plots on hillsides to large irrigated extensions, with an average yield calculated at 2,100 kilos. With an average of 1.4 harvests a year this meant that some 162,000 hectares were dedicated to its culture in plots that averaged 6.5 hectares and cultivated by some 25,000 families. Good yields under irrigation are calculated at 3,000 kilos per harvest with an average of 1.8 harvests or 5,400 kilos a year and 80 hectare units are considered efficient sized. 1,000 such units producing 430 tons each on 80,000 hectares could have met the requirements of the country in 1960 for rice, releasing 24,000 families and possibly double this number of workers for other tasks, if the job opportunities existed, and 80,000 hectares for other uses, if the demand existed. The possibilities of increased productivity through a complete conversion to commercial farming are evidently tremendous, as are likewise the social dangers if the conversion is not accompanied by Operation Colombia.

We will now suppose that Reforma Agraria settles only 200 additional family units in irrigated 80 hectare farms on 16,000 hectares with yields of 3,000 kilos per harvest or 5,400 kilos per year. This could result in an increase in production of 86,000 tons or 20% of the 1960 total national harvest. The impact of this additional supply on prices can be imagined. A good number of the existing 25,000 families growing rice could be ruined and be unable to pay their debts. If they tried to shift into other crops they would encounter the same situation.

Tobacco is a different type of crop requiring much more hand labor and yet the results of unplanned expansion could be equally grave. According to the Tobacco Federation, some 32,000 tons were produced in 1960 on 18,700 hectares for an average yield of 1,780 kilos per hectare. The average sized holding was about 1 hectare so it may be estimated that some 17,000 families were engaged in the cultivation of tobacco. With better techniques and land, it is believed that the average returns could be increased to 3,000 kilos a hectare and that a family, for most of a year, could handle 5 hectares. With full conversion to this type of farming, therefore, the 1960 crop could be produced by 1,840 farms on 9,140 hectares. Since it is estimated that there are some 17,000 families engaged in this cultivation, 15,000 could be released together with 9,000 hectares with full conversion to commercial type farming. Should the Agrarian Reform result in the settlement of an additional 370 families in economic sized, efficiently run farms, the annual production would be increased by 20%, causing a fall in price and distress to 17,000 families.

One more illustration—corn. This is a crop of tremendous importance, for the most part inefficiently cultivated. However, machine cultivation, particularly in the Valle, is taking place. It is estimated by INA [Instituto Nacional de Abasticimientos, the goverment distribution agency controlling prices] that over 850,000 tons are produced a year on some 660,000 hectares; that the average harvest is 1,300 kilos per hectare. Probably nearly 100,000 families are engaged in this cultivation in average holdings of 6-7 hectares. On the other hand, a commercial type operation could average 4,000 kilos per hectare on 80 hectare holdings. With an average of 1.8 harvests a year, full conversion to this type of operation would mean that 1960 crop could be produced by 1,500 units on 120,000 hectares, releasing nearly 100,000 families and probably twice that number of workers, and 540,000 hectares. If the Reforma Agraria resulted in the new settlement of only 300 families in holdings of 80 hectares each, it could increase the harvest by 20% causing great distress to very many poor countrymen. Statistical data are poor, and the 1960 crop is probably overstated, but the point is so obvious that great accuracy is not necessary.

In only these three examples the 1960 crop could, with full conversion to commercial farming, be produced by 4,300 units, instead of 142,000, and on 210,000 hectares instead of 780,000 hectares. Since under a rational agricultural program it appears unlikely that the country will require the use of more land for domestic cultivation, any land reclamation project or forcing of land into cultivation can be justified only on the grounds of increasing productivity and with the full awareness that such moves will or should result in the abandonment of even greater areas of economically less suitable land. . . .

Preliminary studies made by the staff of the foundation for the Progress of Colombia suggest that the number of gainfully employed in agriculture other than coffee could be reduced, under a more technical operation, from 830,000 to 140,000 or from 20.6% of the total gainfully employed in the country to 3%; and that with more economic sized units and concentration in higher yielding districts, the number in coffee growing could be reduced with no reduction in harvests from 360,000 to 120,000, or from 9% to

3% of the total gainfully employed. Probably another 300,-000-400,000 could be released from cattle raising and other rural activities or well over 1,000,000 altogether. This would represent an addition of 50% to the urban working force.

NOTES ON SOURCES

Statistics on Latin America are very hard to obtain. Few countries have staged a census, and fewer still have enough qualified technicians capable of seeing through the lies and distortions thrown out by those in the process of being checked. In Ecuador, for example, the landed oligarchy has tried to convince peons that the census men are Communists, atheists, or baby-snatchers, causing the Indians to stage riots when the census men appeared. For obvious reasons, Latin America's oligarchies are opposed to revealing any information on their living conditions.

Nevertheless, a fairly accurate picture is possible. First, there are the official statistics published monthly and yearly by the United Nations and the Organization of American States. Though the figures of one do not always match those of the other, they offer a good basis for further calculations.

I have relied a great deal on the statistics of ECLA, the United Nation's Economic Commission for Latin America, which has its headquarters in Santiago de Chile. Raul Prebisch (who was then its head and is now Secretary General of the United Nations Conference on Trade and Development), his staff, and especially Jorge Viteri, Chief of Information, were very helpful to me.

Another source available to me was the files of LAFTA, the Latin American Free Trade Association, centered during its first year of operation in Montevideo, where I represented the *New York Times*. Most delegates, and especially Argentina's René Ortuño, as well as the regular staffers, especially Information Chief Mario Raúl Clérico, went out of their way to answer my questions and provide me with the documents I sought.

All the statistics obtainable from these organizations, however, can furnish only a superficial picture, even in terms of statistics. The deeper, more significant figures I obtained in each country, usually from the universities. Almost every Latin American university has an economic bureau or department or institute where professors and literally scores of student-assistants work long hours to come up with detailed, accurate accounts of their countries' economic and social makeup. In addition, many official government reports are extremely well documented and amazingly impartial, to the point that in the *memorias* (yearly summaries) printed by the Banco Central of Chile or of Venezuela, for example, enough documentation can be found to refute all the progress claims of the Banco's ultimate boss, the Chilean or Venezuelan government. Furthermore, most Latin American governments have planning boards or offices, and they too edit statistical material, often proving the very contrary of what their governments are saying. In the bibliography, I have listed a few of these publications.

Much of my information on Latin America was obtained from direct interviews. Everywhere I went, I talked not only to presidents, Cabinet men, and other officials and politicians, but also to businessmen, priests, labor leaders, and military men, as well as to peons, miners, workers, soldiers, and so on, and their families.

Then, of course, I looked. In every country I visited, I tried to see as much as possible, not just capitals, but small towns, even if buried deep in jungles or high in mountains. I compelled my wife, who accompanied me on every trip except throughout Paraguay, to forego a flush toilet for days at a time and hot-water baths for as long as weeks. Since she also took down every word and later transcribed them into piles of notebooks, I owe her much more for making this book possible than can be said here.

In every country, sometimes in a handful of places within a country, I had someone ready, willing, and able to show me what there was to see. Generally, these contacts were journalists, among whom I am glad to note some of Latin America's best writers. Most I had met at the two Punta del Este conferences; some I had known from the days

when I was a *Time* editor; others I had befriended when
we covered some of Latin America's numerous hot stories;
and the rest were friends of friends. These contacts, always
anxious to serve and to show, went far out of their way,
sometimes furnishing transportation and even lodging, to
get me to the right place at the right time. Without them
I would never have been able to talk to Fascists or Communists, guerrillas or bandits, peasant leaders or oligarchs.
Thanks to them, I feel that I got as complete a picture
of Latin America as it is possible for a United States correspondent who may speak its languages (as I do, more or
less) but cannot feel its suffering (as they do). I consider myself
very honored and fortunate to have them all as friends today,
and regret only that I cannot name them all:

Argentina: Rogelio García Lupo, Gregorio Selser, Edgar
    Triveri, and Rodolfo Walsh, journalists.

Bolivia: Teddy Córdoba, journalist; Luis Peñaloza, economist;
    Carlos Ponce Sanginés, archaeologist.

Brazil: Hamilton Chávez, Jayme Dantas, David St. Clair,
    journalists; Franklin de Oliveira, economist-sociologist.

Chile: Mario Planet, journalist; Mario Rafael Vera Valenzuela
    and Helio Varela, economists; Salomón Corbalán Gon-
    zález, senator.

Colombia: Plinio Apuleyo Mendoza and Osiris Troiani,
    journalists.

Dominican Republic: Máximo Luís Vidal, economist.

Ecuador: Antonio Chediac, journalist.

Guatemala: Leonel Mirón, lawyer.

Mexico: Carlos Fuentes, writer; Enrique González Pedrero,
    political scientist; Alonso Aguilar, Félix Espejel and
    Manuel Mesa, economists.

Paraguay: Orlando Rojas, journalist-politician.

Peru: Sebastián Salazar Bondy, journalist.

Uruguay: Vicente Navarro, teacher; Carlos Real de Azúa,
    lawyer-critic; Julio Castro, Emilio Gutiérrez Herrero, Juan
    José López Silveira, and Carlos Quijano, journalists; Alberto
    Methol Ferré, writer; Claudio Williman, economist; Ben-
    jamín Nahum, critic.

Venezuela: José Font Castro, journalist; Salvador de la
    Plaza and Domingo F. Maza Zavala, economists.

And I should also like to thank that oddball Foreign
Service man in every United States Embassy in Latin America
who risked much indeed to help me. He did so, inevitably,

because he believed in the United States and wanted it to do the things, uphold the principles, and follow the policies that would make all of us even more proud of being United States citizens and Latin America a better place to live for Latin Americans.

BIBLIOGRAPHY

Any list of books and documents pertaining to Latin America must be incomplete. Mine will include a few background works in English which any beginner should read—and which will give him a distorted picture; a series of basic statistical and documentary pamphlets or booklets, which any researcher can easily obtain; and a group of books (mostly untranslated into English, unfortunately) which taken together (since some contradict others), I have found, give a much fairer appraisal of Latin America and its problems.

Background Works

Alexander, Robert. *Prophets of the Revolution*. New York: The Macmillan Company, 1962.

——. *Communism in Latin America*. New Brunswick: Rutgers University Press, 1957.

Arciniegas, Germán. *The State of Latin America*. New York: Alfred A. Knopf, 1952.

Benton, William. *The Voice of Latin America*. New York: Harper & Brothers, 1951.

Gunther, John. *Inside Latin America*. New York: Harper & Brothers, 1960.

Hanke, Lewis. *Modern Latin America*. Princeton, N.J.: D. Van Nostrand, 1959.

Herring, Hubert. *A History of Latin America*. New York: Alfred A. Knopf, 1955.

——. *Good Neighbors.* New Haven: Yale University Press, 1961.

James, Preston E. *Latin America.* New York: The Odyssey Press, 1950.

Johnson, John J. *Political Change in Latin America: The Emergence of the Middle Sectors.* Stanford: Stanford University Press, 1958.

Rippy, J. Fred. *Latin America: A Modern History.* Ann Arbor: University of Michigan Press, 1958.

——. *Globe and Hemisphere.* Chicago: H. Regnery Co., 1958.

Documents

Act of Bogotá. Washington, D.C.: Panamerican Union, 1961.

Acta Final. LAFTA (Montevideo), 1962.

Alianza para el Progresso. Visita del Presidente Kennedy a Venezuela. Caracas: Imprenta Nacional, 1962.

América en Cifras. Unión Panamericana. Washington, D.C., yearly.

Annual Reports of the Secretary General of the Organization of American States. Washington, D.C., yearly.

Anuario Estadístico de Costa Rica. Ministerio de Economía y Hacienda, series.

Aplicaciones del Tratado Interamericano de Asistencia Recíproca. Washington, D.C.: Unión Panamericana, 1962.

Asistencia Técnica Directa de la OEA. Washington, D.C.: Unión Panamericana.

Bases y Directivas para programar el Desarrollo Económico del Ecuador. Junta Nacional de Planificación y Coordinación Económica. Quito, 1958.

Betancourt, Rómulo. *IV Mensaje Presidencial.* Caracas: República de Venezuela, 1962.

Boletín Estadístico Mensual. Banco Central de Costa Rica, monthly.

Boletín Mensual. Banco Central de Chile, monthly.

Boletín Mensual de Estadística. Dep. Administrative Nacional de Estadistica, Bogotá, monthly.

Bolivia—10 Años de Revolución. La Paz: Dirección Nacional de Informaciones, 1962.

Bolivia's Ten Year Plan, in "Planeamiento," La Paz: Junta Nacional de Planeamiento (Nos. 3, 4, 5), 1961.

Conference on Education, and Social and Economic Development in Latin America. ECLA (Conf. 10/L. 37—1962).

Convenio Constitutivo del Banco Interamericano de Desarollo (Inter-American Bank). Washington, D.C.: Unión Panamericana, 1959.

The Demographic, Economic, Social and Educational Situation in Latin America. ECLA (Conf. 10/L. 4—1962).

The Economic Regions of Ecuador, Their Integration and Development. Prepared for the Government of Ecuador by Hans Linnemann, appointed by the United Nations Bureau of Technical Assistance Operations. United Nations, mimeograph.

El Financiamiento de la Industria en Chile: Encuesta a los Ejecutivos. Santiago: INSORA, Universidad de Chile, Facultad de Ciencias Económicas, 1962.

Housing Institutions in Bogotá. Panamerican Union, Bogotá, 1961.

Indice de Precios al Consumidor (Costa de la Vida) de las Naciones Americanas. Unión Panamericana, Washington, D.C., yearly and monthly.

Informe Anual. Banco de México, yearly.

Informe y Manual de Extension Agrícola. Misión FAO en el Ecuador. Quito, 1961.

Informe del Seminario Latino Americano de Energía Eléctrica. ECLA. (E/CN. 12/AC. 50/4—1962).

Inmigración y Desarrollo. Universidad de Buenos Aires; Departamento de Sociología. Buenos Aires, 1951.

Instituto de Educación Política [in] San José, Costa Rica. New York: Institute of International Labor Research, Inc., 1960.

Inter-American Treaty of Reciprocal Assistance. Washington, D.C.: Pan American Union, 1961.

Las Inversiones Privadas Extranieras en la Zona Latinoamericana de Libre Comercio. United Nations: 1960.

Latin American Common Market. United Nations, 1959.

Ley de Reforma Agraria. Caracas: Imprenta Nacional, 1960.

Memorandum que el Gobierno de Ecuador presenta al Banco Interamericano de Desarrollo. Quito: Presidencia de la República, 1961.

Memoria Anual. Banco Central de Costa Rica, yearly.

Memoria Anual. Ministerio de Economía y Hacienca, Caracas, yearly.

Memorias. Banco Central de Venezuela, yearly.

Mendes de Almeida, Cândido Antônio. *Perspectiva Atual da América Latina*. Rio de Janeiro: 1959. Ministerio da Educação e Cultûra: Instituto Superior de Estudos Brasileiros.

Plan de Gobierno (1962-1968). IV Congreso Nacional del Partido Aprista Peruano, Trujillo, 22 de febrero de 1962.

Poumaillou, Paul. *Estudio Sobre Inversión y Planificación en el Desarrollo Económico del Paraguay*. Agencia de Desarrollo Internacional; Misión de Operaciones de los Estados Unidos y Banco Central del Paraguay. (Asunción, 1962, but banned by the Government in Paraguay.)

Programa de Cooperación Técnica de la Organización de los Estados Americanos. Washington, D.C.: CIES.

Programa de Gobierno, Movimiento Nacionalista Revolucionario (1960-1964). La Paz.

Programa Nacional de Desarrollo Económico, 1961-1970. Santiago de Chile: CORFO, 1961.

Report of the Conference on Tax Administration. ECLA (E/CN. 12/AC. 50/6—1962).

Respuesta de Costa Rica al Cuestionario de la Comisión Especial de Expertos para el Estudio de las necesidades financieras que Plantea la ejecución de Planos de Reforma Agraria. Preparados por Alvaro Rojas y Claudio Escoto. Ministerio de Agricultura y Ganadería. San José, 1961.

"Revista de la Superintendencia de Sociedades Anónimas." Bogotá, Colombia. Series.

Revista Económica. Banco de la República Oriental del Uruguay. Series.

Serie Economía y Estadística. Universidad de Costa Rica. Series.

Social Progress Trust Fund Agreement. Washington, D.C.: Inter-American Development Bank, 1961.

Special Meeting of IA-ECOSOC, Uruguay, 1961, *Report of the Group of Experts,* I through V, OAS Official Records ES-RE-Doc. 1-7.

Tenth Inter-American Conference. Final Act (1954), Washington, D.C.: Pan American Union, 1954.

United Nations. *Monthly Bulletin of Statistics*.

United States-Latin American Relations. Compilations of Studies Prepared Under the Direction of the Subcommittee on Foreign Relations, United States Senate. Series.

Reference Works

Aguirre, Manuel Agustín. *América latina y el Ecuador*. Quito: Editorial Universitaria, 1959.

Alba, Victor, *Las ideas sociales contemporáneas en México.*

Alessandri, Arturo. *Recuerdos de Gobierno*. Santiago de Chile: Editorial Universitaria, 1952.

Alexander, Robert. *The Bolivian National Revolution*. New Brunswick: Rutgers University Press, 1958.

——. *The Perón Era*. New York: Columbia University Press, 1951.

American Universities Field Staff. New York: *Latin American Reports Service*. Continuous.

Anales de la Universidad de Chile. *Homenaje al Sesquicentenario* Ano CXVIII, Tercer Trimestre de 1960, Número 119.

Anderson, D. W., and Bejarano, Julio. *La industría de la carne en Colombia*. Bogotá: Ferrocarriles Nacionales, 1961.

Arismendi, Rodney. *Problemas de una revolución continental*. Montevideo: Ediciones Pueblos Unidos, 1962.

Bagú, Sergio. *Evolución historica de la estratificación social en la Argentina*. Buenos Aires: Universidad de Buenos Aires, 1961.

Baltra C., Alberto. *Crecimiento económico de America latina*. Santiago de Chile. Editorial de Pacifico, 1960.

Batlle, Jorge (ed.). *Batlle: su vida, su obra*. Montevideo: Editorial Acción, 1956.

Bedregal, Guillermo. *La nacionalización minera y la responsabilidad del sindicalismo*. La Paz: 1959.

——. *Problemas de infrastructura; Régimen monetario y desarrollo económico en Bolivia*. La Paz: Corporación Minera de Bolivia, 1962.

——, and Goosen, Broesma. *El convenio del estaño: Evolución y tendencia de los precios del estañ*. La Paz: Corporación Minera de Bolivia, 1961.

Belaunde Terry, Fernando. *La conquista del Perú por los peruanos*. Lima: Ediciones "Tawantinsuyu," 1959.

Belloni, Alberto. *Del anarquismo al peronismo*. Buenos Aires: La Siringa, 1960.

Betancourt, Rómulo. *Pensamiento y acción*. Mexico, 1951.

——. *Venezuela: política y petróleo*. Mexico: Fondo de Cultura Económica, 1956.

Beveraggi Allende, Walter. *El servicio del capital extranjero y el control de cambios.* Buenos Aires: Fondo de Cultura Económica, 1954.

Blanksten, George I. *Perón's Argentina.* Chicago: University of Chicago Press, 1953.

Caballero Escobar, Enrique. *Capitalización y empleos.* Bogotá: ANDI, 1959.

Cafiero, Antonio F. *Cinco años después.* Buenos Aires, 1961.

Calogeras, João P. *A History of Brazil.* Chapel Hill: The University of North Carolina Press, 1939.

Cardoza y Aragón, Luis. *Guatemala.* Mexico: Fondo de Cultura Económica, 1955.

Cosío Villegas, Daniel. *El pensamiento económico latino-americano.* Mexico: Fondo de Cultura Económica, 1945.

Costa, Cruz. *Esbozo de una historia de las ideas en el Brasil.* Mexico: Fondo de Cultura Económica, 1957.

Council on Foreign Relations (ed.), *Social Change in Latin America Today.* (Esp. Richard W. Patch, "Bolivia: U.S. Assistance in a Revolutionary Setting.") New York: Harper & Brothers, 1960.

Cuadernos Americanos. Bimonthly. Mexico.

Currie, Lauchlin. *Operación Colombia: un programa nacional de desarrollo económico y social.* Bogotá: Fundación Para el Progreso de Colombia, 1961.

de Jesus, Carolina Maria. *Child of the Dark.* New York: E. P. Dutton & Co., 1962.

de la Plaza, Salvador. *El petróleo en la vida venezolana.* Caracas: Pensamiento Vivo, 1962.

——. *Estructura de integración nacional.* Caracas: Pensamiento Vivo, 1959.

——. *Necesidad de la reforma agraria.* Caracas: Editorial "Tierra para quien la trabaje," 1959.

de Oliveira, Franklin. *Revolução e Contra-Revolução no Brasil.* Rio de Janeiro: Editôra Civilizaçao Brasileira S.A., 1962.

del Mazo, Gabriel. *El Radicalismo.* Buenos Aires: Editorial Raigal, 1955.

Dondoli B., César y Torres M., J. *Estudio geoagronómico de la región oriental de la meseta central* (for Costa Rica's Ministerio de Agricultura e Industrías). San José, 1954.

Donoso, Ricardo. *Alessandri: agitador y demoledor* (2 vols.). Mexico: Fondo de Cultura Económica (1952-1954).

Dupray, Norman H. *Aves de rapiña en Venezuela.* Caracas: Editorial Siembra, 1958.

Echavarría Olózaga, Hernán. *El sentido común en la economía colombiana.* Bogotá: Imprenta Nacional, 1958.

Edwards Vives, Alberto. *La Fronda aristocrática, historia politica de Chile.* Santiago de Chile: Editorial del Pacifico S.A., 1945.

Encina, Francisco A. Historia de Chile (3-vol. *resumen* by Castedo, Leopoldo). Santiago: Zig-Zag, 1959.

———. *Neustra inferioridad económica: sus causas, sus consecuencias.* Santiago, 1912.

Figueres, José. *Cartas a un ciudadeno.* San José: Imprenta Nacional, 1954.

———. *Palabras gastadas: democracia, socialismo, libertad.* San José, 1955.

Francovich, Guillermo. *El pensamiento boliviano en el siglo XX.* Mexico: Fondo de Cultura Económica, 1956.

Frankel, Herbert S. *Some Conceptual Aspects of International Economic Development of the Underdeveloped Territories.* "Essays in International Finance," No. IV, May, 1952, Princeton University.

Fredes, Carlos. *Curso de economía: Elementos de economía chilena.* Santiago: Editorial Universitaria, 1962.

Frejat, José. *Capital estrangeiro parasitário.* Rio de Janeiro: Ediçáo de "Panfleto," 1960.

Frente Nacional de Defensa del Petróleo. *Declaración de principios y exposición de motivos.* Lima, 1960.

Freyre, Gilberto. *New World in the Tropics.* New York: Alfred A. Knopf, 1959.

———. *The Masters and the Slaves.* New York: Alfred A. Knopf, 1946.

FUAR. *Programa y Estatuto.* Bogotá: Editorial América Libre, 1962.

Fuentes, Carlos. *La muerte de Artemio Cruz.* Mexico: Fonde de Cultura Económica, 1962.

———. *La Región más transparente.* Mexico: Fondo de Cultura Económica, 1958.

Furtado, Celso. *Formação econômica do Brasil.* Rio de Janeiro: Editôria Fondo de Cultura, 1959.

García Lupo, Rogelio. *La Rebelión de los Generales.* Buenos Aires: Proceso, 1962.

———. "Los Militares Nasseristas en América Latina," prologue to Nasser, Col. Abdel Gamal. *La Revolución Nasserista.* Buenos Aires: Proceso, 1962.

Germani, Gino. *Política e Massa.* Rio de Janeiro: Ediçoes da Revista Brasileira de Estudos Politicos, 1960.

Gonzalez Casanova, Pablo. *La ideología norteamericana sobre inversiones extranjeras.* Mexico: Universidad.

González Pedrero, Enrique. *El gran virage.* Mexico: Ediciones Era, 1961.

Haddad, Jamil Almansur. *Revolução Cubana e Revolução Brasileira.* Rio de Janeiro: Editôra Civilização Brazileira SA., 1961.

Halperin, Maurice. *Desarrollo económico y crisis en America latina.* Mexico: Ediciones de la Universidad Obrera, 1961.

Hanson, S. G. *Economic Development in Latin America.* Washington: Inter-American Affairs Press, 1951.

Haya de la Torre, Victor Raúl. *El antimperialismo y el Apra.* Santiago de Chile. Ediciones Ercilla, 1936.

——. *Y despues de la guerra ¿Qué?* Lima: Editorial PTCM, 1946.

Hayes, Joe C. and Wiltbank, Milford J. *Estudio sobre el problema agrario en Costa Rica.* San José, 1960.

Hernández Arregui, J. J. *La formación de la coinciencia nacional.* Buenos Aires: Ediciones Hachea, 1960.

Hernández Urbina, Alfredo. *Nueva Política Nacional.* Trujillo (Peru): Ediciones Raiz, 1962.

Hirschman, Albert O. (ed.) *Latin American Issues—essays and comments.* New York: The Twentieth Century Fund, 1961.

Horowitz, Irving Louis. *Revolution in Brazil—Politics and Society in a Developing Nation.* New York: E. P. Dutton & Co., 1964.

Julião, Francisco. *Escucha campesino.* Montevideo: "Ediciones Presente," 1962.

Kelly, Sir David Victor. *The Ruling Few.* London: Hollis & Carter, 1952.

Lagos E., Ricardo. *La concentración del poder económico* (in Chile). Santiago de Chile: Editorial del Pacifico S.A., 1962.

"Latin America's Nationalistic Revolutions," 15 articles, in *The Annals of the American Academy of Political and Social Science,* March, 1961.

Leonard, Olen E. *Bolivia: Land, People, and Institutions.*

Washington, D.C., 1952.

Lewis, Oscar. *Five Families: Mexican Case Studies in the Culture of Poverty.* New York: Basic Books, 1959.

——. *Life in a Mexican Village: Tepoztlán Restudied.* Urbana: University of Illinois Press, 1951.

——. *The Children of Sanchez.* New York: Random House, 1961.

Lieuwen, Edwin. *Arms and Politics in Latin America.* New York: Published for the Council on Foreign Relations by Praeger, 1960.

Lievano Aguirre, Indalecio. *Los grandes conflictos sociales y económicos de nuestra historia.* Bogotá: Ediciones Nueva Prensa, 1962.

Machado, Eduardo. *Las primeras agresiones del imperialismo en Venezuela.* Caracas: Magrija, 1958.

——. *Petróleo en Venezuela.* Caracas: Magrija, 1958.

Malave Mata, Hector. *Petróleo y Desarrollo económico en Venezuela.* Caracas: Ediciones Pensamiento Vivo S.A., 1962.

Maldonado, Silvio. *Paraguay.* Mexico: Fondo de Cultura Económica, 1962.

Manuel del elector: La constitution del Perú—El estatuto electoral—Los derechos humanos—Idearios de los partidos—Cifras del censo 1961. Lima: Libraría-Editorial Juan Majia Baca, 1952.

Mariátegui, José Carlos. *Siete ensayos de interpretación de la realidad peruana.* Lima: Bibliotaca "Amauta," 1928.

Matthews, Herbert L. (ed.) *The United States and Latin America.* New York: Foreign Policy Association, 1953.

Maza Zavala, D. F. *Aspectos del desarrollo económico de Venezuela.* Caracas: Universidad Central de Venezuela, 1962.

——. *Dos notas sobre economía venezolana.* Caracas: Editorial Mundo Económico, 1961.

——. *Hacia la independencia económica.* Caracas: 1961.

——. *Paradojas venezolanas.* Caracas, 1959.

Mesa A., Manuel. *Proceso y situación actual de la reforma agraria mexicana.* Mexico, 1960.

Methol Ferré, Alberto. *La crisis del Uruguay y el Imperio Británico.* Buenos Aires: La Siringa, 1959.

——. *La izquierda nacional en la Argentina.* Buenos Aires: Editorial Coyoacan.

Mikesell, R. F. *United States Economic Policy and International Relations*. New York: McGraw-Hill Book Co., 1952.

Movimiento de Liberación Nacional. *Programa y Llamamiento*. Mexico, 1961.

O'Connor, Harvey. *The Empire of Oil*. New York: Monthly Review Press, 1955.

Palacio, Ernesto. *Historia de la Argentina*. Buenos Aires: ALPE, 1954.

Paz, Octavio. *El laberinto de la soledad*. Mexico: Fondo de Cultura Económica, 1949.

Pérez Alfonzo, J. P. *Petróleo, jugo de la tierra*. Caracas.

Pike, Frederick B. (ed.) *Freedom and Reform in Latin America*. Notre Dame: University of Notre Dame Press, 1959.

Pinto S. C., Aníbal. *Ni estabilidad, ni desarrollo: La política del fondo monetario* (IMF). Santiago de Chile, 1960.

Pivel Devoto, Juan E. *Historia de la República Oriental del Uruguay*. Montivedeo: Editorial Medina, 1956.

Prebisch, Raúl. *The Economic Development of Latin America and its Problems*. United Nations, 1961.

Ramírez Necochea, Hernán. *Historia del Imperialismo en Chile*. Santiago de Chile: Empresa Editora Austral Ltda., 1960.

Ramírez Nova, Ezequiel. *América Latina y Estados Unidos*. Lima, 1958.

Real de Azúa, Carlos. *El Patriciado Uruguayo*. Montevideo: ASIR, 1961.

La Realidad Argentian en el siglo XX
   I—Galletti, Alfredo. *La política y los partidos*. Buenos Aires: Fondo de Cultura Económica, 1961.
   II—Portnoy, Leopoldo. *Analisis de la economía*. Buenos Aires: Fondo de Cultura Económica, 1961.
   III—Bagú, Sergio. *Argentina en el mundo*. Buenos Aires: Fondo de Cultura Económica, 1961.

Rennie, Ysabel. *The Argentine Republic*. New York: The Macmillan Company, 1945.

Rodo, José Enrique. *Ariel*. Buenos Aires: Editora del Plata, 1947.

Roel, Virgilio. *La economía agraria peruana*. Lima, 1961.

Romero, José Luis. *Las ideas políticas en la Argentina*. Mexico: Fondo de Cultura Económica, 1956.

Salazar, José Manuel. *Tierras y colonización en Costa Rica*.

San José: Universidad de Costa Rica, 1962.

Santiago Dantas, F. C. de. *Politica externa independente.* Rio de Janeiro: Editôra Civilização Brasileira, 1962.

Scheyven, Raimond. *De Punta del Este a la Habana.* Santiago de Chile: Editorial del Pacífico, 1962.

Selser, Gregorio. *Diplomacia, Garrote y Dólares.* Buenos Aires: Editorial Palestra, 1962.

——. *El Guatamalazo.* Buenos Aires: Ediciones, Iguazu 1961.

Silva Herzog, Jesús. *Historia de la Revolución Mexicana.* Mexico: Fondo de Cultura Económica, 1960. 2 vols.

Silvert, Kalman H. *A Study in Government: Guatemala.* New Orleans: Tulane University, 1954.

——. *The Conflict Society: Reaction and Revolution in Latin America.* New Orleans: The Hauser Press, 1961.

Staley, Eugene. *The Future of Underdeveloped Countries: Political Implications of Economic Development.* 2nd ed. New York: Published for the Council on Foreign Relations by Harper & Brothers, 1961.

Strasser, Carlos (ed.) *Las izquierdas en el proceso político argentino.* Buenos Aires: Editorial Palestra, 1959.

Tannenbaum, Frank. *Mexico: The Struggle for Peace and Bread.* New York: Alfred A. Knopf, 1950.

——. *Peace by Revolution.* New York: Columbia University Press, 1933.

Toriello, Guillermo: *¿A donde va Guatemala?* Mexico: Editorial América Nueva, 1956.

Unión Nacional Paraguaya. *La Tragedia Paraguaya.* Junta central coordinadora en el exilio, 1961.

Universidad Central de Venezuela, Facultad de Economía. *Mesa redonda sobre restricciones petroleras.* Caracas, 1958.

Vera Valenzuela, Mario. *La política económica del cobre en Chile.* Santiago: Ediciones de la Universidad de Chile, 1961.

Viñas, Ismael. *Orden y Progreso.* Buenos Aires, Editorial Palestra, 1960.

Walsh, Rodolfo, *Operación Masacre.* Buenos Aires, 1958.

Whittaker, Arthur. *Argentine Upheaval: Perón's Fall and the New Regime.* New York: Praeger, 1956.

——. *The United States and Argentina.* Cambridge: Harvard University Press, 1956.